Evangelical Anglicans in a
Revolutionary Age
1789–1901

Evangelical Anglicans in a Revolutionary Age 1789–1901

Nigel A.D. Scotland

PATERNOSTER PRESS

First published in 2004 by Paternoster Press

09 08 07 06 05 04 03   7 6 5 4 3 2 1

Paternoster Press is an imprint of Authentic Media,
P.O. Box 300, Carlisle, Cumbria, CA3 0QS, UK

and

P.O. Box 1047, Waynesboro, GA 30830-2047, USA

www.paternoster-publishing.com

British Library Cataloguing in Publication Data
A catalogue record for this book is available from the British Library

ISBN 1-84227-231-4

Cover Design by FourNineZero
Typeset by WestKey Ltd, Falmouth, Cornwall
Printed in Great Britain by Bell & Bain Ltd, Glasgow

Contents

Preface

Since the founding of the Church of England by Henry VIII in the sixteenth century, there have always been Evangelicals among its clergy and people. During the reign of Edward VI, Evangelical politicians such as John Dudley, William Parr and William Paget, together with reformist churchmen such as Thomas Cranmer, Nicholas Ridley and Thomas Goodrich, stamped the established church with Evangelical doctrine and an Evangelical liturgy. The reign of Elizabeth I witnessed a further strengthening of the Evangelical cause with the flowering of Puritanism, which continued to the end of the Cromwellian era.

Whilst it is the case that many nineteenth-century Anglicans found their roots in sixteenth- and seventeenth-century Puritanism, the modern Evangelical movement really emerged from the eighteenth-century revival under the Wesleys. It embraced a number of Anglican clergy, among them John Fletcher of Madeley, Henry Venn of Huddersfield, William Grimshaw of Haworth, Augustus Toplady of Burrington Combe in Somerset and John Newton, first of Olney and later of St Mary Woolnoth in the city of London. It also included the Clapham Sect whose members, led by William Wilberforce, prompted a major social reformation that included the abolition of slavery, and which extended into the nineteenth century and set a pattern for the succeeding generations of Victorian philanthropists who followed them.

The nineteenth century has often been termed 'a revolutionary age' on account of the rapid and radical changes which took place in industry and transport, housing and public health, science and technology, education and social life. Additionally, the fact must not be overlooked that in this 'revolutionary age' religion played a formative part. In particular, Evangelical Christianity shaped the Victorian years. Sheridan Gilley wrote that 'Anglican Evangelicalism was part of a popular Protestant culture which was to flourish and expand for the remainder of the century'.[1] He went on to make the point that 'even in its more secular reaches, popular Protestantism sustained the Puritan ethic of industry, sobriety, thrift and suspicion of godly pleasure, and disapproval of the cruel sports of the eighteenth century, and of the theatre and of novel reading, though the objection to the last was weakened by the emergence of the religious novel itself'.[2]

The nineteenth century was of major importance for Evangelicals because it was then that they emerged as a distinct party within the Church of England. It was also then that the Evangelicals began to grow rapidly in significant numbers and, for the first time, to see some of their own number elevated to the bench of bishops. In Thomas Musgrave and William Thomson they had two Archbishops of York and John Sumner was the first Evangelical to become Archbishop of Canterbury. Many of the nineteenth century's influential politicians and social reformers belonged to the Evangelical party of the Church of England. Among their number were Spencer Perceval, England's only Evangelical Prime Minister, William Wilberforce, Charles Grant, Thomas Fowell Buxton, Lord Shaftesbury, Richard Oastler, George Bull, Florence Nightingale and Josephine Butler. The nineteenth century saw the emergence of Evangelical theologians and Evangelical theology. It was also the era in which they were influential in Parliament and in social reform.

Despite the fact that the nineteenth century was a significant and formative period for Evangelical Anglicans, not a great deal has been written about them. In 1908 G.R. Balleine published *A History of the Evangelical Party in the Church of England*, which traced the history of the party from the Wesleyan revival to 1900. A later edition, published in 1951, included a brief appendix that updated the story from 1900–1950. Balleine's book, which is a mine of useful information, is largely focused on the parishes and mission. Kenneth Hylson-Smith produced *Evangelicals in the Church of England 1734–1984*. His book, to some extent, updated Balleine's work and gives more attention to sources, but it only devotes about 160 pages to the nineteenth century.

This present book is confined solely to the nineteenth century and is based on a wide range of primary and secondary sources.

---

[1] S. Gilley, 'The Church Of England in the Nineteenth Century', in S. Gilley and W.J. Sheils, *A History of Religion in Britain*, p. 297.
[2] Ibid., pp. 295–6.

These include sermons, tracts, private correspondence, newspapers, journals and biographies of the period. Particular attention has been paid to aspects not covered by Balleine or Hylson-Smith, such as nineteenth-century Evangelical Anglican theology, culture and spirituality, together with their role in politics and education.

I owe thanks to many people who have kindly read and commented on the various chapters. Among them were Mr Frank Booth, the Rev Dr Roger Beckwith, Dr Brian Knight, the Rev Dr Alan Munden, Dr Ian Randall, Dr Linda Wilson and the Rev Dr Peter Williams. I am particularly grateful to Tony Graham of Paternoster Press for his careful scrutiny of the manuscript. Any errors and imperfections are, of course, entirely my own.

Nigel Scotland
University of Gloucestershire

Abbreviations

BFBS	British and Foreign Bible Society
BMS	Baptist Missionary Society
CIM	China Inland Mission
CMS	Church Missionary Society
CPAS	Church Pastoral Aid Society
EA	Evangelical Alliance
LCM	London City Mission
LDOS	Lord's Day Observance Society
LMS	London Missionary Society
NSPCC	National Society for the Prevention of Cruelty to Children
RSPCA	The Royal Society for the Prevention of Cruelty to Animals
RSU	Ragged School Union
SPCK	The Society for the Promotion of Christian Knowledge
SPG	Society for the Propagation of the Gospel

1

Who Were the Church of England Evangelicals?

'Remember always that although Evangelicals ... be not the perfection of Christianity yet it is Christianity, vital and essential.'[1] Thomas Arnold penned these words in a private memorandum in 1830, which came to the attention of his brother-in-law and executor when Arnold died in 1842. Coming from a man who was highly critical by nature this was praise indeed. Significantly, in the same memorandum Arnold stated that in the event of his death he wished his children to be brought up 'under the influence of Evangelicals'. The memorandum indicates the growing positive influence that Evangelicals were beginning to make by 1830. It was an influence that was becoming recognised by others also. Among their number was Henry Parry Liddon, one of the inner-circle of the Oxford Movement. He later wrote:

> The deepest and most fervid religion in England during the first three decades of this century was that of the Evangelicals. The world to come with the boundless issues of life and death, the infinite value of the atonement, the regenerating, purifying, guiding action of God the Holy Spirit in respect of the Christian soul, were preached to our grandfathers with a force and earnestness which are beyond controversy.[2]

With the influence of Lord Shaftesbury and the patronage of Lord Palmerston, Frederick Denison Maurice wrote in January 1854 regretfully to the Rev D.J. Vaughan 'of the Evangelicals in the

---

[1] M. Trevor, *The Arnolds – Thomas Arnold and His Family*, cited by J.A.R. Piersenné, *Belonging to No Party: The Christianity of Doctor Arnold*, p. 47.

[2] H.P. Liddon, *The Life of Edward Bouverie Pusey* Vol. 1, p. 255.

Church of England that they are the most influential of all parties, and have the greatest power of bestowing patronage or inflicting injury'.[3] Much later in 1887, John Henry Newman wrote that 'those great and burning truths, which I learned as a boy from Evangelical teaching, I have found impressed upon my heart with fresh and ever increasing vigour'.[4]

As the nineteenth century progressed the Evangelical party began to influence every level of Victorian society from Parliament where they were represented by Wilberforce, the Clapham Sect,[5] Lord Shaftesbury and an increasing number of bishops right down to the poor on whose behalf they campaigned unceasingly. Even Queen Victoria was said to be Evangelical in her sympathies.[6] It has been estimated that at the highest point about one third or 6,000 Anglican clergy were Evangelical. [7] It is very difficult to be precise as to what extent Evangelicalism penetrated the laity and in which classes they found the most adherents. 'The real drama of Evangelicalism', wrote George Eliot (1819–1880), the novelist, 'lies among the middle and the lower classes'.

The Origins of the Evangelical Party in the Church of England

The roots of the Evangelical party, which became so influential in the Victorian years, lay in two important areas: the Protestant Reformation and the Wesleyan revival of the eighteenth century. Clearly, there has always been an Evangelical faith and many Evangelical movements within the Christian church. However, from the middle of the eighteenth century, around about 1750, through to the middle of the nineteenth century, about 1850, a number of scholars have argued for a coherent Evangelical movement. Before this period, and after it, it is quite difficult to

---

[3] F. Maurice, *The Life of Frederick Denison Maurice* Vol. 2, p. 234.

[4] J.H. Newman, 'John H. Cardinal Newman to George Edwards 24 February 1887', in J.H. Newman, *Letters and Diaries* Vol. XXXI, p. 189.

[5] See I.C. Bradley, *The Call to Seriousness*, p. 56.

[6] See N.A.D. Scotland, *John Bird Sumner: Evangelical Archbishop*, p. 112.

[7] B. Hilton, *The Age of Atonement*, p. 26. See also W.J. Conybeare, 'Church Parties', *Edinburgh Review* (Oct 1853), p. 338.

determine how the adjective 'Evangelical' should be applied. This hundred-year period begins with clear manifestations of the Evangelical revival and ends with the so-called 1859 Revival, which, in many ways, looks like the last wave of the eighteenth-century movement.

The Protestant Reformation

The word Evangelical was first used to describe the reforming movements led by Martin Luther and John Calvin that emphasised justification by faith alone. In contrast to the Oxford Movement and the high church party who looked for their roots in the traditions and doctrines of the undivided Catholic Church of the first five centuries, the Evangelicals followed Luther and went back to the Scripture alone as the only source of authority. Luther had asserted his *sola Scriptura* principle in his declaration to the Imperial Diet of Worms in Germany in 1521: 'A simple layman armed with the Scripture is to be believed above a pope or a council without it.'[8] The leading nineteenth-century Evangelical Anglican clergy frequently wrote of their debt to the English Protestant reformers, particularly Cranmer, Ridley, Latimer and Jewel. They also often publicly declared their allegiance to the English Reformation. This was why in 1839, when the Oxford Movement spoke disparagingly of the Reformation, they erected the Martyrs Memorial outside Balliol College as a tribute to three Marian martyrs. Later, when the second generation of the Oxford Movement began to introduce ritualistic and Romish practices into church worship, they formed the Church Association. They also gave support to the Evangelical Alliance (EA), which was founded in 1846 to counteract the rise of Roman Catholicism.[9]

A few examples of the commitment of nineteenth-century Anglican Evangelicals to the principles of the Reformation will suffice to illustrate this point. The first Bishop of Liverpool, John Charles Ryle, in an essay entitled 'Divers and Strange Doctrines', exhorted his readers as to 'try to preserve the Old Protestant principles of the Church of England, and to hand them down uninjured to our children's children. Let us not listen to those faint-hearted Churchmen

---

[8] R. Bainton, *Here I Stand: A Life of Martin Luther*, pp. 116–17.
[9] See I. Randall and D. Hilborn, *One Body in Christ: The History and Significance of the Evangelical Alliance*; and N.M. Railton, *No North Sea*, p. 138.

who would have us forsake the ship, and desert the Church of England in her time of need.'[10]

One of Ryle's contemporaries, and a fellow Evangelical, was Francis Close. Regarded by Alan Munden as a minor national figure,[11] Close was incumbent of Cheltenham from 1826 to 1856, later becoming Dean of Carlisle Cathedral. During his sojourn in Cheltenham, Close had a hand in establishing a number of schools.[12] Speaking in his capacity as vice-president at the opening of the new Cheltenham College buildings in the Bath Road in June 1843, Close referred to the religion to be taught in the school:

> We call it the plain, honest, protestant Evangelical religion of the written Church of England. We pledged our integrity, that … we never would have any master or teacher belonging to the school but such as embraced the religion of the liturgy, the religion of the Homilies and the Creed of the martyred reformers.[13]

Shortly afterwards, in 1847, Close was one of a small group of influential Anglican Evangelicals who founded the Cheltenham Training College to train masters and mistresses on 'strictly Scriptural, Evangelical and Protestant principles'. The prescribed syllabus for students in those early years included a thorough grounding in biblical teaching and Christian history, especially the Reformation.

At Hugh McNeile's (1795–1879) funeral, incumbent of St Jude's, Liverpool and a prominent Evangelical, the Rev Hugh Stowell, a friend, referred to McNeile as 'a genuine successor of our best Reformers':

> His soul beat in true harmony with Hooper and Latimer, and Cranmer and Bradford. He was the trustworthy leader of that great party in the Church, I say again, whose distinguishing characteristic … is the faith of our Reformers. This is the heart and soul, pith and marrow, of our Thirty-nine Articles … This I will say of your pastor's life, that against the fashion of the times … he maintained in simple

---

[10] J.C. Ryle, *Knots Untied*, p. 361.

[11] See A. Munden, *The Church of England in Cheltenham 1826–1856 with Particular Reference to Francis Close.*

[12] N.A.D. Scotland, 'The Centenary of Dean Close School and the Contribution of Francis Close to Education', *History of Education Society Bulletin* (Autumn 1987), pp. 29–40.

[13] *Cheltenham Journal*, 26 June 1843.

dignity the integrity of his testimony for the Protestantism of the Church of England. Protestantism![14]

As well as finding their roots in the Reformation, the early Evangelicals in the Church of England were all in varying degrees influenced by the Wesleyan revival of the eighteenth century. L.E. Elliott-Binns, in *The Early Evangelicals*, played down the extent of Wesley's influence,[15] whereas other writers, such as Ian Bradley, in *The Call to Seriousness*, have attributed a more influential role to Wesley. Bradley wrote

> The origins of Evangelicalism lay in the religious revival that occurred in Britain in the middle of the eighteenth century. During the period between 1736 and 1760, a number of Anglican clergymen went through parallel but apparently spontaneous conversion experiences which involved an intense feeling of their sins being forgiven them and a personal assurance of salvation and which led them to devote the rest of their lives to preaching the Christian Gospel to the masses in a particularly powerful and compelling way.[16]

The nineteenth-century Anglican Evangelicals certainly inherited from Wesley what Bradley terms 'serious' or 'vital' religion. This religion was personal and experiential, and, following Wesley, it emphasised the inward work of the Holy Spirit in achieving new birth in the believer's life and giving assurance of salvation. Bradley mentions that among the first generation of Anglican clergy to be influenced by the Evangelical movement were William Romaine, John Newton, William Grimshaw, Henry Venn and Augustus Toplady.

Romaine (1714–1795), who experienced his Evangelical conversions in the 1740s, was appointed lecturer at St Dunstan's in the East in 1749, a position he held for forty-six years. For a long time he was the only Evangelical Anglican in the City of London. The churchwardens refused to light the building because they disliked Romaine's preaching; as a result, for many months he preached, with a lighted taper in his hand, to a congregation in the dark.[17]

---

[14] J. Marsden, *Memoirs of the Rev Hugh Stowell*, pp. 450–4.
[15] L.E. Elliott-Binns, *The Early Evangelicals*, p. 169.
[16] Bradley, *Call to Seriousness*, p. 15.
[17] See W. Romaine, *The Life, Walk and Triumph of Faith by William Romaine with an Account of His Life and Work by Peter Toon*, pp. v–xxiv.

John Newton (1725–1807) was formerly a hardened sea captain in the slave-trading business. He fell to his knees and was converted during a storm at sea in 1748. He recalled, 'I dreaded death now and my heart foreboded the worst, if the Scriptures, which I had long since opposed, were true'. He wrote, 'I waited with fear and impatience to receive my inevitable doom.' It was then when he felt himself to be on the very brink of eternity that 'the Holy Spirit first raised me to look up to the crucified Saviour'.[18] He later expressed the change that had taken place in his life in the hymn, 'Amazing Grace', which depicts his own Evangelical conversion experience. Newton received deacon's orders on 29 April 1764 and was ordained priest on 17 June in the same year.[19] He became Curate of Olney in the year of his ordination[20] and remained there until 1780 when he moved to London where he served as rector of St Mary Woolnoth, in the inner city, until his death in 1807.[21] Newton's great contribution to the Evangelical movement was his practical theology. His concerns were those of a conscientious pastor, parish evangelist and spiritual counsellor.[22]

William Grimshaw (1708–1763) was incumbent of Haworth from 1742 until his death in 1763. It was a grey village on the Yorkshire Moors, where in later years the Brontë sisters dreamed and died in the morose atmosphere of their father Patrick Brontë's rectory. Grimshaw was altogether different. Ordained priest in 1732, he was Curate of Todmorden from 1731 to 1742.[23] He was brawny, big-hearted, strong-willed and very ready to tackle Sabbath breakers.[24] While the Psalm was being sung immediately before the sermon, Grimshaw would sally forth into the village with a riding crop in his hand to round up the absentees. In one of his letters, John Newton describes how the process struck a visitor:

A friend of mine, passing a public house on a Lord's Day, saw several persons jumping out of the windows and over the wall. He feared the

---

[18] B. Hindmarsh, *John Newton and the Evangelical Tradition*, p. 57. See also J. Bull, *John Newton of Olney and St Mary Woolnoth: An Auto-biography and Narrative*, pp. 24–8.
[19] Ibid., p. 105.
[20] Ibid., pp. 169–220.
[21] Ibid., pp. 289–324.
[22] Ibid., p. 327.
[23] F. Baker, *William Grimshaw 1708–63*.
[24] Ibid., pp. 209–12.

house was on fire, but upon inquiring what was the cause of the commotion he was told that they saw the parson coming. They were more afraid of the parson than of a Justice of the Peace. His reproof was so mild and friendly, that the stoutest sinner could not stand before him.[25]

Along with a number of other Anglican Evangelicals who associated with the Methodists, Grimshaw engaged in extra-parochial activities, including preaching. On receiving complaints about these incursions into his neighbours' territories in 1748, Matthew Hutton, the Archbishop of York, summoned Grimshaw to give an account of his actions. Hutton inquired of Grimshaw, 'How many communicants had you at your quarterly sacraments when you first came to Haworth?' 'Twelve, my Lord,' was Grimshaw's reply. Hutton then asked, 'How many have you now at such solemnities.' Grimshaw replied, 'In the winter from four to five hundred, and sometimes in the summer near twelve hundred.' For Hutton, this harvest of communicants far outweighed the misdemeanour of trespassing in other people's parishes. He dismissed the charge, declaring, 'We cannot find fault with Mr Grimshaw when he is instrumental in bringing so many to the Lord's Table.'[26] Five years later Grimshaw wrote, 'We have lately had Mr Whitefield in these parts ... In my church he assisted me in administering the Lord's Supper to as many communicants as sipped away thirty-five bottles of wine within a gill. It was a high day indeed, a Sabbath of Sabbaths'.[27] In a sermon preached shortly after Grimshaw's death, William Romaine said of him that he 'was one of the most laborious and indefatigable ministers of Christ that I ever knew'.[28]

Augustus Toplady (1740–1778) was profoundly influenced by a Methodist preacher when only sixteen years old. After University, Toplady was ordained in 1762 and became rector of Blagdon in Somerset in the same year. He wrote the hymn 'Rock of Ages Cleft for Me' and took issue in a somewhat bitter fashion with Wesley on the matter of Arminianism,[29] in so far as his health allowed. He was a diligent parish priest loved by his flock.[30]

---

[25] G.R. Balleine, *A History of the Evangelical Party in the Church of England*, p. 67.

[26] Baker, *Grimshaw*, pp. 131–2.

[27] Ibid., pp. 182–3.

[28] J.C. Ryle, *Five Christian Leaders*, p. 58.

[29] Elliott-Binns, *Early Evangelicals*, pp. 205–6.

[30] Ibid., p. 347.

Henry Venn (1729–1797) was ordained in 1749 and served the curacy of Barton, near Cambridge. In 1754 he became Curate of Clapham and remained there for five years. He was Vicar of Huddersfield from 1759 to 1771 and then of Yelling, near Cambridge, until 1797. During his time at Clapham Venn began to associate with John Wesley and the Methodists. Venn was a noted and powerful preacher, and his church at Huddersfield became so crowded that many were unable to gain admission. He wrote *The Complete Duty of Man,* which was published in 1761 and proved to be a popular guide to practical Christian living.[31] Venn is of particular significance because he was the greatest human influence on Charles Simeon who became the leader of the Evangelical party in the first half of the nineteenth century. Simeon later wrote, 'How great a blessing his conversion and example have been to me will never be known till the Day of Judgement.'[32]

Clearly, Wesley's impact on the emergence of Evangelical Anglicanism was significant. Reflecting on this, G.W.E. Russell wrote, 'His influence, combined with that of his brother Charles, acting on such men as Newton and Cecil and Venn and Scott of Aston Sandford: on ... Hannah More; on Howard and Clarkson and William Wilberforce; made a deep mark on the Established Church ... and sensibly affected the character and aspect of secular society'.[33]

Moderates and Extremists

Within nineteenth-century Anglican Evangelicalism it is possible to see two distinctive strands emerging. One of these had its roots in the activities of John Venn, William Wilberforce and the Clapham Sect. Their stance, which was fairly broadly based and issued in generous openhearted social action, was reflected in their journal, *The Christian Observer,* which was founded in 1802. W.J. Conybeare, in his celebrated article entitled 'Church Parties', termed this group 'The Old Evangelical party'.[34] He suggested that their hallmarks were philanthropic work in mines and factories,

[31] See J. Venn, *The Life and A Selection from the Letters of the Late Rev Henry Venn MA*, p. 32.

[32] Ibid., p. 52.

[33] G.W.E. Russell, 'The Evangelical Influence' in *Collections and Recollections*, p. 90.

[34] Conybeare, 'Church Parties', p. 277.

prison reform, the establishment of Ragged Schools, the founding of the Church Missionary Society (CMS) and the British and Foreign Bible Society (BFBS), and the establishment of Church Building Societies.[35] Their supreme achievement was the suppression of the slave trade. These 'Old Evangelicals' were not without their scholars. As a typical example, Conybeare cited Dr Perry, the Bishop of Melbourne,[36] who obtained the highest honours that Cambridge could bestow. By the mid-nineteenth century, Conybeare was of the view that the 'Moderates' were diminishing in their influence and hold on the public.[37]

In contrast, Conybeare designated the second strand of Evangelical Anglicans the 'Recordite party', after their chief organ *The Record*. They were marked out, not by a mere belief in the authority of Scripture, but by a rigid adherence to verbal inspiration. According to the Recordites, 'The Bible is regarded not as a collection of books written by men under Divine guidance, but as a single book, dictated in every word and letter by God himself.'[38] Their favourite society was that which professed to be founded for the conversion of Israelites to Christianity. They taught that the Christian Lord's Day was identical with the Jewish Sabbath and was therefore to be kept with strictness and vigour.

The ministry of a model Recordite clergyman, according to Conybeare, was focused on the preaching of two extempore sermons on Sunday. Their principal concerns were 'the approaching restoration of the Jews, the date of the millennium, the progress of "Tractarian heresy" and the anticipated "perversion" of high church neighbours'.[39] The Recordites had their shibboleths and spoke of 'faithful', 'owned' and 'sealed' ministries and their attitude to culture and public amusement was one of general rejection.[40]

Boyd Hilton, in more recent times, also made a distinction between these two groups, designating them as the Clapham Moderates and the Recordite Extremists. The Moderates preached Christ and him crucified. The Extremists preached the same but also stressed that Christ was coming very soon. The Clapham school generally took a more cheerful view of private and national

---

35 Ibid., pp. 277–85.
36 For Bishop Perry see Conybeare, 'Church Parties', p. 282.
37 Ibid., p. 283.
38 Ibid., p. 287.
39 Ibid., p. 295.
40 Ibid., p. 295.

misfortune, believing, in many cases, it resulted as the natural consequence of misguided action or error. The Extremists saw misfortune as having been caused by sin. Thus the Rev Charles Bell, Francis Close's successor at Cheltenham, when contemplating a nationwide influenza epidemic, which had numbered the Duke of Clarence among its victims, urged the bishops to humiliation and prayer and so to 'publicly recognise the hand of God in our distress'.[41] The Extremists even welcomed disaster as a sign of the last days.[42] The Moderates generally had a more cheerful and affirming attitude to the pleasures of living than the Extremists. Most Moderates were postmillennialists who saw the need to build and work towards the New Jerusalem. The great majority of the Extremists were premillennial and hence believed that social improvement would only materialise after the second coming of Christ. Not surprisingly, therefore, many Extremists became increasingly drawn away from the social activism of the Clapham Moderates.

The Moderate Evangelical Anglicans tended to downplay emotional experiences while in contrast the Extremists set much more store on the prophetic and revivalist campaigns. Again, the Moderates were not antipathetic to scientific discovery,[43] whereas the Recordites opposed any accommodation with science. The Moderates believed the Bible to be inspired but they were not literalists or fundamentalists in the way that Extremists became in the 1840s. Both the Older Clapham Moderates and the Recordite Extremists had their followers during the nineteenth century, but there can be no doubt that it was the Recordites who became the dominant force in the closing decades of the Victorian era.

Centres of Evangelical Anglican Influence

Edward Bickersteth recalled his father say that when he first came as a lad to London in the year 1800, 'he could count upon his fingers all the churches in the metropolis and its environs where Evangelical truth was preached in the pulpit'.[44] Being still very much a minority

---

[41]   *The Times*, 16 January 1892.
[42]   Hilton, *Age of Atonement*, p. 22.
[43]   Ibid., p. 22.
[44]   E.H. Bickersteth, *Evangelical Churchmanship and Evangelical Eclecticism*, p. 13.

in many other places, Evangelical Anglicans tended to group themselves in and around certain centres at the turn of the century. Among the more significant were Cambridge, Clapham, Cheltenham and the Mendip Hills.

Cambridge

At Cambridge the outstanding figure was Charles Simeon (1759–1836). He had been nurtured in the high church tradition and went up from Eton to King's College in 1779, 'a wild undergraduate with a love of horses and extravagant dress'. Being required to attend Holy Communion in his College chapel he was suddenly struck by his unworthiness to attend. He purchased a copy of Bishop Wilson's book, *Lord's Supper*, from which Simeon discovered the meaning of the atonement and consequently, in 1779, he experienced his Evangelical conversion. Simeon wrote: 'The thought rushed into my mind, What! I may transfer all my guilt to another? Has God provided an offering for me, that I may lay my sins on his head? Then God willing, I will not bear them on my soul one moment longer.'[45] He subsequently recalled, 'From the time that I found peace with God myself, I wished to impart to others the benefits I had received.'[46] Three years later, in 1782, he was made a deacon and ordained and appointed perpetual Curate of Holy Trinity Church. The following year, on 28 September, Simeon was ordained as a priest by the Bishop of Peterborough, in Trinity College chapel.

Simeon's early years were marked by hostility from his churchwardens and parishioners, but he won through to become the biggest single influence in the town for nearly fifty years. Lord Macaulay wrote, 'As for Simeon if you knew what his authority and influence were, and how they extend from Cambridge to the most remote corners of England, you would allow that his real sway over the church was far greater than that of any primate.'[47]

Bishop Charles Wordsworth reckoned that 'Simeon had a much larger following of young men than Newman did at Oxford and for a much longer time.'[48] Compared with most Evangelicals, Simeon was a staunch churchman who loved the established church and its

---

[45] W. Carus, *Memoirs of the Life of Charles Simeon MA*, p. 16.
[46] Ibid., p. 17.
[47] G.O. Trevelyan, *Life of Lord Macaulay* Vol. 1, p. 67.
[48] A.R. Vidler, *The Church in an Age of Revolution*, p. 36.

services[49] with a devotion that did much to strengthen the bonds with those who were suspicious about the Evangelical revival. Simeon's maxim was 'The Bible first, the prayer Book next and all other books in subordination to both.'[50]

Simeon had an immense influence over the young undergraduates of the University and, indeed, over many of the teaching staff who flocked to his church on Sundays or made their way to his rooms at King's College to attend one of his classes. Simeon was a great Bible expositor, and his Bible and doctrine classes in the University never failed to attract attention. He published his sermons in twenty-two volumes under the title *Horae Homileticae* (literally, 'hours of sermons'). 'These works,' declared the Rev Edward Bickersteth, 'are a monument of pastoral labour and piety, with much judgement upon doctrinal subjects, and very useful application.'[51]

In order to extend Evangelical influence in the Church of England, Simeon began to purchase advowsons of a number of livings. Eventually this led to the formation of the Simeon Trust in 1833. Simeon wrote: 'Others purchase income, I purchase spheres of work.' At the time of his death in 1836 Simeon had the right to appoint the clergymen to forty-two livings and perpetual curacies.[52] Among those he purchased were Cheltenham and Derby. Like many Evangelicals, Simeon was a great believer in forming societies to promote religious and moral objectives. He played a principal role in the formation of CMS on 12 April 1799 at a meeting held at the Castle-and-Falcon Inn, Aldersgate Street.[53] After a precarious start CMS did splendid work in carrying the gospel to the heathen.[54]

Clapham

The most famous of all early Evangelical groups came into being at Clapham. It was nicknamed the 'Clapham Sect'. In reality it was no sect at all, the members all being staunch adherents of the established church and upholders of the status quo. At the centre of this community was the son of Henry Venn, John (1759–1813) who

---

[49] H.E. Hopkins, *Charles Simeon a Biography*, p. 77.
[50] M. Hennell, *Sons of the Prophets*, p. 21.
[51] *Pulpit*, 1836, p. 217.
[52] Ibid., p. 216.
[53] Carus, *Charles Simeon*, p. 126.
[54] See J. Murray, *Proclaim the Good News: A Short History of the Church Missionary Society*, pp. 163–70.

was rector of Holy Trinity, Clapham, from 1792 to 1813. Most of the members were laymen who were distinguished in various walks of life. Several were Members of Parliament. The most remarkable individual and central figure of the group was William Wilberforce (1759–1833), a Member of Parliament for Hull and a man of some wealth.

Wilberforce, along with many other early Evangelicals, was deeply concerned at the lack of 'real' religion among the people of his own class and this prompted him to publish in 1797, *A Practical View of the Prevailing Religious Systems of Professed Christians in Higher and Middle Classes in this Country contrasted with Real Christianity*. The book, which proclaimed the gospel of seriousness, enjoyed immediate popularity and did a great deal to influence those who its author had in mind. Wilberforce was by all accounts a delightful person. John Jebb (1775–1833), Bishop of Limerick, who belonged to a different school of theology wrote in 1809,

> We had the happiness of meeting Mr Wilberforce ... the pleasantest of men. There is something to me peculiarly delightful in the almost boyish playfulness of a great and good mind; and this I never saw more fully exhibited than in Mr Wilberforce. He absolutely overflows with vivacity.[55]

Other members of the Clapham Sect were Henry Thornton (1765–1815), a wealthy banker; Zachary Macaulay (1768–1838), father of the eminent historian and a businessman of great ability; and James Stephen (1758–1832), a lawyer. Charles Simeon and Isaac Milner, the Cambridge clerics, were occasional visitors to Clapham and sat in on some of their planning meetings.

The group were well-heeled, lived in large houses and drove well-groomed horses, all of which led William Makepeace Thackeray (1811–1863), the novelist, to sneer, 'In Egypt itself there were not more savoury flesh pots.'[56] However, in their defence it must be said that the Claphamites regarded their wealth as God's and not their own. For example, in 1793 Thornton gave £6,680 to charity; all other expenditure that year amounted to only £1,988.[57]

In the eyes of those at Clapham there was nothing so offensive as the slave trade. They took up where Wesley left off and made the

[55] J.H. Overton, *The English Church in the Nineteenth Century*, p. 68, citing C. Forster, *Life of Bishop Jebb*, p. 164.
[56] W.M. Thackeray, *The Newcomes*, chapter 2.
[57] Balleine, *History of the Evangelical Party*, p. 149.

cause their own. They were masters of propaganda and the political pressure group. They had anti-slavery slogans painted on their soup plates so that when their guests finished their soup they would either discern the words 'Abolish all slavery' or find a picture of a Negro with the words, 'A man and brother'. Victory came on 23 February 1807 when Wilberforce finally carried the House of Commons vote to make slave trade illegal by 283 votes to 16.[58] It was not until 1833 that it was finally made a legal offence to own a slave. Bradley calls the ending of the trade 'the outstanding example of what the Evangelicals achieved'.[59]

The members of the Clapham Sect were engaged in numerous other projects. In 1812 Wilberforce was the prime mover of An Association for the Relief of the Manufacturing Poor. The Clapham Sect also promoted Sunday schools and in 1819 Wilberforce pleaded in the House of Commons for the education of the poor. They founded The BFBS, with Henry Thornton spending as much as £2,000 a year in distributing Bibles. They also attacked duelling, bull- and bear-baiting, the state lottery, vice, the use of boys in chimney sweeping and the misuse of the Sabbath.[60]

Somerset and Cheltenham

Two other notable areas where Evangelical Anglican influence was strongly felt were the Mendip Hills around Cheddar and Cheltenham.

Hannah More (1745–1833) was the most influential of the 'Saints' in Somerset. For the first forty years of her life, she enjoyed London's high society, associating with Sir Joshua Reynolds, Johnson and Horace Walpole. Then in 1787 she came under the influence of John Newton and experienced an Evangelical conversion. In 1789, financed by William Wilberforce, Hannah began to work in the village of Cheddar. Wilberforce visited the area and was disturbed by the ignorance, poverty and brutality of the local inhabitants. The Vicar of Cheddar lived in Oxford and the curate in Wells. The thirteen neighbouring parishes were without a resident curate. Hannah had previously written to Wilberforce that the only resident clergyman, the Vicar of Axbridge, 'is intoxicated

---

[58] E.M. Howse, *Saints in Politics*, pp. 118–31.
[59] See Sir J. Stephen, *Essays in Ecclesiastical Biography*, p. 495; Bradley, *Call to Seriousness*, p. 80.
[60] Balleine, *History of the Evangelical Party*, p. 149.

about six times a week and very frequently is prevented from preaching by two black eyes honestly earned by fighting'. Together with her sister, Hannah More gathered more than five hundred children into their various schools and established a variety of schemes for improving the moral and material well-being of the neighbouring countryside. The Mores continued their work until eventually they had founded schools in an area of some seventy-five square miles and were reaching 1,300 children.[61] It was undoubtedly the case that Hannah More's philosophy of education had a strong element of condescension and social control, yet by the standards of her day she did a great deal to improve the lot of the working poor.

Cheltenham came to be dominated by Francis Close (1797–1882) who was incumbent of the parish church from 1826 to 1856. During his time in the town, Close built four churches – St Paul's, Christ Church, St Peter's and St Luke's – and had a hand in the planning of several others. In addition, Close built a dozen infant and junior schools, as well as helping to found the Ladies' and the Gentlemen's College. During his time in Cheltenham he preached against the theatre, the races and the Chartists. The Sabbath was reported to be nowhere better kept outside Scotland than in Cheltenham and when Close left the town people spoke of the end of the 'Close season'.[62]

Writing in 1879, J.C. Ryle noted that outside London there were twelve centres of provincial Evangelicalism: Manchester, Liverpool, Birmingham, Sheffield, Bradford, Hull, Newcastle, Nottingham, Bath, Clifton, Plymouth and Cheltenham.[63] Edward Bickersteth noted in 1883 that 'almost all the great centres of population and influence – Manchester, Liverpool, Leeds, Sheffield, Bradford, Birmingham, Derby, Nottingham, Norwich, Bristol, Dublin, Belfast, and others too numerous to name, as well as the universities of our land, have their fortresses of Evangelical doctrine and discipline'.[64]

---

[61] Howse, *Saints in Politics*, pp. 118–31.

[62] For Close see A. Munden, *Cheltenham's Gamaliel*; G. Berwick, *Life of Francis Close*; G. Hart, *A History of Cheltenham*; Munden, *Church of England in Cheltenham 1826–1856*.

[63] *The Times*, 6 February 1879, cited by K. Hylson-Smith, *Evangelicals in the Church of England 1734–1984*, p. 147.

[64] E.H. Bickersteth, *Evangelical Churchmanship*, p. 13.

The Distinctive Features of Nineteenth-Century Evangelical Anglicans

There are two or possibly three identifiable phases in the history of the nineteenth-century Evangelical Anglicanism. Those who analyse two, take the 'Simeonite phase', which ended in 1836 with the death of Charles Simeon and was largely socially orientated, as the first and the Bickersteth/Shaftesbury/Close phase, which extended from 1836 down to the end of the century, as the second. In this latter period, Evangelical Anglicans increasingly turned their attention to anti-Roman and anti-ritual crusades. They also became less involved in social action and more concerned with other-worldly pietism.

Handley Moule, in his *History of the Evangelical School in the Church of England during the Nineteenth Century*, suggested a third period, 'the age of the Church Missionary Society', which extended from the death of Shaftesbury to the end of the century.[65]

Aside from these identifiable phases, there are several distinctive features that are common to the whole of nineteenth-century Evangelical Anglicanism. David Bebbington, in his seminal work *Evangelicalism in Modern Britain*, sets out four defining core characteristics – 'conversionism', the belief that life changed; 'activism', the expression of the gospel in effort; 'biblicism', a particular regard for the Bible; and 'crucicentrism', a stress on the sacrifice of Christ on the cross.[66] 'Together', he suggests, 'they form a quadrilateral of priorities that is the basis of Evangelicalism',[67] and in the early days of revival the emphasis was often on the first and the last of the core beliefs. Bebbington helpfully elaborates on each of the four characteristics in the opening chapter of his book.

Conversionism was the *sine qua non* of Evangelicalism. Robert Bickersteth, Bishop of Ripon from 1857 to 1884, held 'that no sermon was worthy of the name which did not contain the message of the gospel, urging the sinner to be reconciled to God'.[68] For Evangelicals, conversion was often preceded by acknowledgements of wretchedness, guilt and personal sinfulness. This was followed by what Boyd Hilton called, 'the all important contractual

---

[65] H.G.C. Moule, *The Evangelical School in the Church of England: Its Men and its Work in the Nineteenth Century*, p. 6.

[66] D.W. Bebbington, *Evangelicalism in Modern Britain*, p. 3.

[67] Ibid., p. 3.

[68] Ibid., p. 5.

relationship with Christ'.[69] Conversion for Evangelicals was bound up with theological convictions. Because humans are estranged from God by their sinfulness, there is nothing they can do by themselves to gain salvation. It had 'to be received not achieved'. Conversion for Evangelicals began at the point of initial faith, as Luther had earlier insisted, acceptance comes through faith, not works;[70] for Evangelicals 'conversion is', in the words of Jonathan Edwards, 'a great and glorious work of God's power'.[71] In early Wesleyan Methodism conversion was mostly sudden.[72] On the other hand, Evangelical Anglicans did not doubt the validity of gradual conversions. Charles Simeon was definite that 'we require nothing sudden'.[73]

Activism, for Bebbington, refers to the great desire among Evangelicals, following their conversion, to spread the gospel message. The desire to save souls from a Christless eternity caused Evangelicals to leave centres of learning and to go out into the parishes and the foreign mission fields.

Biblicism, the third feature of the Evangelicals, refers to their devotion to the Bible. In this veneration, Evangelical Anglicans, as will be seen in a later chapter, displayed a variety of views as to the manner of its inspiration and the extent of its reliability. For some, every last word was inspired and the biblical text spoke infallibly on every subject, whether it was science, morality, history or doctrine. For other Evangelicals the Bible was inspired but not infallible in matters of science.

Crucicentrism refers to the centrality of the cross in Evangelical soteriology. Here the doctrine that Christ died as a substitute for a sinful mankind marked Evangelicals off from other sections of Anglicanism. The implications of the cross as a motivating factor for evangelism and service were also important. Henry Venn, for example, maintained that all attempts to promote holiness must be defective unless they were rooted in the cross of Christ.

Reflecting on Bebbington's four cardinal features of Evangelicalism, it is tempting to add 'Pneumatism' as a fifth. For many Evangelical Anglicans, particularly those who identified with the 'Recordites', the doctrine of the witness of the Spirit conveying

---

[69] Hilton, *Age of Atonement*, p. 8.
[70] Bebbington, *Evangelicalism in Modern Britain*, p. 6.
[71] Ibid., p. 7.
[72] S.G. Dimond, *The Psychology of the Methodist Revival*, p. 5.
[73] Bebbington, *Evangelicalism in Modern Britain*, p. 6.

a subjective assurance of the presence of God in the life of the believer was all-important. This was an emphasis that stemmed from John Wesley. In earlier times Evangelical conversion had been understood largely in terms of intellectual assent to biblical and doctrinal truths. As a result of his own heart-warming experience at Aldersgate, Wesley emphasised that the individual can have assurance of salvation as a result of the work of the Spirit of God. Wesley articulated his doctrine in the following statement:

> the testimony of the Spirit is an inward impression whereby the Spirit of God directly witnesses with my spirit that I am a child of God; that Jesus hath loved me and given himself for me; that all my sins are blotted out and I, even I, am reconciled to God.[74]

Notwithstanding these differences of emphasis and understanding, all nineteenth-century Evangelical Anglicans were committed to the following core of doctrine and practice.

Justification by faith

This central Reformation doctrine denotes ways in which the individual was believed to be made (*faceo*) right (just) with God. In a university address, entitled 'On Justification by Faith', Charles Simeon said, 'If there be any one question of more importance than all others, it is this: How shall a man be just with God?'[75] A little later in this sermon Simeon elaborated further on the doctrine:

> What we mean by being justified by faith, we shall explain in a few words. We all, as sinners, are obnoxious to the wrath of God. But the Lord Jesus Christ is set forth in the gospel as having by His own obedience unto death obtained eternal redemption for us. To Him we are commanded to look as to the propitiation offered for the sins of the whole world. And we are assured that, on our doing this with penitence and faith, we shall be justified from all things, from which we would not be justified by the law of Moses ... Thus are we accepted ... or, in other words justified by faith.[76]

---

[74] J.E. Rattenbury, *Wesley's Legacy to the World*, p. 97.
[75] A. Pollard, *Let Wisdom Judge: University Addresses and Sermon Outlines by Charles Simeon*, p. 63.
[76] Ibid., pp. 63–4.

Isaac Milner (1750–1820), President of Queen's College and Simeon's closest friend in Cambridge, said, 'You build for eternity on the righteousness of Christ; you renounce for ever, as a foundation of hope your own righteousness.'[77]

Later in the nineteenth century, as Newman and other Oxford Movement leaders began to reaffirm the medieval teaching that 'justification' was a life-long process initiated by baptism and sustained by an obedient life nurtured on the church's sacramental system, Evangelicals became insistent on the Reformation teaching that justification was through faith in Christ alone who died as the perfect substitute for sinful mankind. As Bishop John Bird Sumner (1780–1862) of Chester put it succinctly in his charge of 1841, 'The scriptural truth is as clear as it is simple ... faith alone can justify, faith alone can appropriate to us that remedy which God has appointed for the healing of our plague.'[78]

The Rev George Stanley Faber (1773–1854) of Durham, an Evangelical theologian, highlighted the only two possible methods of justification in his *Primitive Doctrine of Justification*, which was published in 1837:

> The one system grounds our justification upon our own intrinsic righteousness, infused into us by God, through our faith in the Lord Jesus Christ. The other system grounds our justification upon the Extrinsic Righteousness of Christ appropriated and forensically made our own by faith as an appointed instrument.[79]

Put in absolute simplicity, the issue was whether justification was to be based on what is done *in* the believer or what has been done *for* the believer. The Tractarians, following Pusey and Newman, tended to put the emphasis increasingly on the former, whereas the Evangelicals clung vehemently to the latter. As Bishop John Sumner saw it, the consequence of Tractarian teaching was that man was 'induced to look to himself and not the Redeemer for acceptance with God'.[80]

---

[77] B.M.G. Reardon, *From Coleridge to Gore*, p. 27.

[78] For Sumner on justification, see J.B. Sumner, *The Doctrine of Justification Briefly Stated*.

[79] P. Toon, *Evangelical Theology 1833–1856*, p. 147; see also Hilton, *Age of Atonement*, pp. 23, 141.

[80] Toon, *Evangelical Theology 1833–1856*, p. 148.

The Bible as a divinely-inspired book

The belief that the Scriptures of the Old and New Testaments were divinely inspired was a conviction that was universally held by the early Christian churches. It was lost in the Middle Ages but then emphatically reasserted by the Reformation and Luther's *sola Scriptura* principle. In fact, the Church of England's Articles of Religion, which emerged from the Reformation, describe the Bible as 'God's written Word'. Nineteenth-century Evangelical Anglicans were insistent that the Bible was more than a book penned by men; it was also in their view inspired by God. The celebrated Bible commentator, Thomas Scott (1747–1821), of Aston Sandford, maintained that the biblical authors 'wrote indeed in such language, as their different talents, educations, habits and associations suggested, or rendered natural to them; but the Holy Spirit ... superintended them ... to all which best suited their several subjects'.[81] Daniel Wilson, Bishop of Calcutta, wrote similarly that the Holy Spirit 'suggested and dictated the truths delivered' but 'left the writers to describe the matter revealed in their own way'.[82] Again, Charles Simeon, Fellow of King's College, Cambridge, and the acknowledged leader of the Evangelical party in the established church during the first four decades of the nineteenth century, contended similarly that 'the Scripture was written by God'.[83]

This did not mean that Victorian Evangelicals shared the convictions of the later American fundamentalists whose unthinkingly literal interpretations of the text led to their spending much powder and shot in fighting Darwin's evolutionary theories. Their struggles culminated in the celebrated 'Monkey Trial' of 1925, where William Jennings Bryan declared that 'if the Bible had taught that Jonah had swallowed the whale he'd have believed it'.[84]

The participants at one of Charles Simeon's conversation parties discussed the New Testament passage about 'the rock following Israel in the wilderness'. 'Did the rock really move?' asked one of the undergraduates. 'Oh yes of course', Simeon is alleged to have retorted, 'with a hop skip and a jump!'[85] This was no unbridled or

---

[81] T. Scott, *Introduction to the Study of the Bible*, p. 13.
[82] A. Pollard, 'Anglican Evangelical Views of the Bible 1800–1850', *Churchman* 74.3 (1960), p. 172.
[83] Ibid., p. 169.
[84] See, for example, W.S. Hudson, *Religion in America*, p. 370.
[85] Pollard, *Let Wisdom Judge*, p. 16.

stark literalism. In marked contrast to prevailing opinions, some of the early-Victorian Evangelical Anglicans were among the first to part with a non-scientific approach to the book of Genesis. Among them was John Sumner who wrote in 1816 that 'the account of the creation given by Moses, does not profess to furnish anything like a systematic scheme or elaborate detail of the mode in which the materials of the earth were brought to their actual form and situation'.[86]

Personal religion

A key feature in the lives of Evangelical Anglicans, as indeed all Evangelicals, was their emphasis on personal religion. Not only did they assert that the Holy Spirit influenced the writers of the Scripture, they believed that the same Holy Spirit of God could speak personally and existentially to the individual Christian believer. This 'personal religion' in which the individual shared the whole of life's experiences with Christ was the very hearthstone of all Evangelical religion. Its roots, which are found in early Christianity and in the writings of certain medieval mystics, such as Bernard of Clairvaux and Thomas à Kempis, were firmly re-established by Thomas Cranmer and the Protestant Reformers and the 'religion of the heart and spirit' proclaimed by John Wesley.

Nineteenth-century personal religion found its classic expression in William Wilberforce's *Practical View*, which sold 75,000 copies in its first five months of publication and eventually went through fifteen editions,[87] and Bishop Ryle's *Evangelical Religion*, which also enjoyed widespread popularity. At one significant point in *Evangelical Religion* Ryle pinpoints some significant aspects of this personal religion:

> [A] leading feature of Evangelical religion is the high place which is assigned to the inward work of the Holy Spirit in the heart man ... there can be no real conversion to God, no new creation in Christ, no new birth of the Spirit, where there is nothing felt within. We hold that the witness of the Spirit, however much it may be abused, is a real thing.[88]

---

[86] J.B. Sumner, *A Treatise on the Records of Creation* Vol. 1, p. 272.

[87] W. Wilberforce, *A Practical View of the Prevailing Religious System of Professed Christians in the Higher and Middle Classes in this Country Contrasted with Real Christianity*, p. 7.

[88] Ryle, *Knots Untied*, pp. 6–7.

For Evangelicals, conversion was not primarily an affair of the mind or an intellectual assent to a set of doctrinal propositions; neither was it primarily of the will or a sense of duty; rather, it was a matter of the innermost spirit. It was God's Spirit witnessing with the individual's spirit that he or she is a child of God. In short it was a 'religion of the heart'.

Protestant faith and worship

Not only was the heart of Christianity seen by nineteenth-century Anglican Evangelicals in plain and simple terms, their tastes in matters of faith and worship were similar. They strove always for a faith that was easy to grasp and worship that was unpretentious. This was why they clung so urgently to The Articles of Religion, which they viewed as a straightforward explanation of essential Christian doctrine direct from the Reformation. As Charles Simeon put it, 'The Articles are an authorised exposition of the sense in which all [the Church's] members profess to understand the Scriptures.' Edward Bickersteth the younger reiterated the same point: 'We protest with our Articles and Homilies against the corruptions of Rome. A very large number of us believe the Church of Rome to be the Babylon of the Apocalypse ... We are Protestants, and we are not ashamed of the name.'[89]

The Evangelical taste for simplicity of worship was well put by Bishop Ryle in *Evangelical Religion*: 'But we steadily maintain that simplicity should be the grand characteristic of Christian worship. We firmly believe that the tendency to excessive ornament, and theatrical ceremonial, is to defeat the primary aim for which worship was established, to draw men to Christ.'[90]

Social action

Inheriting the legacy of John Wesley who styled himself 'God's steward of the poor', nineteenth-century Anglican Evangelicals were staunchly and energetically committed to social action. Lord Shaftesbury, who was one of the greatest social reformers of the nineteenth century, asserted in 1884 that 'the most philanthropic movements of the century have sprung from the Evangelicals'. Shaftesbury asserted that he could not remember engaging in any

---

[89] E.H. Bickersteth, *Evangelical Churchmanship*, pp. 18f.
[90] Ryle, *Knots Untied*, p. 13.

one piece of social reform in which he had not been motivated by his faith in Christ. Josephine Butler's (1828–1906) Christian commitment motivated her crusade against prostitution and the unjust treatment of prostitutes in garrison towns and cities. As she said of her work: 'These principles, I have ever believed, and continue to believe, have their foundation in the ethics of Christ.'[91]

The motivation for Evangelical philanthropy was not a sense of duty, but in the main a feeling of altruistic compassion for others that was derived from their personal 'heart' religion. Certainly the record of social action on the part of nineteenth-century Anglican Evangelicals was impressive by any standards and included the anti-slavery campaigns led by William Wilberforce; mining and factory reforms pioneered by George Bull (1799–1865) and Lord Shaftesbury; education work, including the building of schools and colleges, inspired by individuals such as Francis Close and the Sumner brothers; nursing and public health developed by Florence Nightingale; to say nothing of temperance campaigning, prison reform and visiting; improving the status of women and the promotion of child care and orphanages. Kathleen Heasman has justly claimed that nineteenth-century Evangelical social-reformers laid the foundation of the twentieth-century welfare state.[92]

Missionary activity

Ian Bradley wrote that 'Missionary zeal was perhaps the strongest single characteristic of the Evangelicals in the early nineteenth century, it was certainly one of their most powerful legacies to the Victorians.'[93] This missionary impetus stemmed in part from the Evangelical's sense of personal accountability. He or she was accountable before God for the souls of the perishing. The biblical text which hung over the mantelpiece in many Victorian homes, as E.P. Thompson reminded us, was, 'Thou God seest me.'[94] Many Evangelicals believed themselves to be answerable for the way in which they spent every moment of the day. This meant they threw themselves wholeheartedly into visitation campaigns, open air preaching and other forms of evangelistic work.

---

[91] J. Butler, *Personal Reminiscences of a Great Crusade*, p. 39.
[92] K. Heasman, *Evangelicals in Action: An Appraisal of their Social Work in the Victorian Era*, p. 295.
[93] Bradley, *Call to Seriousness*, p. 74.
[94] E.P. Thompson, *The Making of the English Working Class*, p. 406.

The Evangelical Anglicans also drew strongly at this point on the legacy of John Wesley who had declared that 'the world is my parish' and, prompted by his Arminian theology, urged his helpers to go to every corner of the globe to insist 'you must be born again'. Boyd Hilton has made the point that the Moderate Evangelicals in particular were for the most part either explicit or quasi-Arminians. In their preaching they declared God's willingness to save all men.[95] Charles Simeon, who played a principal role in the foundation of CMS in 1799, gave major impetus to Anglican missions at home and overseas.

The huge contribution made by nineteenth-century Evangelical Anglicans to home and overseas mission has been well documented by Donald Lewis,[96] Brian Stanley[97] and William Jacob.[98]

A religion of the home

Finally, it must be said that nineteenth-century Evangelicals succeeded in establishing Christianity as the religion of the home. Here they drew on the legacy of the Elizabethan Puritans who had urged the home as the haven of retreat and the place of Sabbath rest. This should not be taken to imply that Evangelical homes were overly puritanical. George Russell writing at the end of the Victorian era emphasised that 'Austerity, gloom and Pharisaism had no place among the better class of Evangelicals.' He cited the example of William Wilberforce who was pronounced by Madame de Stael to be the most agreeable man in England. In Russell's view he was of 'a most gay and generous disposition' and 'lived in perpetual sunshine, and shed its radiance all around him'.[99]

Evangelicals advocated the need for family prayers and Henry Thornton of the Clapham Sect published a book of *Family Prayers*. Many others produced similar volumes. Evangelicals kept a firm hand on their children at home and the phrase 'Little Children must be seen and not heard' is thought by some to have originated in this context.

---

[95] Hilton, *Age of Atonement*, p. 388.
[96] D.M. Lewis, *Lighten Their Darkness: The Evangelical Mission to Working-Class London 1828–1860*.
[97] B. Stanley, *The Bible and the Flag*.
[98] W.M. Jacob, *The Making of the Anglican Church Worldwide*.
[99] Russell, *Collections and Recollections*, p. 95.

Edward Henry Bickersteth, shortly before his consecration to the See of Exeter, declared that Evangelicals still stood for the Bible as 'the supreme rule of faith and practice', 'the quickening of the human soul to the spiritual life by the direct operation of the Holy Ghost ... justification by faith only in Jesus Christ crucified and risen ... the episcopal form of Church government ... and protest with our Articles and Homilies against the Church of Rome'.

We may conclude that these aspects represent the quintessence of Anglican Evangelicalism in nineteenth-century England. It was a form of religion that had its weak points but was, nevertheless, one of the strongest social and political influences at work in the nineteenth century, as a number of secular historians have recently readily acknowledged.

2

The Clapham Sect

Origins

At the beginning of the nineteenth century Clapham was still a small village with a population of no more than two thousand inhabitants. Three miles of pleasant meadows lay between it and London. Around the common, which was described as 'a glorious wilderness of gorse bushes and gravel pits and ponds', a number of substantial houses had sprung up, built by merchants and a small group of Members of Parliament who wished to live in the country and yet be near to the nation's capital.

The Rev John Venn was the Rector of Clapham during the high period of the Sect's activity. On his arrival in the parish in 1792, in succession to Sir James Stonehouse, a noted Evangelical, Venn was hassled by some of the more influential inhabitants but succeeded in continuing the church on vigorous Evangelical lines. He remained in office till his death in 1813, when William Dealtry (1775–1847) succeeded him. Dealtry was a fellow of Trinity College, Cambridge, and was greatly respected by Charles Simeon.[1]

Venn made two significant innovations. He had a Sunday evening service and he set up a system of district visitors. Evangelicals were still not generally accepted at the time and when a lady who was staying with the Bishop of London at Fulham Palace wanted to visit Venn's Clapham rectory, the prelate only agreed to her using his carriage provided she agreed to get out some distance away and walk to Venn's house. He could not bear the thought that his horses and episcopal carriage might be seen outside an Evangelical rectory.[2]

---

[1] For Dealtry see Overton, *English Church*, p. 66.
[2] Balleine, *History of the Evangelical Party*, p. 147.

The Clapham Sect were a small group of upper class influential lay men and lay women[3] who congregated in Clapham in the late eighteenth century. There was little that was sectarian about them. They were mostly[4] members of the established church who valued the ministry of John Venn at Holy Trinity Church. The designation of 'sect' may have derived from a verbal jibe by the literary critic and wit, Sydney Smith (1771–1845). The name Clapham Sect was made popular by Sir James Stephen, the son of James Stephen, in his famous essay under that title.

A variety of different reasons brought this remarkable group of individuals and their families together at Clapham. They were devoted to the church, fervent in prayer and drew a good deal of inspiration from studying the Bible. The activities of the group seem to have begun soon after Henry Thornton (1760–1815), who was for thirty years MP for Southwark, purchased a mansion on Clapham Common. William Pitt designed a beautiful oval library for the house and this, according to Sir James Stephen, in his *Essays in Ecclesiastical Biography*, became the headquarters of Clapham social action. Stephen wrote, 'the chamber he had thus projected became the scene which amidst his proudest triumphs he might well have envied and witnessed the growth of projects more majestic than any which ever engaged the deliberations of his cabinet'.[5]

Near to Thornton lived William Wilberforce, the vivacious MP for Hull. Pitt and Burke both declared him to be the greatest orator of the age. Indeed, Wilberforce became a real power in the House of Commons at a time when Parliamentary eloquence was at its zenith. Amid many other matters Wilberforce was deeply concerned at the lack of real religion among his own class. For this reason in 1797 he published *A Practical View* in which he compared nominal Christianity with true 'heartfelt' Evangelical Christianity. The book did a great deal to influence the upper classes for whom Wilberforce had written. Although serious about his faith, Wilberforce was no killjoy and many people took delight in his company.

Close to Wilberforce and Thornton's residences lived other people of note. Granville Sharpe (1735–1813) was a scholar and pamphleteer whose work resulted in the decision in 1772 to fight slavery in England. Sharpe became Chairman of The Anti-Slavery

---

[3] Hannah More was associated with the Sect and they sponsored her work in the Mendips.

[4] William Smith was a Unitarian and John Bowdler was high church.

[5] Stephen, *Essays in Ecclesiastical Biography*, p. 524.

Society and was active in the work of the Sierra Leone project and BFBS. James Stephen was an MP and a lawyer of note who had seen the evils of the slave trade at first hand. On his return to England he made contact with Wilberforce and became active in the abolition campaign. Zachary Macaulay had gone at the age of sixteen to work on an estate in the West Indies as an overseer. He arrived back in England obsessed with the barbarity of the slave trade and resolved to throw in his lot with the campaigns of the Saints. Charles Grant (1746–1823) and John Shore (1751–1834), who later became Lord Teignmouth, had both held positions of responsibility in India before and then later, as members of the Sect, became wholehearted backers of missions there.

These men represented the inner core of the Clapham 'Saints' but there were a number of others who were associates in the work. Among them were the Rev Thomas Gisborne (1758–1846), the Squire of Yoxhall in Staffordshire and a Prebendary of Durham Cathedral. He spent part of every year with Wilberforce labouring for their major projects. Sir James Stephen noted that Gisborne who was a close friend of Wilberforce for fifty years,[6] contributed significantly 'to the formation of the national mind on the subject of the highest importance to the national character'. Gisborne was 'one of the greatest preachers of the age'[7] and the expositor of the 'Evangelical system'.[8] Yoxhall Lodge, Gisborne's residence, also became another meeting place for the group.[9] Indeed, Howse refers to it as 'a second Clapham'.[10] Hannah More moved in her later years to Cheddar where the Clapham Sect sponsored her educational work that extended across the Mendip Hills and involved the production and circulation of countless cheap repository tracts. Thomas Babington (1758–1837) joined the Sect's activities, as did Sir Thomas Fowell Buxton (1786–1845), an avid fighter against the slave trade. Although John Venn only involved himself in specifically religious Clapham projects he was nevertheless one of the inner core and his guidance and advice were often requested.[11]

The private lives of the members of the Sect were noteworthy on several counts. They were well heeled and prosperous and

---

[6] Ibid., p. 535.
[7] Ibid., p. 535.
[8] Ibid., p. 533.
[9] Howse, *Saints in Politics*, p. 26.
[10] Ibid., pp. 18, 26.
[11] M. Hennell, *John Venn and the Clapham Sect*, p. 180.

family-orientated individuals who lived in large and comfortable houses. They were well clothed, dined from plentiful tables and rode well-groomed horses. They were men and women of discipline who kept an ordered lifestyle. Some of Wilberforce's daily journals were discovered after he died. They listed periods spent in prayer, so much time for study, and so many hours for business. At the end of each day there was even a column for time wasted. The Saints made prayer a priority[12] and set aside three hours each day for intercessory prayer. They prayed from five to six in the morning, twelve to one at midday and from five to six in the evening. They were also generous with their time and money. For all this, their faith was by no means austere or miserable.[13] Two months before he died John Venn said to his children, 'You can all bear me witness that I have never represented religion to you as a gloomy thing, I have never said you must do this or you will go to hell, but I have set it before you as a scene of joy and happiness unspeakable.'[14]

The Slave Trade

In the eyes of the Evangelicals nothing was so offensive as the slave trade. For many years English seafarers had been engaged in transporting slaves from Africa to the plantations of North America. The usual route was from Bristol and Liverpool to West Africa, where cheap cotton goods were sometimes used to barter for slaves who were then shipped to America and sold to the planters. The ships then returned to England with new cotton, sugar and tobacco. Horace Walpole noted in a letter that about 46,000 slaves were sold to the English plantations every year.[15] By 1770 it was estimated that there were also 14,000 black slaves in England.[16]

In 1774 John Wesley attacked slavery in a tract entitled *Thoughts on Slavery*. In it he exposed some of the brutal practices connected with the trade:

---

[12] Ibid., p. 208.
[13] Ibid., p. 208.
[14] Ibid., p. 159.
[15] P. Cunningham, *Walpole's Letters* (9 Vols.), 'Letter to Sir H. Mann', Vol. 3, p. 197, cited by J.W. Bready, *England: Before and After Wesley*, p. 102.
[16] Ibid., p. 105.

Those selected are marked on the breast with a burning iron. Before going on board, their masters strip them of all that they have on their backs; so that they come on board stark naked, women as well as men ... they are stowed together in as little room as it is possible for them to be crowded.

Wesley described the slave trade as 'the execrable sum of all villainies.' Yet, despite his untiring efforts, he was not to see abolition become a reality. The task was left to Wilberforce.

Wilberforce had first become concerned about the slave trade as a young boy and later, when still only fourteen years of age, he had written 'a precocious letter' to a Yorkshire paper demanding an end to 'the odious traffic in human flesh'.[17] Just six days before he died, Wesley wrote to Wilberforce urging him 'to go on, in the name of God and in the power of His might, till even American slavery, the vilest that ever saw the sun, shall vanish away before it'. Wesley concluded with the words 'That He who has guided you from your youth up, may continue to strengthen you in this and in all things.'[18] Earlier, Thomas Clarkson (1760–1840) and Granville Sharpe had formed an Abolition Committee in 1787 and Clarkson had set out to win Wilberforce to the cause.

Once persuaded, Wilberforce gave the greater part of his life over to the fight. He raised a number of strong objections to the trade in a lengthy work of more than 150 pages and entitled *A Letter on the Abolition of the Slave Trade Addressed to the Freeholders and Other Inhabitants of Yorkshire*.[19] These included the insufficient feeding of slaves, their defective clothing and lodging and their excessive hours of work. He also exposed the cruel and indecent punishments meted out to slaves[20] and offered a number of additional proofs to show that their lives were miserable. Wilberforce concluded by reminding his readers that 'the Jews themselves were expressly commanded not to retain any of their own nation, any of their brethren in slavery'.[21] He emphasised that

Christ has done away all distinctions of nations, and made all mankind one great family, all our fellow creatures are now our brethren; and

---

[17] Howse, *Saints in Politics*, p. 11.
[18] R. Coupland, *William Wilberforce*, p. 141.
[19] W. Wilberforce, *A Letter on the Abolition of the Slave Trade Addressed to the Freeholders and Other Inhabitants of Yorkshire*.
[20] Ibid., p. 67.
[21] Ibid., p. 150.

therefore the very principles and spirit of the Jewish law itself would forbid our keeping the Africans, any more than our fellow subjects in a state of slavery.[22]

In a later plea, entitled *An Appeal to the Religion, Justice and Humanity of the Inhabitants of the British Empire on Behalf of the Negro Slaves in the West Indies*,[23] Wilberforce again attacked 'the driving system – the whip – a brutal instrument'.[24] He also spoke out against the fact that 'no attempt has been made to establish marriage among the slaves' who were left to cohabit by mutual consent.'[25] Victory finally came on 23 February 1807 when Wilberforce carried his bill by a majority of 267 votes.

Although the trade was now outlawed in the British Empire the campaign to end the ownership of slaves continued. When Wilberforce finally retired from the House of Commons in 1825, Thomas Buxton took up the fight, which aimed to end slave ownership in the British Colonies.[26] At a public meeting on 12 May 1832 Buxton concluded his address with the following emphatic declaration.

> When we look at the career of affliction of our brother man, for, after all he is our brother, moulded in the same form, heir to the same immortality, and, although in chains and in suffering, on a level, in the eyes of God, ... when I view him writhing under the lash of his tormentor; when I see him consigned to a premature and unregarded grave, having died of slavery ... there can be but one feeling in my heart, one expression on my lips: 'Great God! How long, how long, is this iniquity to come?'[27]

Slavery was finally ended throughout the British dominions on 7 August 1833. The conscience of the English nation had finally been aroused and Parliament voted the sum of £20,000,000 in compensation to the planters.

---

[22] Ibid., p. 150.
[23] W. Wilberforce, *An Appeal to the Religion, Justice and Humanity of the Inhabitants of the British Empire on Behalf of the Negro Slaves in the West Indies.*
[24] Ibid., p. 13.
[25] Ibid., pp. 14ff.
[26] C. Buxton (ed.), *Memoirs of Sir Thomas Fowell Buxton.*
[27] Ibid., p. 282.

Other Clapham Sect Concerns

The accusation has sometimes been made that William Wilberforce and the Clapham Sect exhausted their energies on the overseas slave trade and failed to devote their attention to issues of greater need at home. Charles Raven, for example, wrote that Wilberforce 'never realised that while he was bringing liberty to the Negroes in the plantation, the white slaves of industry in mine and factory were being made the victims of tyranny a thousand fold more cruel'.[28] Whilst Raven's criticism may have contained an element of truth, the fact is the Saints gave themselves to a number of other projects and concerns.

The Factory Act

In 1802 Wilberforce sided with Sir Robert Peel to establish the first Factory Act, but raised objection that its provisions did not extend far enough. In 1805 he took up on behalf of the oppressed Yorkshire weavers whose plight he knew well. In 1818 Wilberforce supported the further extension to the Factory Act put forward by Peel.

Chimney boys

In the matter of relief for the climbing boys used by chimney sweeps, the *Christian Observer* gave detailed coverage of Lewis Realy who died on 24 November 1809 when he was trapped up a chimney in a house near Temple Bar. Almost no action was taken against those who had ordered the child to do the work. The journal's editor commented that it was time the legislature was 'awakened to the state of these unfortunate sufferers' and an end made of what it referred to as 'the horrors' of this 'slave trade'.[29]

The poor

In 1809 the Saints established The Society of the Refuge for the Destitute, which aimed 'to provide a place of refuge for persons discharged from prisons or hulks, unfortunate and deserted females … and others who … cannot procure an honest maintenance

---

[28] C. Raven, *Christian Socialism 1848–1854*, p. 12.
[29] *Christian Observer*, March 1810, p. 182.

though willing to work.'[30] In 1812 Wilberforce was the prime mover in the formation of An Association for the Relief of the Manufacturing Poor.

During the last decade of the eighteenth century the poor rate proved inadequate to meet the needs of the large numbers of poor at Clapham. As a consequence, John Venn first of all revived the Clapham Poor Society, which provided subsidies to enable the poor to buy bread, coal and potatoes.[31] Then, in 1799, he formed The Society for Bettering the Condition of the Poor at Clapham. The parish was divided into eight districts and each had its own treasurer, and two or three visitors were charged with the responsibility of assessing the needs of those in their area. In fact, Venn's society was criticised because it was thought to discriminate too strongly between the deserving and the undeserving poor. Venn countered that indiscriminate charity weakens resolve: 'In a word let it be the aim of this society to say, not merely this man was hungry and we fed him, but this man was naked and behold he is clothed by his own industry.'[32] Venn also interested himself in the health of his parishioners and in 1800 he made arrangements for the whole parish to be vaccinated.[33]

Education of the poor

A major aspect of the Saints' concern for the poor was the time and energy they devoted to educational projects. From an early point they were enthusiastic backers of Sunday schools. Shortly after Robert Raikes had opened his school in 1780, the first Sunday School Society was formed to promote the organisation of schools and to provide the necessary funds. Henry Thornton was one of the main protagonists and Granville Sharpe and Hannah More were enthusiastic supporters, but some of those in high office, including Bishop Samuel Horsley, believed that Sunday schools were breeding grounds for sedition and democracy. As a consequence, Hannah More experienced considerable opposition when she began her work in Cheddar in 1789.

In reality, More's scheme of education was markedly narrow and subsequent critics denounced it as socially controlling. A farmer's

---

[30] *Christian Observer*, June 1909.
[31] Hennell, *John Venn and the Clapham Sect*, p. 140.
[32] Ibid., p. 145.
[33] Ibid., p. 203.

son, for example, was taught 'beneficial and appropriate knowledge for the boy of this class', but the children of day labourers were to be given 'no writing' and no reading other than the Bible and the catechism and 'such little tracts as may enable them to understand the Church service'.[34]

The work accomplished by Hannah and her sister was substantial. Within a short period they had gathered upwards of 500 children and established schools over an area of seventy-five square miles. Writing in 1801 to the Bishop of Bath and Wells, Richard Beadon (1737–1824), Hannah outlined her motives in setting up schools and gave details of her method of instruction:

> When I settled in the country thirteen years ago, I found the poor in many villages sunk in a deplorable state of ignorance and vice ... This drew me to the more neglected villages, whose distance made it very laborious. Not one school did I ever attempt to establish without the hearty concurrence of the clergyman of the parish. My plan of instruction is extremely simple and limited. They learn, on weekdays, such coarse works as may fit them for servants. I allow of no writing for the poor. My object is not to make them fanatics, but to train up the lower classes in habits of industry and piety. I know of no way of teaching morals but by teaching principles, or inculcating Christian principles without imparting a good knowledge of Scripture.[35]

In 1795 Hannah More started her 'Cheap Repository Tracts', although these were intended more for adults than for children. Her aim was to provide a supply of 'safe' literature that was anti-Jacobin in politics and Evangelical in religion.[36] Among Hannah's early endeavours, *Village Politics by Will Chip* proved to be hugely popular. Will Chip, the author's own creation, caught the imagination of the working classes with his homely wisdom. The tracts sold in thousands, and thousands more were purchased by the wealthy and distributed free of charge. The *Christian Observer* of April 1811 devoted a short paragraph to Hannah More's tracts in which they applauded the fact that 'not only have the poor been taught to read', but 'pains have been taken also to turn this new faculty to account by furnishing them with suitable reading'.[37] In order to keep the

---

[34] Howse, *Saints in Politics*, p. 97.
[35] M.G. Jones, *Hannah More*, p. 152.
[36] Howse, *Saints in Politics*, p. 196.
[37] *Christian Observer*, April 1811, p. 238.

price at a level that the poor could afford, this work had to be subsidised. Henry Thornton, who seems to have made the project his own, donated a large proportion of the money that was needed to fund the publication of these tracts.[38]

In 1809 the Sect formalised their backing of Sunday school work with the formation of The Society for the Support and Encouragement of Sunday Schools in England.[39] Later that year it was reported in the *Christian Observer* that in the half year since their last general meeting the committee had issued 8,995 spelling books, 1,666 New Testaments and thirty-six Bibles for the use in 125 schools that contained upwards of 6,000 children. The same article noted that since the commencement of their institution they had distributed 277,577 spelling books, 60,570 New Testaments and 7,662 Bibles to 3,270 schools containing upwards of 260,000 children, besides £4,176 for the payment of teachers.[40]

The Saints were among the first to see the possibilities of schooling for all poor children. Between 1802 and 1804 Wilberforce and his circle planned and proposed a national scheme of primary schools associated with the Church of England. The idea was for a primary school to be established in each parish. The plan was eventually squeezed out but when the national society was later formed in 1811, it received strong support from the men and women of Clapham.[41] Later, in 1819, Wilberforce spoke in a House of Commons debate on education and made a strong plea for the education of the poor. He declared that 'if people were destined to be free, they must be fit to enjoy their freedom'.[42]

John Venn was one of the first clergymen to introduce parish schools. In Clapham, six schools for poor children were maintained by private subscription. In addition, Henry Thornton and Wilberforce supported schools at Southwark and Sandgate, respectively.[43] Macaulay worked hard to achieve universal education in the colony of Sierra Leone. After his return to England, Venn assisted Joseph Lancaster and also added his support to the *Christian Observer*'s endorsement of Andrew Bell.

Shortly before he died, Venn dictated a 'pastoral farewell address' to his people. The Rev Hugh Pearson read it out at Venn's

---

[38] Howse, *Saints in Politics*, p. 102.
[39] *Christian Observer*, May 1809, p. 332.
[40] Ibid., May 1809, p. 669.
[41] Howse, *Saints in Politics*, p. 99 citing *Christian Observer* 1839, p. 800.
[42] Howse, *Saints in Politics*, p. 99.
[43] Ibid., p. 98.

funeral. In it Venn declared that by the assistance and liberality of his Clapham congregation he had 'been enabled to complete the three things nearest my heart'. One of these was 'the enlargement of our school' by which means 'every child in the parish may be gratu-itously taught to read'.[44] Venn believed that education was a *preparatio evangelica*. For the clergymen, he said, it will produce 'a rising generation of young persons disposed to listen with a lively interest to his sermons ... prepared by good habits to attend regu-larly the ordinances of worship, accustomed to revere him as their guide and attached to him as their friend'.[45]

The suppression of vice

William Wilberforce felt that God had given him two great callings: the abolition of the slave trade and the reformation of manners. The latter objective was progressed when in 1801 proposals were published for establishing a Society for the Suppression of Vice.[46] According to the *Christian Observer* it was composed of 'near four hundred respectable characters, many of them of rank and distinction'.[47] The Society established a number of branches in major towns and cities including Chatham, York, Gloucester, Long Sutton and Reading.[48] They gave themselves to the task of combat-ing vice in a variety of different forms. One of their earliest battles was against the publication of obscene books[49] and the profanation of the Sabbath. The *Christian Observer* reported that the Hull branch focused its endeavours against 'the profanation of the Lord's Day, disorderly houses of every description, lewdness, drunkenness and profane swearing.'[50]

There was a strong element of social control in the Society's work. Persons who employed servants or apprentices for example, were 'strongly recommended ... to take means for regulating their conduct.' This included restraining their servants 'from spending their time in the streets on Sunday evenings', which 'exposes them

---

[44] J. Venn, *Sermons by the Rev John Venn MA Rector of Clapham*, Preface – Brief Life of Venn, p. xxvii.
[45] *Christian Observer*, 1804, p. 542.
[46] Howse, *Saints in Politics*, p. 120.
[47] *Christian Observer*, March 1802, p. 608.
[48] *Christian Observer*, November 1807, p. 756 and 1808 p. 203.
[49] *Christian Observer*, March 1802, p. 608.
[50] *Christian Observer*, March 1808, p. 203.

to great temptation, and is highly injurious to their morals'.[51] By 1810 these efforts were reported to have had 'an extensive influence in the metropolis and its vicinity'.[52] It was reported in May of this same year that 'since the Society's last report there have been nearly 600 prosecutions by the Society.'[53] The bulk of these prosecutions were for Sabbath breaking but they also included five for fortune telling and two for vendors of obscene publications.[54]

Sometimes through the Society, and at other times through their own individual efforts, the Clapham Sect concentrated their energies on other obvious vices that they considered unfit for a Christian country. In particular, they worked hard for the outlawing of duelling, the abolition of the lottery and an end to brutal sports. Sharp wrote a tract against duelling in 1769 and Wilberforce expressed his very strong disapproval at Pitt's duel with Tierney.[55] The *Christian Observer* of April 1803 spoke against the practice of duelling as 'so manifestly at variance with the spirit and precepts of Christianity, that it would be wasting the time of our readers to attempt a formal proof of its criminality.' The journal made reference to the recent unhappy duel between Colonel Montgomery and Captain Macnamara, which resulted in the death of the former. Such scenes, wrote the writer, are 'repugnant to the gospel'.[56]

During his last years in Parliament Wilberforce supported a bill for the prevention of cruelty to animals most notably bull- and bear-baiting. He had to grapple with the fact that respectable society of his age thought that barbarous sports were a necessity for the degraded passions of the lower ranks of society. On the 16 June 1824, the Rev Arthur Broome (1780–1837), the incumbent of St Mary's, Bromley-by-Bow, called a meeting at Old Slaughter's Coffee House, St Martin's Lane, London, at which The Royal Society for the Prevention of Cruelty to Animals (RSPCA) was founded.[57] Thomas Fowell Buxton and William Wilberforce were among the founder members.[58] Broome subsequently resigned his living in order to devote his full energy to the Society's work.[59]

---

[51] Ibid., p. 203.
[52] *Christian Observer*, May 1810.
[53] Ibid.
[54] Ibid., see also *Christian Observer*, November 1807, p. 756.
[55] Howse, *Saints in Politics*, p. 121.
[56] *Christian Observer*, April 1803, p. 252.
[57] A.R. Moss, *Valiant Crusade: The History of the RSPCA*, p. 22.
[58] Ibid., p. 46.
[59] Ibid., p. 34.

The *Christian Observer* of June 1807 stated that it was 'altogether unnecessary to mention the cruel sports of racing and hunting, which are in every view incompatible with Christianity'. Equally, the journal condemned Sunday posting which caused 'multitudes of wretched horses' that laboured under the whip for six days to be denied the rest that God has expressly provided for them on the seventh.[60] Another paragraph regretted that bull-baiting 'has not entirely ceased' and described cock fighting as a 'diabolical amusement'.[61]

Prisons

Since John Wesley's undergraduate days, Evangelicals had begun to demonstrate concern for the state of prisons and the state in which prisoners lived. In 1809 the Clapham Sect formed The Society for the Refuge of the Destitute. It was 'to provide a place of refuge for persons discharged from prisons or the hulks ... and others, who from loss of character or extreme indigence, cannot procure an honest maintenance though willing to work.'[62] Thomas Buxton published *An Inquiry Whether Crime be Produced or Prevented by our Present System of Prison Discipline* in February 1818.[63] In the House of Commons, Sir James Mackintosh described it as being a work 'full of profound information' which had brought prison abuses home to the feelings of every man in the country.[64] On entering Parliament Buxton directed his initial energies to the different forms of judicial punishment.[65]

Wilberforce was hostile towards 'our numerous laws', 'our bloody laws' and 'the barbarous custom of hanging'.[66] In 1819 he spoke out in the Commons against the severity of the criminal code[67] which was a change from his earlier days when in 1795 he gave support to Pitt's repressive Treasonable Practices Act and The Seditious Meetings Act.[68]

---

[60] *Christian Observer*, June 1807, p. 368.
[61] *Christian Observer*, June 1807, p. 368.
[62] *Christian Observer*, June 1809, p. 400.
[63] Buxton, *Memoirs*, p. 74.
[64] Ibid., p. 75.
[65] Ibid., p. 83.
[66] Howse, *Saints in Politics*, p. 128.
[67] Ibid., p. 129.
[68] Ibid., p. 117.

Thomas Gisborne shared Wilberforce's concern for law and order and in his *Friendly Observations Addressed to the Manufacturing Population in Great Britain Now Suffering under the Difficulties of the Times*[69] he urged all members of the manufacturing body to 'conduct themselves with patience, quietude and resignation.'[70] His view was that lawless behaviour would serve no useful purpose. 'What can the wild fury of twenty thousand levellers of factories and breakers of power-looms', he wrote, 'effect against the disciplined valour ... of a thousand dragoons.'[71] Gisborne stressed that machinery would enable them to sell cheaper and better goods on the Continent and then they wouldn't need cheaper bread.[72] He urged his readers to 'reverence the laws' and 'to love your neighbour as yourself.'[73] Gisborne, along with his friend and colleague John Sumner, was an opponent of the Poor Law because 'the idle' and 'the dissolute' were able to obtain relief from the parish.[74]

Sailors

Thomas Clarkson had a particular concern for sailors and the brutality and harsh conditions that many of them suffered. In a publication entitled *The Grievances of our Mercantile Seamen A National and A Crying Evil*[75] he attacked and exposed the cruelty of the ways in which British sailors were treated at sea and in port. Such was the harshness of life at sea that 'at least one quarter of all crews were on the dead list before returning home' and at least another quarter were lost to their country as either 'discharged' or 'deserted'.[76] Those who deserted did so 'generally from the brutal conduct of the captain and the officers.'[77] Clarkson was

---

[69] T. Gisborne, *Friendly Observations Addressed to the Manufacturing Population of Great Britain Now Suffering under the Difficulties of the Times*.

[70] Ibid., pp. 3–4.

[71] Ibid., p. 7.

[72] Ibid., p. 10.

[73] Ibid., p. 12.

[74] Ibid., pp. 20–3.

[75] T. Clarkson, *The Grievances of Our Mercantile Seamen A National and A Crying Evil by Thomas Clarkson, MA*.

[76] Ibid., p. 3.

[77] Ibid., p. 4.

particularly disturbed by the way in which Masters of merchant vessels flogged crew-members sometimes 'with their own hands'.[78] Clarkson did, on one occasion, manage to get an officer tried in a British Court for murdering a crewmember but found that witnesses were bribed out of the way and that magistrates were slave merchants.[79]

While the ships were in port sailors were often forced to live in 'long rooms' close to the dockside. Clarkson found that the land-lords of these places did everything to make the men spend their money: 'Prostitutes in abundance ... and cheerful companions are purposely introduced to them, together with the fiddle and the dance.'[80] Clarkson exposed the ills of the long rooms at the back of the public houses in London's East End where hundreds of sailors danced with local girls. These girls plied the men drinks with laudanum and other drugs to the point 'where they became completely intoxicated'. The girls then induced them back to their lodgings and there the sailors were 'robbed of every penny they possess'. Instances were reported of sailors 'being robbed of fifty pounds or upwards the very day they received it'.[81] Clarkson offered a number of solutions to these evils. Captains could be required to take the crew list to Custom House. They would then be questioned about the behaviour of the crew and the crew in turn would be interrogated as to the conduct of the captain. Complaints would be settled in the law courts.[82] Other measures included the licensing of sailors' lodgings, marine inspectors who would ensure that all seafarers were properly fed, and the building of churches on the docksides.[83]

The sick

Clapham philanthropy also extended to the sick and their concern led them to support the Indigent Blind Institution and the Foundling Hospital. It further extended to 'war widows' and The Refuge for the Destitute.[84]

---

[78] Ibid., p. 11.
[79] Ibid., p. 14.
[80] Ibid., p. 17.
[81] Ibid., p. 17.
[82] Ibid., p. 22.
[83] Ibid., p. 26.
[84] Howse, *Saints in Politics*, p. 127.

Religious projects

The Clapham Sect also committed themselves to a number of specifically religious projects and societies. Among the most noteworthy were the CMS and BFBS.

Church Missionary Society

The Claphamites decided to form a missionary society in 1799. This took place on the 1 April at the Falcon Inn on Aldersgate Street. Only two Clapham representatives were present, John Venn and Charles Elliott. Wilberforce, Grant and James Stephen were made vice-presidents and Henry Thornton, treasurer. Venn laid it down that the society must be conducted 'on the Church principle; but not on the high church principle'.[85] The Rev Josiah Pratt (1768–1844), who was the first editor of the *Christian Observer*, was adamant that the society must be kept in Evangelical hands.[86] The society was first named The Society for Missions in Africa and the East.[87] The word 'church' (Church Missionary Society) was not officially adopted until 1812. Josiah Pratt was secretary for twenty-two years from 1802–1824 in succession to Thomas Scott.

The founders of CMS pleaded that church people should not only support the new society but should also continue to stand behind and give to the work of the Society for the Propagation of the Gospel in Foreign Parts (SPG) and the Society for Promoting Christian Knowledge (SPCK).[88]

The CMS early progress was a mixture of encouragements and setbacks. Several of Simeon's men – among them Henry Martyn (1781–1812), Dr Claudius Buchanan (1766–1815) and Thomas Thomason (1774–1829) – went out to India as chaplains. Buchanan advocated the setting up of an extensive ecclesiastical establishment in India as a way of preserving the country from revolution. He recommended 'the toleration of all religions, and the zealous extension of our own'.[89] Martyn was of the view that the threefold translation of the Bible into Persian, Arabic and Hindustani would be 'the downfall of Mohammedanism' if properly done. He died at the young age of thirty-two with the project all but complete.

---

[85] Ibid., p. 76.
[86] See also Overton, *English Church*, pp. 81–2.
[87] Howse, *Saints in Politics*, p. 76.
[88] For details of these societies see chapter 12 of this book on overseas missions.
[89] Overton, *English Church*, p. 266.

Many of CMS's early discouragements came in the form of the early deaths of missionaries, particularly in West Africa. Notwithstanding these and other difficulties the society became the major overseas Anglican missionary organisation of the nineteenth century.

British and Foreign Bible Society
Representatives of the Clapham Sect also played a significant part in the formation of BFBS in 1804. Early impetus came from Joseph Hughes, a Welsh Baptist minister who presented a paper to a meeting of the Religious Tract Society urging that an association be formed exclusively to promote the circulation of the Scriptures. A meeting, chaired by Granville Sharpe, was held on 7 March 1803 at the London Tavern. At a subsequent meeting, held on 12 March, Hughes' name was put forward as secretary of the new society. Others felt it was important that the new society receive backing from the established church and put forward Josiah Pratt. In the event, Hughes and Pratt were appointed as joint secretaries. Pratt resigned on 23 April and John Owen became clerical secretary. At the same meeting in March Lord Teignmouth was elected first president of the society and among the vice-presidents were the Bishops of London, Durham, Exeter and St David's. The treasurer was Henry Thornton and the committee included Charles Grant, Zachary Macaulay, Granville Sharpe and William Wilberforce.[90]

Despite having received a good deal of hostility from Anglicans, the Bible Society expanded quickly to become one of the largest Evangelical organisations in England. Within the first two decades of its existence it had spent almost £1,000,000 on printing and distributing the Scriptures in 136 languages.[91] By the mid-nineteenth century it had more than 370 branches and an annual income of over £100,000. Henry Thornton was described as 'a very Bible Society in himself' and spent as much as £2,000 a year distributing Bibles.[92]

The Bible Society understandably brought together a heterogeneous group of supporters and this inevitably caused internal difficulties. Among the most prominent was the controversy over the Apocrypha. It had always been the custom to print Bibles on the Continent with the Apocrypha and foreign Protestants were not immediately ready to abandon the practice. Eventually however, after strong objections from Scottish supporters, it was

[90] *Christian Observer*, March 1804, p. 181.
[91] Howse, *Saints in Politics*, p. 111.
[92] Bradley, *Call to Seriousness*, p. 137.

resolved in 1825 'that the funds of the society be applied to the printing and circulation of the canonical books of Scripture to the exclusion of the Apocrypha.'[93] Although this resolution appeared to have settled the issue it had nevertheless caused a good deal of bitter feeling.

Other serious questions arose in 1831 concerning the issues of whether Socinians should be allowed to hold office in the society and whether or not meetings should commence with a reading from Scripture and prayer. The majority defeated the suggestion that those who denied the Trinity and the deity of Christ should be excluded, but a minority resigned and founded The Trinitarian Bible Society. The Bible Society continued to attract opposition from high churchmen, but it nevertheless became one of the largest pan-Evangelical organisations in Victorian England.

The Sect's Methods

Networking

The Clapham Sect's success in many of these projects and societies was due in some measure to the methods that they employed. They extended their efforts through 'networking', both by means of family and church connections. Henry Thornton was Wilberforce's cousin, Gisborne married Babington's sister and Babington married Macaulay's sister. Charles Elliott married John Venn's sister, Stephen married Wilberforce's sister and later, James Stephen's son married John Venn's daughter. Fowell Buxton was a relative of Elizabeth Fry and this undoubtedly aided him in his campaign for penal reform.

Campaigning

The Claphamites were also skilled in the art of campaigning through books, pamphlets and tracts. Most of the inner core of the Saints wrote at least one substantial volume on an aspect of their social concern: Buxton, Clarkson, Sharpe, Stephen and Wilberforce all made significant contributions to the literature on slavery;

---

[93] T.R. Birks, *Memoir of the Rev Edward Bickersteth, Late Rector of Watton* Vol. 2, p. 30.

Clarkson wrote on *The Grievances of Our Mercantile Seamen*; Granville Sharpe produced several important works on the British legal system; Hannah More, perhaps the most prolific author among the Clapham group, reached a wide audience with *Thoughts and Manners of the Great* (1788) and enabled the fashionable world to engage with the challenge of the Evangelical agenda.

Furthermore, Wilberforce and his circle knew how to win friends and influence people in high places. Prime Ministers Pitt and Spencer Perceval were among those whose friendship was courted in support of their various causes.

Motivational Factors

A number of key factors motivated the Clapham Sect in their remarkable wide-ranging social and political achievements. Like all Evangelicals of the period, they believed themselves to be answerable to God for their actions and for the use of their time. This led to their engaging in good works that, as D.W. Bebbington observed, were seen as 'a fundamental element of Christian duty'.[94]

At times, and in some of their projects, the Sect were motivated by the prospect of saving souls. As Sydney Smith once jibed, 'wherever they gain a footing ... proselytism will be their main object; everything else is a mere instrument'.[95] John Venn certainly substantiated Smith's accusation and considered education to be 'a preparation Evangelical.' In the schools which they founded Venn urged that 'the soul may be cultivated and prepared for the reception of heavenly seed.'[96] The rules of the Clapham Bettering Society revealed a similar objective. It was required that all who received financial aid should regularly attend public worship.[97]

It is abundantly clear that the Clapham Sect aimed through many of their projects to control and improve the behaviour of the recipients. Indeed, William Cobbett once declared that 'the mission of the Saints ... was to teach the people to starve without making a noise and keeping the poor from cutting the throats of the rich'.[98] There

---

[94] Bebbington, *Evangelicalism in Modern Britain*, p. 70.
[95] F.K. Brown, *Fathers of the Victorians: The Age of Wilberforce*, p. 5.
[96] Hennell, *John Venn and the Clapham Sect*, pp. 136–7.
[97] Ibid., p. 144.
[98] A. Smith, *The Established Church and Popular Religion*, p. 51.

was without doubt truth in his accusation. It was epitomised by a prayer in Henry Thornton's devotional book for families, 'Give to the poor contentment with their lot, and to the rich a spirit of compassion and benevolence.' The Society for the Suppression of Vice 'strongly recommended to all persons, who employ servants or apprentices, to take means for regulating their conduct, and preventing them from infesting the streets in the evening of the Sabbath.' Such behaviour, it continued, exposed servants to 'great temptation', and is highly injurious to their morals.'[99] In *An Inquiry into the Duties of Men in the Middle Classes of Society in Great Britain*, which was published in 1795, Thomas Gisborne urged employers to put down, albeit mildly, all combinations on the part of their workmen.[100] Hannah More was strongly motivated by social control. Her scheme for education was a narrow one with each child being taught only what was appropriate to his or her social class. She explained the aim which lay behind her tracts as being 'to give to the inferior ranks a new direction to their taste, and to abate their relish for those corrupt and inflammatory publications which in consequences of the French Revolution have been so fatally pouring in upon us'.[101]

Compassion was undoubtedly what most prompted Wilberforce and his associates in the crusade against the slave trade. Wilberforce was moved by the brutality by which slaves were procured, transported, fed, housed and worked under the whip. He urged, 'Christ has done away all distinctions of nations, and made all mankind one great family, all our fellow creatures are now our brethren'.[102]

Of all the factors that goaded the Saints to social reform, fear of divine judgement seems never to have been very far from the surface. In a speech to the House of Commons in May 1789 Wilberforce claimed that the Irish ceased to trade in slaves in the reign of Henry VII when 'a great plague infested the country' and they were 'struck with panic'. Wilberforce suspected 'that the plague was a punishment sent from heaven, for the sin of the slave trade'.[103] 'All I ask, therefore of the people of Bristol', he continued, 'is that they would become as civilised now, as Irishmen were four hundred years ago.' In another

---

[99] *Christian Observer*, March 1808.
[100] T. Gisborne, *An Inquiry into the Duties of Men in the Middle Classes of Society in Great Britain* Vol. 2, p. 375.
[101] Howse, *Saints in Politics*, p. 101.
[102] Wilberforce, *Abolition of the Slave Trade*, pp. 149–50.
[103] Howse, *Saints in Politics*, p. 36.

speech to the House in 1791 he urged that they must continue to combat 'this bloody traffic' until they had released themselves from 'the load of guilt, under which we at present labour'.[104] In his *Letter on the Abolition of the Slave Trade* Wilberforce wrote that to continue to trade in slaves 'must infallibly bring upon us the heaviest judgements of the Almighty'.[105]

The Society for the Suppression of Vice warned in 1803 'that this nation, on account of its irreligion and vices, has just reason rather to dread the displeasure, than to rely on the favour of the Almighty'.[106] The day before the parliamentary session of 1831 commenced, Buxton wrote a meditation in which he prayed, 'May I remember that, ere the year closes, I may be snatched away and hurried before thy judgement seat.'[107]

Assessment of the Clapham Sect

The Saints have been criticised at various points in history and for different reasons.[108] The most frequent accusation is that they spent a great deal of time concerned for the African slaves but not enough for the industrial poor who laboured in furnaces and cotton mills of northern England. Charles Raven, for example, wrote that Wilberforce 'never realised that while he was bringing liberty to the Negroes in the plantations, the white slaves of industry in mine and factory were being made the victims of tyranny a thousand fold more cruel'.[109] Whilst there is clearly substance in this accusation, it is worth pointing out that the generation that followed the Claphamites took up and successfully addressed these issues in Parliament.

It was clearly the case that the abolition campaign was an all-engrossing concern for Wilberforce. Indeed it was essentially his lifetime's work. The Saints – most notably Clarkson, Wilberforce and Sharpe – gave themselves untiringly to research, writings and organising public meetings. Zachary Macaulay actually travelled

---

[104] Ibid., p. 39.
[105] Wilberforce, *Abolition of the Slave Trade*, p. 163.
[106] *Christian Observer*, October 1803, p. 598.
[107] Buxton, *Memoirs*, p. 254.
[108] See for example Bradley, *Call to Seriousness*; and J.L. Hammond and B. Hammond, *The Town Labourer 1760–1832*, p. 216.
[109] Raven, *Christian Socialism 1848–1854*, p. 12.

on a slave ship in 1795 so that he could view the plight of the slaves at first hand. At the height of the campaign, Wilberforce was working nine and a half hours a day gathering and sifting evidence. But it was because the slave trade was, in the words of Sir James Stephen, 'the monster iniquity which fairly outstripped all abhorrence, and baffled all exaggeration'[110] that it justified the attention which the abolitionists gave it.

In a similar vein, charges have been made against the Clapham Sect that they concerned themselves with the vices of the poor but not the conditions of the poor. It is a fact that a number of the issues with which the Saints concerned themselves directly affected the social life and leisure of the poor. The most obvious examples would be the Vice Society's campaigns against the profanation of the Lord's Day, prostitution and drunkenness. Against this view, however, can be set the fact that the group made attacks on horse-racing, hunting, the overuse of horses and Sunday newspapers and the Sunday posting of letters.

The members of the Clapham Sect have been charged with working in such a way as to deal with the manifestations of poverty, but not the roots of poverty. Put another way, they were generous with charity but made no effort to work for better pay and conditions. As John and Barbara Hammond, the Fabian socialist historians, put it:

> It never seems to have crossed the minds of these philanthropists that it was desirable that men and women should have decent wages, or decent homes, or that there was something wrong with the arrangements of a society that left the mass of people in this plight.[111]

However, care must be taken not to assess the Clapham Sect with the wisdom of twentieth- or twenty-first-century hindsight. It was not until a generation later that the Christian socialists began to grapple, albeit inadequately, with these issues. By the standards of their time the Clapham Sect did as much, if not more, for the poor than other sections of the Christian church. It also needs to be recognised that the education that the Claphamites promoted among the poor, particularly through their support of Sunday schools, was a seedbed that with the passing of time produced a more articulate working class who were able to fight for improvements to their lot. The

---

[110] Stephen, *Essays in Ecclesiastical Biography*, p. 538.
[111] Hammond and Hammond, *Town Labourer*, p. 216.

limited education that the Saints provided was a good deal better than none at all and marked the beginnings of what was to become a universal system.

The Claphamites were clearly a people of their own age who believed in a divinely ordered social hierarchy and the subordination of ranks. When Wilberforce introduced the Combination Bill of 1799 to strengthen the laws preventing the combination of workmen against their masters, he did not see it as an attempt to crush the working classes. Rather, he regarded it as a direct means of protecting the poor from manipulation by agitators who were imbued with the spirit of the French Revolution and aimed to hurt the poor by bringing them into conflict with their masters.

There is no doubt that the Clapham Sect accomplished a great deal by their wide-ranging social and philanthropic endeavours – these included charitable institutions such as the Society for the Relief of Persons Imprisoned for Small Debts, and the Society for Bettering the Condition of the Poor at Clapham. In so doing, they set a pattern for subsequent Evangelical social reform in the later nineteenth century. Additionally, the great religious societies that they encouraged and sponsored, CMS and BFBS, were to have a major impact on the religious life of the nation. Sir James Stephen noted that the educational reformers, Andrew Bell and James Lancaster, 'were both their welcome guests' and that schools, prison discipline, Saving Banks, tracts, village libraries, district visiting and church buildings all featured among their many projects.[112]

By 1833, the year of Wilberforce's death and the year in which slavery was abolished in the British Empire, the influence of the Clapham Sect was fading. Notwithstanding the criticisms levelled against them, they had done a great deal to alter the mood of the English nation. G.M. Trevelyan traced the origin of Victorian optimism to their anti-slavery triumph.[113] E.M. Howse concluded that 'they left England with "an earnest of success", and an awakened hope that days still brighter were to come'.[114] K. Hylson-Smith was probably right in his assessment that the Clapham Sect cannot justifiably be dismissed as repressive and reactionary, nor can they be hailed as progressive and reformist. Both claims represent an over-simplification.[115]

---

[112] Stephen, *Essays in Ecclesiastical Biography*, p. 568.
[113] Howse, *Saints in Politics*, p. 185.
[114] Ibid., p. 185.
[115] Hylson-Smith, *Evangelicals in the Church of England*, p. 91.

3

Politics and the Social Order

The Rise of Evangelicals in Parliament

Evangelicals have often been criticised, and with some justification, for concentrating on the world to come and paying only scant attention to the affairs of this world. Such a charge, however, certainly could not be levelled at John Wesley and those who shared his concerns for the state of the British nation. Indeed in his 'Discourse on the Sermon on the Mount' Wesley stated, 'Christianity is essentially a social religion ... to turn it into a solitary religion is indeed to destroy it ... when I say this is essentially a social religion, I mean that it cannot subsist at all without living and conversing with other men.'[1]

Thus it was largely as a result of Wesley's example and impact that in the last quarter of the eighteenth century Evangelicals began to influence public life. In so doing, they were also prompted by the writings of Hannah More, Thomas Gisborne and William Wilberforce. Hannah More's *Thoughts on the Importance of the Manners of the Great to General Society* (1788), Thomas Gisborne's *Enquiry into the Duties of Men in the Higher and Middle Classes* (1794) and Wilberforce's *Practical View* (1797) all gave strong impetus and encouragement to the higher orders of society to bring Christian principles to bear on national life.

From the mid-1780s Evangelicals began to make their presence felt in Parliament. During the following fifty years Ian Bradley identified 112 Evangelical MPs.[2] This represented a 'conservative

---

[1] J. Wesley, 'Discourse on the Sermon on the Mount', in *Works* Vol. 5 (1872 edn.), p. 296.

[2] See I.C. Bradley, *The Politics of Godliness: Evangelicals in Parliament 1784–1832*, p. 15–17.

estimate' and it is quite possible there were more. According to Bradley, most of them were activists and after 1820 aligned themselves with the reforming Tories. The dominant figure in the earlier years was Henry Bankes (1757–1834), Tory MP for Corfe Castle 1780–1826 and Dorset 1826–1830. He was a close friend of William Wilberforce in the early years of his Parliamentary career. Among other responsibilities he chaired a committee set up in 1807 to investigate salaries and sinecures. Bradley observed several different groups of Evangelicals in Parliament in the fifty years preceding 1832; the Saints, the non-Saint Evangelicals and emerging in the later 1820s were a group of Recordite MPs.

William Wilberforce led the Saints and several of their number, including Sir Thomas Fowell Buxton, Charles Grant, William Smith, James Stephen and Henry Thornton, were part of the Clapham circle. Most of the Saints, who numbered about thirty,[3] were Tories and one or two were Whigs. Some, like Buxton and Wilberforce, were more properly independent Tories. The Saints also had important connections. For example, Edward James Eliot's sister was married to William Pitt. Henry Brougham, another Sect member, married Pitt's sister in 1785. Hannah More estimated that the Saints could command about forty votes.[4] After Wilberforce retired from the House in 1825, to be replaced as leader by Buxton, the situation changed and the Evangelicals who began to enter Parliament were those of more extreme Protestant views. The Saints were great supporters of the larger Evangelical societies. Indeed, some of them, such as CMS[5] and BFBS,[6] were Clapham creations.

The Saints also exerted their influence in the affairs and appointments of the Church of England. Charles Grant was elected Director of the East India Company in 1794 and was soon able to get churches built and to secure a succession of able chaplains who were to leave a permanent mark on Anglo-Indian life.[7] Evangelicals had managed to secure Henry Ryder's appointment as Bishop of Gloucester in 1815 despite intense resistance from the Archbishop of Canterbury. Some years later, Charles Grant the Younger and his brother succeeded in getting Daniel Wilson appointed to the See of

---

[3] Ibid., pp. 276–9.
[4] Hannah More to Henry Ryder, 7 May 1819 cited ibid., p. 48.
[5] Howse, *Saints in Politics*, pp. 76–7.
[6] Ibid., p. 110.
[7] Ibid., pp. 79–80.

Calcutta in 1832. Clapham, where nine of the Saints had their homes, was the hub and centre of operations. It was here that their extra-Parliamentary activities were planned and executed. The Saints conscientiously attended parliamentary debates and their commitment to hard work gained them places on important select committees, where they were able to make further impact. Wilberforce was not only the leader of the Saints, but was also widely recognised as the leader of all the MPs who were actively concerned to bring an end to slave trading and, later, slave ownership throughout the British Empire.

In addition to the Saints, Bradley identified a larger group of non-Saint MPs all of whom were Tories.[8] Included in their number were Dudley Ryder, Tory MP for Tiverton (1794–1813), later the First Earl of Harrowby, and Spencer Perceval, Tory MP for Northampton (1796–1812) and Britain's only Evangelical Prime Minister from 1809 until his assassination in 1812. These men, Bradley suggests, were strong Evangelicals, but they did not always follow the dictates of their conscience in reaching an opinion on the debates in the House. They were sometimes governed by other sets of loyalties. This was even the case with some of them in regards to slavery.[9] It seems that a number of these non-Saint MPs did not regularly attend the House of Commons and Parliamentary speeches from their number were few and far between.[10]

A further identifiable group of MPs who began to emerge in the 1820s were the Recordites. They followed the theological and political line adopted by *The Record* newspaper and worked together in Parliament for the advancement of Evangelical causes. They numbered both Tories and Whigs in their ranks. Among them were Captain James Gordon, a Scottish episcopalian, Tory MP for Dundalk and the secretary of the Reformation Society which was established in 1827 and was violently anti-Catholic; Spencer Perceval the Younger, Tory MP for Newport (1827–1831) and Tiverton (1831–1833); and Granville Ryder, Tory MP for Tiverton, and son of the First Earl of Harrowby.

Boyd Hilton, as has been noted,[11] has helpfully distinguished the theological outlooks of the Clapham Moderates from the Recordite

---

[8] Bradley, *Politics of Godliness*, p. 59.
[9] Ibid., p. 48.
[10] Ibid., p. 62.
[11] See chapter 1 of this book.

Extremists.[12] In the later sections of this book, he indicates the ways in which their differing doctrines impacted and influenced their social and political thought. The extreme Evangelicals tended to see God as an interventionist deity ever ready to involve himself in human affairs and to punish sin. Thus every calamity, whether national or individual, was treated with great seriousness and regarded as God speaking, warning, punishing sin or meting out judgement. The Clapham Moderates who included the Saints, Hilton suggests, were in tune with Enlightenment thinking and regarded the world as a well-oiled machine constructed by divine providence to run in accordance with the laws of nature. In social and economic terms the 'Extremists' tended to favour paternalistic interventionist solutions. Thus they supported the Government's protectionist policy in the passing of the Corn Laws in 1815. On the other hand, the 'Moderates', with their theological inclination towards deist non-interventionism, were comfortable with laissez faire economics and the open market. They tended to focus their concern on the salvation of the well to do, the dishonest financier, the exploitive factory owners and the brutal matter forcing climbing boys up the soot-soaked chimneys.

The non-interventionist posture of the 'Moderates' meshed with their view that the poor were part of God's plan in the natural order of things. Poverty was simply the result of the poor breeding too early and too freely and so bringing misfortune on themselves and on society in general. Bishop John Sumner who stood firmly with the Claphamite Moderates[13] drew a distinction in his influential volume, *A Treatise on the Records of Creation* published in 1816, between what he termed 'honourable poverty' 'which is the lot of many' and 'indigence' or extreme poverty which cannot be part of a wise creator's pattern and is most usually self-inflicted by laziness or intemperate behaviour. Sumner pointed up the distinction in the following passage:

> These conditions, it must be remembered, are essentially distinct and separate. Poverty is 'often both honourable and comfortable; but indigence can only be pitiable, and is usually contemptible. Poverty is not only the lot of many, in a well-constituted society, but is necessary that a society many be well constituted'.[14]

---

[12] Hilton, *Age of Atonement*, pp. 10–11.
[13] Scotland, *John Bird Sumner*.
[14] J.B. Sumner, *Creation* Vol. 1, p. 26.

In contrast Sumner saw indigence as reprehensible. It can be avoided given proper motivation and adequate human effort: 'Indigence, on the contrary, is seldom the natural lot of many, but is commonly the state into which intemperance and want of prudent foresight push poverty: the punishment which the moral government of God inflicts in this world upon thoughtlessness and guilty extravagance.'[15]

Sumner suggested a variety of devices for avoiding indigence including postponement of marriage[16] on the part of the lower orders of society. Indigence could not be seen as established by a wise creator and it would not feature in well-balanced civilised societies. Sumner went on to assert that the creator had established a principle of population control that 'will keep a society of various ranks and conditions in a state of balance'.[17] Populations, he argued, will tend to multiply up to the level of the food supply and remain fairly static at that point. When the population level reaches a maximum for the available food supply the resultant pressure will either lead to migrations or famine conditions and then to ill health and subsequent increases in the death rate.

Sumner had taken Thomas Maltnus' theory that poverty, for all except the fortunate few, was inevitable and that redistribution is powerless to effect any lasting change, and given it a specifically biblical and Christian frame of reference. A.M.C. Waterman went further, maintaining that by 1833 political economists had constructed a system on the main features of Sumner's thinking and produced an ideological system which was to dominate popular, if not intellectual, thinking until the end of the nineteenth century.[18] It showed itself in current thought such as laissez-faire economics and pleas for an open market free from import tariffs on foodstuffs and raw materials.

In many ways Sumner's argument in the *Treatise* was very much in keeping with eighteenth-century thinking. Thus the natural world including human relations were seen as God-created and governed by in-built divine laws. Interference with these laws was perilous and could only result in worse disruption. The only ways

---

[15] Ibid., Vol. 1, p. 26.
[16] Ibid., Vol. 2, p. 92.
[17] Ibid., Vol. 2, p. 317.
[18] A.M.C. Waterman, 'The Ideological Alliance of Political Economy and Christian Theology 1897–1833', *Journal of Ecclesiastical History* 34 (April 1983), p. 242.

forward were thus moral improvement and charity, provided it did not undermine the motivation of the poor to work and to improve their situation. Thus, as Sumner saw it, the Speenhamland system was bad because it encouraged idleness and prevented natural law, which would eliminate the weak from running their course.

As the Moderate Evangelicals saw it, the urge to barter and exchange goods was a natural instinct and therefore divinely implanted in man. Consequently, they became supporters of free trade and this led to their opposing any governmental intervention in the market. This meant that they were strongly opposed to the Corn Laws, which provided artificial support to the landed gentry and farmers and raised bread prices beyond the reach of the poor. By the same token, Hilton suggested they opposed the Ten Hours Act since it diminished profits and the wages fund. On the other hand, over-work that caused a glut in the market was unnatural and thus the 'Moderates' were happy to support the sanctity of the Lord's Day. In the light of all this, it does seem a little surprising that the Claphamites were so vehement and strong in the campaign to abolish slavery. Hilton comments of Wilberforce, Thornton and Grant that they all slept through Robert Owen's outlining of his scheme for New Lanark and they only got excited about social reform when there were obvious villains.[19]

Later circumstances led Sumner to be somewhat more restrained in his advocacy of laissez-faire policies. At the end of the French wars, the returning soldiers created a glut of surplus labour and this together with the Corn Laws, which kept bread prices at a high level, led to starvation in some places and rioting and the burning of hayricks. All this meant indigence on a wide scale, which, it seemed, was not likely to be solved by allowing things to run their natural course. In fact, before the end of the nineteenth century, Liberal political theorists were advocating restrictive policies.[20]

Hilton saw the Evangelical age of atonement as coming to an end in the 1850s and being replaced by F.D. Maurice's Christ-centred theology of the incarnation with its emphasis on man rather than a vengeful God. As Hilton put it, 'if God was still working his purpose out, man's task was to work with him in eradicating evil and suffering and to help build Maurice's "organic Christian society"'.[21] Evangelical Extremists had alienated many of the younger generation

[19] Hilton, *Age of Atonement*, p. 208.
[20] Ibid., p. 303.
[21] Ibid., p. 208.

of Evangelicals and pushed potential leaders such as Gladstone, Stanley, Acland, Newman and Robert Wilberforce away towards the high church.[22] In the later years of the century the percentage of Anglican Evangelicals in the House of Commons was less and the bishops and laity in the House of Lords became increasingly focused on moral and ecclesiastical issues.

Evangelical Parliamentary Campaigns

Clearly those members of Parliament who were Evangelicals and members of the established church involved themselves in the wide range of debates, campaigns and legislation in which both Houses of Parliament engaged. An exhaustive treatment of their total impact is not possible within the present context so what follows therefore is a focus on some of the major legislative concerns of the nineteenth-century Evangelical Anglicans.

Their most sustained Parliamentary campaign was, without doubt, the fight to abolish slavery, a struggle that lasted twenty years.[23] Wilberforce first took up the matter in 1787 but it was not until 1807 that trading in slaves was made illegal. Abolition bills were introduced, debated and defeated some eleven times. Public opinion had in consequence to be educated by means of research, publications and pressure groups. In addition, there were almost daily petitions and deputations to cabinet ministers. Victory was finally secured on 23 February 1807 when the Abolition Bill was carried by 283 votes to 16. The historian, William Lecky, described it as one of 'the three or four perfectly virtuous acts recorded in the history of nations'.[24] The slave trade was now illegal, but slavery still remained.

With abolition now achieved, the Saints and their supporters now embarked on a campaign for emancipation. In this second phase of the contest a new leader emerged in the person of Thomas Fowell Buxton, an Evangelical Whig. His struggle was helped considerably by the government's Reform Bill of 1832 that abolished Rotten Boroughs, many of whose MPs were known to represent the slave-owning interest. After a sustained ten year

---

[22] Ibid., p. 10.

[23] Bradley, *Politics of Godliness*, pp. 66–7.

[24] W.E.H. Lecky, *European Morals* Vol. 1, p. 160, cited by Balleine, *History of the Evangelical Party*, p. 119.

campaign, which included pamphlets, public meetings and lectures, victory was accomplished in 1833 when the Emancipation Bill was passed with Parliament granting £20,000,000 to compensate the planters in the British colonies.

For those slaves who wished to return to their home continent, Sierra Leone was established as a refuge for freed slaves. It was a project that was almost entirely the work of members of the Clapham Sect. Begun in 1790, Granville Sharpe was President, Henry Thornton was chairman and Wilberforce, Grant, Lord Teignmouth and Babington were among the directors.[25] Altogether 18,000 liberated slaves had been received in Sierra Leone by 1825.[26]

The Saints, supported by numbers of other Evangelicals, not only concerned themselves with the savagery of the slave plantations in the West Indies, they fought against unfair treatment and cruelty done to native peoples anywhere in the Empire. In 1822 Wilberforce took up the matter of the harsh treatment of slaves in the South African Cape.[27] Several of the Clapham fraternity drew the British Government's attention to the plight of the American Indians who had fought the American Colonists in the War of Independence. The promise of land as their reward had been neglected.[28] Reports from missionaries in India led the Saints to challenge the practice of suttee whereby widows were forced to burn themselves on their husbands' funeral pyres. Buxton pointed out in his Speech to the House in 1821 that the practice had resulted in nearly 2,500 deaths in four years.[29]

In the first years of the nineteenth century, Evangelicals and the Saints, in particular, were concerned with a number of moral issues. The Vice Society, for example, concerned itself with obscene books, the desecration of the Sabbath and prostitution houses, but few such issues found their way into Parliamentary debate. One issue that did was the lottery. Evangelicals fought against the lottery, which they regarded not only as ruinous to many but also as encouraging speculation and idleness. William Smith and Samuel Thornton were both staunch opponents and in 1803 Babington and Wilberforce joined them in trying to persuade the Chancellor of the Exchequer to remove it from the budget. No action was taken and

---

[25] Howse, *Saints in Politics*, pp. 46f.
[26] Ibid., p. 50.
[27] Bradley, *Politics of Godliness*, p. 170.
[28] Ibid., p. 170.
[29] *Hansard* new series 1821, v, 1218 cited ibid., p. 171.

in a debate in 1809 Wilberforce, Smith and Babington were out-spoken in their attacks on it. The Government were extremely reticent to surrender an institution that could raise as much as £500,000 a year for the Exchequer. In 1817 Wilberforce neverthe-less wrote to an Evangelical constituent expressing the hope that 'this national sin will ere long be rooted out of our transgressions'.[30] In 1826 the Government finally surrendered and the budget of that year ended the state lottery.

Among other moral issues to which the Saints gave attention in the early years of the nineteenth century were bull- and bear-baiting, nude bathing, adultery and drunkenness. Evangelical MPs supported various attempts that were made in the early decades of the century to ban the cruel sports of bull- and bear-baiting. Wilber-force declared in a speech in 1802, 'wretched indeed must be the condition of the common people of England, if we suppose that their whole happiness consists in the practice of such barbarity'.[31]

In 1800 Wilberforce, Dudley Ryder and Viscount Sandon spoke in favour of Lord Auckland's bill to prevent adultery by prohibiting the marriage of a divorcée to the co-respondent cited in the divorce case. Although the measure successfully passed its first reading it was subsequently lost. In general the Evangelicals did not overly concern themselves with issues of public decency in Parliamentary debate although Wilberforce did protest against the Thames Bathing Bill of 1815 emphasising that it 'would be a declaration of Parliament that it was expedient that persons should expose their bodies on the banks of the Thames'.[32]

Roman Catholic emancipation

On the 16 April 1829, to the surprise of many, King George IV signed the Roman Catholic Relief Bill. In doing so, many felt that he had been disloyal to his coronation oath. The bill had been brought forward by the Duke of Wellington's administration because they feared that unless the claims of Roman Catholics were acceded to there would be civil war in Ireland. The matter was a pressing one because the Irish population was reckoned at seven million, five and a half million being Roman Catholic. The total population of England and Wales in 1831 was just over fourteen million, which

---

[30] Ibid., p. 121.
[31] *Parliamentary Register* 1802, xviii, p. 501 in ibid., p. 122.
[32] Ibid., p. 178.

meant that one third of the population for whom the Government were responsible were Roman Catholics.

Evangelicals were strongly divided over the issue that the bill raised. Of twelve Whig MPs – identified by Bradley – whose votes were recorded, all voted for emancipation.[33] The Saints also almost all gradually came round to favour relief for the Catholic population. Wilberforce's conversion to the cause seems to have been brought about by his acceptance that it was the only way to solve the nation's problems and stem the tide of rebellion and assassination.[34] John Sumner made his maiden speech during the bill and showed himself to be of moderate Claphamite views. Part of the reason for this mood may well have been the situation in his new diocese of Chester, which had large concentrations of Roman Catholics (particularly in Lancashire), together with clusters of Irish immigrants in Liverpool and Manchester. As Sumner saw it, the nub of the issue was the relative weakness of the Roman Catholic numbers on the ground. He wrote to the Duke of Wellington: 'the safety of the whole measure depends very much on the presumption that the papal cause is a declining cause and will become so more and more'.[35] Other leading Evangelical clerics, including Bishop Henry Ryder (1777–1836), William Dealtry of Clapham and Daniel Wilson (the elder of Islington) shared his views.

In general terms, the Saints, along with the Whig Evangelicals, were progressive and enlightened in their outlook while the Tory Evangelicals, who were traditional upholders of the crown and constitution, were conservative and pessimistic. A growing clutch of Tories identified themselves with the Recordites and those of extreme Protestant views. They were therefore hostile to Roman Catholicism which many of their number regarded as 'the mark of the beast' in the book of Revelation. The Tory Michael Sadler, who wanted to introduce poor laws into Ireland at the expense of the Irish Landlords, typified those who opposed the Relief Bill. This, he argued, would reduce suffering and by the same token prevent the Irish poor from flooding into England and bringing down wages.[36] The King wrote to his Evangelical episcopal protégé, Charles Sumner of Winchester, commanding him not to vote for the bill. Charles Simeon also stood out against emancipation.

---

[33] Ibid., p. 183.
[34] O. Chadwick, *The Victorian Church* Part 1, p. 10.
[35] G.K. Clark, *Churchmen and the Condition of England*, p. 296.
[36] See Scotland, *John Bird Sumner*, p. 68.

Parliamentary reform

In the period immediately following the Emancipation Act there were growing calls for reform. Some Tories even began to feel that had the Whig campaigns for greater Parliamentary representation been heeded they might have prevented relief for Roman Catholics. The issue however was very much larger. The inequalities in the system of representation were grotesque. Large towns such as Leeds, Birmingham and Manchester had no MPs in the House of Commons, while Old Sarum, with seven voters, and Dunwich, half under the sea, had two a piece. Of 658 MPs, landowners or agents of the government nominated 424. The great majority of the clergy at the beginning of the third decade were Tories who identified themselves with the squire and farmers and consequently shared their resistance to reform.

The passage of the Reform Bill into law was a tortuous one. In May 1832 the Lords carried an amendment postponing the vital clause for disenfranchising the pocket boroughs; three archbishops and thirteen bishops voted for the amendment; and the Prime Minister, Earl Grey, resigned when the King refused to create sufficient peers to defeat the opposition. However, when Wellington was unable to form a government, Grey was recalled and the King pledged to create the necessary peers. The bill finally passed through the Lords on 4 June and no bishop dissented. John Sumner[37] and Henry Ryder[38] had supported the bill from the time of second reading whereas others had been subsequently persuaded particularly as the radical press swayed public opinion.

Poor Laws

Expenditure on poor relief had fallen below £7,000,000 in 1820 and below £6,000,000 in 1822, but it began to rise once more after the financial crisis of 1826. By 1831 the figure had topped £7,000,000 once again. Notwithstanding this expense, the Government would have probably continued with the old arrangements had it not been for the Swing Riots of 1830 and the widespread burning of hayricks across much of southern England. These outbursts made it clear that the Poor Law arrangements had not been sufficient to eradicate distress and that new measures had to be

---

[37] Chadwick, *Victorian Church* Part 1, p. 31.
[38] *Napier Papers*, British Museum MSS 34, 613 folio 12.

taken. The reforming Whig government therefore set up a Royal Commission to examine the working of the Poor Laws.

Bishop John Sumner was one of the appointed commissioners. During his years as incumbent of Mapeldurham, a small parish in the Berkshire countryside, Sumner had examined the Poor Laws in detail and indeed wrote articles on the subject for the *Edinburgh Review* (1822) and the *Encyclopaedia Britannica* (1824). When submitting his article to the former journal, he wrote to the editor, Macvey Napier, 'You will perceive that I am a decided enemy of the system; and in fact I become more so every day, from what I see of its effects.'[39]

Until 1834 it had been the practice for individuals who were employed to receive money or supplementary payments from the local magistrates. This procedure could lead to unsatisfactory side effects. It meant that employers sometimes kept wages at a low level knowing that the parish would supplement them. It also encouraged laziness on the part of some labourers who made little effort to find work, knowing that the parish would provide for them. Sumner accepted the conclusion of the Scottish economist, Adam Smith, who asserted that a man would labour if individual satisfaction was adequate. This led him to support proposals that provided that no able-bodied person was to receive relief except in a workhouse. The country was divided into 600 new Poor Law Unions which ignored the familiar parish basis altogether. The result was that many became unemployed in a harsh and hostile environment, and cut off from their familiar local community.

Although Sumner did not speak during the debate in the House of Lords, it was clear that his informal expressions of support for the bill were an influential factor. Nassau Senior, who was the main author of the report, later wrote of Sumner's role, 'I do not believe that we could have ... carried the bill, as it was carried, through the House of Lords, if ... the late Bishop Sumner had not supported us.'[40]

As with the Catholic Emancipation Act, the new Poor Laws divided Anglican Evangelicals. Many were extremely hostile towards the new arrangements believing them to be cruel, and heartless. George Bull and Richard Oastler both weighed in against attempts to curtail outdoor relief. In 1838 alone, some 250,000

---

[39] A.R. Blomfield, *A Memoir of Bishop Blomfield* Vol. 1, p. 204.

[40] Cited by B. Dickey, 'Evangelicals and Poverty', in J. Wolffe (ed.), *Evangelical Faith and Public Zeal*, p. 42.

persons signed protest petitions against the Act. In the later years of the century many Evangelical Anglicans remained decidedly opposed to the new Poor Law, finding it hard to understand how a Christian country could allow parents and children to be wrenched apart and forced into separate workhouses where the food was inadequate and the accommodation unhealthy. A major weakness of the New Poor Law was that it simply failed to distinguish between the genuine poor who were unable to find work and the undeserving poor who were unwilling to work.

Industrial campaigns

Concern about conditions in the mines and the health of the poor in general had featured strongly among John Wesley's concerns. His pleas were taken up by some of the generation who succeeded him. Among those who were members of the established church were Michael Sadler, Richard Oastler (1789–1861) and George Bull.

Michael Sadler (1780–1835) was a MP for Newark. He was a Tory and Wesleyan Methodist who had retained his church connection. He had a passion for education and Sunday schools in particular. He was superintendent of a large Sunday school in Leeds. It was his interest in education that made him aware of the long hours worked in factories by both children and adults. It was this which caused him to declare, 'We are now called upon strictly to observe the command of the Divine Author of our religion to relieve those who have none to help them.'[41] In 1832 Sadler produced a classic parliamentary report on 'Factory Children's Labour'. Because of his untiring labours and powerful influence, Sadler was chosen by common consent as the leader of the Ten Hours Movement in Parliament. In March 1832 he moved the second reading of his Ten Hours Bill in an eloquent speech.[42] Henry Ryder, the Bishop of Lichfield and Coventry, commended the bill to his diocese,[43] but shortly after this, Sadler resigned his Newark constituency in order to take up the safe seat of Aldborough. However, the Reform Act of 1832 disenfranchised the latter, which was a pocket borough, and Sadler found himself out of Parliament.

---

[41] E. Hodder, *The Life and Work of Lord Shaftesbury*, p. 81.
[42] R.A. Soloway, *Prelates and People*, p. 202.
[43] M.S. Edwards, *Purge This Realm: A Life of Joseph Rayner Stephens*, p. 35.

The loss of Sadler was a bitter blow and it was left to the Rev George Bull to find a successor to continue the agitation in Parliament. He, together with Sir Andrew Agnew, visited Lord Ashley, who eventually agreed to take on Sadler's mantle. Ashley received widespread support, including that of Richard Oastler, in this new role.

Described by M.S. Edwards as 'one of the first to relate Christianity to a modern industrial society',[44] Oastler was stimulated by reading the social sermons of the Reformation bishop, Hugh Latimer. Oastler had been a local preacher with the Methodist New Connexion but he parted from their company and joined the Church of England, becoming a disciple of William Wilberforce. The strong support of northern Anglican clergy for the factory reformers drew Oastler away from the Methodists. This was in contrast to many leading Nonconformists who were tending to identify with the Liberal laissez-faire economic policies. Oastler was a vigorous opponent of the New Poor Law that herded the unemployed into workhouses instead of providing them with relief through their parish, as had been the custom since Elizabethan times.

Oastler has been described as 'the Factory Children's King' because he made their cause his own. His eyes had first been opened to the brutal cruelties meted out by managers and charge hands as a result of his friendship with John Wood, a major cotton mill owner. Oastler, who was the resident agent of the Fixby estate, began to campaign against 'white slavery' through the columns of *The Leeds Mercury*. He also developed a powerful platform style and, consequently, the Ten Hours Movement spread rapidly.

Oastler rigorously contended that the factory system was 'the worship of Mammon' and that it did not treat people 'as the children of God, made in the image of God'.[45] Oastler and his associates drew on the growing wave of humanitarian concern that was associated with the abolitionist campaign of the same time. He deliberately made use of some of Wilberforce's methods, including rallies, church sermons and Parliamentary petitions.

Oastler was a man of contrasts. On the one hand, he was a staunch Tory who associated with Ashley and factory owners.[46] On the other, he was given to extreme radical views as he denounced the atrocities of the factory system as belonging to a bygone age and even, on

---

[44] J.C. Gill, *Parson Bull of Byerley*, p. 83.
[45] Ibid., p. 141.
[46] Ibid., p. 140.

occasion, commended sabotage.[47] In 1838 Oastler was imprisoned for a debt of more than £3,000 owed to his former employer and was not finally released until 1844 when his friends organised a liberation fund on his behalf. Notwithstanding his withdrawal from the action, he was clearly a major figure in the Ten Hours campaign. This was forcibly borne out when a great celebration was held on 15 May 1869 at Bradford to uncover Oastler's statue. Lord Shaftesbury who was present for the occasion estimated that 'there must have been one hundred thousand people present'.[48]

A prominent clerical advocate of the cause was George Stringer Bull who became curate of Byerley on the outskirts of Bradford in 1826. There he soon became concerned because children were too exhausted to benefit from the meagre education offered by his Sunday schools. After closely examining the conditions in his own parish he became convinced of the validity of the campaign launched by Oastler at the instigation of the Bradford manufacturer, John Wood. Bull was a staunch Evangelical who supported CMS and conscientiously attended to the needs of his parish. Nevertheless, he gave himself wholeheartedly to the task of supporting the Ten Hours Movement by writing to the newspapers, speaking at public meetings and lobbying Parliament. He was also a prolific pamphleteer and produced more than forty tracts in support of the cause. It was not for nothing that he was dubbed, 'The Ten Hours Parson'. On one occasion the Duke of Wellington said to Oastler, 'that parson of yours preaches nothing but mill owners' duties; he has sent me a sermon full of facts about factories, but ending in every page with an appeal to the mill owners. What do you think of him?' Oastler replied, 'He ought to be a Bishop Your Grace'. To this the Duke replied, 'He is doing much good ... but his sermons will never be fashionable.'[49]

There were of course many other aspects of industrial society with which Evangelicals concerned themselves. Ashley's rigorous condemnation of the ways in which women and children were treated in coalmines won him widespread acclaim. His Mines Act, which became law in 1842 and aimed to prohibit young children going underground, was termed by the Hammonds as 'the most

---

[47] Shaftesbury, *Diary*, 15 May 1969 cited by Hodder, *Life and Work of Lord Shaftesbury*, p. 379.

[48] *Birmingham Journal*, 26 August 1865, cited by Gill, *Parson Bull*, p. 141.

[49] Cited by G. Battiscombe, *Shaftesbury. A Biography of the Seventh Earl 1801–1885*, p. 148.

striking of Ashley's achievements'.[50] The majority of Evangelical bishops seem to have been largely focused on the needs of their clergy, many of whose incomes were low, and the organisational needs of their dioceses. This left little time available to concern themselves with the conditions of the poor in their workplaces. Some bishops, such as John Sumner, visited factories[51] and Henry Ryder, for example, commended the Truck Bill in his charge of 1831, which sought to put an end to the practice of employers paying some of their labourers' wages in kind, often cider or some other alcoholic beverage.[52]

In general terms, it was the Tory Evangelicals who put their efforts into factory reform in the early years of the nineteenth century. It was not until the late 1820s that the Saints and the Moderates began to put their energies into the campaign. By this time many of their number had come to recognise that unrestricted market competition was causing neglect and abuse of the labour force.

The Corn Laws

In 1815 the British Government had passed the Corn Law, which prohibited the import of grain when the price of wheat stood below eighty shillings a quarter. Their aim was quite simply to protect British farmers from being undercut by foreign competition and to make it worth their while to continue production. In this way, the country would remain self-sufficient in time of crisis.

Most Tories were supporters of the establishment. In the country-side where the Church of England was strong, clergy naturally found themselves in an alliance with the squire and farmers in a kind of establishment troika. The laws, however, made corn prices artificially high with the result that poor people found it increasingly difficult to afford bread. A number of the Saints, together with the Moderates who were devoted to free trade, supported Corn Law Repeal. By the 1820s most Tories with the exception of those of extreme views had come to the same opinion. From 1822 the *Christian Observer* maintained strong support for reform.[53] In the 1820s

---

[50] Soloway, *Prelates and People*, p. 210.
[51] H. Ryder, *A Charge to the Clergy of the Diocese of Lichfield and Coventry*, pp. 23f.
[52] Bradley, *Politics of Godliness*, p. 206.
[53] Hilton, *Age of Atonement*, p. 206. See also Bradley, *Politics of Godliness*, p. 279.

the most prominent campaigner in Parliament was the 'Saint', William Whitmore, Tory MP for Bridgnorth in Shropshire (1820–1832).[54] C.P. Villiers subsequently took on Whitmore's role in 1838, although it had been suggested that his motivation might have been as much due to utilitarian philosophy as to religion. Outside Parliament, one of the most prominent supporters of the anti-Corn Law league was the Honorable Rev Baptist Noel (1798–1861). He believed that 'our national distress' had been brought about by 'this inhuman legislation', which he saw as a departure 'from the spirit and mandates of the divine law'.[55]

John Sumner supported the repeal of the Corn Law in 1846. A number of reasons persuaded him in favour of the bill. As a political economist he was still convinced of the benefits of laissez-faire economics and believed that the market should be allowed to find the best interests of the poor.[56] He also saw the importance of the church siding with a popular opinion that was so obviously rooted in social justice. E. Roy Moore commented on Sumner's position that 'he had fully come to the conclusion that if the church was to become credible in the eyes of the working classes, the physical and social conditions of the poor must be improved, and the church no only be seen to be sympathetic, but also active in their welfare'.[57]

Anthony Ashley was deeply exercised by the issue of the repeal. He recognised its rightness and felt he must surrender his protectionist views. Out of loyalty to the farmers of his constituency he therefore resigned his seat.[58]

Suffrage

Arising out of the failure of the Great Reform Bill to give the vote to substantial numbers of working men, the Chartist movement came into being with its six-point charter for further electoral reform. The most significant of the six was the demand for 'universal suffrage'. Advocates, many of them Nonconformists, stomped the countryside preaching and holding public meetings on behalf of the charter which was presented to Parliament on several occasions. As part of their campaign, in 1839 male and female Chartists paraded

---

[54] Hilton, *Age of Atonement*, p. 207.
[55] Ibid., p. 247.
[56] Scotland, *John Bird Sumner*, p. 69.
[57] E.R. Moore, *John Bird Sumner, Bishop of Chester 1828–1848*, p. 203.
[58] See Battiscombe, *Shaftesbury. A Biography*, pp. 185–8.

through the streets of the town or city in which their branch was situated to attend the Sunday worship of their parish church. In most cases they requested the rector or vicar to preach to them on a text that they supplied beforehand.[59]

Evangelical Anglican clergy seemed particularly hostile towards the Chartists. From the first days there were innumerable sermon titles such as 'The Sin of Despising Dominion', 'The Powers that be are Ordained of God' and 'Fear God and Honour the King'. Some were even more explicit such as 'Chartism Unmasked'. One of the assistant clergy was asked to preach to Sheffield Chartists on James 5:1–6. Instead, he selected Proverbs 24: 'My Son, fear thou the Lord and the King: and meddle not with them that are given to change' and warned the labouring men and women who had assembled before him of the wickedness and desperate hazard they were pursuing, and 'exhorted them to a serious and diligent pursuit of those better things which the Gospel of Christ held out to them'.[60] The Vicar of Preston, the Rev Roger Carus Wilson, asked in his sermon to the town's Chartists, 'Was there anything in the state of the country to justify a discontented spirit and to call for turbulence and trouble? No, because social inequality was inevitable.'[61]

When Cheltenham Chartists paraded through the town to the parish church on 18 August 1839, the usual congregation deserted. However, Francis Close ascended the pulpit and held the mob spellbound for an hour. He condemned the Chartists for going to church with no intention of praying. They were guilty of 'high crime coming to God's temple in an unhallowed spirit'.[62] Later in the same sermon Close urged that 'socialism is rebellion against God and Chartism is rebellion against man'.[63] In his address to the female Chartists of Cheltenham a little later, Close told his hearers to return home to their fireside duties and to be in submission to their husbands.[64] He likened their behaviour to their French sisters who 'glutted themselves with blood and danced like maniacs amidst the

---

[59] See E. Yeo, 'Christianity in the Chartist Struggle', *Past and Present* (May 1981), pp. 109–39.

[60] E.R. Wickham, *Church and People in An Industrial City*, p. 100.

[61] Ibid., p. 100.

[62] F. Close, *Sermon on the Occasion of the Visit of the Chartists to Cheltenham Parish Church*, p. 18.

[63] Ibid., p. 18.

[64] F. Close, *A Sermon Addressed to the Female Chartists of Cheltenham Sunday 25th August 1839*, p. 3.

most fearful scenes of the reign of terror'.[65] There is no doubt that the hostility of Church of England clergy to working-class movements alienated the poor still further from their congregations.

Although Chartism did not achieve any of its goals within the period of its activity, it brought key issues into the public arena and helped to make churchmen aware of the social injustices they were perpetrating. The end result of this was the Second Reform Act of 1867 and the Third Reform Act of 1884. The Act of 1867 enfranchised a good many new voters in the boroughs and some in the counties. The Act of 1884 completed the process giving the vote to all working men in the counties. In the earlier years of the century, Church of England clergy in particular were apprehensive when it came to any moves to widen the franchise. Their fear was that it would result in disestablishment and their consequent loss of status and influence in the parish and community. By the close of the century the situation was changing. It had become clear that the Church of England would be able to provide for itself even if was no longer the official church of the nation. A sign of the changing attitude was the fact that only one bishop, Charles Ellicott of Bristol, voted against the 1884 Franchise Bill.[66]

Trade unions

Trade unions became increasingly important in the period 1825–1881 following the Repeal of the Combination Acts in 1825. The early period witnessed the brief crescendo and collapse of Robert Owen's Grand National Consolidated Trades Unions. Most of the early trade unions of the 1830s and 1840s were combinations of skilled or semi-skilled workers. They tended to act on more conventional lines by negotiation rather than by strike action. After 1881 there developed what is often misleadingly termed the 'New Unionism'. These were, generally speaking, unions of unskilled workers such as the Dockworkers' Union and the Transport and General Workers' Union.

The Church of England as a whole gave very little encouragement to the trade union movement. What little support there was came from the Christian socialists, most notably Thomas Hughes[67]

---

[65] Ibid., p. 18.
[66] G.I.T. Machin, *Politics and the Churches in Great Britain 1869–1921*, p. 148.
[67] S. Mayor, *The Churches and the Labour Movement*, p. 90.

and a little later some of those who were associated with the Settlement Movement in London's East End.[68] In the early part of the century most clergy viewed combinations in the same way they regarded the Chartists. They saw them as disturbers of the status quo and as a threat to what they believed was a divinely ordered social hierarchy.

Clerical opposition to trade unions appeared to be at its most vehement in the countryside where the Church of England was at its strongest. The bitterness of the rural conflict between the squire and the parson and farm labourers was mirrored in the campaigns of the National Agricultural Labourers Union formed by Joseph Arch in 1872.[69] It was the case that there were one or two notable Church of England clergy who supported Arch, most obviously J.C. Cox of Belper;[70] James Fraser, later Bishop of Manchester; and Edward Girdlestone (1805–1884),[71] the Evangelical rector of Halberton in Devon, who subsequently became known as 'the agricultural labourers' friend'. However, the great majority of agricultural union delegates and speakers perceived the clergy to be the enemy and bishops such as William Magee of Peterborough and Charles Ellicott of Bristol were regularly denounced at union meetings. Ellicott was dubbed 'the horse-pond bishop' for suggesting union officials be thrown into the village pond and Magee was shouted down for likening union delegates to 'ravenous birds of prey ... which led by their carnivorous instincts, found out sickly diseased animals, perched on their heads and picked out their eyes'.[72] The farm labourers bitterly resented the clerical magistracy who were often harsh in the sentences they meted out to the rural poor and were perceived as heartless as a result of their role in administering the Poor Law with its brutal workhouse regime.

The 'Sheffield Outrages' led to bad publicity for trade unions in general in the later 1860s[73] but by the 1880s a different picture was beginning to emerge. The good management and organisation of the celebrated London Dock Strike of 1889 further enhanced this. The

---

[68] Clark, *Churchmen*, p. 255.

[69] N.A.D. Scotland, 'Rural War in Later Victorian Norfolk', *Norfolk Archaeology* 38.1 (1981), pp. 82–7.

[70] See Mayor, *Churches and the Labour Movement*, p. 102; see also Clark, *Churchmen*, pp. 254–5.

[71] J.S. Reynolds, *The Evangelicals at Oxford 1735–1871*, p. 92.

[72] N.A.D. Scotland, *Methodism and the Revolt of the Field in Lincolnshire, Norfolk and Suffolk 1872–1896*, p. 301.

[73] See Wickham, *Church and People in An Industrial City*, pp. 124–5.

public at large were impressed that the dockers behaved, in the words of the *Church Times*, 'with an admirable quietness and self-restraint'.[74] Many of the British public came to the view that a general union would benefit the country. The fact that a number of prominent trade union leaders, men such as Henry Broadhurst, Tom Mann and Ben Tillet, were Christians of some sort also helped to reduce suspicion and break down barriers. Even the prominent Evangelical, Bishop John Ryle, who in earlier days had opposed the agricultural unions in Suffolk,[75] changed his tune. Addressing the fourteenth Liverpool Diocesan Conference in November 1895 he said:

> you cannot find fault with the formation of trade unions in the present day. For anything I can see, they are likely to do good and promote peace, provided they are reasonably conducted, and do not interfere with the liberty of those who object to join them. So long as business is conducted in the vast scale of modern times, the working classes must not be blamed if they co-operate, combine, and endeavour to protect their interests and defend their rights in every legal way.[76]

The Later Victorian Years

In the later Victorian years the number of Evangelical Anglicans in the House of Commons diminished. Increasingly, the Evangelical members in the House were identified with the Nonconformists rather than with the established church. The impact of American revivalism and Keswick holiness teaching was also generating a world-denying spirituality that tended to draw Evangelical Anglicans away from social and political issues that had no direct connection with the church. In addition, there emerged, with the passing of the century, what David Smith has aptly described as 'growing social conservatism among Anglicans' and this 'opened up a chasm between them and their Dissenting brothers'.[77]

---

[74] *Church Times*, 6 September 1889, cited by Mayor, *Churches and the Labour Movement*, p. 109.

[75] Scotland, *Methodism*.

[76] J.C. Ryle, 'What is Wanted? The Opening Address at Fourteenth Liverpool Diocesan Conference, 5 November 1895', in *Charges and Addresses*, p. 293.

[77] D.W. Smith, *Transforming the World? The Social Impact of British Evangelicalism*, p. 30.

During the 1880s and 1890s it was the Wesleyan Evangelicals, led by Hugh Price Hughes and his Forward Movement, who began to influence and inform Government policy rather than the Church of England Evangelicals. The chief concerns of Evangelical clergy and laity were now with the role of the church in education, opposition to ritualism and Romanism and the promotion of temperance, each of which are the focus of subsequent chapters in this volume.

Taken as a whole, there can be no doubt that the Evangelical clergy and laity of the Church of England made a significant impact on the social and political issues of the nineteenth century. They had abolished the slave trade, achieved major changes in factory and working conditions, established Sunday as a day of rest for the labouring poor, promoted temperance and been major players in the field of education. Along the way they had developed effective means of making their point of view heard. These included the use of pressure groups, pamphleteering and networking. Theirs was indeed an enduring legacy.

4

Evangelical Anglicans and Social Action

Lord Shaftesbury maintained in 1884 that 'most of the great philanthropic movements of the century have sprung from the Evangelicals'.[1] Although there were plenty of critics of their work, Evangelicals, and not least those who were members of the established church, made a major contribution to the moral and social needs of Victorian England. As has been noted, some have seen Evangelical Anglicanism as having two or possibly three phases: an earlier Wesley-Simeonite[2] phase which extended to Simeon's death in 1836, and subsequent Bickersteth-Shaftesbury and CMS phases which extended to the end of the century. The Wesley-Simeonite Evangelicals, who were more moderate in their views, tended to put greater energy into social reforming activities than their later counterparts who became somewhat more concerned with internal matters such as ritualism and spirituality.

The history of Evangelical social reform is, to a significant degree, the story of a number of prominent individuals. Most obvious were William Wilberforce and members of the Clapham Sect (discussed in the previous chapter) and the Seventh Earl of Shaftesbury, but there were a host of other members of the established church who made important contributions in their respective fields. They included Richard Oastler, Michael Sadler and George Bull in factory reform. Dr Thomas Barnado undertook major work on behalf of homeless children; Florence Nightingale and Ellen Ranyard developed nursing training; Josephine Butler campaigned

---

[1] E. Hodder, *The Life and Work of the Seventh Earl of Shaftesbury, KG* Vol. 2, p. 3.

[2] A 'Wesley-Wilberforce' rather than a 'Wesley-Simeonite' phase might make the point more adequately that the first phase was more socially orientated.

against the harsh treatment of prostitutes; John Howard demonstrated humanitarian concern for prisoners; Agnes Weston devoted her life to the cause of sailors; and Quinton Hogg pioneered technical education and clubs for young men.

Lord Shaftesbury

Without doubt Lord Shaftesbury (1801–1885) was the most influential Evangelical social reformer in Victorian England. By birth Anthony Ashley Cooper was 'an aristocrat to his fingertips'[3] but his whole life was dedicated to the works and activities which earned him the title, 'The People's Earl'.

Anthony and his three older sisters were treated harshly by their parents who were of the opinion that 'to render a child obedient, it should be in a constant fear of its father and mother'.[4] Notwithstanding the coldness of his parents, Anthony found love and affection through the care of Maria Millis. She had gone into service as a personal maid to his mother and had moved with her when she married Lord Ashley. She was an Evangelical of a generous, loving disposition and the Bible stories she repeated to young Ashley and her simple prayers sowed the seeds of his strong Christian faith.[5]

Ashley's motivation to social action began early while he was still a pupil at Harrow School when he witnessed a pauper's funeral. The memory of the drunken pallbearers dropping the coffin was, he later wrote, 'the origin of my public career'. After taking a first-class degree in Classics at Christ Church, Oxford, in 1822 he entered Parliament as a Tory in 1826.[6]

One of his first assignments as a member of the House of Commons was to serve on the Select Committee that investigated the whole issue of lunacy. His first Parliamentary speech on 19 February 1828 was a seconding of Robert Gordon's Bill to Amend the Law for the Regulation of Lunatic Asylums, in which he pointed out 'the illegal detention and coercion of sane persons, and of gross neglect and cruelty to unfortunate lunatics'.[7] Within his speech Ashley gave evidence that demonstrated that the existing system

---

[3] Balleine, *History of the Evangelical Party*, p. 190.
[4] Hodder, *Life and Work of Lord Shaftesbury*, p. 26.
[5] See Battiscombe, *Shaftesbury. A Biography*, pp. 6–7.
[6] Shaftesbury, *Diary*, 28 April 1826.
[7] Hodder, *Life and Work of Lord Shaftesbury*, p. 52.

needed drastic overhaul. A number of reforms followed in the wake of this Act, one of which was a requirement that fifteen commissioners be appointed by the Home Secretary to replace the existing five. They were to have wider powers of control over all asylums in and around London.[8] It was stated that five of the commissioners were to be doctors and were to receive a salary, whilst the remaining ten became one of the unpaid commissioners. In the following year, he became chairman of the Commission and remained in that post until his death, a period of fifty-seven years.[9] For the rest of his life Ashley was constant in his concern for the mentally ill. He visited many asylums in London and the provinces and saw for himself the filthy conditions and the degradation of the inmates, many of whom were chained to their beds.[10]

In July 1845 Ashley succeeded in passing two Bills into law that aimed to improve the conditions in asylums. Sometimes referred to as the 'Magna Charta' of the insane, these two Acts were For the Regulation of Lunatic Asylums and For the Better Care and Treatment of Lunatics in England and Wales. The latter Act made it obligatory for each county to make adequate provision of asylums. The background to this was the fact that there were 17,000 registered insane persons but only 4,000 places in the counties. As a result, 9,000 were detained in workhouses, prisons and other unsuitable accommodation.[11] Bready remarked that these two Acts humanised the treatment of the insane to a position where they were no longer regarded as 'prisoners' but as 'patients'.[12] In 1852, in a speech to the Lords, Ashley reported a picture of progress in the treatment of the mentally ill. Nine years later he gave his support to the endeavour to establish a Benevolent Asylum for the Insane of the Middle Classes. The reason for this was that the number of insane was increasing and many who failed to qualify for a place in a pauper asylum could not afford the fees. Despite his many other commitments, Shaftesbury remained active in the cause of the mentally ill until the end of his days.

In 1833 Ashley began his involvement in the campaign to reform and regulate the conditions and hours of employment in the nation's mills, mines and factories. This was a movement which was forever to be associated with his name. It began when Michael Sadler lost his

---

[8] Ibid., p. 53.
[9] Ibid., p. 53.
[10] Ibid., p. 53.
[11] J.W. Bready, *Lord Shaftesbury and Social Industrial Progress*, p. 90.
[12] Ibid., p. 93.

Parliamentary seat in Hull in the elections that followed the Great Reform Bill. Sadler had been highly valued as a spokesman in Westminster for those who were seeking to aid industrial employees. Aware of his successful work on behalf of the mentally ill, George Stringer Bull, a Yorkshire incumbent and leading campaigner for a ten-hour day, urged Shaftesbury to take Sadler's mantle.

Shaftesbury immediately set about personally visiting factories so that he could obtain first-hand information. The result was that he was able to put a Bill before the house in March 1833 which proposed to restrict the hours of those aged nine to eighteen years to ten a day, and eight hours on Saturday. No person under the age of twenty-one was to undertake any night work. The Bill passed through the second reading but was amended so that only those between nine and thirteen could work a ten-hour day, as opposed to those aged nine to eighteen. Although this 1833 Factory Act was a disappointment to Ashley, it had brought a number of significant changes.[13] No child aged between nine and thirteen was allowed to work more than forty-eight hours a week and no more than nine hours in any day. Those aged between thirteen and eighteen were prohibited from working more than 12 hours a day. Perhaps the most significant provision of the Act was the appointment of inspectors to ensure that factories did not infringe the measures.

Notwithstanding the success of his Act, Ashley was resolved to continue the struggle until the ten-hour day was standard. Eventually in May 1847 the Ten Hours Bill became law, with John Fielden, speaking on Ashley's behalf.[14] Even then its success was limited since factory owners could evade the new law by utilising a relay system which kept machines running from 5.30 a.m. to 8.30 a.m. It was not until much later in the century, under Disraeli's government, that a ten-hour day for all young workers was firmly established.

Another major aspect of Shaftesbury's work on behalf of the industrial poor commenced in 1840 when he led an inquiry into the conditions of work and employment for children in the mines and collieries. In a speech to the House in 1842 Ashley used some of his findings to make clear the urgency of the situation. He reported that 'about Halifax and the neighbourhood children are sometimes brought to the pit at the age of six, and are taken out of their beds at

---

[13] Ibid., pp. 80–1.
[14] See Battiscombe, *Shaftesbury. A Biography*, pp. 202–3.

four o'clock'.[15] He went on to describe in graphic detail the extreme conditions in which many of these little ones were forced to work:

> In the West Riding of Yorkshire it appears that there are very few collieries with thin seams where the main roadways exceed a yard in height, and in some it does not exceed 26 or 28 inches; nay in some the height is as little even as 22 inches; so that the youngest child cannot work without the most constrained posture. The ventilation, besides, in general is very bad, and the drainage worse. In Oldham the mountain seams are wrought in a very rude manner. There is very insufficient drainage. The ways are so low that only little boys can work in them, which they do naked, and often in mud and water, dragging sledge-tubs by the girdle and chain. In North Lancashire 'the drainage is often extremely bad; a pit of not above 20 inches seam', says a witness, 'had a foot of water in it, so that he could hardly keep his head out of water'.[16]

These disturbing revelations drew the support of many in public life. Shaftesbury recorded in his diary, 'the feeling in my favour has become quite enthusiastic; the press on all sides is working most vigorously. Wrote pointedly to thank the editor of the *Morning Chronicle* for his support, which is most effective'.[17] John and Barbara Hammond described the Mines Act of 1842 as 'the most striking of Ashley's personal achievements'.[18] Among other things the Act made it illegal to employ women and girls in the mines under the age of thirteen and boys under the age of ten. Ashley was pleased with his success and recorded in his diary that he

> took the sacrament on Sunday in joyful and humble thankfulness to almighty God, for the undeserved measure of success with which he has blessed my effort for the glory of his name, and the welfare of His creatures. Oh that it may be the beginning of good to all mankind.[19]

Another of Shaftesbury's concerns was the 'climbing boys' who were used by their employers to sweep chimneys. Many were forced screaming into narrow chimneys, others died of burns, suffocation or 'sooty cancer'. In 1840 Ashley brought a Bill before the House of

---

[15] Extract from a speech by Ashley in 1842.
[16] Ibid.
[17] Hodder, *Seventh Earl of Shaftesbury* Vol. 1, p. 418.
[18] J.L. Hammond and B. Hammond, *Shaftesbury*, p. 83.
[19] Hodder, *Seventh Earl of Shaftesbury* Vol. 1, pp. 431–2.

Commons that aimed to entirely prohibit the use of climbing boys. He was disturbed to find opposition from both Conservatives and Evangelicals but supported by radicals.[20] The Bill, however, successfully passed through both Houses. Although the use of young boys came to a complete end in London as a result of the Act, in other places the magistrates turned a blind eye to the practice. As a result, the Climbing Boys Society was formed with Ashley as chairman and with the express object of the total abolition of the practice. In 1864 Ashley succeeded in bringing another Bill into law but, like its predecessor, it proved ineffectual. Finally, in 1875 he succeeded in piloting a further Bill through both Houses that enforced the annual licensing of chimney sweeps and gave the enforcement of the law into the hands of the police. By this time, machines for sweeping chimneys had become available and their use approved by many insurance companies.[21]

For many years Ashley also worked in partnership with Edwin Chadwick at the Board of Health. He was in fact the Board's only unpaid member. In all his work in the cause of sanitary reform Ashley's declared intention was to 'Christianise' the condition of the working classes. Chadwick by contrast was a radical with no such agenda, but the two men nevertheless worked well together.[22] Ashley's aristocratic grace and charm did much to improve the Board's public image. Ashley's popularity also did much to counteract Chadwick's poor communication skills and sullen temperament.

In 1844 Chadwick's report, entitled 'A Commission on the Health of Towns', exposed impure or imperfect water supply and inadequate drainage in many of the nation's largest towns and cities. The report prompted the foundation of the Health of Towns Association and Ashley became chairman of the London branch. In 1847 he took on a further responsibility when he was appointed a member of the recently established Metropolitan Commission of Sewers. This body was charged with the planning and construction of public works for all that part of London outside the city boundaries. Ashley won the hearts of many Londoners when he remained in the city during the height of the cholera outbreaks in August and September 1849 bearing the brunt of the organisation and appointing additional medical superintendents on his own responsibility to treat the many thousands of suffering and dying. Ashley wrote with

---

[20] Battiscombe, *Shaftesbury. A Biography*, p. 126.
[21] Ibid., p. 127.
[22] Ibid., p. 220.

thoughtfulness in his diary for 9 September, 'Have been mercifully preserved through this pestilence. Have not I, thank God, shrunk from one hour of duty in the midst of this city of the plague, and yet it has not approached either me or my dwelling.'[23]

Ashley continued his work in the area of public health until his later years. He gave active support to the Artisans and Labourers Dwelling Act of 1868, which provided for the demolition of unsanitary housing. He also supported the Artisans Dwelling Act of 1875 in an able speech in which he showed the difficulty faced by Government in finding housing for people whose homes had been demolished to make way for improvements.[24]

The huge scope of Shaftesbury's many interests makes it impossible, in the present context, to do full justice to his contribution and influence on Victorian social action. Suffice it to say, however, that his commitments included the crippled, for whom, with the help of Lord Kinnaird, he opened several homes in the 1850s.[25] The London cabmen, for whom he started the Cabmen's Shelter Fund in 1875, were another of his concerns. This helped to make possible the construction of forty night shelters, which could accommodate some 3,000 cab drivers in various parts of London.[26] Shaftesbury was not oblivious to the problems resulting from sweated labour and for this reason he tendered his support to the Needlewoman's Institute in Manchester Square, London. He was also a strong advocate of the temperance movement and gave major impetus to the Ragged School Union, which is considered separately in the chapter on education. He also took a keen interest in some of the Ragged School Union's activities such as the Shoe Black Brigade,[27] the refuges and dormitories.[28] In November 1866 when the government gave him the *Chichester*, a fifty-gun frigate, as a training ship for homeless boys, he recorded in his diary, 'it has been a dream of fifteen years'.[29]

After the death of his wife, Shaftesbury established The Emily Loan Fund in her memory in 1872. This was to aid the watercress and flower girls to earn a living during the winter months when

---

[23] Hodder, *Life and Work of Lord Shaftesbury*, p. 418.
[24] Ibid., p. 690.
[25] Heasman, *Evangelicals in Action*, p. 220.
[26] Ibid., p. 274.
[27] Hodder, *Life and Work of Lord Shaftesbury*, p. 437.
[28] Ibid., p. 614.
[29] Ibid., p. 614.

watercress and flowers were scarce or unavailable. In this period, poor women would be able to apply for the loan of a baked-potato oven, a coffee stall or a barrow and board for the sale of whelks.[30] Loans were usually £1 or £2. Shaftesbury later reported that between 800 and 1,000 loans had been made and a total of not more than £50 had been lost. 'Of all the movements I have been connected with,' he said, 'I look upon this Watercress Girl Movement as the most successful.'[31]

Shaftesbury also concerned himself with prison visiting[32] and cruelty to animals.[33] On the latter subject, he spoke in the House of Lords in May 1876 in support of Lord Carnarvon's Bill for restricting cruelty to animals. He also assisted in the formation of the Victoria Society for the Protection of Animals from Vivisection.[34] Shaftesbury also emerged as a strong campaigner on behalf of the Negro slaves of America and entertained Mrs Beecher-Stowe to dinner along with the Archbishop of Canterbury and others.[35]

Despite his overwhelming concern for the poor, Shaftesbury nevertheless had a dislike for democracy. Geoffrey Best has suggested that this was particularly apparent in the Factory Act of 1833 in which he expressed the view that factory workers who should be treated with respect should nevertheless look to the mill owners as their superiors.[36] He was strongly opposed to trade unionism[37] and Chartism and spoke of socialism and Chartism as, 'the two great demons in morals and politics'.[38]

John and Barbara Hammond highlighted Shaftesbury's paternalistic nature suggesting that even though he improved children spiritually, he did not teach them how to improve their status in life. Their social problems were not therefore solved and they were left dependent on the church.[39] J.W. Bready asserted that Ashley's methods tended to be 'preventive rather than curative',[40] a view which is perhaps only partially true. It was the case that Shaftesbury's

---

[30] Ibid., p. 671.
[31] Ibid., p. 671.
[32] Ibid., p. 311.
[33] Ibid., p. 696.
[34] Ibid., p. 696.
[35] Ibid., p. 376.
[36] G. Best, *Shaftesbury*, p. 83.
[37] Hodder, *Seventh Earl of Shaftesbury* Vol. 1, p. 156.
[38] Hodder, *Life and Work of Lord Shaftesbury*, p. 173.
[39] Hammond and Hammond, *Shaftesbury*, p. 258.
[40] Bready, *Lord Shaftesbury*, p. 92.

solution to many issues was the formation of charitable societies, but, on the other hand, he worked through the legislature, and the bills he successfully steered through Parliament did put a stop to excessive working hours and brought to an end social evils such as the use of climbing boys or the hard-treatment of the mentally ill.

Geoffrey Finlayson was of the view that Shaftesbury was paternalistic and condescending in his attitude to the poor.[41] This is perhaps a more obvious criticism, but, on the other hand, there were few Victorian reformers for whom this was not the case. It's too much to expect a Victorian aristocrat such as Shaftesbury to operate with twenty-first century attitudes.

Shaftesbury was elected to Parliament as a Tory but he never sided wholly with the Tories. His overriding concern was always to work on behalf of those who were the victims of Victorian society and this often involved opposition from his fellow Tories. He recorded in his diary of 24 November 1845:

> I have no political party; the Whigs, I know, regard me as leaning very decidedly to the Conservatives; the Conservatives declare that I have greatly injured the Government of Sir Robert Peel. I have, thus, the approval and support of neither; the floating men of all sides, opinions, ranks and professions, who dislike what they call a 'saint', join in the hatred, and rejoice in it.[42]

Shaftesbury's principle can perhaps best be illustrated by the repeal of the Corn Laws. Since 1815 foreign corn had been taxed and therefore the price of bread was high. Landowners and farmers were clearly strong supporters of this measure and they had chosen Ashley to stand for their views in Parliament. Ashley eventually came to support the Anti-Corn Law League's agenda because he saw the terrible distress that the high price of a loaf of bread was causing the poor. In 1846 he therefore resigned his seat since he could no longer subscribe to the Tory protectionist lobby. He was returned to Parliament as the MP for Bath in the following year.

Throughout his life, whether within Parliament, or in the world outside working to improve the social life of the nation, Shaftesbury was always motivated by his Christian faith. His uncomplicated Evangelical personal religion coloured and impacted his every

---

[41] G.B.A.M. Finlayson, *The Seventh Earl of Shaftesbury 1801–1885*, p. 515.

[42] Hodder, *Life and Work of Lord Shaftesbury*, p. 336.

action. During the 1830s he became friendly with Edward Bickersteth who convinced him of the premillennial end-time theology. From this point on, Ashley's hopes became more and more fixed on Christ's second coming and earthly reign.[43] He believed physical bodies were a temple of the Holy Spirit and 'conceived it a religious duty to provide for them a clean social environment'.[44] His convictions concerning the Second Advent gave him an increasing sense of urgency that 'man must co-operate with God to fill the world with the knowledge of his glory so that the "last days" may not be delayed'.[45]

Regardless of how Lord Shaftesbury is viewed, his achievements were remarkable by any standards. The sheer scope and volume of his concerns and his workload set him head and shoulders above his contemporaries. He was an outstanding leader and men and women of all parties respected him for his high principles and sheer hard work. It was the case that he had his blind spots, particularly in regard to his own estate at St Giles, where his agent Robert Short Waters mismanaged his affairs.[46] It seems clear that Waters not only ill-served the labourers on the estate but also embezzled large sums of Shaftesbury's money.[47] The matter was eventually settled out of court in June 1868.[48] Notwithstanding these aberrations Shaftesbury was, without doubt, the greatest social reformer of the Victorian era. As Georgina Battiscombe put it, 'No man has in fact ever done more to lessen the extent of human misery or to add to the sum total of human happiness.'[49]

Evangelical Societies

When Lord Shaftesbury died the nation honoured him with a memorial service in Westminster Abbey on Thursday 8 October 1885. 189 religious and philanthropic institutions, with which he had been more or less associated, were represented.[50] Shaftesbury's

---

[43] Battiscombe, *Shaftesbury. A Biography*, p. 101.
[44] Bready, *Lord Shaftesbury*, p. 34.
[45] Finlayson, *Seventh Earl of Shaftesbury*, p. 17.
[46] Battiscombe, *Shaftesbury. A Biography*, pp. 282–3.
[47] Ibid., p. 286–7.
[48] Ibid., p. 287.
[49] Ibid., p. 334.
[50] Brown, *Fathers of the Victorians*, p. 328.

life was testimony to the immense value that Evangelicals placed on societies. They promoted and fostered social action by means of charitable societies which were focused on particular issues. Ford K. Brown makes the point that 'the mushroom growth' of Evangelical societies came in the years after the French Revolution.[51] He lists more than 250 societies that were formed between 1800 and 1841.[52] The origins of such societies are traceable to John Wesley who not only referred to himself as 'God's steward of poor', but also organised his Methodist congregations into small groups in which each member was urged to make a weekly contribution in support of the needy.[53] The Charitable Societies of the Victorian era were probably therefore patterned on the Wesleyan 'Strangers Friend and Benevolent Societies'. The first such was founded in London in 1785 and others followed at Leeds in 1789 and at Manchester in 1791.

With such an expansive array of Evangelical societies active in Victorian Britain it is impossible to attempt anything approaching a comprehensive coverage in a chapter of this nature. What can be offered is consideration of the more prominent societies, most of which were focused on moral, humanitarian and public health concerns.

An important factor in all of these societies was the obligation to engage in charity. For Evangelicals, this was simply the insistence that good works result from justification and indeed evidence justification. As Martin Luther had put it, at the time of the Reformation, 'Good works do not make a good man, but a good man does good works.'[54]

One of those responsible for promoting the necessity of charitable giving was John Bird Sumner. Along with his contemporaries, he was convinced of 'the vast disproportion observable between the wealth of the few, and the poverty of many'.[55] From this he went on to argue that the situation made 'the exercise of judicious charity still more imperative'. Indeed, he continued, it 'demands of the affluent not only a denial of some luxurious vanities, but what is more reluctantly sacrificed, a portion of their time, and a sound exertion of discriminating judgement'.[56]

---

[51] Ibid., pp. 331–40.
[52] See Hodder, *Life and Work of Lord Shaftesbury*, Appendix, pp. 777–9, which gives a list of these societies.
[53] See Heasman, *Evangelicals in Action*.
[54] M. Luther, *A Treatise on Christian Liberty*, p. 24.
[55] J.B. Sumner, *Creation* Vol. 1, p. 26.
[56] Ibid., Vol. 2, p. 85.

Although Sumner's thinking on this matter belonged essentially to the eighteenth century, it was followed with little questioning by most Evangelicals in the first half of the nineteenth century. Indeed, it wasn't until the middle Victorian years that churchmen fully recognised that charity and charity alone would never be sufficient to meet the needs of the poor and disadvantaged sections of British society.

Humanitarian Concerns

The most prominent of all Evangelical humanitarian concerns was undoubtedly the abolition of slavery, which was considered in detail in the preceding chapter. Of this great achievement Ian Bradley wrote:

> The outstanding example of what the Evangelicals achieved with public opinion behind them was, of course, the ending of the British slave trade in 1807 and the total abolition of all slavery in the British colonies twenty-six years later. Recent attempts to debunk the Abolition Movement and call into question the motives of those engaged in it have failed to provide any substantial evidence to support their case.[57]

A significant feature of Evangelical humanitarian concern was seen in their treatment of the mentally ill. The old physical method of dealing with the insane by bleeding them and forcibly chaining them to their beds was gradually replaced by more respectful approaches. In this Lord Shaftesbury had played a major role. The Evangelicals in general fostered a spirit of kindness and sympathy that stemmed from their religious beliefs. It was this that helped the authorities to come to the realisation that there was a difference between those who were 'insane' and those who were 'mentally retarded'. This distinction was finally recognised by The Idiots Act of 1886 and, as a result, institutions were set up where various kinds of training were given to those who were capable of receiving limited instruction. Evangelicals also promoted care for epileptics. The Meath Home of Comfort was founded in 1892 close to the outskirts of Godalming to provide care for women and girls, particularly those connected with the Girls' Friendly Society. Lord

---

[57] Bradley, *Call to Seriousness*, p. 80.

Shaftesbury and Lord Kinnaird were concerned at the lack of educational opportunity for crippled children. Through their help several homes for this purpose were opened in the 1850s. Miss Caroline Blunt opened the Winchmore Home in Marylebone Road for crippled girls in 1851 and an institution for boys was founded in 1866 at Kensington. A little later the Moor Street Home was started in the Edgware Road for younger boys of eight to thirteen.[58] Later in the century orphanages such as Dr Barnado's began to make special provision for crippled children.[59]

Among the many individuals who played a prominent part in humanitarian endeavours in the Victorian years was Thomas Barnado (1845–1905). Barnado grew up in Dublin and attended St Werburgh's Church, where he was confirmed. The minister was Dr Marrable, an earnest Evangelical preacher, and, according to Barnado, 'a man of great breadth and liberality'.[60] It was during this time that he experienced his Evangelical conversion, which he always referred to as, 'the most momentous event in his life'.[61] In 1903 he wrote:

> I was brought to Christ in the year 1862. A gentleman, a personal friend of mine Dr Hunt of Harcourt Street, Dublin, a charming man, had been the means in God's hands of awakening inquiry in the mind of my brother George ... and of myself a little later on... I actually found Christ without any human intervention, when alone some few days after a special interview.[62]

In 1866 Thomas Barnado left Ireland and settled in Stepney in the East End of London where he set up a Ragged School. It was possibly in this same year that he encountered Jim Jarvis, the first destitute child he had come across.[63] Barnado established mission and temperance work in London, Edinburgh and elsewhere. It was out of his East End Juvenile Mission that the world-famous Dr Barnado's homes were developed.

Interestingly, the title 'doctor' seems to have been assumed and there is no evidence, according to Gillian Wagner's researches, that

---

[58] See Heasman, *Evangelicals in Action*, pp. 220–1.
[59] Ibid., p. 221.
[60] G. Wagner, *Barnardo*.
[61] Ibid., p. 9.
[62] Ibid., p. 10.
[63] Ibid., p. 30.

he was ever granted an honorary diploma.[64] Indeed, up until 1873 when orders were given that he was to be known as Dr Barnado, he was always 'Brother Barnado' or plain 'Mr Barnado'.[65]

The scope of Barnado's work was immense and led to his children being called 'the largest Family in the World'. In addition to the boarding-out centres, the homes had nearly 200 separate cottages and households which cared for and instructed 8,500 children.[66] Barnado lastingly impacted juvenile legislation and it was largely through his influence that the 1891 Custody of Children Act came into being, preventing the exploitation of children by heartless parents. When Barnado died in 1905 at the age of sixty, his homes had brought up 60,000 once destitute youngsters.

Barnado had also had a hand in the formation of the Society for the Prevention of Cruelty to Children in London, which was later to become the National Society for the Prevention of Cruelty to Children (NSPCC).[67] A meeting was held at the Mansion House. Lord Shaftesbury, who moved the founding of the NSPCC, chaired it. Another Evangelical, Lord Aberdeen, who proposed the election of a council to carry forward the business of the NSPCC, followed him.[68] Barnado was among those elected though he resigned some six years later maintaining that the society was coming too much under the influence of Rome.[69] Along with Shaftesbury, Barnado was convinced of the value of emigration. By the end of Barnado's life, over 11,000 children had been sent to Canada.[70]

Evangelicals also inspired compassion for animals. In 1809 a Society for the Suppression and Prevention of Wanton Cruelty to Animals was founded at the Crown and Anchor, in Bold Street, Liverpool. No further information about the society has come to light, but there is mention in the minutes of the London Branch of the society.[71] As has been noted in the earlier chapter on the Clapham Sect, in 1822 the Rev Arthur Broome called a meeting

---

[64] Ibid., pp. 62–3, 315–17.
[65] Ibid., p. 62.
[66] Bready, *England: Before and After Wesley*, p. 420. See also J.W. Bready, *Dr Barnardo, Physician, Pioneer, Prophet, Child Life Yesterday and Today*.
[67] Wagner, *Barnardo*, pp. 215–17.
[68] Ibid., p. 216.
[69] Ibid., p. 216.
[70] Ibid., p. 251.
[71] Moss, *Valiant Crusade*, p. 21.

in London to consider the whole issue of animal welfare. On 16 June 1824 a meeting was held and the RSPCA was launched. Fowell Buxton took the chair and the Rev Arthur Broome and the Rev G.A. Hatch were among the speakers.[72] A committee was set up which included William Wilberforce MP and the Rev A. Broome, Rev G.A. Hatch and the Rev G. Bonner.[73] The committee sponsored publications and also adopted measures for inspecting street markets, slaughterhouses and the conduct of coachmen. Strenuous efforts were also made to halt bull fighting. Shortly after having taken up full-time work with the RSPCA Broome employed, at his own expense, the first full-time inspector the movement ever had.[74]

Public Health

Evangelicals, along with other sections of the established church, were concerned at the degrading conditions in which the poor lived and worked. Some were reticent to be too outspoken in connecting social conditions with clerical effectiveness.[75] Others, such as Thomas Musgrave, and later in the century John Charles Ryle were more forthright in their approach. Musgrave, for example, was adamant that the miserable living conditions of the poor must be improved. He warned that if the church was to succeed as a national institution 'it must promote the temporal as well as the religious good of the poor'.[76] Ryle was one of the main promoters of the Commission of Inquiry into Unemployment in Liverpool, which was set up in 1894,[77] and he was a forthright opponent of the excessive levels of alcoholic drink consumed by the city's inhabitants.[78]

In his later years as Primate, Archbishop Sumner recognised that church extension and education were making few inroads in the slum areas of the metropolis or the towns of his former industrial

---

[72] Ibid., p. 22.
[73] Ibid., p. 22.
[74] Ibid., p. 34.
[75] Soloway, *Prelates and People*, p. 210.
[76] T. Musgrave, *A Charge Delivered to the Clergy of the Diocese of York, June and July 1853*, pp. 12–13, cited by Soloway, *Prelates and People*, p. 211.
[77] I.D. Farley, *J.C. Ryle: First Bishop of Liverpool*, p. 124.
[78] Ibid., p. 150.

diocese. In 1852 he supported Shaftesbury's efforts to get stronger legislation to enforce the clearing up of the slums. His view was that there was no other way forward.[79] In an attempt to address this issue, Lord Shaftesbury had earlier assisted in 1842 in founding what was first known as The Labourers' Friend Society. It later became The Society for Improving the Condition of the Labouring Classes whose main object was 'to keep in view the erection of model dwellings for all varieties and grades of industrial life'.[80]

Two particular aspects of public health where Evangelicals made significant contributions were the introduction of nursing and help for prostitutes. The development of nursing in England owed much to the inspiration derived from the care for the sick on the part of deaconesses at Kaiserworth in Germany. Florence Nightingale (1820–1910) visited the German town in 1849 and again in 1851. She was an Evangelical by upbringing, her maternal grandfather, William Smith, having connections with the Clapham Sect. She also worked in concert with Lord Shaftesbury and always gave him credit for having originated the Sanitary Commission for the East, which led to major improvements in the Crimea. In her later years Florence moved away from her roots and was inclined to identify herself with the Christian socialists.

Nightingale trained her nurses as professionals combining the devotion exhibited by the Evangelical sisters of Kaiserworth and the scientific knowledge she had learned through her experiences in Crimea. Together with a Liverpool Unitarian businessman, William Rathbone, she introduced improved district and workhouse nursing into that city. In the middle Victorian years two other nursing organisations – The East London Nursing Association and the Ranyard Nurses – came into being. Both had Evangelical connections. The former group was started by the Honourable Mrs James Stuart-Wortley to nurse cholera patients. The Ranyard nurses were the nursing section of The London Bible and Domestic Female Mission founded in 1857 by Ellen H. Ranyard (1810–1879). Leading figures behind Ranyard's organisation were Anthony Thorold, Rector of St Giles-in-the-Field (later to become Bishop of Rochester), Lord Shaftesbury and Arthur Kinnaird.[81] In 1868 Ranyard began training poor women as itinerant nurses in the wards of Guy's Hospital. She called them 'Bible-nurses'. This contrasted with Nightingale's

---

[79] *Hansard* CXX (1852), pp. 1299–1300.
[80] Hodder, *Life and Work of Lord Shaftesbury*, p. 352.
[81] Lewis, *Lighten Their Darkness*, pp. 221–2.

approach which confined trainees solely to nursing activities. Together with his wife, William Pennefather began training women for parochial mission work and a house for training deaconesses was set up in 1860. In this Pennefather drew on the example of the Protestant Deaconess house in Germany. Following the cholera outbreak of 1866 his Mildmay Deaconesses began to engage in visiting and nursing the sick and dying, and a small hospital and Medical Mission was established.[82]

A significant Evangelical contribution in the area of public health was their work among prostitutes. In the first decades of the nineteenth century there were a number of societies that worked to close down brothels. Religious institutions called 'Magdalens' were set up with the specific objective of reforming the prostitute. Three large Evangelical societies were set up with the specific aim of helping dissolute women, The Rescue Society in 1853 under the presidency of Lord Shaftesbury, The London Female Preventive Society and Reforming Institute in 1857 and The Homes of Hope in 1860. In the same year the Midnight Meetings Movement was established by a group of Evangelicals, among them the Rev Baptist Noel and the Rev Daniel Wilson, the younger, of Islington.

Midnight helpers and volunteers invited women of the street for a free meal at designated restaurants after which there was a short talk at which an invitation was given and help offered to any who wanted to change their way of life. As each person left, they were presented with a sealed envelope that contained the name and address of a female worker if they wanted further help. Brian Dickey has suggested that in the early part of the century the problem of prostitution was seen largely as one of indiscipline but by the later Victorian years it was regarded by most as a moral issue.[83]

The most prominent Evangelical figure in the work among prostitutes was Josephine Butler. She had a strong Evangelical upbringing and at the age of seventeen had a deeply religious experience that remained with her throughout her life.[84] In 1852 she married George Butler (1819 1890) and they had what proved to be a deep and special relationship. In the biography of her husband Josephine described it as 'a perfectly equal union, with absolute freedom on both sides for personal initiative in thought and action

---

[82] R. Braithwaite, *The Life and Letters of Rev William Pennefather*, p. 409.

[83] Dickey, 'Evangelicals and Poverty', p. 52.

[84] G.W. Johnson and L.A. Johnson (eds.), *Josephine Butler: An Autobiographical Memoir*, pp. 15–16.

and for individual development'.[85] After a period in Cheltenham, George was appointed Principal of Liverpool College and the Butlers moved to the northwest in January 1866. It was here that Josephine began her work among the prostitutes.

She believed the underlying problem to be a socio-economic one rather than a sexual one. She was convinced that if the employment opportunities for women were extended the number of prostitutes would be decreased. Her researches revealed that nine thousand women in the city were earning their living by prostitution, 1,500 of them were under fifteen years of age.[86]

In 1869 Josephine began to work for the repeal of the Contagious Diseases Acts, which had become law in 1864, 1866 and 1868 and applied to prostitutes in garrison and naval towns. The Acts were a double standard since for women prostitution was an offence committed for financial gain whereas for men it was an irregular indulgence of a natural impulse. Josephine also objected to the compulsory inspection of women for venereal disease by doctors (all male), after being arrested by a police constable on the grounds of suspicion only. Her struggles led to a Royal Commission being established in 1871 to which she gave evidence. Her other major campaign was to get the age of consent for lawful sexual intercourse raised from twelve to sixteen. This resulted in the Criminal Law Amendment Act of 1885.

The role of individuals such as Ranyard, Nightingale and Butler was certainly encouraged by growing numbers of women who were taking up careers in a variety of fields.[87] Mary Clare Martin's work on Walthamstow and Leyton has shown there was a widening of public philanthropic roles for women in the middle years of the nineteenth century.[88]

Other Concerns

Evangelicals of the established church involved themselves in a wide range of campaigns and societies that were concerned with moral issues and social injustice. One of their most notable institutions

---

[85] Cited ibid., p. 20.
[86] Ibid., p. 246.
[87] Lewis, *Lighten Their Darkness*, p. 221.
[88] M.C. Martin, 'Women and Philanthropy in Walthamstow and Leyton 1740–1870', *London Journal* 2.19 (1995), pp. 126–7, 131.

was The Society for the Suppression of Vice founded in 1802 by members of the Clapham Sect and a number of London parish clergy and professional men.[89] The objectives of the society were taken over from William Wilberforce's earlier Proclamation Society. They included action against the profanation of the Lord's Day and profane swearing, the publication of blasphemous and obscene books and prints, selling by false weights and measures, the keeping of brothels and gaming houses, illegal lotteries and cruelty to animals.[90] By the end of 1804 membership stood at 1,200 and income ranged from £900 to £1,400 every year between 1803 and 1807.[91] The society's membership shrank during the Napoleonic Wars but recovered during the 1820s when obscene and blasphemous publications became a particular focus of its attention. Its membership then began to decline once more as new societies that overlapped with its concerns began to emerge. Among these were the RSPCA, visiting societies and societies preventing child prostitution.[92] By 1879 the Vice Society's membership had dwindled to a mere 130 and by that time the scope of its activities was very limited. It was involved in a short-lived crusade against West End Prostitution in 1857–1858, a campaign against betting shops in the mid 1850s and indecent popular journalism in the 1860s and 1870s.[93] In 1886 the society handed over its funds to and merged with the National Vigilance Association. Despite its demise, M.J.D. Roberts has maintained that the society was nevertheless 'effective as an embodiment of community standards, particularly in the field of literary decency'.[94] In addition, the society, he asserted, 'played a leading part in identifying "deviant" social groups and activities for later official surveillance and/or informal social regulation'.[95]

Church of England Evangelicals, along with their Nonconformist counterparts, were particularly concerned about the dangers of alcoholic drink. Most of their parochial clergy warned of the evils of beer and spirits in their sermons and supported temperance

---

[89] M.J. Roberts, 'Making Victorian Morals? The Society for the Suppression of Vice and its Critics', *Historical Studies* 21.83 (Oct 1981), pp. 157–73.

[90] Ibid., p. 160.

[91] Ibid., p. 161.

[92] Ibid., pp. 164–5.

[93] Ibid., p. 168.

[94] Ibid., p. 173.

[95] Ibid., p. 173.

societies. Bishop Robert Bickersteth of Ripon was a zealous advocate of temperance societies,[96] and John Ryle of Liverpool declared that 'of all the gigantic evils we have to face in the Church of England there is none to be compared with the enormous evil of intemperance'.[97] Reformers such as Thomas Barnado[98] and Josephine Butler also gave their support to temperance endeavours of various kinds. The Church of England clergy and parishes gave support to both temperance and teetotalism but it was not until the early 1860s that the first formal organisation began. Francis Close gave strong support to the temperance cause and helped to form The Church Temperance Reformation Society. In 1862 it became The Church of England Temperance Society and included in its membership both abstainers and moderate drinkers. Close served as chairman in 1873.

The nineteenth-century temperance movement was rooted in the teaching of John Wesley who urged members of his societies to avoid buying and selling spirituous liquor. In the 1820s and 1830s many local temperance societies sprang up, particularly as a result of the influence of the Primitive Methodists. By the middle of the century the temperance movement was well established and two national societies had come into existence, The United Kingdom Alliance in 1853 and The National Temperance League in 1856. Although the former had some Evangelical support, the latter organisation was much more closely linked with Evangelical work. Its prominent supporters included the Earl of Aberdeen, Lord Mount-Temple and Lord Kinnaird.

Prompted by the American gospel temperance movement there was a growing opinion on the part of those who were engaged in rescue and humanitarian social work that a definite and strong line needed to be taken in regard to alcoholic drink and its associated problems. Mrs C.L. Wightman (1817–1896), the wife of the Vicar of St Alkmund's, Shrewsbury, became the leading figure in the British gospel temperance movement. She was the author of an influential teetotal tract, *Haste to the Rescue*, which was published in 1859. It recounted the evil and damage caused by drink in the homes of the poor. 26,000 copies were sold in the first six months.[99] A copy of Mrs

---

[96] See entry for Robert Bickersteth, *D.N.B.*, p. 468.
[97] Farley, *Ryle*, p. 144.
[98] Wagner, *Barnardo*, p. 58, and Heasman, *Evangelicals in Action*, p. 133.
[99] Heasman, *Evangelicals in Action*, p. 131, and Bradley, *Call to Seriousness*, p. 101; see also B. Harrison, *Drink and the Victorians*, p. 169.

Wightman's *Haste to the Rescue* was distributed to every clergyman and theological college in the country. This prompted the start of temperance work in many parishes and was an important factor in the formation of the Church of England Temperance Society in 1862.[100] Catherine Marsh (1818–1912), the daughter of William Marsh, worked with navvies at the Crystal Palace and made use of the pledge which she found to be successful.

Working class women had not joined temperance societies in any great numbers and this prompted the founding of The British Women's Temperance Association in 1876. A closely related organisation, The Temperance Union of Christian Workers, had come into being a year earlier with the specific aim of making improvements in the homes of the poor. Among its members were Charlotte Mason and Agnes Weston.

The emergence of gospel temperance had the effect of moving the drink question from being a social campaign to a religious one. Notwithstanding hostility on the part of some, its influence undoubtedly reached sections of the lower classes and helped to reduce the consumption of alcohol on the part of the poor. Evangelicals recognised that prohibition alone was not sufficient and many of their number, such as William Pennefather[101] and Bishop John Ryle,[102] put time and energy into opening coffee and cocoa houses. The Coffee Tavern Company was formed in 1876 under the presidency of the Honourable W.F. Cowper-Temple and opened twenty-seven houses in London and the provinces. By 1882 more than one hundred such companies were known to be in existence.[103]

One other significant concern among Evangelicals was the state of the nation's prisons. At the middle point of the nineteenth century these consisted of a variety of institutions. These were fifty-six short-sentence gaols in the more important counties and boroughs; there were convict prisons at Pentonville, Millbank, Brixton and several other locations. There were also detention centres for those awaiting trial. Among them were Clerkenwell, Newgate and the Horsemonger gaols.

In the later years of the eighteenth century, John Howard (1726–1790) had opened the eyes of the British public to the deplorable state of the prisons. His detailed researches included many

---

[100] Heasman, *Evangelicals in Action*, p. 132.
[101] Braithwaite, *William Pennefather*, pp. 312–13.
[102] Farley, *Ryle*, p. 148.
[103] Heasman, *Evangelicals in Action*, p. 141.

European countries and he travelled an estimated 50,000 miles and spent some £30,000 of his own personal fortune in the cause of the prisoner. Among those who came to share Howard's concerns were William Wilberforce, Henry Thornton and Charles Grant of the Clapham Sect. Wilberforce in particular spoke out strongly in the Commons in favour of several Bills that proposed to reduce the number of crimes for which a person could be hanged.[104] Wilberforce also became a member of a Select Committee on 'death penalty for felonies'[105] and his influence gave considerable help to humanising the country's criminal code. By the middle of the nineteenth century most prisons had at least one chaplain and some of these, such as the Rev John Clay who worked at Preston from 1821 to 1858, did a great deal to make life for their inmates considerably more humane. Clay's work was subsequently published by his son and had widespread influence on other chaplains.[106]

Many Evangelicals were inspired by the example of John Wesley's Holy Club and the Quaker, Elizabeth Fry, and in consequence concerned themselves with prison visiting. Others gave time to helping ex-prisoners find their way back into society or caring for juvenile offenders. The Royal Society for Discharged Prisoners was set up at Charing Cross, with the aid of Lord Kinnaird, for this purpose and a cluster of similar organisations were formed in its wake.[107] The Church Army also began to take a more active concern for prisoners in the 1880s.[108] In general terms, it was the case that Evangelicals urged and promoted a reformative rather than a punitive approach to the criminal.

It is not difficult to find flaws in Victorian Evangelical social concern even by nineteenth-century standards. Much of what was done was curative rather than preventative in nature and left the recipients dependent on the churches and societies concerned. Men such as Wilberforce, Shaftesbury and Kinnaird were firm believers in a fixed social hierarchy with the result that they inevitably found it difficult to demonstrate to their beneficiaries how to improve their status in life. It was perhaps for this reason that Anglican Evangelicals gave almost no support to the emerging trade union

---

[104] Bready, *England: Before and After Wesley*, p. 372.
[105] Ibid., p. 372.
[106] Heasman, *Evangelicals in Action*, p. 179.
[107] Ibid., p. 178.
[108] See S. Dark, *Wilson Carlisle The Laughing Cavalier*, pp. 101–12.

movements of the 1870s and 1880s. Many, like Archbishop John Sumner, also remained suspicious of state intervention, feeling that it might conspire to take away self-motivation and so result in apathy and laziness on the part of the poor and unemployed.

Nevertheless, Evangelical social concern covered a very wide spectrum. It also encompassed the blind and the deaf, the sick and the aged, the sailor and the soldier and specific working groups such as the police, cabmen, railway workers, navvies, postmen and gypsies. Evangelical enterprise also gave public and separate roles for women in the sphere of social reform. Anglican Evangelicals did not evade their responsibilities. Their sacrificial involvement and efforts generated a climate of care and compassion that laid the foundations of the state-run social services which emerged in the twentieth century.

5

Evangelical Bishops

Early Bishops

As has been noted, at the beginning of the nineteenth century the Evangelicals were a small minority. It was therefore no surprise that they had no representatives on the episcopal bench. One or two bishops were however sympathetic to their cause in a somewhat reticent manner. Beilby Porteous (1731–1808) of London shared some of the concerns of the Clapham Sect. He was a decided opponent of the slave trade and an early patron of CMS. He urged on his clergy the importance of residing in their parishes and ministering to the needs of their people. Shute Barrington (1734–1825) who was translated to the See of Durham in 1791 was noted for his piety and generosity and along with Porteous he encouraged Hannah More in the production of her cheap repository tracts. Among those whom Barrington raised to Prebendal Stalls in his Cathedral were John Bird Sumner and Thomas Gisborne who both had strong links with Clapham. Bishop Burgess (1756–1837) who was a close friend of Barrington was first consecrated to the See of St David's and later translated to Salisbury. He had a particular concern for the disadvantaged and urged that those who gave money to the poor should not be overly concerned as to whether they were deserving or not. God was the best judge of the sincerity and the motivation of both receiver and giver.[1] Burgess was also active in the campaign to end the slave trade.

It was not until 1815 that the Evangelicals obtained their first bishopric when Henry Ryder was consecrated as the first Bishop of Gloucester. Ryder was the youngest son of Nathaniel, the first Baron Harrowby, and Elizabeth, his wife, who was the daughter and

---

[1] Soloway, *Prelates and People*, p. 24.

co-heiress of Dr Richard Terrick (1710–1777), successively Bishop of Peterborough and London. Educated at St John's College, Cambridge, he emerged from the University with 'a generally high character' and a man with 'literary tastes, studious habits and outwardly at least of irreproachable conduct'.[2] He was ordained in 1800 by Bishop Cornwallis of Lichfield to the curacy of Sandon, the family living in Staffordshire. In 1801 he was appointed Rector of Lutterworth in Leicestershire and in addition in 1805 Vicar of the adjoining parish of Claybrook. In 1808 he was made a Prebendary of Windsor and in 1812 he became Dean of Wells. In 1802 he married Sophie, the second daughter of Thomas March Phillipps of Garendon, Leicestershire, by whom he had ten sons and three daughters.

In his early days Ryder was reckoned to have been a high churchman with a strong prejudice against the Calvinistic doctrines held by the more extreme sections of the Evangelical party. A change in his opinions came about in 1807 as a result of his having been selected to preach at the Archdeacon's visitation at Leicester. He used the occasion to attack the doctrines of the Evangelicals which he believed to be contrary to the teaching of the Church of England. His words were taken to be particularly focused on Thomas Robinson whose forty-year ministry in Leicester attracted very large congregations and exercised a major influence in the town. In 1808 Robinson was given the task of giving the visitation sermon and it was widely expected that he would use the opportunity to reply to Ryder's attack. However, he made no reference to the matter and Ryder was much impressed by his forbearance and forgiving spirit. Later in the same year the two men unexpectedly met and a friendship was forged which prompted a major change in Ryder's spiritual life.[3] By 1810 Ryder had begun to read the commentaries of Henry and Scott, and his changed views were soon apparent in his preaching and ministry. Ryder began holding family prayer and Bible reading each day instead of just on Sunday and he commenced the practice of reading the Scriptures and praying at the cottage meetings. His Windsor canonry brought no change to his views and when he preached at St George's Chapel, 'he faithfully confessed his Saviour, and was an honoured instrument for good'.[4] In 1811

[2] *Christian Observer*, August 1836, p. 503.
[3] G.C.B. Davies, *The First Evangelical Bishop: Some Aspects of the Life of Henry Ryder*, p. 5.
[4] Ibid., p. 5.

Ryder took the chair at the annual meeting of the Bible Society at
Leicester and expressed strong support for its work. In 1814, as
Dean of Wells, he preached CMS's anniversary sermon, being the
first cleric in a high office to do so.

During his time at Wells, Ryder was noted for his compassion
and concern for the poor and his effective preaching. He ran soup
kitchens for the needy and personally distributed food and
clothing in the parishes of the Deanery.[5] In 1813 when he took his
Doctor of Divinity degree at Cambridge he preached in Holy
Trinity Church and his friendship with Simeon grew. Simeon had
in fact warned him on his coming to the Cathedral that 'you may
be sometimes urged to do things which though desirable in themselves, are not expedient'. Ryder responded that he would 'treasure
up your written counsel and hope to have it often confirmed by
personal intercourse'.[6]

By the time Ryder was offered the See of Gloucester his views
which were well known aroused considerable opposition. There is
no doubt however that he owed his appointment to the influence of
his older brother, Lord Harrowby, who was himself an Evangelical.
Ryder's elevation was resented by both Archbishop Manners
Sutton because he was 'a religious bishop' and by the wider church.
For this reason the Prime Minister, Lord Liverpool, held back for
some months before issuing the *conge d'élire*. Lord Harrowby
helped to overcome the opposition when he declared in the House
of Lords, 'If Dr Ryder is not fit to be a bishop, Lord Harrowby is not
fit to be Lord President of the Council.' This was a response that the
Prime Minister could not afford to ignore.

Ryder's Evangelical views were soon apparent in both his visitation charges and his preaching. On the matter of baptism, for example, he said, 'I would solemnly protest against that most serious
error of contemplating all individuals of a baptised congregation, as
converted, as having all once known the truth, and entered upon the
right path'.[7] Ryder enjoined his hearers to urge their parishioners 'to
come in true repentance and lively faith to the Saviour and receive
their portion of his meritorious atonement'.[8]

---

[5] Ryder to Dudley Ryder, 15 April 1812, cited by Soloway, *Prelates and People*, p. 186.

[6] Davies, *First Evangelical Bishop*, p. 8.

[7] Ibid., p. 9.

[8] H. Ryder, *Visitation Charge* 1816, pp. 20–2, cited by Davies, *First Evangelical Bishop*, p. 9.

Ryder soon showed himself to be a conscientious bishop who gave himself unstintingly to teaching and pastoral care. Hannah More wrote in 1818 that

> The Bishop of Gloucester has been almost the only visitor in my sick room. When I saw him, he had confirmed some thousands, consecrated one church and two churchyards, and preached nine sermons in ten days; if the Spirit is as able as it is willing, the flesh must sink under such labours.[9]

At Gloucester the Dean and Chapter made efforts to exclude Ryder from the pulpit but his tact and humility overcame their prejudices. It was his custom to preach twice and often three times on a Sunday, and, in addition, he regularly instructed the children of the national school during the afternoons.

Ryder's elevation to the episcopal bench was a particular encouragement to CMS.[10] No previous bishop had been willing, as Ryder was, to ordain men for work outside the diocese and every missionary had therefore been forced to serve a curacy in an English parish before going out to the foreign field.[11] So great was Ryder's influence over CMS that he spoke fourteen times at their annual meetings.[12] In his later years at Lichfield, Ryder was a noted supporter of the Church Pastoral Aid Society (CPAS), which had been formed in 1836 to raise the salaries not only of curates but also of lay assistants.

In his charge to the Gloucester diocese in 1819 Ryder gave teaching on the Holy Communion. He urged his clergy to explain the real nature of the service to their people and to caution them against 'formal reliance upon an outward ordinance'. The sacrament must be represented he urged, 'as an act of faith in the love and power of Jesus'.[13] Ryder did not discuss either the real presence or the nature of sacramental grace but he urged attendance at the Lord's Supper as an important part of people's spiritual provision.[14]

In 1824 Ryder was translated to Lichfield which with its larger population and industrial centres offered greater scope for his

---

[9] *Christian Observer*, 1836, p. 635, cited by Davies, *First Evangelical Bishop.*, p. 12.

[10] Davies, *First Evangelical Bishop*, p. 16.

[11] Balleine, *History of the Evangelical Party*, p. 193.

[12] Davies, *First Evangelical Bishop*, p. 17.

[13] H. Ryder, *Charge 1819*, p. 64f. cited by Davies, *First Evangelical Bishop*, p. 11.

[14] Ibid., p. 11.

organisation and evangelistic concerns. With the assistance of Archdeacon George Hodson he formed a diocesan Church Building Association and with the help of Archdeacon William Spooner £15,000 was subscribed during the first year. The cause of Evangelicalism was advanced in Birmingham. After eight years in his new diocese Ryder had consecrated twenty new churches and ten more were in the process of construction. Ryder discovered that the efforts of his new society fell well behind what was needed and he therefore experimented with the building of proprietary chapels which led to a complaint from Walter Hook, the future Vicar of Leeds, that he was co-operating with 'fanatical ministers' and laymen in creating new chapels in crowded districts.

In his charge of 1832 Ryder continued his focus on the needs of the working classes and the manufacturing districts. He gave encouragement to those employers who paid 'conscientious and kind attention to the comforts and morals of the poor'. He was able to report that there had been an increase of forty resident clergy in the diocese over the previous four years. He also urged the greater use of district visitors from each congregation to support the work of the incumbent in discovering the sick and those in need of help and support.[15]

Ryder's view of the role of the clergyman was increasingly hard to realise in nineteenth-century England. In 1824 he spoke of the parish minister as 'the cementer of social union, the organ of kindly communication between the rich and the poor of the land. He is at once the object of respect and the friend to each.'[16] The fact was the gap between rich and poor was growing steadily and the prospects of the working classes being drawn into the worshipping life of the local church patronised by mill owners and company managers was becoming increasingly unlikely.

The pastoral oversight of a diocese that included the present dioceses of Coventry, Birmingham and Derby was a huge task and Ryder's health suffered. After only twelve years in office he died at the relatively young age of fifty-eight. William Wilberforce referred to him as 'the highly-prized and loved Bishop Ryder' and as a prelate after his own heart, 'who united to the zeal of an apostle the most amiable and endearing qualities, and the polished manners of

---

[15] H. Ryder, *Charge 1832*, cited by Davies, *First Evangelical Bishop*, p. 28.

[16] H. Ryder, *A Charge to the Clergy of the Diocese of Lichfield and Coventry, at the Primary Visitation*, p. 13, cited by Soloway, *Prelates and People*, pp. 232–3.

the best society'.[17] Augustus Shirley, later to be Bishop of Sodor and Man, wrote from Ashbourne in Derbyshire of a confirmation service held by Ryder in September 1824:

> The confirmation took place on Friday last, and was conducted in a most impressive manner by our apostolical bishop (Ryder), who addressed the young people after the service, in that pious, simple, affectionate and earnest manner, by which his personal character and writing are so eminently distinguished.[18]

Shirley continued in a subsequent paragraph, 'His manners are particularly elegant, and he has the happy art, which so few possess, of making conversation profitable without being constrained.'[19]

Charles and John Sumner

It was to be more than a decade after Ryder's consecration before the Evangelicals were able to add to their number on the episcopal bench. Charles Richard Sumner (1790–1874) was consecrated as Bishop of Llandaff in 1826. He and his elder brother, John, were the sons of Robert Sumner, the rector of Kenilworth in Warwickshire. Both boys were educated at Eton College where their grandfather had been Headmaster. John Sumner who was some ten years older than Charles went up to King's College, Cambridge, from where he received his BA degree in 1802 and returned to Eton as a schoolmaster. In the same year their father died and John and his wife, Mary Ann, had the responsibility of keeping an eye on Charles and providing him with breakfast and tea.[20] In 1810 Charles entered Trinity College, Cambridge, and graduated BA in 1814. He was ordained deacon in 1814 and priest in 1817 and was curate of Highclere from 1816–1821. While still in this junior position he tutored the children of the King's mistress, the Marchioness of Conyngham, and this resulted in his having a number of Royal audiences. It was not long before George IV

---

[17] Hylson-Smith, *Evangelicals in the Church of England*, p. 70.
[18] T. Hill, *Letters and A Memoir of the Late Walter Augustus Shirley DD. Lord Bishop of Sodor and Man*, p. 66.
[19] Ibid., p. 67.
[20] See Scotland, *John Bird Sumner*, p. 13.

made Charles one of his domestic chaplains.[21] Here Sumner quickly showed his mettle.

On one occasion the King had requested to receive Holy Communion. Sumner arrived to find that he had just dismissed a servant in anger and 'told him plainly that he did not seem in a fit state to receive the communion, that he must learn to restrain his passion, and must forgive'.[22] Sumner then asked for permission to withdraw so that the King could think the matter over. The King took the rebuke in good heart and later knelt to receive communion with the rest of his household including the servant who had been at fault.[23]

The King's warmth towards Sumner increased steadily and resulted in a string of appointments, including the Vicarage of St Helen's, Abingdon 1821–1822, Canon of Worcester 1822–1825 and Canon of Canterbury in 1827. In 1826 he was appointed Bishop of Llandaff and was consecrated on 21 May 1826. His year in office gave indications of what was to follow in subsequent years. There was no episcopal palace at Llandaff and Sumner's immediate priority was to provide himself with a suitable residence in Wales. Being himself opposed to the non-residence of his clergy it was essential that he set an example himself. He was able to rent a convenient house at Llansanfraed between Abergavenny and Monmouth where he was joined by his wife and family.[24] He immediately set about a visitation of the diocese.[25] His son later recorded:

> Searching enquiries were made of every incumbent as to the state of his parish ... In that part of Glamorganshire which was in the Llandaff diocese, sixty-two out of one hundred and seven incumbencies were provided with glebe-houses, seventy-two had none, and in the whole diocese, one hundred and thirty-seven out of two hundred and thirty-four parishes were without a resident clergyman and one hundred and forty-one parishes had neither Sunday nor day school.[26]

---

[21] Hylson-Smith, *Evangelicals in the Church of England*, p. 154.
[22] Balleine, *History of the Evangelical Party*, p. 193.
[23] G.H. Sumner, *Life of Charles Richard Sumner DD Bishop of Winchester*, pp. 78–9.
[24] Ibid., p. 114.
[25] Ibid., p. 115.
[26] Ibid., p. 115.

The Church in Wales had fallen into deplorably bad times and in his short time in office Charles Sumner did his uppermost to stir his diocese and clergy from their state of indifference and sloth.

On 18 November 1827 Sumner received a letter from the King in which he wrote, 'The very moment I was informed of the death of the Bishop of Winchester, I nominated you his successor.' Sumner remained in office for forty years and during that time he was able to set a new pattern of episcopacy. His biographer reported:

> It is not too much say that, during the term of his tenure of the See, a revolution was effected in the episcopal office. Prelates with wigs, great state and corresponding haughtiness of manner gave place to real overseers of the clergy, sympathising in the pastors' struggles, cheering them in their disappointments, counselling them in their difficulties. Bishop Blomfield, Kaye and the two Sumners were in the van of the movement. The perfunctory discharge of customary duties was felt to be no longer the ideal of perfection to be aimed at. Real hard work was the order of the day.[27]

Charles Sumner very quickly identified himself with the Evangelical party by preaching on behalf of CMS.[28] He constantly urged both his clergy and ordination candidates to 'Preach Christ' as the 'grand centre of the Christian system',[29] and to be unswerving in their attachment to 'justification in and by Christ through faith'.[30] His convictions were strongly Protestant and he attacked those who designated 'the blessed Reformation' as 'that great schism' and spoke of the sacraments 'not as seals and pledges, but as instruments of salvation'.[31] In his charge of 1845 Charles Sumner urged upon the clergy a twofold duty: 'First, to vindicate the anti-Romish character of our own church, and next, to guard against the aggressive pretensions of such a power as Romanism'.[32] In his charge of 1850, Sumner spoke at length on the question of baptismal regeneration following the Gorham affair. He stressed that when the child came of age, 'I must look, notwithstanding his baptism for the

---

[27] Ibid., p. 135.
[28] Ibid., pp. 140–1.
[29] Ibid., p. 143.
[30] Ibid., p. 143.
[31] C.R. Sumner, *A Charge to the Clergy of Winchester 1841*, pp. 30–9.
[32] C.R. Sumner, *Charge to the Clergy of Winchester 1841*, p. 299.

Scriptural evidence of his being a child of God.'[33] He spoke out strongly on the matter of the restoration of the Roman Catholic hierarchy and used the occasion to urge on his clergy the additional duty 'of holding fast and pure their own reformed faith'.[34] He also denounced Private Confession 'as foreign to the spirit of the Gospel'.[35]

Charles Sumner, together with his brother John, was in many ways a herald of change in the character of English episcopacy. As Arthur Burns has reminded us, he established a quadrennial visitation pattern at Winchester[36] and focused attention on areas of deficiency and weakness[37]. His charges contained a statistical section in which he analysed the information he had received and suggested courses for action. He set a particular trend by including among his statistics a tally of clergy surviving from his primary visitation and noting those who had died since his previous address.[38] Sumner's publication of statistics was done with the objective of indicating and demonstrating diocesan improvement.[39]

Sumner was deeply concerned at the lack of church building particularly in areas such as Southwark and Lambeth, which were then a part of Winchester diocese, and Portsea. A Winchester Diocesan Church Building Society was started in 1837 and the symbolic importance of a simultaneous appeal on its behalf throughout the diocese was not lost on Sumner. 'May it not remind us that we are all members of one body', he said, during the course of his 1841 visitation address.[40] Sumner noted in his 1833 charge that there were only nine clergy for 91,500 people in Southwark and in one Surrey parish there were only 150 free sittings for fourteen thousand.[41] Twenty years later Sumner saw clearly that before a congregation could be formed its members in the towns 'must be sought out as the wounded and the dying in the battlefield' and brought

---

[33] C.R. Sumner, *A Charge 1850*, cited by G.H. Sumner, *Life of Charles Richard Sumner*, p. 343.

[34] Ibid., p. 345.

[35] Ibid., p. 350.

[36] A. Burns, *The Diocesan Revival in the Church of England c. 1800–1870*, p. 28.

[37] Ibid., p. 28.

[38] Ibid., pp. 33–4.

[39] C.R. Sumner, *A Charge Delivered to the Clergy of the Diocese of Winchester in October 1833*, pp. 16–18.

[40] Burns, *Diocesan Revival*, pp. 122–3.

[41] C.R. Sumner, *A Charge 1833*, pp. 16–18.

to safety.[42] He also argued that parochial clergy must be involved in working for improved sanitation and housing and the promotion of education.[43]

Charles Sumner was a remarkable bishop by any standards. He took meticulous care over his confirmation[44] preparation. In earlier times he met with both farmers and the leaders of their aggrieved labourers. He obtained a general promise from the farmers to put up the men's wages.[45] One evening, a few days later, he met outside his palace gates with an angry mob still dissatisfied with the terms they had received and agreed to make further efforts on their behalf.[46] Like many of his contemporaries Sumner was immensely hard working. His son reported that in 1867, the year before his resignation, he wrote upwards of 3,500 letters on matters of business.[47] When his older brother John died, Samuel Wilberforce informed William Gladstone that Charles would be the best man to succeed to the primacy. Wilberforce declared

> He is a capital administrator, an Eton Scholar of that old school dying out among us, entirely good, sound on all points of the faith, a gentleman, a man of surpassing prudence ... It would be thoroughly welcomed by the Evangelical party; it would excite no anger in others.[48]

Once having gained the ear of the King, Charles was able to introduce his brother John Bird to George IV and, with the continued favour of the Marchioness of Conyngham, obtained for him the bishopric of Chester.[49] John Sumner was consecrated at York on 14 September 1828 and his friend Thomas Gisborne of Yoxhall Lodge, a fellow Prebend of Durham, preached the sermon. His nineteen years at Chester were widely acclaimed as a model of leadership, pastoral care and clear-sighted strategy.

Sumner's strategy for the diocese had four key aspects to it: the greater provision of church accommodation, especially for the

---

[42] C.R. Sumner, *The Home Work of the Parochial Ministry: A Charge*, pp. 19–21.

[43] Ibid., pp. 32–3.

[44] G.H. Sumner, *Life of Charles Richard Sumner*, pp. 216f.

[45] Ibid., p. 192.

[46] Ibid., p. 193.

[47] Ibid., p. 212.

[48] R.G. Wilberforce, *The Life of the Right Reverend Samuel Wilberforce* Vol. 3, pp. 63–4.

[49] S. Baring-Gould, *The Evangelical Revival*, p. 265.

poor; the encouragement and support of the clergy; the advocacy of lay visitors and lay helpers: and the provision of education. Sumner aimed to increase the number of new churches by initiating and supporting church building societies, such as the Chester Diocesan Society for Building Chapels in Rural Districts, which was founded in 1836, and The Chester Diocesan Building Society, which he established in 1843. In all, he consecrated 233 new churches, which caused Geoffrey Best to describe him as 'one of the greatest promoters of new churches'.[50] Sumner was quick to point out, however, that these churches were not built as ends in themselves, or as centres where the working classes could be civilised and instructed in Christian principles. At the beginning of his first charge to the diocese in 1829, he said: 'wherever an assemblage of men is collected together, provision should be made for their souls; that is provision that they should be brought to God through Jesus Christ'.[51]

Unlike many earlier nineteenth-century prelates, Sumner saw one of his major roles as that of 'pastor pastorium'. Something of his meticulous care for his clergy can be seen by glancing at his detailed notes on the many parishes of his diocese. Besides giving full details about communicant numbers, Sunday schools and midweek meetings, Sumner adds details about their stipends and snippets of information such as 'his wife is ill'.[52] Although Sumner did deal with national issues in his visitation addresses he invariably made the task of the clergyman one of his central concerns.

Sumner recognised that many clergy were simply unable to cope with their task single-handed. He therefore urged them to appoint and use lay helpers in the work of their parishes. In these proposals he was probably influenced by Charles Simeon's use of district visitors in his Cambridge parish. 'Such visitors', Sumner declared, 'would lessen the clergyman's own labour by visiting and examining the schools, by reading and praying with the infirm and aged, by consoling the fatherless and widows in their affliction.'[53] Sumner encouraged the work of societies such as the Lancaster District Visiting Society, which dealt with the needs of 1,250 families in 1832.[54]

---

[50] G. Best, *Temporal Pillars*, p. 163.

[51] J.B. Sumner, *A Charge Delivered to the Clergy of the Diocese of Chester at the Primary Visitation in August and September 1829.*

[52] J.B. Sumner, *Handwritten Notes on the Parishes of the Diocese of Chester* (Chester Records Office), MS EDR 5/BOX5.

[53] J.B. Sumner, *A Charge 1829*, p. 23.

[54] W.R. Ward, *Religion and Society in England 1790–1850*, p. 136.

Sumner was a remarkable promoter of education. He remained convinced that unless children and young people grew up at least being able to read and to write, there would be little long term hope of their spiritual and social well-being improving. During John Sumner's time in Chester, 671 new day schools were built and many Sunday schools strengthened and improved. Sumner also emerged as possibly the major influence in the founding of Chester Training College in January 1830.[55] It was the first of its kind in the country and was soon 'able to send forth thirty masters annually'.[56]

Along with his brother, Charles, John Sumner was a staunch opponent of the Oxford Movement. In his charge of 1838 he urged that it 'threatened a revival of the worst evils of the Romish system'.[57] Sumner's opposition was twofold. Tractarian theology did not regard Scripture as 'sufficient to make a man wise unto salvation' and it undermined the doctrine of justification by faith.[58] In *The Doctrine of Justification Briefly Stated* he pointed out that 'the Romish system' conflated justification and sanctification thus making human endeavour a contributory factor in salvation. He argued that in the New Testament justification and sanctification were entirely separate.[59]

Sumner was a committed supporter and encourager of Evangelical societies. His presence seems to have been prominent on the platforms and at meetings of those societies which had their roots in Clapham, namely CMS, BFBS and the Lord's Day Observance Society (LDOS). According to Eugene Stock, Sumner and his brother Charles, 'threw themselves heart and soul into the work of the Church Missionary Society'.[60] John Sumner was the National Anniversary speaker no less than twelve times between 1815 and 1848. In his later years when he was Primate, Sumner gave considerable time and support to Henry Venn discussing strategies and helping him to establish new dioceses overseas.

---

[55] J.L. Bradbury, *Chester College and the Training of Teachers 1839–1875*, p. 25.

[56] J.B. Sumner, *A Charge Delivered to the Clergy of the Diocese of Chester 1832*.

[57] J.B. Sumner, *A Charge Delivered to the Clergy of the Diocese of Chester at the Triennial Visitation in 1838*, pp. 1f.

[58] *Loc. cit.*

[59] J.B. Sumner, *Doctrine of Justification*, p. 7.

[60] E. Stock, *The History of the Church Missionary Society* Vol. 1, p. 58.

In 1848 Sumner was elevated to the Primacy, a move that delighted Queen Victoria.[61] His time as archbishop was beset with controversies: they included the Gorham Affair, the restoration of the Roman Catholic hierarchy, the revival of Convocation and the publication of *Essays and Reviews*. In addition he had to cope with the rising tide of ritualism that was particularly marked in England. He presided over the secular court that declared in opposition to the Arches' decision that Gorham's denial of baptismal regeneration was contrary to the teaching of the Church of England.[62] He further directed Gorham's institution to the living of Brampford Speke against the wishes of Bishop Henry Phillpotts. The Gorham Affair eventually led to calls for the revival of convocations. Along with Lord John Russell, Sumner opposed these proposals believing that they would result in growing Rome-ward moves.[63] When however in 1854 convocation was finally recalled Sumner was magnanimous in his attitude. He willingly accepted the Lower House of Convocation's own nomination of prolocutor when he had the power to make his own appointment.[64]

It was often supposed in earlier times that no nineteenth-century biography of Sumner was produced on account of his ineffectual primacy. However, with hindsight, it is clear that even in his fading years as archbishop Sumner has much to commend him. He was a man of enlightened opinions as was witnessed in his stance on issues such as Roman Catholic emancipation, the Great Reform Bill and the repeal of the Corn Laws. The controversies that he was called upon to handle demanded a gracious fair-mindedness which Sumner displayed to effect in his dealings over the Hampden and Gorham Affairs. At the same time he had stood firm in the face of threats from the writers of *Essays and Reviews* and the rising tide of ritualism. Sumner was widely respected in the House of Lords to the end of his days and remembered by his generation as a thoughtful scholar and a man given to prayer and the habits of study and writing. *The Times* reported he was 'a ripe scholar, a fluent writer, a sound divine, a not illiberal thinker with moderate views'.[65]

---

[61] See letter from Prince Albert to Lord John Russell, 16 February 1848 (Windsor Royal Archives) MS C18.

[62] J.C.S. Nias, *Gorham and the Bishop of Exeter*, pp. 97f.

[63] Russell to J.B. Sumner, 15 March 1850, *Russell Papers*, Folio 218/219.

[64] See Scotland, *John Bird Sumner*, p. 121.

[65] *The Times*, 8 September 1862.

Thomas Musgrave

It was not until 1837 that the Evangelicals saw another from their ranks raised to the bench of bishops. This was Thomas Musgrave (1788–1860) who was the son of a wealthy Cambridge tailor and draper. Musgrave had a long and distinguished career at the university of his native town where he held office as a professor. In 1834 he had been one of several academics who petitioned Parliament for the removal of all tests before taking degrees. Lord Melbourne reportedly wanted to encourage friends of his Government in both Oxford and Cambridge and accordingly he raised a number of academics in both institutions to high ecclesiastical office. Among their number Dr Musgrave of Trinity was given the See of Hereford.[66] Despite his liberal stance in politics, Musgrave was 'a very conservative Evangelical churchman'.[67] Two years after his appointment to Hereford he married the daughter of Lord Waterpark.

Musgrave shared the Sumner brothers' concern for the needs of the many labouring poor in his rural diocese. He warned his clergy that they should not confine their ministry solely to the spiritual welfare of their parishioners. If the Church of England was to be successful as the nation's church it must concern itself with the temporal as well as the religious needs of the poor. 'It is idle', he retorted, 'to expect that persons depressed by severe poverty and wretchedness will always be so well conducted, or so accessible to the pastor's warnings and advice, as those who are in easier and more comfortable circumstances.' Musgrave was particularly concerned at the condition in which the Herefordshire agricultural labourers lived. 'Their dwellings,' he said, 'are often dark and confined, sordid and cheerless, with little or no space for profitable employment on their own, or recreation.'[68] Musgrave appealed to his clergy to use their influences on local landowners 'to elevate the honest and industrious poor' in the social scale.[69] In November 1847 Lord John Russell raised Musgrave to the archiepiscopal See of York. On coming to his new diocese, Musgrave continued to emphasise his concern for the poor. He stressed to his clergy that atrocious housing and sanitation both demoralised the labouring

---

[66] Chadwick, *Victorian Church* Part 1, p. 113.
[67] Soloway, *Prelates and People*, p. 7.
[68] T. Musgrave, *A Charge Delivered to the Clergy of the Diocese of Hereford June 1845*, pp. 21–2.
[69] Ibid., pp. 21–2.

poor and numbed them to their ministers' spiritual message.[70] Musgrave also concerned himself with educational issues and underlined the importance of a schools system which was based on religion and morality.[71]

Musgrave was a strong opponent of the Oxford Movement and issued a charge in which he held that the effects of infant baptism were an open question and declared that George Gorham's views on the subject were legitimate within the Church of England.[72] In his 1849 charge, Musgrave commended William Goode's *Effects of Infant Baptism* and said that the 'sixteenth-century English reformers were Calvinists and taught that spiritual regeneration in baptism could only result in the case of those who had been from all eternity elected to everlasting life'.[73] Musgrave attended the judgement of the Judicial Committee of the Privy Council in March 1850 and approved their decision.[74] Along with Sumner, Musgrave had no appetite for the revival of convocation. At York he locked the meeting place and by this action prevented any business being conducted.[75] Although the Canterbury convocation met in 1854 Musgrave resisted to the end declaring that the convocation of York would serve no useful purpose. His death in 1860 brought an end to the ban with his successor, Charles Longley, immediately allowing business to be transacted.

Walter Augustus Shirley

Following the death of Longley, it was another decade before any further Evangelicals were raised to the episcopate. On 10 January 1847 Walter Augustus Shirley (1797–1847), Archdeacon of Derby, was consecrated as Bishop of Sodor and Man. He took up residence on the island almost immediately and his wife and son followed some weeks later. He held his first confirmation on 14 February

[70] Musgrave, *A Charge 1853*, pp. 12–13, cited by Soloway, *Prelates and People*, pp. 211–12.

[71] T. Musgrave, *A Charge Delivered to the Clergy of the Diocese of Hereford 1839*, p. 20, cited by Soloway, *Prelates and People*, p. 406.

[72] Chadwick, *Victorian Church* Part 1, p. 256.

[73] T. Musgrave, *A Charge Delivered to the Clergy of the Diocese of York, June 1849*, cited by Nias, *Gorham*, p. 167.

[74] Ibid., p. 97.

[75] Chadwick, *Victorian Church* Part 1, p. 315.

1847 with twenty-nine candidates.[76] Walter Shirley was a compelling preacher and he reported that 'the people here crowd to hear
me preach'.[77] In company with other Evangelicals Shirley was a
decided opponent of what he termed 'Puseyism'.[78] Referring to the
ritualists he wrote, 'most of those whom I have met are painful
supercilious coxcombs'.[79]

Well before his consecration Shirley was already burnt out with
overwork. Shortly after taking office he said, 'My constitution is
gone; the fact is, I have done two days' work in one. You know what
my maxim has always been – better to wear out than to rust.'[80] Amid
the turmoil of moving and all his other commitments, Shirley had
been struggling to complete his Bampton Lectures, which he was to
have given at Oxford in April. He delivered his first two on 14 and
21 March, but illness prevented him from delivering any more. He
contracted pneumonia and died peacefully on 21 April surrounded
by his friends and family.

John Graham

The following year John Graham (1794–1865) was appointed
Bishop of Chester in 1848 in succession to Sumner. He came from a
middle-class family, his father being a managing clerk in the city of
Durham. He was a Fellow and Tutor, and later Master of Christ
College, Cambridge. On two occasions he filled the office of
Vice-Chancellor of the University. The Prince Consort honoured
him by appointing him his chaplain and it was through his favour
that he was raised to the episcopal bench.[81]

Graham was universally loved and respected by all classes
throughout his large diocese. He was a staunch defender of the
amended Poor Laws which he believed would bring the working
classes 'back to habits of industry and frugality and temperance; by
rekindling in their breasts a spirit of honest independence'.[82]

---

[76] Hill, *Augustus Shirley*, p. 472.
[77] Letter to Ven Archdeacon Hill, 22 February 1847 in ibid., p. 479.
[78] Ibid., p. 482.
[79] Ibid., p. 482.
[80] Ibid., p. 497.
[81] *The Chester Chronicle*, 24 June 1865.
[82] J. Graham, *A Sermon Preached … March 16, 1841, Being the Day on
Which the Foundation Stone was Laid of the Cambridge Victoria Benefit
Asylum*, pp. 6–7 in Soloway, *Prelates and People*, p. 189.

Notwithstanding his support of the harsh provisions of the Poor Law, Graham was deeply concerned for the needs of the lower sections of society. He was a strong supporter of the Friendly Benefit Societies which he believed could be of real help to workers during periods of unemployment without destroying their independence as the old law did.[83]

During his time at Chester, Graham cultivated warm relationships with Nonconformists which caused some friction with high churchmen. Throughout his time as bishop he was an ardent supporter of BFBS and chairman of the diocesan auxiliary.[84] During a sermon preached in St John Street Wesleyan Chapel, shortly after the bishop's death, the Rev J.F. Moody stated that

> During the past three years I have had several opportunities of observing him in public and never heard a word escape his lips inconsistent with the pure protestant evangelical faith which he was set apart to defend, nor witnessed an act inconsistent with the genius of experimental religion.[85]

The Palmerstonian Bishops

In 1855 there began a decade which put a new complexion on the English episcopate. In that year Lord Palmerston succeeded Lord Aberdeen as Prime Minister. Save for a short interval in 1858, he remained in office until his death in 1865. Palmerston took his religious obligations lightly, although he did attend Church of England services at Romsey Abbey. In matters of church patronage he came increasingly to rely on his step son-in-law, Lord Shaftesbury. In fact, Shaftesbury wrote of him, 'He does not know in theology, Moses from Sydney Smith.'[86]

In his period of office, Palmerston appointed three English archbishops, one to Canterbury and two to York, nineteen diocesan bishops, six Irish bishops and thirteen English deans. Shaftesbury later recalled that Palmerston only ever made one ecclesiastical appointment (Blakesby, Canon of Canterbury) without consulting

---

[83] Ibid., p. 189.
[84] *The Chester Chronicle*, 24 June 1865.
[85] *The Chester Chronicle*, 24 June 1875.
[86] Shaftesbury to Evelyn Ashley, in Hodder, *Seventh Earl of Shaftesbury* Vol. 2, p. 505.

him in the matter.[87] Of the fourteen English diocesans appointed by Palmerston only eight were Evangelicals: Montagu Villiers of Carlisle (1856–1860) and Durham (1860–1861), Charles Baring of Gloucester and Bristol (1856–1861) and Durham (1861–1879), John Pelham of Norwich (1857–1893), Robert Bickersteth of Ripon (1857–1884), Joseph Wigram of Rochester (1860–1867), Samuel Waldegrave of Carlisle (1860–1869), William Thomson of Gloucester and Bristol (1861–1862) and York (1862–1890) and Francis Jeune of Peterborough (1864–1868). Of the other seven, Archibald Tait was described as being 'evangelical without fanatical',[88] and Harold Browne often called himself both 'evangelical' and 'a high churchman'.[89]

Of the eight Palmerston appointees who were Evangelicals, Baring, Waldegrave and Jeune achieved first-class honours degrees and Joseph Cotton Wigram graduated sixth wrangler at Cambridge in 1819. In addition, William Thomson achieved distinction as an academic and was Bampton lecturer in 1849. These men were also strongly committed to the doctrines of justification by faith and personal conversion that their party prized highly. Bickersteth in his charge of 1861, for example, urged his clergy 'to dwell much upon the central truth of the whole scheme of the gospel, and the atonement effected by our Saviour Jesus Christ, when He died upon the cross'.[90]

The majority of the Palmerston bishops, and particularly the Evangelicals among them, were men who had themselves had a wide experience in parochial work. On coming to office, they emerged as strong pastors both to their clergy and their people. In this matter John Pelham was well known. He would arrive at a country parsonage on a Saturday afternoon and spend the evening with the clergyman and his family. On the Sunday he would take part in all the church services and speak to the Sunday school teachers.[91] Robert Bickersteth, according to his son and biographer, 'was never happier than when he could arrange to spend a whole Sunday with an earnest clergyman'.[92] In his second charge to the

---

87   Ibid., Vol. 3, p. 191.
88   *The Church of England Quarterly Review* Vol. XL, p. 459.
89   G.W. Kitchen, *Edward Harold Browne DD. Lord Bishop of Winchester, A Memoir*, p. 398.
90   M.C. Bickersteth, *A Sketch of the Life and Episcopate of the Right Reverend Robert Bickersteth DD Bishop of Ripon 1857–1884*, p. 44.
91   *The Times*, 2 May 1894.
92   M.C. Bickersteth, *Robert Bickersteth*, p. 110.

clergy of Rochester, Joseph Wigram stated that he had established a fund with a view to raising the value of all the smaller livings in the diocese to £200 per year.[93] Montagu Villiers also expressed his dissatisfaction that the value of the benefices in his Carlisle diocese were so low.[94]

The Palmerston bishops made good use of rural deans and several of their number revived the office in areas where it had fallen into disuse. Villiers, for example, created eighteen rural deaneries within his two archdeaconries of Carlisle and Westmorland,[95] and William Thomson created five new rural deaneries in the diocese of York.[96]

Another aspect of Palmerstonian episcopal diocesan strategy was that of church building. In this matter they were the heirs of the Sumners who had seen it as vitally important to take the church into places where the people were resident. During his episcopate Robert Bickersteth consecrated 158 churches, of which 92 were new parish churches, 47 were enlargements of existing buildings and 19 were chapels of ease.[97] While Charles Baring was Bishop of Durham 119 new churches were erected at a cost of £363,830.[98] William Thomson promoted local church extension societies in the main towns and centres of the diocese supported by a Central Society, which had been established in 1861. Between 1861 and 1889 they had promoted the building of 91 new churches, 31 mission chapels, as well as the enlargement of 105 churches.[99]

Hand in hand with the promotion of church building almost all of the bishops shared a major concern for education. This was seen in the encouragement of Sunday schools, the building of national schools and in the training of teachers. Several of the Evangelicals

---

[93] J.C. Wigram, *A Charge to the Clergy and Churchwardens of the Diocese of Rochester at his Second General Visitation in November 1864*, p. 26.

[94] H.M. Villiers, *A Charge Delivered to the Clergy of the Diocese of Carlisle at the First visitation of the Hon. Montagu Villiers, DD, Lord Bishop of Carlisle 1858*, p. 4.

[95] A.F. Munden, 'The First Palmerston Bishop: Henry Montagu Villiers, Bishop of Carlisle 1856–1860 and Bishop of Durham 1860–1861', *Northern History* 26 (1990), p. 194.

[96] H. Kirk-Smith, *William Thomson, His Life and Times 1819–1890*, p. 147.

[97] M.C. Bickersteth, *Robert Bickersteth*, p. 145.

[98] *Durham County Advertiser*, 19 September 1879.

[99] Kirk-Smith, *William Thomson*, p. 67.

among them provided statistical information in their diocesan charges. In 1865 John Pelham reported that 'inspite of many hindrances' the work of education 'is making progress in the diocese'. He continued, 'The provision of 130 new schools since my last visitation is one palpable proof of it.'[100] Francis Jeune expressed his satisfaction that there were only 46 parishes in the diocese of Peterborough in which there was no school.[101]

The Palmerston bishops were firm believers in the value of the parochial system of pastoral care and from time to time they said so in their charges and addresses. The Evangelical bishops in particular recognised that the parish clergy simply could not cope single-handedly with the demands of a large urban parish. They would all have endorsed Villiers' view that it was 'a positive duty' that lay agency should be employed.[102] Joseph Wigram pioneered the use of 'Mission women' who he declared 'are invaluable aids to a clergyman'.[103]

As well as utilising the laity, Palmerston's appointees sought to raise the quality of their clergy. Villiers saw the number of graduate clergy increased during his Carlisle episcopate.[104] In his visitation address of 1861 Robert Bickersteth reported his wish 'to raise the standard both of intellectual and spiritual qualification for the work of ministry'.[105] During William Thomson's archiepiscopate 810 deacons were in the diocese of York, 71 per cent of whom were graduates.[106]

The Palmerston bishops paid particular attention to improving the quality of public worship. They wanted the services to be relevant to the needs of the poor with good plain preaching. Charles Baring in particular was concerned that too many of his Gloucestershire clergy were failing to use 'homely illustrations' and

---

[100] J.T. Pelham, *A Charge Delivered to the Clergy and Churchwardens of the Diocese of Norwich by John Thomas, Lord Bishop of Norwich at His Visitation in 1865*, pp. 16–17.

[101] F. Jeune, *A Charge Delivered to the Clergy and Churchwardens of the Diocese of Peterborough at his Primary Visitation in October 1867 by Francis, Lord Bishop of Peterborough*, p. 11.

[102] H.M. Villiers, *On the Necessity of Lay Agency in the Church*, p. 84.

[103] Wigram, *A Charge 1864*, p. 19.

[104] Munden, 'First Palmerston Bishop', p. 197.

[105] R. Bickersteth, *A Charge Delivered to the Clergy of the Diocese of Ripon at his Triennial Visitation, April 1861 by Robert, Lord Bishop of Ripon*, p. 11.

[106] Kirk-Smith, *William Thomson*, p. 54.

'every day expressions'. Baring also recommended writing full notes and then committing the sermon to memory.[107] Baptism was another focus of attention and there was a common desire to make it a public occasion. Joseph Wigram, for example, observed that in 423 of his churches, baptism took place during Sunday morning or evening services, but this was not the case in 221 of his churches. 'Would that public baptisms were celebrated in all!' he said.[108] Confirmation was another area of concern. It had been a custom in some dioceses to hold large-scale confirmation services in central market towns with children and young people being brought in from the surrounding parishes. This often resulted in large numbers going straight from the church to pubs and other hostelries for refreshment. Frequently, disorderly conduct followed and there were even occasions where the police had to be called in.[109] Charles Baring regretted that some Gloucestershire confirmations were 'a season of dissipation' for which reason he tried always to hold services on Sunday so that parents and sponsors could attend and exercise a restraining hand.[110] Bickersteth, Baring and Pelham urged on their clergy the need to prepare their candidates carefully and all three increased the number of confirmation services within their dioceses. This had the effect of creating smaller numbers and thus improving the general tenor of the occasion.[111] With their increased endeavours not surprisingly most saw a significant rise in the number of candidates.[112]

Somewhat surprisingly, perhaps, the Palmerston bishops, Evangelicals as much as the others, were advocates of more frequent services of Holy Communion. In the earlier years of the century many Evangelical clergy held only three or four communions during the course of a year. Robert Bickersteth said that it was desirable that the Lord's Supper should be celebrated in every church at least once a month.[113] William Thomson made it clear in an address to the York diocese that too many clergy were neglecting 'to give

---

[107] C. Baring, *A Charge Delivered to the clergy of the Diocese of Gloucester and Bristol at His Primary Visitation in October 1857*, pp. 31–2.

[108] Wigram, *A Charge 1864*, p. 8.

[109] F. Knight, *The Nineteenth-Century Church and English Society*, p. 92.

[110] See N.A.D. Scotland, *Good and Proper Men: Lord Palmerston and the Bench of Bishops*, p. 112.

[111] Ibid., p. 113.

[112] Ibid., pp. 113–14.

[113] M.C. Bickersteth, *Robert Bickersteth*, p. 114.

sufficient opportunity to their people to attend Holy Communion'.[114] Bishops such as Thomson, Wigram and Bickersteth helped to make Evangelicals aware of the importance of a more frequent attendance at these services.

Notwithstanding this sacramental emphasis, the Palmerston bishops shared in Lord Shaftesbury's inbuilt fear of all things ritualistic and Roman. They attacked the doctrine of the 'real presence', the mixed chalice, lighted candles, the use of vestments, the eastward position of the celebrant and a number of other 'Romanising' practices.[115] They were also solid in their support of the 1874 Public Worship Regulation Act and several of their number dealt firmly with ritualist clergy in their dioceses. Charles Baring, for example, refused to license the Rev George Peake as curate to Oswald's Church unless he received pledges that he would not engage in specified ritualistic practices that had been declared illegal.[116] He also suspended the Rev Francis Grey, the Rector of Morpeth, from the office of rural dean because he had worn a black stole with three crosses embroidered on it.[117] William Thomson refused to license a curate at St Martin's Scarborough, on account of the parish's use of coloured stoles, the mixed chalice, wafer bread and the practice of placing bread fragments in the chalice.[118]

Palmerston's Evangelical bishops were conservative theologically and rigorously opposed *Essays and Reviews* when it was published in 1860.[119] William Thomson edited *Aids to Faith* which was a response designed to help 'those whose faith may have been shaken'.[120] With the exception of Joseph Wigram they were Whig bishops who generally aligned themselves with the Whig cause. They were not given to making frequent addresses in the House of Lords but when they did speak it was mostly on religious or educational matters.

Ecclesiastics from the high church party judged the Palmerston bishops somewhat harshly. Samuel Wilberforce called their

---

[114] W. Thomson, *A Charge to the Clergy of the Diocese of York Delivered at His Primary Visitation in October 1865 by the Most Reverent William Lord Archbishop of York, Primate of England and Metropolitan*, p. 24.

[115] Scotland, *Good and Proper Men*, pp. 136–57.

[116] *Durham County Advertiser*, 19 September 1879.

[117] W.H.B. Proby, *Annals of the Low Church Party*, p. 42.

[118] Scotland, *Good and Proper Men*, p. 42

[119] Ibid., pp. 90–5.

[120] *Christian Observer*, May 1862, p. 372.

appointments 'wicked' and Sabine Baring-Gould thought them pastoral ignoramuses who knew little theology. History however has shown them to be 'good and proper men'[121] who were accessible to their clergy and deeply involved in the affairs of their dioceses. Together they established a new emphasis on pastoral care and the bishop as the manager of the diocese.

Later Victorian Evangelical Bishops

The Evangelical party was not again to know the same level of patronage that Palmerston had shown during his two terms of office. It was not until 1875 that they received another representative when Anthony Thorold (1825–1895) was appointed to Rochester. Five years later, Disraeli appointed John Charles Ryle as the first Bishop of Liverpool. In 1885 Thorold's friend, Edward Henry Bickersteth (1825–1906), incumbent of Christ Church Hampstead, succeeded Frederick Temple as Bishop of Exeter. In 1892 John Bardsley (1835–1904) was translated to the See of Carlisle from Sodor and Man where another Evangelical, Norman Stratton, who was Archdeacon of Huddersfield, succeeded him.

Anthony Thorold

Following in the steps of the Palmerston Evangelical bishops, Anthony Thorold came from successful pastoral ministries in London at St Giles and St Pancras. His second marriage to Emily Labouchere 'a pronounced Evangelical' but 'a fascinating, gentle, clever and witty' woman kept him strictly within the Evangelical party.[122] He was a close friend and trusted adviser to William Thomson for thirty-five years. Indeed he had served as Thomson's examining Chaplain at Gloucester[123] and later been appointed by him as Canon Residentiary at York. During his period of residence he frequently acted as Thomson's commissary.[124]

---

[121] Letter from Lord Shaftesbury to Edwin Hodder (undated) commenting on Lord Palmerston's episcopal appointments: 'He ever sought good and proper men ...'. In Hodder, *Life and Work of Lord Shaftesbury*, p. 607.

[122] C.H. Simpkinson, *The Life and Work of Bishop Thorold of Rochester 1877–1891, Winchester 1891–1895*, p. 47.

[123] Ibid., pp. 65, 323.

[124] Ibid., p. 70.

Thorold was consecrated bishop of the newly organised See of Rochester in Westminster Abbey on 25 July 1877. In the new arrangements the diocese had taken on a large part of South London from the Winchester diocese. Balleine stated Thorold found it 'chaos, a mere bundle of jarring and discordant fragments, loosely tied together by an Act of Parliament'.[125] However, he soon set to work and began by organising a series of conferences for his clergy in different centres[126] at which he set out his strategy.[127] This included remodelling the disparate evangelistic agencies and bringing about a greater co-ordination among them, sustaining and increasing voluntary elementary schools provision, and promoting theological learning and spiritual life among the clergy. In addition, he urged a great fight for temperance, especially in the populous suburbs of South London by means of the Church of England Temperance Society.[128]

Thorold was an inveterate traveller. He preached twice each Sunday in different churches and passed his weekdays speaking, visiting and discussing the needs of the diocese. He was particularly troubled to see the lack of clergy in the enormous urban parishes and saddened to observe how sparsely occupied their churches were for Sunday worship.[129] In the spring of 1878 he launched The Rochester Diocesan Society to unite the diocese for evangelistic work[130] and asked individuals and churches to contribute a total of £10,000 a year towards its work.[131] A key aspect of Thorold's strategy was establishing small mission parishes of some 3,000–5,000 working people. These would be separated off from large urban parishes and in their midst he would plant a young clergyman and would hire for him a loft, hall or schoolroom. By diligent visiting, teaching and praying a group would be formed which would eventually become a new church without impairing the life of the original church.[132] In his first charge of 1878 Thorold proposed to organise a series of devotional retreats for his clergy and also to ensure that time was made available for study and for improving their teaching and

[125] Balleine, *History of the Evangelical Party*, p. 281.
[126] Simpkinson, *Bishop Thorold*, p. 90.
[127] Ibid., p. 92.
[128] Ibid., pp. 92–3.
[129] Ibid., p. 95.
[130] Ibid., p. 105.
[131] Ibid., p. 109.
[132] Ibid., p. 107.

preaching. Another key aim was to build up a Lay Workers Association to assist the clergy and enable the church to be the church of the people.[133] Thorold also welcomed the arrival of a number of University missions into the diocese.[134]

In his early years at Rochester Thorold was rigid in his stance against the ritualists and refused to visit ritualist churches. As he put it in his charge of 1885, 'I belong to the flint age'.[135] With the passing of the years, however, he mellowed in his attitude to ritualist clergy and came to recognise that 'a man's voice means much more than his garments and his doctrine much more than his ceremonial'.[136] Thorold was an immensely hard-working bishop who took particular care over his confirmations.[137] In 1884 he wrote 6,258 letters with his own hand. When he became Bishop of Winchester in 1891 he left behind him a united and mission-orientated diocese.

John Charles Ryle

In 1880 John Charles Ryle was appointed first Bishop of Liverpool having only a few days previously accepted the Deanery of Salisbury.[138] Ryle came to office having been incumbent of the two Suffolk parishes of Helmingham (1844–1861) and Stradbroke from 1861 to 1880. In 1870 he was made rural dean of Hoxne and in 1872 Canon of Norwich. During this lengthy period of rural ministry Ryle had emerged as the undisputed leader of the Evangelical party in the Church of England. He was described by his successor as 'a man of granite with the heart of a little child'.[139]

Ryle was 'the prince of tract writers' and by the time of his consecration he had published more than 130 tracts and several widely read books, the most notable being *Knots Untied* 1874, *Holiness* 1877, *Practical Religion* 1878 and *Expository Thoughts on the Gospels* 1873. In all Ryle wrote more than two hundred tracts and twenty books. Ryle's tracts were written to convey the essentials of the Evangelical faith to ordinary people. They were priced at a penny and sold in huge quantities.

---

[133] Ibid., p. 118.
[134] S.C. Carpenter, *Church and People 1789–1889*, pp. 284–5.
[135] Simpkinson, *Bishop Thorold*, p. 145.
[136] Ibid., p. 146.
[137] Ibid., p. 201.
[138] A.R.M. Finlayson, *Life of Canon Fleming*, pp. 178–9.
[139] Balleine, *History of the Evangelical Party*, p. 279.

During the 1850s onwards Ryle frequently spoke in London churches[140] and in the 1860s and 1870s he began to play an increasing part in the church congresses appearing on the platform at gatherings in Nottingham and Leeds in 1871, Brighton in 1872 and Croydon in 1874 and 1877, Sheffield and Swansea in 1873 and 1879, and Leicester in 1880. He was Select Preacher at the University of Cambridge in 1873 and 1874, and for the University of Oxford in 1874, 1875, 1876, 1879 and 1880. He was also closely involved in the founding of Wycliffe Hall, Oxford, in 1877 and Ridley Hall in 1879. Ryle was a staunch member of and frequent speaker at the Church Association and he also regularly addressed the Islington Clerical Conference. He was also a keen supporter of CMS and spoke every year in St Silas Church on its behalf.[141] Significantly, unlike many Evangelicals, Ryle supported the revival of convocation. He believed that their re-establishment was inevitable and for that reason urged his fellow Evangelicals to be involved.[142]

On his arrival in his new diocese Ryle was unequivocal as to his views: 'I come among you a Protestant and Evangelical: but I come with a desire to hold out the right hand to all loyal churchmen, holding at the same time my own opinions determinedly.'[143] Ryle had to begin from scratch and establish diocesan machinery. He began by appointing two Archdeacons, both of whom were Evangelicals, one for Liverpool and the other for Warrington. He also appointed twenty-four honorary canons, half of whom were Evangelicals and the others drawn from other sections of the church.

Following Anthony Thorold, Ryle believed that the parochial system was inadequate to meet the needs of the industrial nineteenth century. In a published tract entitled *Can They Be Brought In?*, Ryle contended that the Church of England had made an idol out of the parish system and forgotten that it was defective at a number of points particularly in an urban context.[144] Ryle proposed to remedy the defect of the system by abandoning parochial autonomy and establishing missionary curates.[145] Ryle saw the task of his clergy was to preach and to visit, not administrate.[146] His top priority for the

---

[140] Farley, *Ryle*, p. 4.

[141] Ibid., p. 89.

[142] Hylson-Smith, *Evangelicals in the Church of England*, p. 161.

[143] *Guardian*, 28 April 1880, cited by Balleine, *History of the Evangelical Party*, p. 279.

[144] J.C. Ryle, *Can They Be Brought In?*, p. 28, cited by Farley, *Ryle*, p. 28.

[145] Farley, *Ryle*, p. 110.

[146] Ibid., p. 101.

parish minister was 'patient, house to house visiting'.[147] Ryle promoted the building of mission rooms where non-liturgical services
could be held and where the clergy could make use of lay help.[148] Ryle
was also an enthusiastic supporter of increased roles for women as
church visitors and Scripture readers.[149] During his episcopate
forty-eight mission halls were built and licensed for worship. He
established a Bible Women's Society whose members visited the slum
quarters. At the close of Ryle's years in the diocese there were
forty-five Scripture readers and thirty-one Bible women.

Ryle saw increased educational provision as a key phase in his
strategy for the diocese. He regarded Sunday schools as an important means of plugging the gap in areas where there were only
secularist day schools. He saw the number of Sunday school pupils
rise from 36,000 in 1881 to 50,000, but this growth was not
sustained.[150] Ryle believed that Christianity was the only solid
basis for education, but he was not prepared to condemn the
Board Schools.[151] Indeed, he praised the Liverpool Council of
Education for its handling of the Bible in the secular schools.[152]

Ryle shared Thorold's hostility to alcoholic drink – he believed it
was the greatest evil faced by the Church of England.[153] He opposed
social drinking between meals, which he regarded as the seeds
of drunkenness. In 1884 it was calculated that there were 2,402
drinking houses in the city, or one for every 299 inhabitants.[154] Ryle
established a Temperance Sunday each January in the diocese when
temperance sermons would be given. By the time of his retirement
191 out of 205 churches held a Temperance Sunday.[155] Ryle was a
great backer of cocoa houses in Liverpool and by the mid 1880s
four hundred people were running fifty-one houses, eight cafes and
two carts.[156] Ryle's hostility to alcoholic beverage had a marked
effect in curtailing drunkenness in Liverpool.[157]

---

[147] Ibid., p. 106.
[148] Ibid., p. 114.
[149] Ibid., p. 136.
[150] Ibid., p. 140.
[151] Ibid., p. 141.
[152] Ibid., p. 142.
[153] Ibid., pp. 143–4.
[154] Ibid., p. 145.
[155] Ibid., p. 147.
[156] Ibid., p. 148.
[157] Ibid., p. 150.

Contrary to what some have asserted, Ryle was socially concerned. He was aware of the needs of the unemployed, he promoted medical work, he was active on behalf of the seamen and their families, and he gave a good deal of time to supporting charities. Ryle remained hostile to ritualism to the end and his allowing James Bell Cox to be prosecuted and imprisoned attracted widespread criticism.

Ryle set his new diocese on a firm footing. He had begun with 120 curates and by 1897 there were 220. In his first year of office he confirmed 4,500 young people, in 1896 he had 8,300 candidates. He established diocesan organisations and diocesan societies and promoted the building of numerous mission halls and churches.

Edward Henry Bickersteth

Edward Henry Bickersteth was appointed to the See of Exeter in 1885. He was the son of Edward Bickersteth who had been secretary of CMS and rector of Watton in Hertfordshire. He was nurtured in an atmosphere of prayer and devotion and not surprisingly had an Evangelical conversion experience at the age of fourteen.[158] He was a lifelong Evangelical and, like his father, was a devoted supporter of missionary work.

As a diocesan Bickersteth took particular care and trouble over his confirmations, which averaged about one hundred and twenty a year.[159] He enjoyed good relationships with the clergy of all schools of churchmanship despite his opposition to illegal ritualistic practices.[160] Bickersteth stipulated that the residentiary canons he appointed resign their pastoral cures and devote themselves to an aspect of diocesan work such as education or foreign missions.[161] The bishop was a committed visitor and adopted the practice of visiting a certain number of rural deaneries each year, sometimes staying as long as ten days in a particular area meeting clergy, church wardens and Sunday school teachers.[162] He also fostered and promoted good relationships with Nonconformist clergy and on one occasion more than 200 of their number spent a day at the Bishop's palace.[163] He particularly

---

[158] F.K. Algionby, *The Life of Edward Henry Bickersteth: Bishop and Poet*, p. 10.
[159] Ibid., p. 59.
[160] Ibid., p. 62.
[161] Ibid., p. 64.
[162] Ibid., p. 65.
[163] Ibid., p. 72.

concerned himself with the superannuation of the clergy, the promotion of church schools and temperance campaigns. He described intemperance as 'a national abscess' that 'needed the surgeon's lancet'.[164]

Bickersteth's commitment to mission led him to inaugurate a scheme in 1884 in which £18,000 was given to CMS 'in memory of departed brothers and sisters in Christ'. In this way it became possible for the society to extend its offices without taking money that had been designated for overseas missionary work.[165] Bickersteth was three times a speaker at the annual meeting of CMS and preached the annual sermon in 1888.[166] Bishop Bickersteth was frequently invited to speak in the church congress.[167] He was remembered for his saintly living and many of the clergy took strength from his deep spirituality and valued the Quiet Days and Retreats he organised for them. In 1870 he produced the *Hymnal Companion to the Book of Common Prayer* to replace his father's earlier *Christian Psalmody*. The book quickly became popular and in 1893 was used in 1,478 English churches.

Two other Evangelical bishops of note were John Bardsley (1835–1904) and Norman Stratton who had been Archdeacon of Warrington and chaplain to the Bishop of Liverpool. Bardsley was promoted to Sodor and Man in 1887 and to Carlisle in 1892.[168] Stratton had been Archdeacon of Huddersfield before being nominated to Sodor and Man in 1892. There he achieved remarkable success preaching during the summer months to crowds, sometimes of ten thousand and more, on Douglas Head.[169]

Conclusion

It's not easy to assess the impact of Evangelical bishops in the nineteenth century but several things can be said. There can be no doubt that Henry Ryder and Charles and John Sumner led the way for a new pattern of episcopacy. They were the first genuinely pastoral bishops who grappled with the needs of the industrial towns and

---

[164] Ibid., p. 77.
[165] Ibid., p. 167.
[166] Ibid., p. 167.
[167] Ibid., p. 169.
[168] Ibid., p. 169.
[169] Balleine, *History of the Evangelical Party*, pp. 282–3.

cities and promoted the building of schools and churches on a large scale. The bishops appointed by Lord Palmerston built on the diocesan reforms which, as Arthur Burns has shown, began to emerge in the 1830s and 1840s.[170] Had it not been for their presence on the Bench at a time when the tide of ritualism was rising, the worship of the established church might well have taken on a very different aspect. Had Archbishops Sumner and Musgrave not been in office at the time of the Gorham controversy, life for Evangelicals in the Church of England might have been very difficult if not, in many cases, impossible.

Whilst it is true that there were few theologians among their number, the Evangelical bishops of the nineteenth century kept alive the importance of evangelism, mission and the need to give pastoral support to their clergy. Although they were for the most part a small minority, the Evangelical prelates made their voice heard and exerted an influence that was above their numbers.

---

[170] See A. Burns, *The Diocesan Revival in the Church of England c. 1800–1870*, pp. 5–8.

6

The Battle for the Bible

Although the Victorian years were to witness considerable argument and debate as to the nature and inspiration of Scripture, few Evangelicals in the earlier years of the century were troubled by doubts as to its veracity or infallibility. Most would have shared the view of the Rev Theobald Pontifex, the central figure in Samuel Butler's novel, *The Way of All Flesh*.[1] Of him Butler wrote:

> It had never so much as crossed Theobald's mind to doubt the literal accuracy of any syllable in the Bible. He had never seen any book in which this was disputed, nor met with anyone who doubted it. True, there was just a little scare about geology, but there was nothing in it. If it said that God made the world in six days, why He did make it in six days, neither in more nor less; if it was said that He put Adam to sleep, took out one of his ribs and made a woman of it, why it was so as a matter of course. He, Adam, went to sleep as it might be himself, Theobald Pontifex, in a garden, as it might be the garden at Crampsford Rectory during the summer months when it was so pretty, only that it was larger, and had some tame wild animals in it. Then God came upon him, as it might be Mr Allaby or his father, dexterously took out one of his ribs without waking him, and miraculously healed the wound so that no trace of the operation remained. Finally, God had taken the rib perhaps into the greenhouse, and had turned it into just such another young woman as Christina. That was how it was done; there was neither difficulty nor shadow of difficulty about the matter. Could not God do anything he liked, and had He not in His own inspired Book told us that he had done this?[2]

---

[1] S. Butler, *The Way of All Flesh*, first published posthumously in 1903. Butler died in 1902.

[2] Ibid., pp. 52–3.

Butler commented, 'This was the average attitude of fairly educated young men and women towards the Mosaic cosmogony fifty, forty or even twenty years ago.'[3]

The main root of this Evangelical understanding of Scripture derived from Greek thought in the early Christian centuries which had been further reinforced by the Reformation. Calvin, for example, spoke of the apostles as 'pens in the hands of the Holy Spirit'. He could even go so far as to speak of 'the style of the Holy Spirit'. Eighteenth- and nineteenth-century Evangelicals endorsed these Reformation convictions as the solid bedrock on which they stood. It followed on from this that many of their number thought in terms of God literally breathing the Scripture into the writers of the biblical documents. The result was that the canonical books were held to speak authoritatively on all matters, whether they related to man's relationships to God or to the scientific origins of the universe. Indeed, most ordinary men and women in the closing years of the eighteenth century and the beginning of the nineteenth regarded the Judeo-Christian religion as an historical religion. It concerned the story of God's dealings with his people in history. It was therefore understandable that the accounts of the Creation and the Fall should have been regarded as historical events. Most Evangelicals who opened their Bibles at Genesis accepted without question Archbishop James Ussher's marginal note alongside the first verse which dated the creation at 4004 BC.[4] In fact even scientists did not seriously question Ussher's contention until the beginning of the nineteenth century. As late as 1826 George Bugg's *Scriptural Geology* showed that Evangelicals were still capable of closing their eyes to the new findings of geology.

Early Nineteenth Century

As the new century dawned evangelicals were, for the most part, all of a piece in their attitude to the sacred text. They believed it to be fully inspired and 'the word of God'. At the same time they were not rigid literalists when it came to the interpretation of the text.

---

[3] Ibid., p. 53.
[4] James Ussher (1581–1656), Archbishop of Armagh, calculated on the basis of the biblical narrative and a bit of guess-work that the creation had taken place in 4004 BC, a date which began to be printed by University presses from 1701 onwards.

Among their number was Thomas Scott of Aston Sandford, the distinguished Bible commentator, whose celebrated commentary was first published in 1796 and then went through a further five editions during the author's lifetime. In the preface to this work Scott set out a detailed understanding of the divine inspiration of Scripture in which he emphasised the role of the Holy Spirit whose 'effectual superintendency' of the sacred writers 'sufficed absolutely to preserve them from every degree of error in all things which could in the least affect any of the doctrines or precepts contained in their writings, or mislead any person who considered them as a divine and infallible standard of truth and duty'.[5] This did not mean that there was no human element in the transmission of the divine revelation. Scott was clear that the biblical authors 'wrote, indeed, in such language, as their different talents, educations, habits, and associations suggested, or rendered natural to them'. Nevertheless, he continued, 'the Holy Spirit so entirely superintended them, when writing, as to exclude every improper expression and to guide them to all those which best suited their several subjects'.[6]

However, Scott was by no means a literalist and he clearly distinguished the different genres in the biblical writings. He recognised that prophecy should be read as prophecy and that poetry could not be read as historical fact. Scott also stressed the importance of faith and reason in interpreting the meaning of the text: 'Faith, receiving and appropriating the testimony of God, is to reason, not unlike what the telescope is to the eye of the astronomer who by it discerns objects invisible to all others, and sees clearly and distinctly those things which to others appear obscure and confused.'[7] Reason has a wider function enabling the reader 'to discern the excellency of the things revealed to us', 'to bow in humble submission to the divine teaching', and 'to receive in adoring faith what we cannot comprehend'. Scott had no detailed knowledge of Hebrew, Greek or Latin and so to interpret the text his method was to compare Scripture with Scripture.[8]

The great Charles Simeon held views that were in many ways similar to those of Scott. He was adamant that Scripture was inspired but he was not a rigid literalist. He also shared Scott's view

---

[5] Preface, reprinted as Scott, *Introduction to the Study of the Bible*, p. 13, cited by Pollard, 'Anglican Evangelical Views of the Bible', p. 167.

[6] Scott, *Introduction to the Study of the Bible*, p. 13.

[7] Ibid., p. 47.

[8] Ibid., p. 49.

that Scripture should be understood by comparing it with other Scripture. In his theory of inspiration Simeon stressed the role of the Holy Spirit. The Scriptures

> were indeed written by men; but men were only the agents and instruments that God made use of: they wrote only what God by His Spirit dictated to them: so that, in reality, the whole Scripture was as much written by the finger of God as the laws were, which He inscribed on two tablets of stone, and delivered to His servant Moses.[9]

As Simeon perceived it, the biblical writers were not mere pens in the hands of the Holy Spirit, their humanity showed in the character and style of their writings. They were, however, preserved from error by the Spirit of truth.[10] In his hermeneutic Simeon was certainly no rigid fundamentalist. It was clear to him that Scripture was written in human words which were not fully capable of conveying the total meaning of their divine subject matter. Commenting on Hebrews 6:4–6 he wrote, 'Scripture often uses stronger language than will admit of literal interpretation'. In another place he cited Jesus' saying about a camel going through a needle's eye to show that Scripture cannot always be understood literally.[11]

Simeon was ready to admit that there may perhaps have been some minor errors in the transmission of the biblical text. He also on one occasion maintained that Scripture contains 'inexactnesses in reference to philosophical and scientific matters'. Nevertheless, he was quite clear that there was no 'error in doctrine or other important matter'.[12] Simeon also saw the importance of reason and it was this which kept him from the growing preference for premillennial speculations about the end times. Henry Martyn (1781–1812), one of Simeon's curates and a distinguished Cambridge scholar, left the University and travelled to Persia where he served as a missionary. On one occasion he was questioned by one of the country's high-ranking officials who believed in the verbal inspiration of the Koran as to whether he believed the same

---

[9] *Horae Homileticae* 1833, sermon 2133. See also M. Hennell and A. Pollard (eds.), *Charles Simeon 1759–1836*, p. 46.

[10] Pollard, 'Anglican Evangelical Views of the Bible', p. 169.

[11] Hennell and Pollard, *Charles Simeon*, p. 44.

[12] W.W. Brown, *Recollections of the Conversation-Parties of the Rev. Charles Simeon*, p. 100; see also Hennell and Pollard, *Charles Simeon*, p. 44.

of the New Testament. Martyn replied that he believed, 'The sense from God but the expression from the different writers of it.'[13] Martyn, unlike many of his contemporaries, did not hold to verbal inspiration.[14]

Daniel Wilson (1778–1858), Vicar of St Mary's, Islington (1828) and consecrated bishop of Calcutta in 1832, published a two-volume work, *Evidences of Christianity* (1828 and 1830) in which he, like Simeon, insisted upon the divine superintendence of the Holy Spirit in prompting the biblical writers. Nevertheless, he not only also acknowledged the human element in the language and structure of the text, he maintained that the Bible had only been pre-served from 'every kind and degree of error relating to religion'.[15]

The main focus of debate in the early years of the century appears to have been the mode of inspiration and the relative degrees of inspiration in differing passages of Scripture. Bebbington suggests that the 'chief court of appeal' in much of this debate was the Non-conformist, Philip Doddridge (1702–1775).[16] He recognised that some biblical passages offered greater revelation into the divine mind than others. It was this reason that led him to distinguish different modes of inspiration. For example, in a meeting of London's Evangelical leaders in 1800 Doddridge's views were the focus of the debate. Richard Cecil asserted that 'there is some danger in considering all Scripture as equally inspired'.[17] Although Henry Foster, 'a plain and deeply pious man', argued for a theory of verbal inspiration, John Davies contended that 'it is the ideas and not the words which were inspired'.

Simeonite Moderates

As has been noted, by the close of the second decade of the century Anglican Evangelicals were beginning to separate into two factions. On the one hand, there were the 'Moderates' who tended to identify

---

[13] J. Sargent, *Memoir of the Rev Henry Martyn BD*, p. 426.
[14] Bebbington, *Evangelicalism in Modern Britain*, p. 86.
[15] D. Wilson, *Lectures on the Evidences of Christianity* Vol. 1, p. 455.
[16] Bebbington, *Evangelicalism in Modern Britain*, p. 87.
[17] J.H. Pratt (ed.), *The Thought of the Evangelical Leaders: Notes of the Discussions of the Eclectic Society, London, During the Years 1798–1814*, pp. 152f, cited by Bebbington, *Evangelicalism in Modern Britain*, p. 87.

with the earlier generation, who looked to Simeon, John Venn, William Wilberforce and members of the Clapham Sect. Their views on the nature and inspiration of Scripture tended to be less rigid and more open to the impact of geological discovery. In very general terms, they recognised, as Luther had before them, that not all Scripture was equally inspired in the sense that some passages clearly provided divine and salvific revelation while others were merely historical narrative, poetry or ceremonial law. The 'Moderates' also tended to avoid giving a blunt, literal interpretation of every text as this enabled them to avoid the extremes of premillennial eschatological speculation which identified the 'Big Horn' in the Book of Daniel and the 'Beast' of Revelation with specific contemporary individuals.

On the other side, from about 1820 onwards and influenced by two Scottish Nonconformists, Alexander and Robert Haldane, there emerged what Boyd Hilton and others have termed the Extremists or Recordites because they were readers of *The Record*. This paper, which was edited by Alexander Haldane (1800–1882) from the early 1830s, fostered a much more rigorous understanding that held to the twin concepts of verbal inspiration and infallibility of Scripture. It was this group who were to find more difficulty in coming to terms not only with the discoveries in science but also with the emerging developments in biblical criticism.

The Moderates

The Moderates continued to stand in the tradition that had been established by individuals such as Venn, Simeon and Wilson. Prominent among their number was John Bird Sumner whose major work, *A Treatise on the Records of Creation*, was published by Hatchard in 1816. In it he dismissed the arguments of the Early Church Fathers that the Genesis account of the formation of the world must be seen as allegory: 'I would promise ... that two unanswerable reasons must forbid us, however pressed with difficulties from resorting to the explanation ... My inquiry ... supposes the Mosaic account to contain not allegory but fact.'[18]

---

[18] J.B. Sumner, *Creation* Vol. 1, p. 26.

Even so, Sumner did not feel compelled to assert that every detail must be interpreted as historical fact.[19] He commented in an appendix at the end of Volume 1 that Moses' account of creation 'does not profess to furnish anything like systematic or elaborate detail of the mode in which the materials of the earth were brought to their actual form and situation'. Sumner summarised what in his view the Genesis account of the creation demanded of its readers:

> First that God was the original Creator of all things: secondly, that at the formation of the globe ... the whole of its materials were in a state of chaos and confusion: and thirdly, that at a period not exceeding five thousand years ago ... the whole earth underwent a mighty catastrophe.[20]

At this moment in time, geology was at a point where it did not substantially conflict with what was seen as the Mosaic account of the origins of the universe. Sumner concluded: 'All I am concerned to establish is the unreasonableness of supposing that geological discoveries as they have hitherto proceeded are hostile to the Mosaic account of creation.'[21]

Walter Augustus Shirley gave the Bampton Lectures in 1847, but died before completing them. Entitled *The Supremacy of the Holy Scriptures*, they were significant on several counts. First and foremost, Shirley contended for the supremacy of the Scriptures as 'the one rule of faith and practice ... the only divine record we possess, and the one standard of truth and error, to which all must appeal, and by which all may be guided into truth'.[22] But secondly, it was clear that he did not hold to any particular mode of inspiration. In fact, he made the point that Jesus revealed God's will 'by oral teaching and did not, during his personal ministration, dictate any written document'.[23] He was also clear that the Lord's teaching was 'for several years ... verbally handed on and confirmed to the faithful by those who heard him'.[24] In this H.D. McDonald observed that 'Shirley can be said to anticipate the work of more recent form criticism'.[25]

[19] Ibid., pp. 30–1.
[20] Ibid., pp. 39–40.
[21] Ibid., pp. 269–70.
[22] F.W.A. Shirley, *Bampton Lectures* 1847, p. 25.
[23] Ibid., p. 13.
[24] Ibid., p. 14.
[25] H.D. McDonald, *Ideas of Revelation 1700–1860*, p. 137.

The Recordites and the Move Towards Infallibility

As we have noted, it was during the third decade of the nineteenth century that more rigid views of biblical inspiration and infallibility began to emerge. David Bebbington observed that 'around 1830' there was 'a change of direction in Evangelicalism'. Ford K. Brown also noted the change, but his explanation was little more than the observation that the older generation of Simeonite Evangelicals were passing away. As he saw it, in the years immediately following Wilberforce, 'the Evangelical Party is slowly reconstituted by a different kind of Evangelical'.[26] Ian Bradley observed 'a new obscurantism and fanaticism' but offered little further explanation. 'Evangelicalism in the second half of the nineteenth century', he wrote, 'was very different from what it had been in the first: there was a good deal more cant and a great less practical piety'.[27] Alec Vidler assessed the change as, in part, a reaction against the Oxford Movement. He was of the view that the Evangelical movement was far from being 'a spent force' in the 1830s, although it had hardened into a party,[28] but as Bebbington pointed out, 'this change was well under way before the Oxford Movement began'.[29] Many of the Evangelicals who moved in this new direction were doubtless impacted by Haldane's views which were expressed through the columns of *The Record*. In addition Haldane came to have a strong influence on Lord Shaftesbury with whom he became a close friend in the 1850s. Alexander's uncle, Robert Haldane (1764–1842), who changed the focus of his attention to Europe after considerable home mission work in Scotland, further extended the 'Haldane Spirit'. In 1816 he settled in Geneva where he found religious life in a weakened state. He gave lectures on the letter to the Romans and sought to re-establish the teachings of Calvin in the city's churches.

Robert Haldane was particularly disturbed at the low view of Scripture he found among many of the clergy in the birthplace of Calvinism. To some extent this may have been generated by the influences of the Romantic movement which was pervading much of Europe at the time. This led many to imagine that the Bible was inspired in much the same way as poetry was held to be inspired.

---

[26] F.K. Brown, *Fathers of the Victorians*, pp. 518f.

[27] Bradley, *Call to Seriousness*, p. 194.

[28] Vidler, *Age of Revolution*, p. 49.

[29] Bebbington, *Evangelicalism in Modern Britain*. pp. 75–6.

Haldane determined to make a strong apologetic for the authority of Scripture and published *The Evidence and Authority of Divine Revelation* in 1816, in which he argued against the Enlightenment view that Scripture must be assessed according to human reason and wisdom. He contended that the whole of Scripture was to be exalted as divine teaching, despite containing 'things evidently mysterious'.[30] The Scriptures, he asserted, make 'a claim of infallibility and of perfection' for their own inspiration. He rejected outright the view of many English Evangelicals that the various biblical books evidenced different levels of inspiration.

At this point in time Haldane's views were largely unheeded and would possibly have remained so, had it not been for the fact that in 1821 he began a twelve-year struggle against the inclusion of the Apocrypha in Bibles distributed by BFBS.[31] For some considerable time the organisation had produced Bibles that included the Apocrypha for use in European countries. Haldane viewed this practice as unacceptable since it placed literature of a more speculative kind alongside the canonical books and therefore weakened their authority. The society, whose supporters included Simeon and other Evangelical clergy who held a less rigid view of inspiration, were reticent to change their practice, particularly since Bibles with the Apocrypha were acceptable to the majority Continental Catholics and Protestants.

Although by 1826 BFBS had gone some way to amending its policy in this matter, not all the subscribers were happy, and the Edinburgh and Glasgow auxiliaries withdrew their support. In 1828 Haldane further intensified the debate when he produced a 176–page book entitled *On the Inspiration of Scripture*. In it, he argued that 'our knowledge of the inspiration of the Bible, like every other doctrine it contains, must be collected from itself'.[32] He took his definition of inspiration from 2 Timothy 3:16 which he interpreted as, 'God breathed words', clearly implying 'dictated'. Haldane contended that where the text stated that 'all Scripture is given by inspiration of God', it meant, 'all writing'. He wrote, 'The words then of which the whole Scriptures are composed, are dictated by God and written by men.'[33] His claim therefore was both

---

[30] R. Haldane, *The Evidence and Authority of Divine Revelation*, pp. 134f., in Bebbington, *Evangelicalism in Modern Britain*, p. 87.
[31] Railton, *No North Sea*, p. 154.
[32] R. Haldane, *On the Inspiration of Scripture*, p. 88.
[33] Ibid., p. 43.

one of 'infallibility and perfection'.[34] It was 'also a claim of absolute authority which demands unlimited submission'.[35]

Francis Close, who was incumbent of Cheltenham from 1826–1856 and subsequently Dean of Carlisle, was a prominent Recordite. His convictions on scriptural authority resonated with those of Haldane. In the preface to *The Book of Genesis*, he underlined his conviction that 'All Scripture is given by inspiration of God.' He then proceeded to expand this conviction in the following more detailed paragraph:

> Let it always be remembered, that however the sacred penmen might differ from each other with regard to the situations in which they were placed and the time in which they lived, but one Spirit taught them all, and that the holy book has properly one author, that it declares 'the whole council of God'; and consequently, if we would ascertain his will, we must patiently investigate, and in a spirit of humility and prayer, cautiously study, the whole of his revelation, tracing through the various records of the Old Testament the doctrines and promises of the New.[36]

In his classic text entitled *Theopneustia* (literally 'God-breathed'), which was published in 1841, Louis Gaussen stated this new and more rigorous understanding of Scripture in forthright manner. François Samuel Robert Louis Gaussen (1790–1863) had been converted as a result of the impact of English and Scottish Evangelicalism on Switzerland. He was ordained on 10 March 1814 and became pastor at Satigny in 1816[37] and later went on to be a professor of theology in Geneva.

Gaussen was greatly influenced by Haldane from whom he derived his doctrine of inspiration. He called Haldane 'the grandfather of the Genevan Church'.[38] Gaussen's book was intended as a riposte to Schleiermacher and others of the German liberal school who denied that the Holy Spirit inspired the biblical writers. At the same time, he was contending against English Evangelicals who were of the opinion that not all parts of the Bible were equally

---

[34] Ibid., p. 88.
[35] Ibid., p. 88.
[36] F. Close, *The Book of Genesis*, p. vi.
[37] Railton, *No North Sea*, p. 157.
[38] A. Haldane, *The Lives of Robert Haldane of Airthrey and his Brother, James Alexander Haldane*, pp. 429f.

inspired to the same level. It was also significant that his volume was published in 1841, the year in which Newman published *Tract 90*, which was an attempt to give a Roman Catholic interpretation to *The Thirty Nine Articles*. Gaussen's doctrine of inspiration was a response to both German liberals and Newman. Gaussen was also strongly anti-Roman and wrote in his book that the Bible does not

> require that men should worship the Virgin, do homage to angels, purchase pardons, adore images, confess in the ears of a priest; does it forbid marriages, prohibit meals, teach us to pray in a foreign language; interdict the Scriptures to the people and have a sovereign pontiff.[39]

He went on to conclude that those who wish to set the Bible above everything must cling to the motto, 'All the written word is inspired by God, even to a single iota, and particle of a letter and the Scripture cannot be destroyed.'[40] It is clear from this that Gaussen asserted the plenary inspiration of the whole Bible. David Bebbington has helpfully pointed out that two terms accurately define the distinctiveness of Gaussen's doctrine, 'verbal inspiration' and 'inerrancy'.

Gaussen's teaching on the former comes in a section of his book that deals with what he termed 'evasion', the notion that it is the ideas rather than the words of the Bible that are inspired. This view, which was held by a number of Evangelical Anglicans, Gaussen stoutly rejected in his succinct articulation of inerrancy: '*Theopneustia* is that inexplicable power which the Divine Spirit, afore time, exercised upon the authors of Holy Scripture, to guide them even to the words which they have employed, and to preserve them from all error, as well as from any omission.'[41]

Gaussen is often considered to have accepted a mechanical theory of inspiration, but despite an insistence that what the writer penned is 'dictated from on High' he considered that God still 'employs, in various degrees, their personality'.[42] As to the precise manner in which inspiration took place, Gaussen commented, 'Scripture never presents to us either its mode or its measure, as an object of study.'[43]

---

[39] F.S.R.L. Gaussen, *Theopneustia: The Plenary Inspiration of the Holy Scriptures*, p. 433.

[40] Ibid., p. 433.

[41] Ibid., p. 37.

[42] Ibid., Chapter 1.

[43] W.J. Abraham, *The Divine Inspiration of Holy Scripture*, p. 33.

Gaussen's convictions as to verbal inspiration led logically to his rigorous assertion of 'infallibility'. 'Is the Bible from God? Or, is it true (as has been affirmed) that it contains sentences purely human, inaccurate narratives, vulgar conceits, defective arguments …?' Such a view, which was held by significant numbers of nineteenth-century British Evangelicals, was in Gaussen's opinion a degrading one and undermined the miraculous nature of Scripture. On this understanding 'inspiration … would be unequal, often imperfect, accompanied with harmless errors, and meted out according to the nature of the passages, in very different measure, of which they constitute themselves to be more or less the judges'.[44] As Gaussen saw it, there could be no errors in any matters, whether religious, moral, scientific or historical, if the Bible was to be God's authoritative word to mankind. 'These pretended errors', he wrote, 'do not exist';[45] if 'any physical errors could be proved to exist in sacred writ it would not be a book from God'.[46]

A number of Evangelical Anglicans embraced views that were very similar to those of Gaussen, including Joseph Baylee (1808–1883), the Principal of St Aidan's Theological College, Birkenhead (1856–1869), and subsequently Rector of a Gloucestershire country village. Baylee wanted his students to be able to stand firm in their future ministries and so drummed into them that the Bible 'can have no mistake in history, no error in science, no corruption in morals, no deficiency in metaphysics, no ignorance respecting heaven, no defectiveness respecting our relations to eternal ages'.[47] If it were to be 'anything short of this', it 'would not be God's word with all its awful sanctions'.[48]

At an earlier point in his volume Baylee attempted to distinguish between 'ordinary' and 'extraordinary' inspiration with reference to the Apostle Paul's consideration of marriage in 1 Corinthians 7. 'Clearly', Baylee argued, 'he was inspired to write the whole letter but he had no extraordinary inspiration on specific matter.'[49] Following Gaussen, Baylee expounded both 'infallibility' and its concomitant, 'verbal inspiration'. Of the infallibility of the Bible he

---

[44] Gaussen, *Theopneustia*, pp. ii, 27; cited by Bebbington, *Evangelicalism in Modern Britain*, p. 90.
[45] Ibid., p. 134.
[46] Ibid., p. 171.
[47] J. Baylee, *Verbal Inspiration*, p. 47.
[48] Ibid., p. 47.
[49] Ibid., p. 47.

contended that were it anything short of this, it 'would not be God's word with all its awful sanctions'.[50]

From this contention Baylee went on to argue for verbal inspiration. If infallibility is asserted, he claimed, 'the Bible cannot be less than verbally inspired. Every word, every syllable, every letter is just what it would be, had God spoken it from heaven without any human invention.'[51] By his own admission Baylee acknowledged this 'is indeed a large claim to make for the Bible',[52] but he fully believed it to be fully demonstrable. In summing up his contention he wrote:

> The Bible is the Word of God. In it He reveals His will, and communicates knowledge through human instruments, and in human language ... Every natural image is found to be most wonderfully true, every scientific statement is infallibly accurate, all its history and narrations of every kind are without any inaccuracy. Its words and phrases have a grammatical and philological accuracy, such as is possessed by no human composition.[53]

In a later volume entitled *Genesis and Geology: The Holy Word of God Defended from its Assailants*, which was published in 1857, Baylee grappled with the Genesis account of creation. He stressed that the Bible never says the world was created in six days. In his opinion, Moses' words were that, 'In six days the Lord created heaven and earth.' Baylee distinguished between 'God creating' the heaven and the earth and the creation of this world which 'the Bible never says ... was created in six days'.[54] Whatever the merits of his attempts to draw this distinction, Baylee was still happy to endorse Bishop Ussher's chronology and to assert that in the Mosaic account we have 'scientific statements'.[55]

Essays and Reviews: A Parting of the Ways

The publication in 1861 of *Essays and Reviews*, an avowedly liberal Anglican collection of writings, had the effect of widening the

---

[50] Ibid., p. 47.

[51] Ibid., p. 48.

[52] Ibid., p. 49.

[53] Ibid., p. 61.

[54] J. Baylee, *Genesis and Geology: The Holy Word of God Defended from its Assailants*, p. 9.

[55] Ibid., p. 13.

gap between the Moderates and the Recordites. The latter were singularly hostile in their response, whilst the former were prepared to recognise the validity of some of the points that the essayists had raised, most notably in matters of cosmology and the authorship of the Pentateuch.

Although outwardly speaking the churches appeared confident and were for the most part well attended in the middle-Victorian years, cracks were beginning to emerge beneath the surface. Not only were scholars and clergy contending with doubt arising from scientific discovery, their faith in the reliability of the Bible was also being challenged by the newly emerging discipline of higher criticism. Arising initially in Germany, biblical critics began to question traditional views on authorship and to challenge the historicity of the Gospels. They maintained the narratives were biased accounts written by people of faith and, more than that, they were overlain with mythical imagery that obscured historical fact.

The seven liberal Anglican churchmen who wrote *Essays and Reviews* were influenced by this kind of thinking. Their stated aim was to 'think freely within the limits of the Church of England'.[56] As things turned out, their thinking extended well beyond the confines of what many Anglican clergy and laity, and, indeed, what the Church courts regarded as acceptable.

The contributions to *Essays and Reviews* were varied; some were more obviously divergent from historic creedal Christianity than others. Rowland Williams, for instance, questioned the Mosaic authorship of the Pentateuch, asserted that the Book of Daniel was not authentic history and that the servant in Isaiah 53 did not refer to Christ, but was in all probability Jeremiah or possibly Baruch. These conclusions led Williams to state that 'the Bible is, before all things, the written voice of the congregation'.[57]

Particularly disturbing to most Evangelicals were the views of Benjamin Jowett (1817–1893) whose essay was on the interpretation of Scripture. He was well acquainted with the findings of German biblical criticism and was convinced that it had much to teach English students who had been sheltered from such influences 'by the blind veneration in which ... the very letter of Scripture was usually held'.[58] On the issue of inspiration, Jowett

---

[56] Vidler, *Age of Revolution*, p. 124.
[57] H.B. Wilson (ed.), *Essays and Reviews*, p. 47.
[58] Reardon, *From Coleridge to Gore*, p. 333.

asserted that the Bible must be treated 'like any other book' and attention must therefore be paid to personal, local, historical and linguistic points of character. This can only be done 'in the same careful and impartial way that we ascertain the meaning of Sophocles or Plato'.[59]

Most Evangelical Anglicans were unequivocal in their denunciation of the essayists contending that they had denied the unique inspiration of the Scripture and undermined people's Christian faith. A number of rural deaneries and clerical groups sent written protests to the primate, John Bird Sumner, himself an Evangelical. The memorandum from a Dorsetshire rural deanery typified the shock felt by many evangelical clergy: 'We wish to make known to your Grace and to all the Bishops the alarm we feel at ... the denial of a Divine Inspiration of the canonical Scriptures of the Old and New Testament.'[60] Sumner replied on behalf of the episcopal bench that 'we cannot understand how the opinions can be held consistently with an honest subscription to the formularies of our Church, with many of the fundamental doctrines of which they appear to us essentially at variance'.[61]

The publication of *Essays and Reviews* further emphasised the already emerging differences among Evangelicals regarding the nature of the inspiration and authority of Scripture. Those whose roots and sympathies lay for the most part, with the Simeonite Moderates continued to stand aside from a rigid doctrine of verbal inspiration and infallibility. The Recordites, on the other hand, still drawing on the theology of Haldane and François Gaussen, pursued these doctrines with the same continuing rigour down to the end of the century.

One of those who stoutly defended the infallibility of Scripture was Charles Waller (1840–1910). He read *Essays and Reviews* whilst studying at Oxford and it had shaken his previous confidence in the inspiration of Scripture. One man in Oxford, however, appeared to understand the position and know how to hold his ground. The Rev John William Burgon (1813–1888) of Oriel College was an old-fashioned high churchman. In 1861 he preached a sermon before the University that encouraged the then youthful Waller. In it he declared, "The Bible is none other than the

---

[59] Ibid., p. 328.
[60] R.T. Davidson and W. Benham, *Life of Archibald Campbell Tait* Vol. 1, p. 281.
[61] Ibid., p. 284.

word of God, not some part of it more, some part of it less, but all alike the utterance of Him who sitteth on the throne, faultless, unerring supreme'.[62]

After a brief curacy with William Pennefather at Mildmay, Waller became a tutor at the London College of Divinity in 1865, under the leadership of the Principal, T.C. Boultbee. Waller was examining chaplain to Bishop J.C. Ryle and succeeded Boultbee as Principal in 1884 remaining in office until 1899. Later, Waller wrote, 'The Authoritative Inspiration of Holy Scripture as Distinct from the Inspiration of its Human Authors', which appeared in the *Imperial Bible Dictionary* in 1885 and was then republished separately in 1887, with a preface by J.C. Ryle.[63]

Waller was clear that the problem that many of his contemporaries had over inspiration was simply that they came to the issue from the standpoint of the inspiration of the biblical writers. This approach as he saw it could not be valid since a number of the biblical books are anonymous and, where the authors are known, we have very little knowledge of them. Waller's main point was that inspiration could not therefore be about the process by which the biblical authors were prompted to write, but rather must be grounded in Scripture itself: 'The Scripture is the book in which He [God] dwells'.[64]

For Waller the question of the infallibility of Scripture turned on Jesus' reading of it.[65] When Jesus read the Scripture, 'He would read it without any imperfection of thought or motive ... It is only in this sense, as He would have read it, that we claim infallibility for Holy Scripture'.[66] If Jesus had 'undertaken to fulfil, i.e. to fill full, the whole of Scripture with His own personality; then in relation to Him we may, we must, take the whole Scripture to be perfect and infallible'.[67] On Waller's understanding, therefore, 'infallibility was not a matter of human judgement of the text but of the Lord's endorsement of it'.

---

[62] E.M. Goulburn, *John William Burgon* Vol. 1, p. 273.
[63] C.H. Waller 'The Authoritative Inspiration of Holy Scripture as Distinct from the Inspiration of its Human Authors', *Imperial Bible Dictionary* (1885) and republished under the same title in 1887, pp. 1–58.
[64] Ibid., p. 29.
[65] Ibid., p. 30.
[66] Ibid., p. 30.
[67] Ibid., p. 30.

Some years later, Waller wrote *The Word of God and the Testimony of Jesus*[68] in which he reiterated the same opinions. Regarding 'verbal inspiration', he wrote that it will be found that the more carefully the life of Jesus is read, 'the more absolutely is He committed to the veracity and authority of every word of the Canonical Scriptures'.[69] At a later point in the book Waller stated emphatically: 'We maintain the infallibility of the Scripture ... Not a syllable of what is really God's word can be lost. One jot or one title shall in no wise pass from Law or Prophet or Psalm or Gospel or Acts or epistle or Apocalypse till all things are done.'[70]

In the same year 1861 John Cale Miller (1814–1880), the Rector of St Martin's Church in Birmingham, joined with Waller in protesting against *Essays and Reviews*. The object of Miller's publication, entitled *Bible Inspiration Vindicated: An Essay on Essays and Reviews*, was 'to set forth, simply and in popular form, the true doctrine of inspiration'.[71] He rejected 'mechanical inspiration' for the reason that 'the books of the Bible bear upon them, in so many cases, the stamp of a peculiar distinctive style – Paul's style so different from John's, as Ezekiel is so different from Isaiah's'.[72] Miller favoured what he termed 'dynamical inspiration' whereby 'the Holy Spirit exercised His enlightening, guiding, controlling influence' on the biblical writers, 'working through the natural laws of their understandings'.[73] Miller supported the infallibility of the Old Testament on the grounds of Jesus' use and acceptance of it. He also pinpointed the facts that Jesus endorsed the historicity of Jonah and the Apostle Paul regarded the account of the Fall as factual. Miller was clear that his doctrine was 'infallible inspiration without question'.[74] He spelt out what this meant in practical terms towards the end of the book:

> Our contention is ... that the writers have, in no single instance, given us legend or myth in place of historic fact. And yet further, that there are no blunders in the Bible; but that when astronomy, or geology, or any

---

[68] C.H. Waller, *The Word of God and the Testimony of Jesus.*

[69] Ibid., p. 15.

[70] Ibid., p. 70.

[71] J.C. Miller, *Bible Inspiration Vindicated: An Essay on Essays and Reviews*, p. v.

[72] Ibid., p. 17.

[73] Ibid., p. 18.

[74] Ibid., p. 33.

other science, rightly interprets the phenomena, works, and laws of God in nature, those phenomena, works and laws will be found to harmonise with the right interpretation of His Written Word.[75]

Joseph Baylee returned to the fray when he addressed the theological students at Trinity College, Dublin, in a series of lectures. He still vigorously championed 'verbal inspiration' arguing that it had dominical precedent. Jesus had allayed the anxieties of those who feared that he had come to destroy the law and the prophets when he declared that 'until heaven and earth pass, one jot or one title of the law should not fail ... could He have made a stronger assertion of the Divine authority of every word and letter of written law?'[76]

Lord Shaftesbury was convinced that the entire Bible must be accepted in its literal sense, or its whole authority would be shaken. He told CPAS in 1862 that 'there is no security whatever except in standing upon the faith of our fathers, and saying with them that the blessed old book is God's from the very first syllable to the very last, and from the last back to the first'.[77] In 1866 he denounced J.R. Seeley's *Ecce Homo*, which described Jesus primarily as the founder of a morality that changed history, as 'the most pestilential book that has ever been vomited forth from the jaws of hell'.[78]

Francis Close shared Lord Shaftesbury's concern at the weakening views being expressed with regard to the authority of Scripture. He joined the fray in 1863 with the publication of *Footsteps of Error*, a collection of earlier anti-Roman fifth of November sermons. He included one called, 'The Written Tradition'. In it he referred to 'the corruption of the divine infallible rule of faith and practice [and] the substitution of patristic tradition for the written tradition of God – the oral for the written word'.[79]

In the closing years of the century John Charles Ryle emerged as one of the most forthright defenders of verbal inspiration. As a country clergyman in East Anglia, Ryle had thundered out his views in *Knots Untied* (1874) and *The Authoritative Interpretation of Holy Scripture* (1877). In the latter volume he wrote if human history appeared to run contrary to the Bible, 'it is generally safer

---

[75] Ibid., p. 48.
[76] J. Baylee, *Verbal Inspiration: The True Characteristic of God's Holy Word*, p. 35.
[77] Hodder, *Seventh Earl of Shaftesbury* Vol. 3, p. 7.
[78] Ibid., p. 164.
[79] F. Close, *Footsteps of Error*, p. 15.

and wiser to believe that the Bible history is right and the other history is wrong'.[80] As a law book, its impact would be nullified if there was even the slightest error of detail. Ryle however was adamant that 'every book, and chapter, and verse and syllable of the Bible was given by inspiration of God'.[81] In *Is All Scripture Inspired? An Attempt to Answer the Question* Ryle urged that if the Bible was not inspired by God 'throughout' then 'it is not a safe guide to heaven'.[82] He supported his conviction that the Bible was inspired on the grounds of the richness of its contents, its reasonable account of history, its faithful account of human nature and its answers to ultimate questions.[83] Regarding the thorny questions such as the tempting serpent, Balaam's talking ass and Jonah and the Whale [sic], Ryle's response was, 'do we not believe in miracles?' He reminded his readers of the resurrection of Christ from the dead, the greatest miracle of all.

Ryle was particularly impressed by the coherence of Scripture. Referring to the biblical writers, he wrote:

> They lived at different intervals over a space of 1,500 years; and the greater part of them never saw each other face to face. And yet there is a perfect harmony among all these writers! They all write as if they were under one dictation. The style and handwriting may vary, but the mind that runs through their work is always one and the same.[84]

Ryle was of the opinion that every honest and unprejudiced reader must see that there is a gulf between the Bible and any other book.[85] He referred to the Bible as 'the book of God' written by 'Divine Inspiration'. He also came close to articulating the 'dictation theory' and asserted that while the Bible writers were 'not machines' the Holy Spirit put the thoughts and ideas into their minds and guided their pens. Ryle's understanding of Scripture, a view he recognised 'was not accepted by many good Christians', was that of verbal inspiration. He wrote:

---

[80] J.C. Ryle, *Biblical Inspiration: Its Reality and Nature*, p. 41.

[81] Ibid., p. 41.

[82] J.C. Ryle, *Is All Scripture Inspired? An Attempt to Answer the Question*, p. 6.

[83] Ibid., pp. 12–17.

[84] Ibid., p. 20.

[85] Ibid., p. 23.

The view which I maintain is that every book, and chapter, and verse, and syllable of the Bible was given by inspiration of God. I hold that not only the substance of the Bible, but its language – not only certain parts of the Bible, but every chapter of the book – that all and each are of Divine authority. I hold that the Scripture not only contains the Word of God, but is the Word of God.[86]

Ryle concluded the matter by stating that if the Bible is not fully inspired, the statements that it makes about itself – such as 'the oracles of God', 'He saith' and 'God saith' – make no sense.[87]

Ryle was not the only prominent Evangelical churchman to proffer the doctrine of verbal inspiration. The saintly scholar, Handley Moule (1841–1920), who was Principal of Ridley Hall, Cambridge, endorsed his views. In *Outlines of Christian Doctrine*, which was published in 1896, he wrote of the Holy Scriptures as 'one of the great phenomena of the world'.[88] Like Ryle, Moule was particularly impressed by the coherence of Scripture. 'No other collections of writings', he wrote, 'exists which mysteriously combines, as they do, the widest diversities of date and authorship with the deepest pervading harmonies and unities'.[89] For Moule, the divine authority of the Old Testament could be confidently assessed because of Jesus' 'profound veneration for it'.[90] As he put it in another place, 'the attitude of Christ to the Old Testament Scriptures is decisive proof that they rightly claim ultimate spiritual authority'.[91] From this position, Moule went on to assert that the spiritual and moral power of the New Testament demonstrates it to have been 'of the same order of the older Scriptures'.[92] He stressed the fact that the New Testament canon was widely accepted 'within three centuries from the death of Jesus Christ'[93] and almost universally endorsed in the writings of the Early Fathers. Whilst he also recognised each biblical writer's individuality, he was emphatic that the Old and New Testament documents are 'divine Scriptures' and 'divinely moulded' for the Holy Spirit's infallible use'.[94]

---

[86] Ibid., p. 41.
[87] Ibid., p. 48.
[88] H.C.G. Moule, *Outlines of Christian Doctrine*, p. 4.
[89] Ibid., pp. 5–6.
[90] Ibid., p. 5.
[91] Ibid., p. 7.
[92] Ibid., p. 6.
[93] Ibid., p. 6.
[94] Ibid., p. 141.

So while on the one hand the 'Recordites' clung strongly to 'verbal inspiration' and 'infallibility', other Evangelicals tended to distance themselves from these concepts. In 1861 William Thomson, soon to be enthroned as Bishop of Gloucester and less than two years later as Archbishop of York, edited *Aids to Faith*, which was a rebuttal to *Essays and Reviews*. In the preface Thomson stated the objectives of the writers were 'to offer aid to those whose faith may have been shaken by recent assaults' and to 'set forth their reasons for believing the Bible, out of which they teach, to be the inspired Word of God'.[95]

Thomson's approach to the Bible was more in keeping with the views of the earlier Simeonite 'Moderates'. In his Pastoral Letter to the clergy and laity of the Province of York he pointed out that 'The Bible is termed the word of God in the 19th, 20th, 22nd and 24th Articles.' And he further pointed out that 'in Article 22 Scripture and the Word of God are treated as interchangeable terms'.[96] In the light of this, Thomson contended that 'If the Bible is not the Word of God, but contains the Word of God ... There is no touchstone which shall test us whether a given passage is part of the Word of God or the word of man therewith entangled.'[97] Having made this assertion Thomson pointed out that 'the Church has laid down no theory in inspiration'. 'But,' he continued, 'she does lay down that the declarations of Scripture are of supreme authority'.[98]

Thomas Rawson Birks (1810–1883), who was elected Professor of Moral Theology at Cambridge in 1872, was another Evangelical who inclined to the views of Thomson. According to Bebbington, Birks rejected dogmatic inerrancy on the ground that 'we should engage in inquiry into the mode of inspiration'.[99] In 1861 Birks published *The Bible and Modern Thought*, as a counterblast to *Essays and Reviews*. In it he accepted that the Bible could be studied like any other book, intelligently and naturally, but he also took the view that it was unlike any other book, being the Word of the Holy Ghost. As such, it could contain no error in 'details, the phrases, the form, the historical circumstances'.[100]

---

[95] W. Thomson (ed.), *Aids to Faith*, Preface.

[96] W. Thomson, *A Pastoral Letter to the Clergy and Laity of the Province of York by William Lord Archbishop of York, Primate of England and Metropolitan*, p. 8.

[97] Ibid., p. 10.

[98] Ibid., p. 10.

[99] Bebbington, *Evangelicalism in Modern Britain*, p. 90.

[100] T.R. Birks, *The Bible and Modern Thought*, p. 266.

Birks did not hold with a rigid dictation theory of inspiration and wrote:

> There is a mechanical view of Bible inspiration, which shuts out, and practically denies, the human element in its composition. It reduces the whole process ... by which the Spirit of God overruled and guided the sacred penmen, to one dull monitory of mere verbal dictation.[101]

Birks took the view that the biblical books did not come down to the church 'absolutely perfect, without speck or flaw'.[102] Minor errors have occurred during the process of translation and transcription.[103] He acknowledged the presence of 'a few slight inaccuracies in the Gospels' such as the differing location of Jesus' anointing at Galilee in Luke and at Bethany in the other three Gospels. His conclusion, however, was that 'the presence of a few slight inaccuracies in the Gospels, or in other histories of Scripture, would be no decisive argument for a lowered theory of their inspiration'.[104]

Henry Wace (1836–1924), who became Dean of Canterbury in 1903, had a high view of Scripture but stopped short of verbal inspiration. He was of the opinion that 'criticism will properly inquire into the genuineness of authenticity of the sacred writings' but there could be 'no substantial inaccuracy or it would not be inspired'.[105]

In 1890 a further volume of essays was produced, entitled *Lux Mundi* ('Light of the World'). The authors, a group of liberal Anglo-Catholics, expressed their faith in historic creedal Christianity but at the same time sought to embrace some aspects of critical scholarship. One of the more controversial doctrines was Charles Gore's 'kenotic theory', which was drawn from Philippians 2 where Jesus is said to have emptied (*ekenosen*) himself. Gore maintained that at the incarnation Jesus emptied himself of his divinity. His understanding and knowledge was therefore that of a first century man. Canon Hay Aitken (1841–1927), who was one of the Church of England's best known nineteenth-century Evangelists, declared his belief in the kenotic theory, asserting that Christ as a man was not infallible.[106]

---

[101]   Ibid., p. 249.
[102]   Ibid., p. 319.
[103]   Ibid., p. 319.
[104]   Ibid., p. 89.
[105]   H. Wace, *The Bible and Modern Investigation: An Address on the Authority of Scripture*, p. 87.
[106]   Hylson-Smith, *Evangelicals in the Church of England*, p. 142.

Aitken was asked by the editor of *The Record* to state his views with perfect frankness regarding the contentions of modern critical scholarship with particular reference to Jesus' acceptance of the traditional authorship of the psalms.[107]

Aitken's approach to the question was to point out that Christ was clearly limited in knowledge. He did not know the time of his Second Advent. He learnt by hearing and answering questions. From this Aitken went on to make the following assertion concerning Jesus:

> If this is the true view of the way in which Christ acquired knowledge, it follows that in his manhood Christ could only form his conclusions with respect to the truth of certain traditional views held by his contemporaries as to the authorship of certain parts of the Old Testament, by the information within His reach as man, unless a specific revelation were made to Him on this subject by His Heavenly Father.[108]

Aitken was clearly advanced in his views even by the standards of the Evangelical Moderates. He penned a letter to a friend who had tried to persuade him to confess his belief that 'All Scriptures are given by Inspiration of God.' In it he wrote, 'No statement that I could make would give satisfaction to those who hold the extreme traditional theory of plenary inspiration, and thus the "rent would only be made worse".'[109]

The Recordites rejected the propositions of the kenotic theory. For instance, the Islington Clerical Conference in January 1891 discussed and affirmed the testimony of Christ to Holy Scripture,[110] and in the *Churchman* Stanley Leathes and others attacked the consequences of extreme criticism and strongly defended Christ's infallibility.[111] *The Record* provided an independent, Evangelical reply to *Lux Mundi* and modern criticism in a series entitled 'The Authority and Accuracy of Christ's Teaching'. The Rev R.B. Girdlestone of Wycliffe Hall provided the first few articles. *The Record* set out what was becoming the view of most of their readers that Christ's attitude to the Old Testament was indisputable and to question the reliability of its text was to

---

[107] *The Record*, 22 January 1892.
[108] C.E. Woods, *Memoirs and Letters of Canon Hay Aitken*, pp. 256–7.
[109] Ibid., p. 258.
[110] *The Record*, 3 October 1890.
[111] *Churchman*, September–October 1891 and January 1892.

compromise the Lord's authority, and to make Christian belief impossible.[112]

The close of the nineteenth century thus saw a divergence of opinion among Evangelicals. The Moderates, following men such as William Thomson, Thomas Birks and Hay Aitken, tended to distance themselves from assertions of plenary inspiration and infallibility. They were unwilling to commit themselves to specific theories of inspiration and continued to emphasise the human element in the process. Many of their number were mindful of Sir Leslie Stephen's (1832–1904) belief that he must accept every word in the Bible as literal truth or cease to be a Christian, which led him to renounce his father's religion.[113] The Moderates were unable to run with the view that to concede to a single point of biblical critical thought amounted to abandonment of the faith. On the contrary, it might be a positive way to embrace a changing culture. The Recordites, however, for their part, remained despondent at such a prospect and clung to John Ryle's assertion in his fifth triennial charge to the Diocese of Liverpool in 1893:

> I can only advise all my clergy, who want counsel on the subject of Higher Criticism, to cultivate a very cautious attitude of judgment. Beware of taking up loose and confused views of the doctrine of inspiration. Stand firm on the grand old text, 'All Scripture is given by inspiration of God' (2 Timothy 3:16) ... do not be carried off your feet by the first clever new book you come across, and especially if you have never examined this branch of study before.[114]

It was partly on account of the strident and outspoken views of men such as Ryle, supported by other bishops, such as Thorold and Bardsley, together with prominent clergy such as Canon Alfred Christopher (1820–1913) of St Aldates, Oxford, that a large number of Evangelicals at the end of the nineteenth century continued to take their stand on the plenary inspiration and the infallibility of Scripture. Nevertheless, it is also clear that there were a significant number of others who were no longer comfortable with these terms. They were still confident that the Old and

---

[112] *The Record*, 8 January 1892. See also A. Bentley, *The Transformation of the Evangelical Party in the Church of England in the Later Nineteenth Century*, p. 172.

[113] Chadwick, *Victorian Church* Part 1, p. 113.

[114] Ryle, *Charges and Addresses*, pp. 276–7.

New Testaments contained all that was necessary for salvation, doctrine and church practice but they felt the necessity of taking on board at least some of the findings of the higher critics.

7

Evangelical Anglicans and Theology

Background

At the beginning of the nineteenth century a significant number of Evangelical Anglicans had their roots in the Wesleyan revival. Their energies had been given to preaching the gospel and engaging in pastoral work. It is therefore not surprising that there was little, if any, doctrinal theology emerging from the pens of Evangelical Anglicans. George Stanley Faber was perhaps the only exception. A Bampton lecturer, he was already publishing in 1801. What little Evangelical theology there was therefore centred on practical and soteriological issues. John Wesley, for example, had written a *Treatise on Baptism* (1756) and Samuel Walker of Truro produced *A Short Introduction to the Lord's Supper*. Charles Simeon did write and preach on theological issues but his concerns were largely focused on justification, the atonement and the second coming of Christ.

In the second quarter of the century, as the Evangelicals began to emerge as a distinct party within the Church of England, some of their number began to give more attention to theological concerns. In particular, their output was increased with emergence of the Oxford Movement following John Keble's Assize Sermon in 1833. Significantly, Peter Toon argued that much of the Evangelical theology which emerged in the years 1833–1856 took firm shape on the anvil of Tractarianism.[1] He supported this contention partly on the basis that a number of distinctively Evangelical Anglican societies were founded in this period in direct opposition to similar ones founded by the followers of Newman and Pusey.

---

[1] See Toon, *Evangelical Theology 1833–1856.*

The leaders of the Oxford Movement had an explicit concern to rediscover the witness of medieval theology and to assert that the Anglican Church was a part of the one true Catholic Church. In order to facilitate this contention Pusey began translating the lives of the Early Church Fathers. Within a short space of time this provoked the newly emerging Evangelicals to rediscover their roots in the English Reformation. As part of that process, the Parker Society was formed in 1840 under the presidency of Lord Ashley, and began faithfully to publish the works of the sixteenth-century English Reformers. Not surprisingly, much Evangelical theology in the Victorian years was rooted in the writings of Cranmer, Ridley, Latimer and the Edwardian and Elizabethan Protestants. Whilst it was the case that William Goode (1801–1868) the Younger made wide use of the Early Church Fathers, later generations in particular shared the views of Bishop John Ryle who was sometimes heard to remark that the Fathers were 'greatly over-rated as commentators and expositors'.

The Content of Evangelical Theology

Authority

After John Keble had preached his celebrated Assize Sermon on national apostasy, which marked the beginning of the Oxford Movement, the Tractarians began to put their faith in Newman's doctrine of the apostolic succession. By this he argued that there was a direct link through the unbroken line of successive bishops between the Church of England and the undivided Catholic Church of the first five centuries. This led the Tractarians to place consider-able authority on the writings of the Early Church Fathers and other traditions including the creeds and the rule of faith. In short, they adopted the view that these writings contained authoritative divine revelation in the same way as the New Testament documents. Keble's *Primitive Tradition* (1836), Newman's *The Prophetical Office of the Church* (1837) and Manning's *The Rule of Faith* (1838) all suggested an elevated position for tradition as equal with Scripture. Manning in his volume stated, 'All interpretations of Holy Scripture must be made in accordance with the faith of those on whose evidence we receive the written Word of God itself.'[2]

---

[2] Ibid., pp. 113–14.

In the light of these contentions, the Evangelicals not unnaturally began to vigorously assert the supreme authority of Scripture in all matters of faith and practice as set out in Article 6, 'Of the Sufficiency of Holy Scripture'. Bishop Daniel Wilson set out his views on the matter in 1841 in a sermon entitled, *The Sufficiency of Holy Scripture as the Rule of Faith*.[3] He argued that if tradition must be the interpreter of Scripture, Scripture is no longer inspired by the Holy Spirit.[4]

Without doubt, the most learned and comprehensive counterblast to the Tractarian stance on tradition came from the pen of William Goode the Younger (1801–1868). Goode was the most able and prominent theologian of the Evangelical Anglican party. *The Divine Rule of Faith and Practice*, which was first published in 1842 and reprinted in 1855, was 1,500 pages long and asserted that Holy Scripture has always been and is the sole, divine rule of faith and practice to the church. Goode claimed that there is nothing in the form or substance of the Fathers that we are bound to receive as the word of God. Volume 3 contains an extensive mass of quotations from the Early Church Fathers themselves, and from the Laudian divines, prized highly by the Oxford Movement, showing that they viewed the Scripture as the sole and complete rule of faith and judge of controversies. Goode summarised his findings in this way:

> I conclude the whole with the following decisive testimony of this last witness. The deference which the Fathers always paid to the Holy Scriptures as the sole authoritive rule of faith is sufficient to guide us in the deference which they would have admitted to be due to themselves.[5]

In the light of this, he asserted, the Church of England requires nothing to be believed as an Article of the Christian faith 'but what, in her judgement, has good indubitable foundation for it in the Holy Scriptures'.[6]

Isaac Taylor, an Anglican Evangelical layman, approached the issue from a slightly different angle. In a two-volume work entitled *Ancient Christianity*[7] he attempted to show that the Catholic

---

[3] D. Wilson, *The Sufficiency of Holy Scripture as the Rule of Faith*.
[4] Ibid.
[5] See W. Goode, *The Divine Rule of Faith and Practice* Vol. 3, p. 521.
[6] Ibid., p. 543.
[7] Toon, *Evangelical Theology 1833–1856*, p. 122, citing I. Taylor, *Ancient Christianity* Vol. 2, p. 365.

Church of the first five centuries corrupted teaching of Scripture. One of the examples he gave was the teaching on celibacy, which he described as a 'perversion' of the teaching of Jesus in Matthew 19:12. Taylor also examined the spirituality and the morals of the undivided Catholic Church, describing them as 'far more gross, violent and sensual than could be found in any protestant country'. Taylor further spent pen and ink on the worship of the same period, noting that it included such aspects as 'the veneration of relics, the invocation of dead saints, and worship at shrines'. He termed it 'idolatry and blasphemy'.[8]

Goode also showed that the patristic literature was *not* unanimous in its testimony on a number of key doctrines. For example, there were several different voices speaking on issues such as the divinity and generation of the Son, the procession of the Holy Spirit from the Father and the Son, the Nestorian, Eutychian and Pelagian errors, the millennium and the re-baptism of heretics. Goode summed the matter up as follows:

> If Holy Scripture is thus the sole infallible and authoritative Rule of Faith it follows, of course, that it is to its decision alone that we must appeal … in controversies concerning the faith; and hence it is justly called the sole infallible Judge of controversies of the faith.

Goode continued on the same page to make the point that Holy Scripture is also 'the sole infallible Rule of Faith to every individual' and that all Christians have the right of private judgement in determining the meaning of Scripture.[9]

All this is not to say that nineteenth-century Evangelical Anglicans saw no value in patristic tradition. For Goode, it could, on occasion, elucidate what a careful study of the Scripture revealed. Other leading Evangelicals, especially those who were more pastorally orientated (such as Hugh Stowell of Manchester, Hugh McNeile of Liverpool or Francis Close of Cheltenham) had rather less time for tradition. As Bishop Ryle said, 'Infallibility is not to be found in the early Fathers, but in the Bible.'[10] Again he urged

> Let us settle it next in our minds that there is no other rule of faith, and judge of controversies, but that simple one to which Christ always

---

[8] Ibid.

[9] Goode, *Divine Rule of Faith and Practice* Vol. 2, p. 61.

[10] Ryle, 'The Fallibility of Ministers', *Knots Untied*, p. 368.

referred the written Word of God. Let no man disturb our souls by such value expressions as 'the Voice of the Church', primitive antiquity the judgement of the early Fathers, and the like tall talk. Let our only standard of truth be the Bible, God's Word written.[11]

Much later, at the close of the century, Handley Moule was still making the same point which Goode had argued in 1842. In his *Outlines of Christian Doctrine*, Moule considered various kinds of authority that 'may be real, yet not ultimate'.[12] As examples, he cited the fact that 'a creed has authority; a Council has authority; a Father has authority, and still more, many consenting Fathers, witnessing the facts of belief'.[13] Yet as far as Moule was concerned none of these could claim ultimate authority. Only the Scriptures can make such a claim. Moule was adamant: 'Reverently, but still lawfully and firmly, if the deplorable necessity should arise, the individual may appeal, from even Creed or Council, to the Holy Scriptures, asking to be tested by their sacred verdict alone, as the basis of the authority of all other lawful courts.'[14]

Justification

The central aspect of Evangelical theology was the doctrine of justification. Frederick W. Robertson of Christ Church, Cheltenham, St Ebbe's, Oxford, and Trinity Chapel, Brighton, wrote in a letter dated 4 March 1841 that 'justification by faith alone' is 'that cardinal doctrine of our best hopes'.[15] Charles Simeon began his celebrated sermon *On Justification by Faith* before the University in 1815 with these words: 'If there be any one question of more importance than all others, it is this: "How shall a man be just with God?"'[16]

The Oxford Movement led to developments in the traditional Anglican understanding of justification as expressed in the Articles of Religion, notably in articles 11, 12 and 13. The change began when Newman published his *Lectures on Justification* in 1838 in which he attempted to fuse together Protestant and Catholic ideas. In particular, he brought together the notion of the external righteousness

---

[11] Ryle, 'Apostolic Fears', *Knots Untied*, p. 395.
[12] Moule, *Outlines of Christian Doctrine*, p. 7.
[13] Ibid., p. 7.
[14] Ibid., p. 8.
[15] S.A. Brooke, *Life and Letters of Frederick W. Robertson*, p. 59.
[16] C. Simeon, 'On Justification by Faith', in *Let Wisdom Judge*, p. 63.

of Christ being reckoned or (imputed) to the believing Christian and the righteousness of Christ being (infused) into the soul by the Holy Spirit at regeneration. For Newman, 'justification' was both a declaration made to us and an action *in* us. As he put it in the lectures; 'almighty God declares ... the soul righteous, and in that declaration ... makes it actually righteous'. Again he wrote: 'Christ ... our righteousness fulfils the law *in* us as well as for us'.[17] To be justified for Newman and the Tractarians was therefore 'to receive Divine Presence within us'.[18]

To the Evangelical party of the Church of England these assertions were simply a restatement of the views of the schoolmen and later medieval churchmen. The root problem, as they saw it, was that 'infused' or 'internal' righteousness is, to some extent at least, a human action. Thus justification was seen as man's endeavour as well as God's action. It meant in effect that the individual contributed to his or her standing before God in the matter of salvation. Newman, with his Evangelical upbringing, was aware of the problem this raised and tried to answer it with what his Evangelical contemporaries regarded as a mere sophism. Newman proposed the concept of 'adherent' righteousness. God, according to him, indwells the soul but he does not mix in with the human soul. He does this in the same way that he indwells the wider creation without actually submerging into it in some animistic way.

In their opposition to these Tractarian teachings, the Evangelicals of Church of England took their stand wholly on the Articles of Religion and the teaching of the sixteenth-century English Reformers. Canon Charles Heurtley (1806–1895), who later became Lady Margaret Professor of Divinity, sought in his Bampton Lectures on *Justification*[19] to show that 'our justification consists not, as the Church of Rome teaches, in our being made righteous ... but as our own church teaches in our being accounted righteous'. Again he puts it more explicitly:

> Justification is one of the precious gifts thus bestowed upon us, and it consists, not in an imperfect righteousness of our own inherent in us, but in Christ's perfect righteousness imputed *to* us – ours because we are one with Christ, and Christ with us. In Hooker's forcible

---

[17] J.H. Newman, *Lectures on Justification*; cited by Toon, *Evangelical Theology 1833–1856*, p. 151.

[18] Ibid., p. 152.

[19] C.A. Heurtley, *Justification – Eight Sermons*, p. 86.

enunciation of this doctrine, 'Christ hath merited righteousness for as many as are found in Him'.[20]

Charles Simeon put it with equal emphasis: 'That the doctrine is true is beyond doubt. We are only justified by the righteousness of Christ imputed to us'.[21] The Rev Edward Bickersteth in a sermon on the subject of justification, which he preached in December 1827, made the same point. He began by asserting that justification 'is the very heart and core of our common Christianity',[22] and then went on to make clear that the Greek term *logizomai*, signifying to reckon or impute, is used on the subject of justification eleven times in one chapter (Romans 4).[23] Again he stated, 'When we believe in Christ, we are then immediately justified: though sinful in ourselves, yet according to the revealed will of God, we are accounted and dealt with as righteous in his sight'.[24]

During his years as Bishop of Chester, John Bird Sumner became increasingly concerned that justification by faith alone, 'the fundamental and characteristic article of all Reformed churches', was becoming obscured by the teachings of the Oxford Movement. In his Charge to the clergy of the diocese in 1841 he was adamant 'that we are accounted righteous before God through the merit of 'Christ alone, and not for our own works or deservings'.[25]

Two years later Sumner wrote *The Doctrine of Justification Briefly Stated.*[26] Having set out what is meant by justification, Sumner cited the conversion of the Ethiopian official in Acts 8 as a paradigm for laying hold justification:

---

[20] Ibid., p. 335–6.
[21] A.W. Brown, 'Notes on Calvinism and Arminianism', in *Recollections of Conversation Parties of the Rev Charles Simeon*, pp. 267–88, in E. Jay, *The Evangelical and Oxford Movements*, p. 27. Abner William Brown attended Simeon's conversation parties between 1827 and 1830 and took notes which he published in 1863 hoping that they would convey something of 'the raciness' of Simeon's remarks and responses to his questions which are not captured in his other published work.
[22] E. Bickersteth, *A Discourse on Justification by Faith: Preached in the Course of Sermons on Points of Controversy between the Romish and Protestant Churches at Tavistock Chapel, Drury Lane on Tuesday 11 December 1827*, p. 3.
[23] Ibid., p. 12.
[24] Ibid., p. 17.
[25] J.B. Sumner, *A Charge 1838*, p. 25.
[26] J.B. Sumner, *Doctrine of Justification*.

He perceived that what he needed was in Christ Jesus; that peace with God was to be procured through his propitiation; he believed that Jesus was the Son of God, 'the Lamb of God, which taketh away the sins of the world'. And thus he was accounted righteous before God.[27]

Sumner argued that the Roman Church confused two things: 'what has been done for us,' namely, Christ's sacrifice for sin, and 'what is being done in us', namely, Christ's working in the believer's life. If a person puts their hope in this second proposition, he is 'induced to look to himself, and not to his Redeemer, for acceptance with God'.[28] Sumner was at pains to point out that our own righteousness is 'an imperfect righteousness':

There is a righteousness which is inherent, and a righteousness which is not inherent. The righteousness whereby we are sanctified is inherent, but not perfect. The righteousness whereby we are justified is perfect, but not inherent. This is the fundamental and characteristic article of all Reformed Churches: laid as it were their corner-stone; that we are accounted righteous before God through the merits of Christ alone, and not for our own deserving.[29]

Although following the Protestant Reformers Sumner was vehement that our works play no part in the individual's justification, he followed them in maintaining that good works are the fruit of true faith. Answering what he held to be the 'erroneous' teaching of the Tractarians Sumner asserted that a man is

not accepted with God, because he is a new creature, but because Christ has made atonement for the wrath which in his old nature he had incurred. His faith in that atonement which led to his acceptance, leads also to his doing works meet for one who is accepted; but the works which follow his being justified, and are its effect, can never also be the cause of justification.[30]

While he was rector of Stradbroke in Suffolk, John Ryle wrote a piece entitled, 'Evangelical Religion', which was published in 1877. In it he stated that the third leading feature of Evangelical religion is 'the paramount importance it attaches to the work and office of our

---

[27] Ibid., p. 13.
[28] J.B. Sumner, *Charge 1841*, p. 22.
[29] Ibid., p. 22.
[30] Ibid., p. 24.

Lord Jesus Christ'. By dying as 'our Representative and Substitute', he 'obtained a complete salvation for sinners and a redemption from the guilt, power and consequences of sin'.[31] He went on to state exactly the same point, which both Simeon and Sumner before him had made, that 'all who believe in Him are, while they live, completely forgiven and justified from all things, are reckoned completely righteous before God'.[32]

On the matter of 'justification', Church of England Evangelicals stood firm throughout the Victorian years in their assertion that justification was 'extrinsic', that is rooted in what Christ had done, that it was by faith alone in his atoning death that 'righteousness' is accounted to us. Even at the close of the century, Handley Moule noted that 'the Imputed Righteousness of Christ' is 'now much disputed'.[33] 'But', he continued, 'it rests securely upon Romans IV.6 with its context'.[34]

The Tractarians also clashed swords with the Evangelicals in one further aspect of this doctrine. They readopted the medieval view that baptism is the instrument which sets in motion the process of regeneration which is then sustained by the sacraments of the church, especially the Eucharist, and later also confession and absolution. Newman of course recognised that Article XI was un-equivocal in its assertion that 'we are justified by faith *only*'. He therefore proposed that faith is the sole 'internal instrument' whereas baptism is 'the external instrument'. For Newman, Pusey and the Tractarians justification was received at baptism as the instrument 'whereby the love of God is shed abroad in our hearts and makes our faith a regenerate and lively faith'.[35] To the Evangelicals all of this was anathema and resulted in some of the hottest and keenly fought theological controversies of the century.

The Church

The issue of baptism, particularly infant baptism, leads naturally to a consideration of the doctrines of church, ministry and sacraments. Here also, there was lively controversy between the theologians and

---

[31] Ryle, *Knots Untied*, p. 5. *Knots Untied* was first published in 1874.
[32] Ibid., p. 5.
[33] Moule, *Outlines of Christian Doctrine*, p. 188.
[34] Ibid., p. 188.
[35] 1 Timothy 2:19.

clergy of both parties. The Tractarians developed a high view of the visible church ruled by bishops. They claimed that men are joined to 'Christ by being joined to His Church'. The visible church, as they saw it, was the body of Christ and thus the extension of Christ the Head. To be joined to the body was to be joined in union with the head of that body. For the Oxford Movement the visible Episcopal Church was one and the same as Christ's mystical body.

The Evangelicals took their stand on the Articles and the teaching of the Protestant Reformers and drew a distinction between the mystical body of Christ, 'the one holy catholic apostolic church' and the visible local church. As far as the Evangelicals saw it, by no means all members of the local visible Episcopal Church were members of Christ's 'true church'. The true church, as they perceived it, was 'invisible' not visible. Only God ultimately knows the elect. Evangelicals took their stand on the apostle Paul's words to Timothy that 'the Lord knows them that are his'.[36]

In 1846 Hugh McNeile produced a volume entitled, *The Church of God in Christ and the Churches of Christ Militant Here on Earth*. In it he dealt with the credal statement, 'One Holy, Catholic and Apostolic Church'. His argument was that the 'Church Militant Here on Earth' is the 'invisible Church' consisting of all true believers in every place. Its oneness was derived from its union with Christ in the one Holy Spirit. The visible church, on the other hand, embraced members of this church together with 'false professors of Christianity'. Edward Arthur Litton who was successively Dean of Oriel, Vice President of St Edmund's Hall, Rector of St Clement's Oxford and Rector of Naunton, near Cheltenham, took the view which McNeile also shared: the key is not that the individual church is joined to Christ, the head of the body, but *rather* the Scripture is plain that it is the individual members who are joined with the head of the body. Litton drew on Ephesians 4:15–16 which makes it clear that it is each individual member who grows up into Christ. In Litton's words: 'The union of the members with the head here described is such, that the vital energy which animates the whole Body flows directly ... from the Head into each member.'[37] Litton further underlined the point: 'If Christian communities, as such, may be said to have Christ as their Head, it is not by direct union, but mediately; that is, it is because

---

[36] 1 Timothy 2:19.
[37] E.A. Litton, *The Church of Christ in Its Idea, Attributes and Ministry*, p. 313.

the individuals of which they are composed are, presumably at least, in life-giving union with Him.'[38]

Desmond Bowen was critical of Litton's lack of faith in Hooker's view of the church in the nation because 'there is nothing in the state, as such, directly leading to Christ'.[39] However, the issue, as Litton saw it, was that the state put too much emphasis on seeking to improve society by means of better social institutions and educational endeavour instead of aiming to 'recover man from the moral ruin occasioned by the Fall'.[40] Litton clarified what Protestants meant 'when they say that the body of Christ, is invisible, they mean nothing more than that which makes us members of the body of Christ, or the true Church – viz. saving faith in Christ – is invisible'.[41] He then went on to indicate that there must always be a link between the visible and invisible body of Christ:

> The point of inseparable connexion between the Church as invisible and the same Church as visible will now be understood. It is this: the members of Christ's body are never to be sought for save in the visible Churches of Christ ... The true Church cannot, at present, manifest itself otherwise than under the form of local Christian communities; where they are, therefore, there, and not elsewhere is where it is.[42]

Litton's views were typical of nineteenth-century Evangelicals. Their primary loyalty was always to the invisible church but they nevertheless valued the visible established church. Indeed as far as they were concerned they showed themselves to be decidedly more loyal to her formularies than most of their Tractarian counterparts. Several of the Evangelical bishops appointed by Lord Palmerston expressed their strong support for the Church of England as the national church. Samuel Waldegrave, for instance,

---

[38] Ibid., p. 313. Litton was described by F.J. Chavasse, Principal of Wycliffe Hall, as 'peculiarly well qualified to act as the spokesman of the Evangelical School. In University distinction he had few superiors. He was a double first class man, and had been a Fellow of Oriel'. See F.J. Chavasse's introduction to the second edition of *The Church of Christ*.

[39] See D. Bowen, *The Idea of the Victorian Church*, p. 149, citing E.A. Litton, *Connection of the Church and the State: The Question of the Irish Church*, p. 5.

[40] Bowen, *Idea of the Victorian Church*, p. 149.

[41] Litton, *Church of Christ*, p. 322.

[42] Ibid., p. 327.

preached a sermon in Carlisle Cathedral in August 1868 entitled 'Ministering Kings to Our Established Church a favour from God'. In it he underlined the fact that the Church of England 'is a Reformed Church' which was 'reformed by the Ministration of Kings'.[43] He went on to point out that it is 'our national church' whose organisation is designed to make it 'the channel of blessing to every quarter of our land'.[44] William Thomson preached a sermon entitled 'The National Church' at the opening of the Cathedral of St Albans in October 1885. He spoke warmly in favour of the established church and in particular the great contributions it had made to education and the needs of the sick and the poor.[45]

Geoffrey Best, summing up nineteenth-century Evangelical Anglican attitudes to the established church, suggested that their conviction that sin corrupted every human institution 'prevented their putting too full a confidence in a national Church establishment'.[46] 'Nevertheless,' he continued, 'the Church of England was, all in all, the best establishment within the power of sinful men to construct.'[47]

The ministry

As the Tractarians saw it, what made or guaranteed the church visible to be the 'divine society' or 'mystical body' was the episcopal order. In short, it was their doctrine of ministry which guaranteed the status of the church and validity and efficaciousness of its sacraments.

Newman in *Tract 1* had set out what he termed the 'branch theory' in which he claimed a direct linkage between the Church of England and the undivided church of the first five Christian centuries. The link was the passing down the sacramental grace of God, through a direct unbroken line of bishops. In his own words, 'The Lord Jesus Christ gave His Spirit to His apostles, they in turn laid their hands on those who should succeed them; and those again on

---

[43] Waldegrave, S., *Ministering Kings to Our Established Church a Favour from God*, p. 11.

[44] Ibid., p. 12.

[45] W. Thomson, *The National Church. A Sermon Preached at the Opening of the Cathedral of St Albans on 2nd October 1885 by William Lord Archbishop of York*, pp. 1–4.

[46] G.F.A. Best, 'The Evangelicals and the Established Church in the Early Nineteenth Century', *Journal of Theological Studies* 10.1 (1959), p. 68.

[47] Ibid., p. 68.

others; and so the sacred gift has been handed down to our present bishops.'[48] For the Tractarians therefore 'episcopacy' was essential to the being of the church. It was needed to guarantee the orders of presbyters who then administered efficacious grace, especially through the Eucharist. This was the position that had been earlier expressed by Cyprian, the third-century Bishop of Carthage in North Africa who declared that 'The bishop is in the church and the church is in the bishop.'[49]

The majority of Evangelicals appear to have held the view that the episcopal form of government was apostolic in origin and God's intended norm for the established church. Litton, for example, basing his argument on the fact that Paul consecrated Timothy and Titus, wrote: 'it is an historical fact that towards the close of the apostolic age the ministry is found to have assumed the episcopal form, and that to the bishop was reserved the rights of ordaining'.[50] Again, Hugh McNeile, in his *Lectures on the Church of England*, gave full vent to his belief in episcopacy. In summary he declared:

> And now I feel emboldened, in the combined light of these several scriptural applications of the true church, to declare ... that the Church of England in ... her episcopal constitution and diocesan superintendence as the church collective, is comprehensively in accordance with the word and will of the Lord Jesus Christ, to the glory of God the Father.[51]

Nevertheless, most Evangelicals were unwilling to deny the validity of dissenting ministries. In the words of Hugh Stowell, 'We are bound to love the pious dissenter as a brother, we are not bound to love him as a dissenter.'[52] Furthermore, nineteenth-century Evangelical Anglicans did not subscribe to Newman's view of the apostolic succession. For them, the key factor was not the apostolic laying on of hands but the proclamation of the apostolic doctrine. Bishop Ryle wrote in *Knots Untied*:

---

[48] J.H. Newman, Tract 1 'The Ministerial Commission', p. 8 in W.G. Hutchinson, *The Oxford Movement. Being a Selection from Tracts for the Times*.

[49] Cyprian, Letter 68 in J.C. Ayer, *A Source Book for Ancient Church History*, p. 238.

[50] Litton, *Church of Christ*, p. 577.

[51] H. McNeile, *Lectures on the Church of England*, p. 45.

[52] H. Stowell, *Tractarianism Tested by Scripture* Vol. 1, p. 260.

But what are bishops, priests and deacons? What are the best of ministers but men – dust, ashes, and clay – men of like passions with ourselves, men exposed to temptations, men liable to weaknesses and infirmities? ... The greatest errors have been begun by ministers ... we should follow them so far as they teach according to the Bible, but no further ... Infallibility is not to be found in ordained men, but in the Bible.[53]

Evangelical Anglicans shared Ryle's strongly expressed view that the Church of England ministry was in no sense a priestly office.[54] Edward Litton was among those who expressed this conviction in writing. He stressed that 'In Scripture various terms are used to describe the office of Christian ministers – they are pastors, rulers, teachers, ministers, evangelists: but not even once is the term Hiereus – i.e. sacrificing priest – applied to them, or the Eucharist spoken of as a sacrifice.'[55]

In a significant passage in another part of the same book, Litton underlined the fact that the word 'ordination' and its derivatives in no sense convey 'any idea of a sacred or sacramental character'.[56] He pointed out that the word *ordo*, from which the Latin verb ordinaire is derived, was the technical term for the senate or council, to which, in the colonies and municipal towns of the Roman Empire, the administration of local affairs was committed, and the members of which were called *Decuriones*. The *ordo* were not the priesthood as opposed to the laity, but the magistracy as distinguished from the plebs or private citizens. In fact, Litton wrote, 'the word ordinare was never used by the classical writers to signify consecration to a sacred office'. Thus, 'to be ordained' merely signified that a person 'had been chosen as a member of the governing body or presbytery in a Christian society'.[57] From this Litton warned that 'to transfer the notions which in later times became connected with "ordination" into the apostolic age, or the narrative, is a ready way to fall into serious errors of scriptural interpretation'.[58]

---

[53] Ryle, *Knots Untied*, p. 369.
[54] Ibid., p. 257; see also his entire Chapter 11 'The Priest', pp. 242–59.
[55] Litton, *Church of Christ*, p. 611.
[56] Ibid., p. 565.
[57] Ibid., p. 565.
[58] Ibid., p. 566.

The Eucharist

Central to the sacramental teaching of the Tractarians was their assertion that though the bread and wine remain, yet there is by the act of consecration a real, though spiritual presence of the body and blood of Christ united with the bread and wine to form with them one compound whole. In a celebrated sermon entitled 'The Holy Eucharist a Comfort to the Penitent', which he preached in 1843, Edward Pusey spoke of 'that bread which is his flesh' and of 'touching with our very lips the cleansing blood'.[59] A decade later, George Denison, Archdeacon of Taunton, accelerated the controversy over 'the real presence' when he asserted during the course of sermon that

> The body and blood of Christ, present naturally in heaven, are really, though supernaturally and invisibly present in the Lord's Supper under the elements by virtue of consecration that both parts of the sacrament are given to and received by all who communicate and that worship is due to the body and blood of Christ present under the form of the bread and wine.[60]

Toon pointed out that there were three major doctrines of the Eucharist found within the established church in the century before the Oxford Movement – the 'virtualist', the 'memorialist' and the 'receptionist'.[61] According to the virtualist understanding the bread and wine do not change in themselves nor is the presence of Christ in them. After the consecration the elements become the vehicle by which the grace of God is conveyed to the recipients. In the memorialist position, which was originally associated with Bishop Benjamin Hoadly (1676–1761), it was asserted that Christ was present only in the same way as he was present in all worship and fellowship. In the receptionist position, which had been earlier taught by Daniel Waterland (1683–1740), it was held that a sacrifice presence was received if the communicant exercised due and proper faith. This view had been that of Cranmer's second prayer book of 1552 and of Charles Wesley's hymns.

Tractarian teaching had its roots in virtualist and the receptionist positions reaching its mature expression after 1845. Evangelical

---

[59] E.B. Pusey, *The Holy Eucharist a Comfort to the Penitent*, pp. 16, 23.
[60] See Scotland, *John Bird Sumner*, p. 117.
[61] Toon, *Evangelical Theology 1833–1856*, p. 195.

Anglicans favoured either the memorialist or the receptionist view. William Goode's position was that the Church of England teaching views the bread and wine, not as memorials but as 'effective instruments' whereby 'the communicants receive in a state of communion with Christ'.[62] Goode therefore inclined to the receptionist view although he did not exclude the virtualist position totally.

Alongside Goode, Nathanel Dimmock and T.S.L. Vogan made valuable Evangelical contributions to the Eucharistic debate. Vogan published *The Doctrine of the Eucharist* (1871) and Dimock wrote *The Doctrine of the Sacraments* (1871). Reynolds noted that 'Dimock wrote magisterially on the atonement, the sacraments and the Church of Rome.'[63]

Bishop Edward Bickersteth of Exeter expressed a similar view in his diocesan charge of 1888. 'We steadfastly believe', he declared, 'that in the Holy Communion Feast, the souls of the faithful are strengthened and refreshed by the Body and Blood of Christ as their bodies are by the bread and wine; but we utterly repudiate Transubstantiation in the Supper of the Lord.'[64] John Charles Ryle had earlier expressed this same view:

> There is a real spiritual 'presence' of Christ within the hearts of all truehearted communicants in the Lord's Supper. Rejecting as I do, with all my heart, the baseless notion of any bodily presence of Christ on the Lord's Table, I can never doubt that the great ordinance appointed by Christ has a peculiar blessing attached to it. That blessing, I believe, consists in a special and peculiar presence of Christ, vouchsafed to the heart of every believing communicant ... In a word, there is a special spiritual 'presence' of Christ in the Lord's Supper, which they only know who are faithful communicants, and which they who are not communicants miss altogether.[65]

Baptism

A major controversy between Evangelical Anglicans and high churchmen focused on the spiritual effects of infant baptism. Tractarians returned to the position of Thomas Aquinas and

---

[62] W. Goode, cited by Toon, *Evangelical Theology 1833–1856*, p. 201.
[63] See J.S. Reynolds, *The Oxford Evangelicals 1871–1905*, pp. 94, 118; and Toon, *Evangelical Theology 1833–1856*, p. 197.
[64] Algionby, *Edward Henry Bickersteth*, pp. 211–12.
[65] Ryle, *Knots Untied*, p. 199.

regarded baptism as the instrumental cause of regeneration. They interpreted the language of *The Book of Common Prayer* service literally, believing, as the priest was required to state, that the baptised infant was regenerate. Edward Pusey articulated the views of most high churchmen in his *Tract 67* on baptism. He endorsed the words of the catechism which speak of baptism 'wherein I was made a member of Christ, the Child of God an inheritor of the Kingdom of heaven'.[66] Pusey regarded baptism as the means whereby the individual is 'engrafted into Christ and thereby receives a fuller principle of life'.[67] Again, he wrote in 1836 that the regeneration of baptism is indeed a new birth. This implied 'new nature, existence imparted; and this is actual not metaphorical'.[68]

The most celebrated clash over infant baptism was that between the Evangelical George Gorham (1787–1857), who was the incumbent of St Just-with-Penwith, and his bishop, Henry Phillpotts (1778–1869), of Exeter. Phillpotts was a staunch high churchman who vehemently asserted that the baptised infant was automatically regenerate. George Gorham was perhaps unusual among Evangelical clergy in that he was prepared to assert that such might be the case, but that it did not always necessarily follow. Gorham had aroused Phillpotts's hostility while still at his Cornish parish when he advertised in the *Ecclesiastical Gazette* for a curate 'free from Tractarian error'.[69] When, therefore, Gorham sought a move to the parish of Brampford Speke just outside Exeter, the bishop demanded to test his views on baptism. The examination began on Friday 17 December 1847 and lasted for fifty-two hours over a period of eight days, with only short breaks for meals.[70] There were fourteen further hours from 8–10 March 1848.

Both Gorham and the bishop were agreed that the Scripture and the church linked baptism with regeneration. Phillpotts followed the teachings of the medieval schoolmen that asserted that infants who had committed no actual sin were unable to resist the grace of regeneration. He maintained that the language of the service for the public baptism of infants in *The Book of Common Prayer* supported his view. Immediately the baby was baptised the priest was required to say unconditionally, 'seeing now this child is regenerate'. Phillpotts

---

[66] G. Rowell, *Hell and the Victorians*, p. 17.
[67] Ibid., p. 17.
[68] Ibid., p. 17.
[69] Chadwick, *Victorian Church* Part 1, p. 251.
[70] Nias, *Gorham*, p. 11.

also supported his contention with the answer to the second question in the catechism in which the child was taught to affirm that in his baptism 'he was made a child of God and an inheritor of the Kingdom of heaven'. Gorham however countered that infants received no spiritual grace from baptism because they were by nature 'unworthy recipients, being born in sin, and the children of wrath'.[71] Gorham further responded by reference to Article 25, which asserts that the sacraments only have 'a wholesome effect or operation' upon such as 'worthily receive the same'.[72]

At the conclusion of the examination, Gorham received notice from the Bishop of Exeter that he refused to induct him to the living that he had been offered by the Crown. The bishop's injunction found him 'unfit to fill the said Vicarage, by reason of your holding doctrines contrary to the true Christian faith, and the doctrines contained ... especially in *The Book of Common Prayer* and the Administration of the Sacraments'.[73] Gorham was unwilling to accept the verdict and appealed to the Court of Arches where Dr Bayford, an eminent ecclesiastical lawyer, stoutly defended him. Bayford pointed out that Gorham's difference with the bishop was in regard to 'worthy recipients'[74] and he went on to question Phillpotts' view that all infant candidates for baptism were worthy recipients.[75] Despite Bayford's efforts the decision of the Court on 2 August 1849 went against Gorham. Sir Herbert Jenner Fust was of the view that although the meaning of 'regeneration' was not totally clear the doctrine of the Church of England was that children are regenerated in baptism.[76]

To most Evangelicals the decision, if upheld, was a fatal blow[77] because they had always stressed the need for people to repent, believe and be converted. Now it appeared that all that was necessary was holy water at the font. Many Evangelical Anglicans were not Calvinists and tended to regard the sacraments as pledges of a future regeneration.

Despite the fact that judgement had gone against him, Gorham remained convinced that his doctrine of baptism was in keeping

---

[71] Ibid., p. 18.
[72] Ibid., p. 29.
[73] Ibid., p. 44.
[74] Ibid., p. 48.
[75] Ibid., p. 48.
[76] Ibid., p. 48.
[77] Ibid., p. 73.

with the Church of England and he therefore made recourse to the final court of appeal in ecclesiastical matters, the Judicial Committee of the Privy Council. At the same time, a number of Evangelicals began to voice their opinions declaring that Bishop Phillpotts' doctrine was 'a popish fiction' which destroyed souls.[78] In his charge of 1849, the Archbishop of York, Thomas Musgrave (1788–1860), declared the effects of infant baptism were an open question. 'We cannot,' he said, 'insist on it as a ruled doctrine of our Church that all baptised children are, as such, spiritually regenerate'.[79] William Goode, the leading Evangelical theologian of the time, published *The Doctrine of the Church of England as to the Effects of Baptism in the Case of Infants* in 1849. In it he underlined the crucial importance of faith if the baptised person is to experience regeneration: 'in the spiritual new birth, life, a living principle of faith must have been implanted to make the birth by baptism effectual to the production of a being spiritually alive'.[80]

The Judicial Committee of the Privy Council gave judgement on 8 March 1850 that Gorham's doctrine was not contrary or repugnant to the declared doctrine of the Church of England. The actual wording included the following lines: 'We judge that baptism is a sacrament generally necessary to salvation, but that the grace of regeneration does not so necessarily accompany the act of baptism that regeneration invariably takes place in baptism … in no case is regeneration in Baptism unconditional.'[81]

Following the reversal in Gorham's favour the Bishop of Exeter excommunicated the Archbishop of Canterbury and publicly declared that the Primate, or any other person who instituted Gorham to the living of Brampford Speke, would be guilty of favouring heretical doctrines. Despite the vehemence of Phillppotts' words Gorham was instituted and ministered quietly in the parish until his death. The majority of Evangelical clergy clearly shared his views on the baptism of infants and many of them subscribed to the memorial restoration in Brampford Speke out of thankfulness to Gorham for the stand he had taken. Significantly, as early as 1816

---

[78] Chadwick, *Victorian Church* Part 1, p. 255.

[79] T. Musgrave, *A Charge Delivered to the Clergy of the Diocese of York, June 1849* cited by Nias, *Gorham*, p. 167.

[80] W. Goode, *The Doctrine of the Church of England as to the Effects of Baptism in the Case of Infants*, p. 22.

[81] For a full statement see Carpenter, *Church and People 1789–1889*, pp. 198–9.

Henry Ryder in his first charge to the clergy of the diocese of Gloucester had taken issue with a tract on baptismal regeneration, written by Dr Mant, who was later to become Bishop of Down, and produced by SPCK. Ryder declared, 'I would solemnly protest against that most serious error of contemplating all the individuals of a baptised congregation, as converted'.[82] He urged his hearers 'to come in true repentance and lively faith to the Saviour and receive their portion in his meritorious atonement'.[83]

Eschatology

The nineteenth century witnessed considerable developments in the Evangelical eschatology. The latter half of the previous century had been marked by a growing postmillennial optimism. As the revival under the Wesleys had spread many preachers began to imagine that it would be the prelude to the millennium after which the Lord himself would return. However, with the coming of the Napoleonic Wars in the first two decades of the new century, there was a growing erosion of the earlier confidence. People were no longer confident in the progress of good in the world. In fact, many began to feel pessimistic and expected only 'the progress of evil'. A number of prominent Evangelicals, among them George Faber, identified Napoleon as the Anti-Christ, heading up a revived Roman Empire.[84] J. Hatley Frere also identified Napoleon as 'the Beast of Revelation', his hatred of the British being a characteristic that Scripture foretells.

The defeat of Napoleon did not end millennial speculation. The 1820s were a decade of confusion and political uncertainty following the ending of the war. Bread prices were high, unemployment was still fairly widespread and, in addition, there was still talk of revolution. A number of Evangelicals came to the conviction that the latter days were beginning and though the end was not yet, it was not far off. In 1821 James Haldane Stewart, incumbent of Percy Chapel in Charlotte Street, London, wrote a tract entitled *Thoughts on the Importance of Special Prayer for the General Outpouring of*

---

[82] H. Ryder, *A Charge 1816*, pp. 20–2, cited by Davies, *First Evangelical Bishop*, p. 9.

[83] Ibid., p. 9.

[84] See G.S. Faber, *Dissertations on the Prophecies*, and *A General and Connected View of the Prophecies*, cited by Railton, *No North Sea*, p. 197.

the Holy Spirit, and over the next thirty years 90,000 copies were distributed. Stewart noted the failures of religious societies to transform the world and he began to preach that there would be no millennium before the second coming of Christ.[85]

Associated with this new premillennialism there emerged a growing new support for Jewish projects. These were motivated by their study of the Old Testament prophets who declared that in the last days God's people would return to their own land. In earlier times these passages were held to refer to the return of the Jews from Exile but in the second and third decades there emerged a penchant for more literal interpretation on the biblical text. Hugh McNeile's *Popular Lectures on the Prophecies Relative to the Jewish Nation*,[86] which was published in 1830, may be taken as a representative example.

In Lecture 4, entitled 'The Jews shall be restored to their own land', McNeile considered the various interpretations that have been given to the text – first, the return of the Jews from Babylon; secondly, the conversion and sanctification of the Christian Church; thirdly, the mixture of the two; and, finally, the literal reoccupation of Palestine by the twelve tribes.[87] The last understanding, according to McNeile, is 'proved to be the correct one, by its being the only one which is consistent throughout'.[88] He summed up his conviction in the following lines:

> The King has been preserved in heaven, where he sitteth on the right hand of God. We are plainly informed, that he shall come again from heaven in like manner as he went up to heaven (Acts 1 v. 11). Thus King and people shall meet; and the literal, lineal descendants of David's subjects shall be governed by the literal, lineal descendant of King David himself, and 'He shall reign over the house of Jacob for ever, and of his Kingdom there shall be no end'.[89]

In 1825 The London Society for the Promotion of Christianity Amongst the Jews became increasingly aware in their discussions that Jerusalem was to be the capital of Christ's millennial kingdom.

---

[85] S.C. Orchard, *English Evangelical Theology 1790–1850*, p. 70.
[86] H. McNeile, *Popular Lectures on the Prophecies Relative to the Jewish Nation*.
[87] Ibid., pp. 123–42.
[88] Ibid., p. xxii.
[89] Ibid., pp. 141–2.

This led to their establishing a permanent post in Jerusalem. Early in 1826 Johann Nicolayson, a Dane, was appointed with instructions to buy ground for a church. In April 1841 the London Society set out plans for an enlarged mission in Jerusalem with a school, a hospital and a scheme to provide work for converts.[90] Even Charles Simeon was initially swept along with the enthusiasm and for a while he campaigned earnestly on behalf of the London Society. He made a number of preaching tours with William Marsh as his companion.[91] Simeon wrote,

> In the Apostolic Age a number of Jews were first called, and then Gentiles. So in the Millennial period, the awakening will commence among the Gentiles; and then shall come the conversion of the Jews; who, being turned to faith, will be God's instruments for the bringing in of the whole Gentile world.[92]

Edward Bickersteth preached and published on the restoration of the Jews to Israel. In fact, in a single day, Whit Sunday 19 May 1839, Bickersteth gave four sermons in the city of Edinburgh on the theme of Jewish restoration. They were subsequently printed and distributed by the London Society to the clergy.[93] In 1841 Bickersteth published a lengthy volume entitled *The Restoration of the Jews to Their Own Land and the Final Blessedness of our Earth*.[94] In it he urged his readers 'to discern the times of the times. They are so distinct that he may run who reads them.'[95] He continued,

> The Turkish Empire is wasting; the unclean spirits of Popery, lawlessness and infidelity are stirring up and gathering the Kings of the earth to last war. The way of the Jews is preparing. It is even now seen that Palestine is to be the battlefield of Europe ... Any day may remove the remaining obstacles of the return of the Jews to their own land.[96]

---

[90] Orchard, *English Evangelical Theology*, pp. 206–10.
[91] Ibid., p. 123.
[92] Simeon MSS p. 617, cited by Orchard, *English Evangelical Theology*, p. 123.
[93] *London Society Minute Book* minute 1526, 23 July 1839, cited by Orchard, *English Evangelical Theology*, p. 211.
[94] E. Bickersteth, *The Restoration of the Jews to Their Own Land and the Final Blessedness of our Earth*.
[95] Ibid., p. 163.
[96] Ibid., p. 163.

Such was the interest in the end times that a number of prophetic societies and conferences came into being. Among them were the Bloomsbury Meetings and The Winchester Prophetical Investigation Society. Montagu Villiers, the Rector of St George's, Bloomsbury, started the Bloomsbury gatherings in 1843 and they continued until he left the parish in 1856. S.C. Orchard remarked that the list of lectures were 'an Evangelical roll-call' and included Edward Bickersteth until his death, his son, Edward H. Bickersteth, who was later Bishop of Exeter, and his nephews, Robert, who was later Bishop of Ripon, and Edward, who was later Dean of Lichfield. Edward Hoare, Vicar of St John's, Holloway, Edward Auriol, Rector of St Dunstan's in the West, and Charles Goodhart of Park Chapel, Chelsea, were also among the regular lecturers.[97]

The Winchester meetings were organised by the Canon of Winchester, William Carus Wilson. He had taken part in the Bloomsbury lectures in 1848 and organised two similar conferences that focused on premillennial themes in 1849 and 1850. One of those who lectured in 1850 was Joseph Wigram who was then Archdeacon of Southampton. His topic was 'The Advent of the Lord the Present Glory of the Church'.[98] He made the point that when the Lord returns, such is God's covenant with Israel, He will take away their sins and 'reign over the house of Jacob for ever'.[99] Then will follow the thousand-year period.[100]

Of all those Evangelicals who became so taken up with the end times and the premillennial scheme it seems to have been Edward Bickersteth who most influenced Lord Shaftesbury.[101] As a result, between 1838 and 1840 Ashley encouraged Lord Palmerston, who was Foreign Secretary, to sponsor Jewish settlement in Palestine in order to counteract Russian influence in the region. Matters further developed when in the summer of 1841 Frederick William IV, the King of Prussia, suggested to the British Government that a Protestant bishopric should be set up at Jerusalem. The Prussian monarch was undoubtedly a man with a deep Christian commitment but Shaftesbury, who shared his strong Protestant and

---

[97] Orchard, *English Evangelical Theology*, p. 157.

[98] J.C. Wigram, 'The Advent of the Lord the Present Glory of the Church', in W.C. Wilson (ed.), *The Blessing of the Lord's Second Advent: Six Lectures During Lent.*

[99] Ibid., p. 46.

[100] Ibid., p. 53.

[101] Railton, *No North Sea*, p. 204.

anti-Roman convictions, seemed somewhat unaware that his agenda was in part political. 'Prussia,' as R.W. Greaves observed, 'was not yet a first class power' but was 'seeking to climb to a greater influence in the near East, with the help of Britain'.[102] The resulting project was a confused mixture of ecclesiastical and political agendas with different groups of politicians and churchmen offering their support for a variety of reasons.[103]

King Frederick worked through his special envoy, Chevalier Bunsen who, like Shaftesbury, had a deep interest in the Holy Land. The proposal was that the bishopric should be shared by Britain and Prussia. The bishop would be consecrated by the English bishops but nominated alternately by the English and Prussian crown. Despite a change of government, which saw Palmerston replaced as Foreign Secretary by Lord Aberdeen, the situation moved according to plan. The position was offered in the first instance to Shaftesbury's 'extremely Protestant' friend, Alexander McCaul. He, however, declined it, feeling that the task demanded 'a true Son of Israel'. The bishopric was then offered to and accepted by Michael Solomon Alexander who seemed admirably qualified. He had been born in Poland, was a subject of Prussia, a true Jew, British by naturalisation and a Christian by conversion. At the time when he was nominated for office he was professor of Hebrew and Rabbinic Literature at King's College, London. Alexander was consecrated in the chapel at Lambeth Palace on 7 November 1841 by the Archbishop of Canterbury assisted by the Bishops of London and Rochester, together with George Augustus Selwyn, the first Bishop of New Zealand who had himself been raised to the episcopate just three weeks earlier in the same place.

The Jerusalem bishopric met with a variety of reactions. For those Tractarians who shared Newman's view that Lutheranism and Calvinism were heresies, it was a bitter blow. Newman later wrote in his autobiography that it was 'the third blow that finally shattered my faith in the Anglican Church'.[104] Others who shared Newman's dislike of Lutheranism and Calvinism nevertheless were glad to see the Anglican Church established in the Holy City. Among their number was William Gladstone who proposed Bishop Alexander's health at a dinner given by Bunsen. Shaftesbury also

---

[102] R.W. Greeves, 'The Jerusalem Bishopric, 1841', *English Historical Review* 44 (July 1949), p. 340.

[103] See for example Battiscombe, *Shaftesbury. A Biography*, p. 138.

[104] J.H. Newman, *Apologia Pro Vita Sua*, pp. 204–9.

noted in his diary for 26 October, 'Very glad to have heard that many of the High Church are warmly in favour of the Hebrew Bishopric, Archdeacons Samuel Wilberforce and Manning. Palmer, too, of Worcester, supposed to be among the most violent, spoke to Bunsen in terms of the greatest delight.'[105]

For Ashley and the Evangelicals the Jerusalem bishopric was rooted in their belief that it was another sign of Christ's imminent return and the start of the millennial reign. Alexander McCaul, who turned down the offer of the bishopric, called the experiment 'one of the noblest projects that ever emanated from the piety of earthly Kings to promote the glory of the King of Heaven'.[106] The bishopric, he later wrote in 1858, was 'a most powerful instrument for the spread of the gospel amongst the Jews, and for the reformation of the churches'.[107] Not all Evangelicals saw the Jewish people in an eschatological light. Baptist Noel is said to have taken 'a noble stand against the Romance of Jewish Missions founded on millenarianism'.[108] Conybeare in his essay on 'Church Parties' emphasised that it was the Recordites who interpreted 'those glorious prophecies of the restoration of Israel and the blessedness of the New Jerusalem' to 'the carnal seed of Abraham, to the pawnbrokers of Monmouth Street, and the slop-sellers of St Giles' rather than to the Christian Church'.[109] It was, he said, his misfortune, on one occasion, to hear one of these Judaizers advocate the notion that the 'Lost Tribes' are identical with Saxons on the ground that *Saxon* is an abridgement of 'Isaac's son'.[110]

Among those who persisted with older postmillennial schemes proclaimed by John Wesley and the earlier generations of Evangelicals were William Wilberforce, John Venn and Samuel Wilberforce. John Venn, son of Henry Venn, informed a meeting of the Eclectic Society that Scripture clearly predicted a period of peace and glory for the church. Richard Cecil and Thomas Scott concurred. Samuel Waldegrave, who was shortly to become Bishop of Carlisle, devoted his Bampton Lectures to an extended argument in support of postmillennialism. He did not view Jerusalem as having a dominant role in the end time and saw the future kingdom as essentially

---

[105] Hodder, *Life and Work of Lord Shaftesbury*, p. 202.
[106] Railton, *No North Sea*, p. 224.
[107] Ibid., pp. 224–5.
[108] Ibid., p. 205.
[109] Conybeare, 'Church Parties', p. 228.
[110] Bebbington, *Evangelicalism in Modern Britain*, p. 62.

spiritual. Waldegrave argued that when Christ the perfect comes, the imperfect must be done away. Since, during the millennium Satan is not yet destroyed, Christ must return after the thousand-year period has come to an end.[111] The future millennial age remained a matter of contention among Evangelicals and wise scholars such as Handley Moule urged that the subject be left with 'a reverent avowal of the conditions of mystery'.[112] His final counsel was: 'On no topic of revelation should believing students be more watchful against premature conclusions and unloving mutual criticisms than on the details of our blessed Lord's most certain, literal, glorious and desirable Return.'[113]

The final state

The other aspect of eschatology over which Evangelical Anglicans felt keenly was the matter of hell and eternal punishment. For Evangelicals hell and eternal punishment were the motivation for preaching the gospel and overseas missionary work. Typical of their number was William Cadman (1815–1891), Rector of St George the Martyr in Southwark. Preaching in 1856 he made it clear to his comfortably well-off congregation that hell was a distinct possibility and that not all would be saved.[114] John Ryle was also among those who were adamant about a literal hell which he described as 'the hopeless prison, the bottomless pit, the lake that burns with fire and brimstone'.[115] The thought filled Ryle with urgency and he spoke out strongly against those ministers who tried to sidestep the matters of death and hell. In 1855 he wrote,

> I believe the time is come when it is a positive duty to speak plainly about the reality and eternity of hell … it is a question which lies at the very foundation of the gospel … The grand object of the gospel is to persuade men to flee from the wrath to come and it is vain to expect men to flee unless they are afraid.[116]

---

[111] S. Waldegrave, *New Testament Millenarianism: or the Kingdom and Coming of Christ as Taught by Himself and His Apostles by the Rt. Hon., and Right Rev Samuel Waldegrave DD, Lord Bishop of Carlisle*, pp. 13, 83, 136.

[112] Moule, *Outlines of Christian Doctrine*, p. 114.

[113] Ibid., p. 114.

[114] W. Cadman, 'The Sin of Neglecting the Poor', *The Pulpit* 69 (1856), pp. 516–22, cited by Hilton, *Age of Atonement*, p. 280.

[115] J.C. Ryle, *Repent or Perish*, as cited by Farley, *Ryle*, p. 17.

[116] J.C. Ryle, *Lot's Wife*, as cited by Farley, *Ryle*, p. 17.

While Evangelicals clung tenaciously to the creedal assertions of the final judgement to come, the more liberally minded were of the view that eternal punishment was overly vindictive and could not be justified on moral grounds, particularly in the case of those who had never received the Christian revelation. In 1860 matters came to a head with the publication of *Essays and Reviews* in which some of the contributors undermined traditional creedal eschatology. One result was the emergence of what was described as 'an unholy alliance' between Evangelicals and high churchmen. Lord Shaftesbury wrote to Edward Pusey on 26 February 1864 urging that they sink their differences of many years and 'struggle ... for the very Atonement itself, for the sole hope of fallen man, the vicarious sacrifice of the Cross'.[117] The result was a campaign backed by *The Record* in which 11,000 clergy and 137,000 laity were prevailed upon to sign an address in which they declared their firm belief that the canonical Scriptures teach 'in the words of our blessed Lord, that the punishment of the 'cursed equally with the life of the righteous is everlasting'.[118]

In 1864 William Thomson wrote a *Pastoral Letter to the Province of York* in which he was adamant that 'Everlasting must mean forever, never coming to an end. The Church of England believes in a life that lasts for ever for the good, and in an everlasting punishment for the wicked.'[119] Other Evangelical bishops soon followed suit. Samuel Waldegrave for example urged his clergy to faithfully declare that 'there is a great assize near at hand' and that 'the dead shall be judged out of the things written in the books'.[120] 'Everyone unwashed in His Blood', he declared, 'shall without doubt perish everlastingly'.[121] These episcopal pronouncements did not settle the issue. Indeed, only three years after Thomson's pronouncement, Thomas R. Birks, the Honorary Secretary of the Evangelical Alliance, published a book entitled *The Victory of Divine Goodness*[122] that revealed a sharp difference of opinion even among Evangelicals. Birks asserted that unbelievers would be consigned to an

---

[117] Hodder, *Life and Work of Lord Shaftesbury*, p. 593.
[118] Vidler, *Age of Revolution*, p. 128.
[119] Thomson, *Pastoral Letter*, p. 13.
[120] S. Waldegrave, *The Charge Delivered in July and August 1864 at His Second Episcopal Visitation by the Hon. And Right Rev Samuel Waldegrave DD Lord Bishop of Carlisle*, p. 59.
[121] Ibid., p. 60.
[122] T.R. Birks, *The Victory of Divine Goodness*.

eternal realm that was separated from heaven.[123] However, he went on to take a restitutionist line in which he suggested the possibility that in that state they might be raised 'into a trance of holy adoration in the presence of infinite and unsearchable goodness'.[124] These speculative views brought about a deep rift in the Evangelical Alliance and as a result Birks tendered his resignation which was accepted by the Executive Council on 12 January 1870. For its part, the Executive passed a resolution which denounced 'the assertion that there will be mercy in some form or other extended to the souls under the solemn sentence of eternal judgement'.[125]

Clearly, Evangelical clergy, both Moderates and Extremists, took their stand on the doctrines of the creed. They held firmly the Great Reformation doctrines of the supreme authority of Scripture and justification by faith alone. In their doctrine of the church they tended to emphasise the invisible nature of Christ's body. In the matter of the ministry and sacraments, they turned aside from teaching which accorded the clergy a sacerdotal function or regarded baptism and the Eucharist as automatic purveyors of regeneration grace.

---

[123] Randall and Hilborn, *One Body in Christ*, p. 122.
[124] Ibid., p. 123.
[125] Ibid., p. 127.

8

Sunday Observance

Victorian attitudes to Sunday observance were largely rooted in the sixteenth-century Reformation and the ideals of the Puritans in particular. Early Protestants relaxed the stringency of the medieval church, but there were reactions in the later stages of the Reformation. The Marian legislation repealed the Act of Edward VI which had permitted harvest work on Sunday. The Elizabethan Articles of Religion endorsed the Second Book of Homilies as containing 'a godly and wholesome Doctrine'. The eighth homily, entitled 'Of the Place and Time of Prayer', was based on Cranmer's earlier work and rejected Jewish authority proposing in its place the law of nature. It included a list of religious duties and attacked idleness and dissipation without making any allowance for public or harvest work. The homily pointed out that 'this commandment of God doth not bind Christian people so strictly to observe ... the Sabbath day as it was given to Jews: yet it ought to be retained and kept of all good Christian people'.[1]

During Elizabeth's reign Bibles became more freely available and pious clergy and laity began to reach their own conclusions as to what were sound morals and appropriate Christian living. As they searched through the Scriptures most concluded that Sunday was in some degree at least a Sabbath and should be kept holy by avoiding labour and recreation. In the 1580s there was a flowering of English Puritanism, much of which drew on the theology of John Calvin (1509–1564). In his *Institutes of the Christian Religion* Calvin had asserted that the Sabbath was a day on which 'believers were to cease from their own works and allow God to work in them'. Again

---

[1] 'Of the Place and Time of Prayer', *Second Book of Homilies*, pp. 359–72.

he asserted, 'The Sabbath was appointed for no other purpose than to render men conformable to their creator.'[2]

Two books, both published in 1592, were influential as far as Sabbath keeping was concerned: Richard Greenham's (1535–1594) *Treatise on the Sabbath*, and Dr Nicholas Bownde's *The Doctrine of the Sabbath*. Bownde argued that the Sabbath as Sunday was a 'naturally moral and perpetual' law binding on all humanity. It was not merely a ceremonial law binding only on ancient Israel. Therefore, the adoption of Sunday as a Sabbath was a divine mandate that came ultimately from Christ himself and was transmitted through the apostles.

Bownde demanded that the fourth commandment be incorporated into the laws of the land. 'It behoveth', he wrote, 'all Princes and magistrates, that bee in highest authority, to provide that laws be enacted for the preservation of this rest, with civil punishments to be inflicted upon them that shall break it.' Furthermore, Bownde asserted:

> It is … certain that we are … commanded to rest … from … all … things which might hinder us from the sanctifying of the Sabbath … We must not think it sufficient that we do not work on the Sabbath, and … be occupied about all manner of delights, but we must cease from the one as from the other.[3]

William Perkins (1558–1602) wrote, 'It is a notable abuse of many to make the Lord's Day a set day of sport and pastime, which should be a day set apart for the worship of God and the increase of true religion.'[4] John Dod (1565–1645) asserted: 'The Sabbath is the market-day of the soul, on which we lay in spiritual food for the following week.' 'It is a day', he continued, 'that doth the saints enrich'.[5]

Teaching about Sunday and Sunday observance was the first major doctrinal difference between the contending factions of the English Protestant Church. On the one hand, there were those who,

---

[2] J. Calvin, *Institutes of the Christian Religion*, cited by C. Hill, *Society and Puritanism*, p. 171.

[3] N. Bownde, *The Doctrine of the Sabbath*, cited by J. Premus, 'The Lord's Day as a Sabbath', in T. Eskenazi et al. (eds.), *The Sabbath in Jewish and Christian Traditions*, pp. 108–9.

[4] Hill, *Society and Puritanism*, p. 174.

[5] Ibid., p. 175.

together with Puritans, such as Bownde and Dod, took a sabbat-arian view, holding that the fourth commandment demanded strict attention to worship and tight restrictions on all leisure activities. On the other side, there were those who took what was sometimes termed as the dominical view, asserting that Jesus' view of Sunday observance was altogether more relaxed. Such individuals noted that the Lord allowed the disciples to pluck ears of corn and that he healed the man with the withered hand, the man with the unclean spirit, the infirm woman, the crippled man and the blind man all on the Sabbath.[6]

During the Cromwellian period sabbatarians received state endorsement of their views. The Westminster Confession of 1644 was emphatic that God by his word endorsed the fourth command-ment as 'binding all men in all ages'.[7] Its exposition continued,

> The Sabbath is then kept holy unto the Lord, when men, after a due preparing of their hearts, and ordering of their common affairs before-hand, do not only observe an holy rest all the day from their own works, words, recreations; but also are taken up the whole time in the public and private exercise of His worship, and in the duties of necessity and mercy.[8]

With the arrival of the Restoration in 1660 the alliance between sabbatarianism and Parliament was somewhat weakened. In many of the rural areas magistrates were still able to enforce church atten-dance and put a stop to Sunday trading and recreational activities. In the larger towns and cities, however, it proved as much as many of them could do to urge the duty of public worship without having to regulate the rest of the day's activities. Nevertheless, many of the middle classes kept Sunday special by having the best meal of the week on that day and avoiding amusements and pastimes.

In 1726 the Non-juror, William Law (1686–1761), first pub-lished *A Serious Call to a Devout and Holy Life*. Through the imagi-nary figure of Flavia he makes it clear that a Sunday spent in religious worship was of little account unless it issued in a virtuous life, which was caring of the poor.[9] John Wesley whose thinking was

---

[6] See Matthew 12:9–13; Mark 2:23–28; Luke 13:11–13; John 5:1–9, 9:13–16.
[7] *The Westminster Catechism*, cited by J. Wigley, *The Rise and Fall of the Victorian Sunday*, p. 23.
[8] Ibid., p. 23.
[9] W. Law, *A Serious Call to a Devout and Holy Life*, pp. 64–5.

greatly influenced by Law thought that activities that did not specifically strengthen religious commitment were unsuitable for Sundays. Both he and his brother Charles demanded strict observance
of the Sabbath. He was an active member of The Society for the Reformation of Manners and in 1763 rejoiced at the large number of
prosecutions for Sabbath-breaking that the society had brought
before the courts.[10] Two of Wesley's associates, William Grimshaw,
the incumbent of Haworth, and John Newton, first captain of a
slave-trading ship and then successively Vicar of Olney and St Mary
Woolnoth in the city of London, were both careful about their
observance of Sunday. Grimshaw achieved something of a reputation for stopping Sunday football matches and ensuring that even
the unwilling were present for morning worship. He had local
publicans fined for drawing beer during the time of divine service
and summoned the disorderly to the archdeacon's court.[11] John
Newton, likewise, held strongly to the vital importance of retaining
a strict Sabbath observance. Against the backcloth of the French
Wars and the Government's proposals to authorise the drilling of
the militia on Sundays, Newton declared, 'if the breach of the
Sabbath was authorised by law, it would alarm me much more,
than to hear that fifty or a hundred thousand French were landed or
that our Grand Fleet was totally destroyed. I should consider it as a
decided token that God had given us up'.[12]

During the 1780s, in the wake of the Wesleyan revival, there was
a rekindling of sabbatarianism in which many of its nineteenth-
century features began to emerge. These developments were further
reinforced as a result of the introduction of a ten-day week and the
abolition of Sunday in post-revolutionary France. Churchmen and
others in authority were determined that no such anarchy should
take root on English soil. For this reason, Evangelicals set up what
later became known as The Society for the Suppression of Vice.
Within twelve months of its founding the society had brought
convictions for breaches of the Sabbath against 623 people and
censured a further 3,000 of the offence in London alone. In 1809
The Society for Promoting the Observance of the Sabbath was
established to assume the responsibility for this area of morality.
Against this background, William Wilberforce and Lord Belgrave

[10] S. Ayling, *John Wesley*, pp. 71, 262.
[11] Baker, *Grimshaw*, pp. 210–14.
[12] J. Newton, *Wrangham MSS*, Box 3, cited by Bradley, *Call to Seriousness*,
     p. 15.

unsuccessfully tried to introduce a Bill to suppress Sunday newspapers in 1795.[13] Hopes were again lifted when Spencer Perceval
became Prime Minister in 1809. He had a penchant for scanning the
text of the book of Revelation and looking for parallels between
Napoleon and the Anti-Christ.[14] John Wigley has made it clear that
by the 1820s 'the sabbatarians had emerged as a determined group,
with a strong sense of mission'. More significantly, 'They had overwhelmed most non-sabbatarian theologies, notably those which argued that Christ, the Apostles or the Early Church had relaxed the
fourth commandment, technically called the Dominical school, and
sought to enforce their own views.'[15]

Early Nineteenth-Century Sunday Observance

By and large, Evangelical Anglicans adopted one of two attitudes to
Sunday observance. On the one hand, there were those who took
the view that the Lord's Day must be kept in strict accordance with
the provisions of the fourth commandment. This, the 'sabbatarian
view', was held by most of the Recordites. On the other hand, the
Moderates were of the opinion that Jesus adopted a less rigorous
understanding of the Sabbath day. Theirs can be designated as a
'dominical view'. Both groups supported moves to preserve Sunday
as a day for rest and worship, but the Recordites were more rigid as
to what was permissible and what was not. They were also more
rigorous in their pursuit and support of legislative campaigns and
action.

It needs to be recognised that nineteenth-century Sunday observance was intertwined with both spiritual and economic considerations. For instance, Sir Andrew Agnew MP (1793–1849) recognised
that Sunday working would overstock the labour market.[16] While the
Moderate Evangelicals supported sabbatarianism for this reason,
the Recordites were concerned that an ill-kept Sabbath day would
incur the 'special' wrath of God. Premillennial sabbatarians therefore
gave great prominence to railway accidents that happened on the
Sabbath and engaged in vigorous campaigns to persuade shopkeepers to desist from Sunday trading. It was this which caused

---

[13] Wigley, *Victorian Sunday*, p. 28.
[14] Ibid., p. 28.
[15] Ibid., p. 30.
[16] Hilton, *Age of Atonement*, p. 209.

Donald Lewis to comment, 'It was thus the lot of the Record to hold high the sabbatarian standard during the 1830s.'[17] He further underlines the important link between sabbatarianism and evangelism, since many Evangelicals considered a well-kept Sabbath not only as a means of grace for Christians, but also a means of grace for the unbeliever.

Among early nineteenth-century Evangelicals the members of the Clapham Sect were by no means rigorous in their observance of Sunday. They were essentially men and women of the Enlightenment and as such they were flexible, tolerant and utilitarian. Sunday at Clapham was a day for God and the family. Apart from family prayers and two church services a Claphamite Sunday consisted of 'rational' recreations such as walking, reading and quiet games.

According to his contemporaries, Wilberforce 'delighted in the noisy exuberance of playing children' and he and his contemporaries had a very positive attitude to their Sundays. Wilberforce also advocated Sunday letter writing. He firmly believed that recreations were intended 'to refresh our exhausted, bodily and mental powers and restore us with renewed vigour'. In the best-selling book, *A Practical View*, Wilberforce advocated a moderate attitude to the Sabbath.[18] He reiterated those views when he wrote in 1821, 'Often good people have been led by the terms of the fourth commandment to lay more stress on the strictness of the Sunday than on its spirituality.'[19]

Zachary Macaulay, another Clapham Sect member, kept open house on Sunday and his residence presented a cheerful outlook with many children happily engaged in playful activities. The ideal of the Clapham Sunday was the rural Puritan one in which the parish gathered round its squire. Domestic servants were encouraged to go to their own services and were given time to rest. The atmosphere was relaxed but regulated.

In later years, however, Hannah More, whose educational and social work in the Mendips was endorsed and supported by the Clapham fraternity, adopted a strict sabbatarian dimension to her Sunday. She devoted the day to prayer and serious reading. When

---

[17] Lewis, *Lighten Their Darkness*, p. 233.

[18] W. Wilberforce, *A Practical View of the Prevailing Religious System of Professed Christians in the Higher and Middle Classes in this Country Contrasted with Real Christianity*, pp. 76–80.

[19] R.I. Wilberforce and S. Wilberforce, *The Correspondence of William Wilberforce* Vol. 2, pp. 451–2, cited by Wigley, *Victorian Sunday*, p. 29.

inclement weather prevented her going on the rounds of her Sunday schools, she tried to occupy the time in such a way that not a moment was wasted. She wrote: 'I have seldom a Sabbath to spend on myself. Let me not trifle away this precious opportunity but pass it in extraordinary prayer, reading and meditation. Enable me to make conversation one of my pious exercises.'[20]

Another who had associations with the Clapham Sect and who was related to Wilberforce was John Bird Sumner. In his *Treatise on the Records of Creation*, which was first published in 1818, he argued that the main difference between the heathen and Christian nations is the 'reverence and due observance of a Sabbath'.[21] 'England as a nation', he wrote, 'stands or falls on its keeping of Sunday ... civil society is contained and held together by the Sabbath.'[22]

Daniel Wilson and the Lord's Day Observance Society

During the autumn of 1827 Daniel Wilson, Vicar of Islington and later Bishop of Calcutta, preached a series of three sermons on the Lord's Day. The sermons were later published as a book in 1831 under the title *The Divine Authority and Perpetual Obligation of the Lord's Day*.[23] In the third sermon, Wilson argued that the Lord 'never violated the Mosaic enactments, but honoured them in His whole ministry, and left the Sabbath in its full force'. Wilson did, however, point out that the Jewish Sabbath with its particular animal sacrifices was no more in force. After the resurrection, he declared, even 'the Mosaic covenant "decayed and waxed old, and vanished away"', and 'the Evangelical covenant took its place'.[24] The primary essential law of this new covenant is 'one day's religious rest, after six days' labour'.[25] In the sixth sermon, Wilson set out 'the unspeakable importance of a right observation of the Lord's Day, with the evils of the opposite abuse'.[26] On a very

---

[20] W. Roberts, *Memoirs of the Life and Correspondence of Mrs Hannah More* Vol. 2, p. 421, cited by J. Gordon, *Evangelical Spirituality*, p. 11.
[21] J.B. Sumner, *Creation*, cited by Scotland, *John Bird Sumner*, p. 101.
[22] Ibid., p. 101.
[23] D. Wilson, *The Divine Authority and Perpetual Obligation of the Lord's Day*.
[24] Ibid., p. 81.
[25] Ibid., p. 81.
[26] Ibid., p. 166.

practical note, he reiterated the fact that the Lord's Day was not only a day of duty and rest 'but the restoring, the awakening day – the day of recovery and reformation'.[27] 'Man', he urged, 'was created for six days work not seven.'[28] As John Bird Sumner had done before him, so Wilson pointed out that the main difference between heathen and Christian nations 'is the recurrence and due observation of a Sabbath'.[29] The violation of this day is 'a brand on the forehead of nominal religion'. Wilson was specific as to the nature of that violation:

> See the Sabbath-breaker opening his shop, writing his letters, preparing his accounts; see him entering his office; see him imposing upon his servants, his clerks, his dependants, the yoke of unpermitted and unholy labour. Observe him in languid carelessness, idling away the morning hours, and disgracing, by excess and worldly company, the evening.[30]

Wilson laid down rules for keeping the Sabbath on Sunday: only works of real necessity and mercy may be done;[31] there must be no letter writing, accounts, bargaining, payment of wages, luxurious meals, walking, riding or visits to pleasure gardens and 'the abominations of Sunday newspapers must be avoided'.[32]

Wilson's first three sermons inspired the people of his parish to found a Lord's Day Society during 1827. Then following the publication of his book he and his brother, Joseph, organised a meeting in the latter's residence near Clapham. A committee was formed with Joseph as Secretary and on 8 February 1831 the LDOS was formed. During the following month office space was taken up in the Exeter Hall, the Evangelicals' headquarters, and it was resolved to press for further legal measures to protect the institution of the Lord's Day. After a series of inquiries they persuaded the Scottish Whig MP Sir Andrew Agnew (1793–1849) to take up their cause in Parliament.

The first committee consisted of three clergymen and eighteen laity. The Rev Henry Blunt, the incumbent of Trinity Church, Sloane Street, was a prominent Evangelical pastor and preacher. The Rev Samuel Charles Wilkes was Rector of Nursling in

[27] Ibid., p. 171.
[28] Ibid., p. 171.
[29] Ibid., p. 173.
[30] Ibid., p. 173.
[31] Ibid., p. 150.
[32] Ibid., p. 152.

Hampshire from 1847 to 1872 and editor of the *Christian Observer* from 1816 to 1850.[33] The laity included Sir George Grey and Henry Maxwell but neither was able to give the society their substantial support. The membership of the LDOS, which was on the basis of an annual subscription of 10s 6d, came largely from the middle classes, with only a smattering coming from the gentry and aristocracy. Among the bishops who gave their support to the society were George Davys (1780–1864), the Bishop of Peterborough from 1839 to 1864, Edward Grey (1782–1837), the Bishop of Hereford, and the brothers Charles Richard Sumner and John Bird Sumner. The latter in particular was an active supporter of the society and took the Chair of the Chester branch on a number of occasions during his episcopate. According to the *Chester Chronicle* of 21 February 1834, Sumner spoke of the incalculable blessing arising to man from due observance of the Sabbath. He went on to remark very favourably on the way in which the Sabbath was kept in the city. Passing through the streets a few Sabbaths ago, Sumner had observed with pleasure the great decorum generally manifested.[34]

The LDOS soon established auxiliaries across the country, most of which were organised by local Evangelical clergy without any permanent full-time officers. The majority of these outposts were located in the south of England where their membership included members of the professions and some gentry. Their three strongest local branches were Bath, Derby and York, all of which attracted added support for their opposition to Sunday rail travel. Another well-supported auxiliary was Cheltenham whose ebullient rector, Francis Close, proved himself to be an ardent sabbatarian and opponent of excursion trains on the Lord's Day. Sir Andrew Agnew was strongly of the opinion that the area societies had a particular role to play in bringing pressure to bear on their local MPs. In Bath for example, the LDOS branch was particularly strong and made its influence felt in the local press. During the election campaign of 1837 the *Bath Chronicle* laid bare J.A. Roebuck's anti-sabbatarian views with the result that he came bottom of the poll with only 900 votes.[35] In the 1847 election at Bath the local LDOS secretary spoke on behalf of Anthony Ashley who was contesting the seat and at about the same time the city's auxiliary hired a local policeman

---

[33] For Samuel Charles Wilkes see Reynolds, *Evangelicals at Oxford*, p. 83.

[34] See Scotland, *John Bird Sumner*, pp. 101–2.

[35] *Bath Chronicle* 20 July 1837, cited by Wigley, *Victorian Sunday*, p. 49.

to keep a watch on the Lansdown revel which took place on a Sunday.[36]

By 1841 it had become clear that if the organisation was to significantly impact Government legislation, let alone the wider society, a full-time secretary was going to be needed. For this reason Joseph Wilson retired into the background and the committee employed the Rev J.T. Baylee following a recommendation from the Rev Hugh Stowell, the leader among the Evangelical clergy of Manchester 1828–1865.[37] Much of Baylee's early work was concerned with the issues connected to the growing network of railways and the increasing volume of Sunday traffic. It soon became clear to him and to others that a number of the railway companies respected their principles. The Liverpool and Manchester railway ran only a reduced Sunday service and devised an arrangement that enabled sabbatarian shareholders, if they so wished, to donate to charitable causes that part of their dividend which derived from Sunday trains. In the second half of the century the LDOS focused its energies against the Post Office transmitting Sunday mail and issues relating to the opening of museums and places of amusement.

As the Victorian era progressed a number of smaller sabbatarian societies came into being with more confined local objectives. In 1857 The Cab and Omnibus Men's Sunday Rest Association was set up with the objective of reducing Sunday working hours. However, its practice of giving out Bibles at the meetings failed to gain the support of the men and the society closed down in 1866.[38] In the early summer of 1858 Bishop Archibald Tait of London and Bishop Charles Sumner of Winchester brought together a number of prominent Anglican clergymen and laymen and founded The Metropolitan Rest Association. Sixteen bishops proffered their support as vice-presidents and a number of prominent Evangelical clergy became members. Among them were William Cadman, Rector of St George's Southwark, William Champneys (1807–1875) and Thomas Dale.[39] However, it was the LDOS that continued to make the most significant impact in the later Victorian years. In 1895 its general secretary, Frederick Peake, was still contending for a strict sabbatarianism when he told the House of Lords' Select Committee:

---

[36] Ibid., p. 57.
[37] Reynolds, *Evangelicals at Oxford*, p. 91.
[38] Wigley, *Victorian Sunday*, p. 110.
[39] Ibid., p. 110.

Anything [on Sundays] that is not distinctly religious is wrong ...
We should hardly make it purely a question of 'rest'. We ... seek the
religious observance of the Lord's Day as the primary thing, and the
question of human rest ... as a secondary matter arising out of that.[40]

Key Sabbatarian Issues

Sabbatarians believed that it was not only work but also Sunday
amusements that would destroy the sanctity of the Sabbath. They
therefore gave themselves to fighting on both fronts. Their hand
was strengthened by a series of 'essay competitions' in which
individuals were invited to write essays on the advantage of Sabbath
observance. In 1847 John Henderson, a Glasgow Merchant, invited
members of the working classes to write essays on the benefits
of keeping Sunday according to the provisions of the fourth
commandment. In 1848 Lord Ashley adopted Henderson's idea in
an English context when he established the Albertian Essays. They
were so called because he had persuaded Prince Albert to donate
£50 in prize money. The EA, the Religious Tract Society and a
Leicester sabbatarian group set up other similar competitions. The
prize-winning entries from these organisations were published and
did much to foster interest in the campaign. Queen Victoria, it
should be noted, although she never missed divine worship, happily
spent the rest of the day as she pleased. She travelled by train on
Sundays, rode out with Prince Albert in her carriage and attended
race meetings. The Earl of Shaftesbury went through great agonies
of conscience one day in 1841 when the Queen invited him to go
with her to a Sunday race meeting at Ascot. After much
heart-searching he decided he must accept her offer and prayed that
his time with her 'may not be productive of any mischief to the slight
influence I may have in the world for carrying forward measures
and designs of good to mankind'.[41]

Sunday trading

The prohibition of Sunday trading was obviously one of the crucial
concerns among sabbatarians. Indeed it was an object which they

---

[40] First Select Committee of the House of Lords, *Lord's Day Act*, 100,
128–9, cited by Wigley, *Victorian Sunday*, p. 153.
[41] G.W.E. Russell, *A Short History of the Evangelical Movement*, p. 133.

shared with the Chartists and other radical groups. With backing from the LDOS, Sir Andrew Agnew had brought forward legislation to prohibit shopkeepers from opening on Sunday. The Bill, which he introduced in 1833, 1834 and 1836, included stringent fines for those who broke the law. It was however defeated on all three occasions and still failed, though in a slightly revised form, in 1837. Daniel Wilson in his sixth sermon pointed out that Scripture was clear that 'man was enjoined to work for six days, not seven: his faculties cannot bear an unremitted strain'. 'The six days, if given up to religious acts, would be idleness, superstition and tempting of God,' he wrote, but 'the seventh, if not dedicated to them, is impiety, pride, and contempt of the Almighty'.[42]

Francis Close had strong views on the Sabbath which he believed to be 'really beneficial to man, suited to his necessities, adapted to his wants, calculated to sooth his sorrows and is highly conducive to his present peace and enjoyment'.[43] Close was therefore a strong objector to the shops remaining open on Sundays and formed a Sabbath committee that succeeded in persuading almost all the town's 400 shopkeepers to cease from trading on the Lord's Day. In 1855 Lord Grosvenor introduced a Sunday Trading Bill and its prospect of success caused large-scale demonstrations on three successive Sundays in Hyde Park. Its provisions hit the working classes particularly hard since they were often paid too late on a Saturday and would have no hope of buying food until Monday. The meeting on 23 June had to be broken up by the police.

Sunday drinking

Integrally related to the issue of Sunday trading was the issue of Sunday drinking. The Vice Society reduced the incidence of drunkenness considerably when they persuaded employers to alter their practice of paying wages in public houses on Saturday evenings. In 1830 Evangelical peers in the House of Lords secured an amendment to the Beer Act.[44] This ensured that public houses would remain closed during the times of Sunday worship. The provisions of the legislation required beer houses to restrict their hours to 1.00 p.m. to 3.00 p.m. and 5.00 p.m. to 10.00 p.m. Clergy were not only concerned about drinking but also with the recreational activities

---

[42] Wilson, *Divine Authority*, pp. 172, 187.
[43] *Cheltenham Journal*, 15 January 1844.
[44] Bradley, *Call to Seriousness*, p. 101.

that were associated with beer shops. These included gambling and cruel sports. In fact, sabbatarians were somewhat dilatory in curtailing drinking on Sundays.[45] In part, this may have been due to the fact that the water supply was impure in many of the country's large towns and cities.[46] Beer was seen as a safer alternative to polluted water at a time when cholera epidemics were not infrequent.[47] Indeed, it was not unusual for Evangelical Sunday schools to provide beer and cake for the youngsters at their parties. Additionally, Evangelical Anglicans were not generally teetotallers and did not therefore believe in the prohibition of alcoholic beverages. Significantly, Daniel Wilson appears not to have been against the drinking of beer. In his sermon on the 'National Guilt of Violating the Lord's Day' he bemoaned the fact that 'formerly decent alehouses' had been 'converted into spirit shops, with doors ever open to attract careless youth'.[48]

It is noteworthy that several prominent Evangelical families were engaged in brewing, among them T.F. Buxton and the Hanbury and Guinness families. Furthermore, many Evangelical MPs were behind measures to lift the restrictions on the beer trade in the hope that it would diminish the trade in spirituous liquor. In 1854 J.T. Baylee told the Commons Select Committee on Public Houses, 'I am not a teetotaller and I do not think that it [alcoholic drink] is in itself wrong.'[49] Likewise, Edward Bickersteth when Bishop of Exeter spoke of intemperance as 'a national abscess' but at the same time recognised that the public house 'is necessary for the comfort, recreation and social intercourse of the people'. In view of this he contended that 'reform, rather than abolition must be the aim of a sound temperance policy'.[50]

As the century progressed there was a growing move among some Evangelical Anglicans in favour of both temperance and teetotalism; clergymen such as Francis Close and Alfred Christopher spoke out strongly in favour of abstinence. The latter produced

---

[45] Harrison, *Drink and the Victorians*, p. 81.

[46] Ibid., p. 291.

[47] There were major cholera outbreaks in 1831, 1848–1849, 1855; see L.C.B. Seaman, *Victorian England*, pp. 50–1.

[48] Wilson, *Divine Authority*, p. 196.

[49] *Parliamentary Papers*, 1854, XIV, Report of the House of Commons Select Committee on Public Houses, Sections 6, 7 and 18, cited by Wigley, *Victorian Sunday*, p. 87.

[50] Algionby, *Edward Henry Bickersteth*, p. 76.

some cogent arguments for prohibition. He reprinted a letter to *The Times* from forty-seven publicans in support of Sunday closing. He also drew attention to the fact that in 1854–55 there were more people in the drink shops of the parish of St Mary-le-bone in the city of London than there were in all the churches.[51] It was against this background that the Tory MP, Colonel Wilson Patten, managed to secure the rapid passage of His bill through both Houses to restrict Sunday drinking hours from 1.00 p.m. to 2.00 p.m. and 6.00 p.m. to 10.00 p.m.[52] Wilson Patten's success was short-lived when Sunday trading riots followed in 1855. This resulted in the Radicals overturning his legislation and replacing it with an Act which increased the hours of Sunday drinking from 1.00 p.m. to 3.00 p.m. and 5.00 p.m. to 11.00 p.m.[53] After 1855 the will to further restrict Sunday drinking was gone. Many Evangelicals were of the opinion that it would not only be counter-productive but bring the law into disrepute.

Sunday mail delivery

Lord Shaftesbury was an influential and respected figure because of his humanitarian concerns. In the matter of Sunday observance he was more willing to work behind the scenes. But in 1850 the LDOS did succeed in persuading him to speak in the House of Commons against the collection and delivery of Sunday mail. On 30 May he defeated Lord John Russell's Whig government on the matter. His advocacy had been helped by the fact that each member had previously received a bound copy of the *Albertian Essays* which had been triggered by the same controversy. Shaftesbury was strongly of the view that sabbatarian legislation would benefit the poor and the working classes. Not everyone shared his views, which made him unpopular in some quarters. The stoppage of Sunday mail pleased Post Office workers but was resented as an inconvenience by many with the result that Parliament reversed the legislation after only a short period.[54] Among Evangelical Clergy who opposed Sunday postal services were John Cale Miller, a prominent Birmingham Evangelical, who was

---

[51] J.S. Reynolds, *Canon Christopher of St Aldate's, Oxford*, p. 142.
[52] Wigley, *Victorian Sunday*, p. 86.
[53] Ibid., p. 87.
[54] I. Rennie, *Evangelicalism and English Public Life 1823–1850*, cited by Lewis, *Lighten Their Darkness*, p. 233.

incumbent of St Martin's Church, and Henry Venn Elliott, the incumbent of St Mary's, Brighton.[55]

Sunday rail travel

Railway travel was extremely hazardous in the early days of the industry and there were a number of serious crashes. However, by the later 1840s rapidly improving technology was ensuring much greater safety and rail companies began to see the possibilities of increased income from Sunday travel. As far as sabbatarians were concerned this was a clear infringement of the fourth commandment. The battle began in earnest in 1850 when the Great Western began a series of cheap Sunday excursions out of London. By 1854 other companies followed suit, among them the Blackwall, the Tilbury and Southend, the South Western and the Brighton Companies. In 1858 a Captain Young stood out at a meeting of the latter company to try to prevent them from running Sunday excursion trains. The directors took the view that their task was solely a financial one and that matters of religious concern were not part of the remit of a business meeting. However, in Venn Elliott they had a doughty opponent. On the occasion of a terrible accident at the Clayton tunnel, on the Brighton line, Elliott and others remonstrated with the company's directors. He preached a sermon on the matter to his congregation which was based on the Lord's comments on the collapse of the Tower of Siloam. He drew up a strong memorial that was signed by eighty-three clergy resident in the town and 5,000 laity. It was more than eighty feet long and its prayer was 'that excursion trains might be transferred from the Sunday to a weekday'.[56] Sir Andrew Agnew tried another tack in his efforts to curtail Sunday excursion trains in Scotland. He simply bought up sufficient shares in Scottish railway companies to be able to vote down the directors' plans to run Sunday trains.[57]

Francis Close of Cheltenham was another staunch opponent of Sunday rail travel. He made a direct approach to Hudson, 'the railway king', and for six years his efforts prevented the age of steam interrupting the town. It seemed, however, that part of the reason for this vehement opposition to Sunday rail travel was that the working classes of Birmingham would journey to Cheltenham

---

[55] J. Bateman, *The Life of the Rev Henry Venn Elliott*, p. 225.

[56] Ibid., p. 225.

[57] Bradley, *Call to Seriousness*, p. 104.

and pollute the atmosphere of the town. Close said 'if they wanted fresh air a 6d bus ride was quite sufficient to air them, and once in the country they cooled themselves by large potations of porter and liquor. That suited them better than paying four or five shillings for a ride to Cheltenham to drink its salt waters.'[58]

Close also concerned himself with the proposal to build the new St James' station in St George's Place. He realised it would be convenient for many town's people but it was in danger of disturbing the parish on Sundays. Close was adamant that 'the great bulk of our townspeople have no wish or inclination to travel on the Lord's Day. Then why should we have the bubbling, hissing, roaring, bellowing monster coming within a few yards of our parish church and interrupting our devotion?'[59]

The campaign against Sunday trains continued on into the second half of the century with the LDOS setting up the Central Committee for Securing the Cessation of Sunday Excursion Trains. Its Dover branch typified the activities of other local auxiliaries in its extended debate with the South Eastern Railway's cheap Sunday excursion trains. The issue ultimately was one of supply and demand as Anthony Trollope made clear in his novel, *Barchester Towers*. On his arrival at Barchester, Obadiah Slope, the Bishop's Evangelical chaplain, expressed his fear that there was a great amount of Sunday travelling with three trains in and out of the city every Sabbath. 'Could nothing be done to induce the company to withdraw them?' he remarked. To which Dr Grantley replied, 'If you can withdraw the passengers, the company, I dare say, will withdraw the trains.'[60]

Places of entertainment

Sabbatarians were quick to point out that European nations such as France, Spain and Italy, which neglected the Sabbath, had for that reason been the victims of revolution and bloodshed. When therefore the Great Exhibition of 1851 was kept firmly closed on Sundays, sabbatarians were convinced that it was heralded as a sign of God's favour on the nation. It should be noted however that Evangelicals had caused considerable backlash to their vigorous

---

[58] *Cheltenham Journal*, 15 January 1844.
[59] Cited by O. Ashton, 'Clerical Control and Radical Responses in Cheltenham', *Midland History* Vol. VIII (1983), p. 124.
[60] A. Trollope, *Barchester Towers*, pp. 34–5.

demands for fig leaves to be placed over the genitalia of the Exhibition's nude statues. Early in 1852, however, the Crystal Palace was moved to Sydenham and the controlling company decided to open the building to the public on Sunday afternoons. Five people visited Lord Derby, the Prime Minister. They were John Bird Sumner (Archbishop of Canterbury), Charles Sumner (Bishop of Winchester), Charles Blomfield (Bishop of London), Lord Shaftesbury and Sir Robert Inglis. Their remonstrations marked the start of a public debate in which concern was voiced that the Queen was transgressing God's laws. When the directors acceded to the request for closure and expressed their willingness to attempt to find a sufficient supply of fig leaves, Evangelical spirits were quickly raised. Their success gave impetus for further restrictions on Sunday leisure and entertainment.

In 1856 Shaftesbury and Sumner persuaded Lord Palmerston to order the Sunday closure of the British Museum and the National Gallery.[61] Sir Joshua Wellesley, the radical MP, was incensed by this restriction and put down a motion in the House of Commons to open both places after morning services[62] but his proposal was overwhelmingly defeated by 328 votes to 48.[63] This after *The Record* had described the proposal as 'a more portentous calamity to England, and a greater blow to her greatness, than if her army had actually perished to a man on the shores of the Crimea'.[64]

Strengthened by this success the Evangelicals turned their attention to the question of military bands giving Sunday concerts in London's parks. Lord Palmerston, who was not a strict sabbatarian, had allowed Sir Benjamin Hall, the Commissioner of Works, to organise for the Horse Guards band to play in Kensington Gardens and the Band of the Second Life Guards in Regent's Park and another military band in Victoria Park. Such was their popularity that it was reckoned that 140,000 people had gathered in the parks on Sunday 4 May 1856 to hear the bands. On the Sunday following, 250,000 listened to martial music.[65] Sabbatarians were deeply concerned that bandsmen were being made to do extra work beyond the call of military duties, and that on a Sunday. Lord Shaftesbury therefore persuaded Archbishop Sumner to write a

---

[61] Bradley, *Call to Seriousness*, p. 105.
[62] Lewis, *Lighten Their Darkness*, p. 236.
[63] Chadwick, *Victorian Church* Part 1, p. 465.
[64] Lewis, *Lighten Their Darkness*, p. 236.
[65] Chadwick, *Victorian Church* Part 1, p. 466.

letter to the Prime Minister urging him to bring the concerts to an end. Somewhat surprisingly Palmerston complied and told the House of Commons that he had yielded to the Primate's request. Palmerston wrote to Sumner that although he thought the bands would 'afford the inhabitants of the metropolis innocent recreation combined with fresh air', he had received 'representations from other quarters' which had caused him to 'look upon the matter from a different point of view'. 'I shall', he continued, 'take steps for the discontinuing of the Band playing in Kensington Gardens and in the parks on Sundays'. Behind the scenes it was rumoured that the Scottish members were intent on bringing the Government down had he not bowed to Sumner's letter.[66]

The sabbatarians kept up the pressure against the Sunday opening of the British Museum, although with diminishing support, until the end of the century. Gradually, with growing numbers of provincial libraries and museums open, the pressure grew on members of both Houses of Parliament to follow suit. Edward Bickersteth of Exeter spoke against opening in 1894 declaring that if the established church condoned it, working people would move their allegiance to the free churches. Notwithstanding his urgent pleas the feeling in both Houses was moving in the opposite direction. On 10 March 1896 the Tory Member for Finsbury Central put down a motion to allow national museums and galleries to open on Sunday afternoons with the proviso that no staff worked for more than six days in any one week. The bill was carried with a majority of 178 votes to 93.[67]

Prominent Sabbatarians

Throughout the nineteenth century the campaign in support of Sunday observance had been well supported by a sizeable number of Evangelical Anglican clergy and laity. Indeed, Wigley has shown that it was the Evangelical sector within the established church which proved to be the most significant influence.[68] He acknowledged that sabbatarianism was strong in rural areas, but observed that its most active supporters were to be found among

---

[66] Lord Palmerston to Archbishop Sumner 10 May 1856, *Broadlands Papers* Ms GC/CA/319.
[67] Wigley, *Victorian Sunday*, pp. 146–7.
[68] Ibid., p. 182.

the respectable middle class of the small towns in the south of England.[69] Owen Chadwick agreed that the leaders of the movement were Evangelicals of the Church of England, but pointed out that their power rested on a wider constituency which consisted of Wesleyans, Baptists and other free church members.[70] The campaign for a godly Sunday was, as he asserted, a part of what became known as the Nonconformist Conscience.[71]

Prominent among the later Evangelical Anglican leaders of the movement to honour the Sabbath day were the Seventh Earl of Shaftesbury, Archbishop Sumner and Bishops Edward Bickersteth and John Charles Ryle. Shaftesbury believed that England's laws should be made to conform to the laws of God. For this reason he campaigned in Parliament for the proper religious observance of Sunday. Edwin Hodder wrote of him:

> In defence of the Christian Sabbath – its claims, duties and privileges – Lord Ashley was, throughout his life, always on the alert. Any encroachment upon its sanctity, from whatever quarter, was sure to bring him to the front; any effort to guard and honour it was equally sure of his co-operation and support.[72]

In addition to his opposition to Sunday trading and Sunday postal deliveries and bands in the parks, Shaftesbury was president of both the LDOS and the Working Men's Lord's Day Rest Association.[73] In his addresses at the annual meetings of these two organisations Shaftesbury spoke of the rights, duties and privileges of the Sabbath in relation to social, domestic, political and religious life.[74] His one great fear was that the English Sunday might become like that in France. He wrote in his diary for 23 September 1855: 'The stir in

---

[69] Ibid., p. 182.

[70] Chadwick, *Victorian Church* Part 2, p. 464.

[71] Ibid., p. 464 The following lines from the President's address to the Primitive Methodist Annual Conference of 1869 are indicative of the Nonconformist Conscience on Sunday Observance. 'Permit us to exhort you to hallow the Lord's Day. We deeply deplore the persistent and systematic efforts put forward to secularise the Sabbath, and by railway trips draw the artisan from his family and the house of God ... We earnestly and affectionately exhort all our members to honour the sanctity of this day and by both precept and example teach this duty to others'.

[72] Hodder, *Seventh Earl of Shaftesbury*, p. 419.

[73] See ibid., pp. 531f.

[74] Ibid., p. 531.

Paris on the Lord's Day is like the breaking of a mill dam ... It is terrible, painful, alarming to see a wholesale resolute national desecration of the Lord's Day.'[75] Although Shaftesbury's attitude appeared strict and confining, even to many of his contemporaries, he was, as Georgina Battiscombe pointed out, 'acting in what he believed to be interest of men, and especially the poor'.[76]

Sumner, like Shaftesbury, held strong views about Sunday. He was an active supporter of the LDOS from its inception. Along with the earlier Clapham Sect members, Sumner was convinced of the importance of achieving Sunday observance by Government legislation. Unlike them he was not apparently motivated by a fear of national judgement in the event of failure. Speaking at the National Annual General Meeting of the society held at Exeter Hall in May 1834, Sumner sought to counter those who argued against legislation.[77] People had urged that the poor would be the losers as a result of parliamentary action. Sumner contended on the contrary that 'the poor man would be the greater gainer by a measure which would prevent him from being forced to work on the Sabbath'.[78] Despite provoking a hostile reaction, he fought throughout his career in support of the legislative measures promoted by the LDOS. As has been noted, Sumner was one of those who successfully prevailed on Lord Palmerston to order the Sunday closure of the National Gallery and British Museum in 1856. In the same year, he also succeeded in stopping Sunday afternoon military band concerts in all London parks. In May 1860 he spoke forcibly in the House of Lords against widening the scope of Sunday trading in the debate on the Selling and Hawking Goods on Sunday Bill. He 'feared there would be great difficulty in dealing with certain branches of Sunday trading. If they permitted newspapers, for example, how were they to deal with periodicals?'[79]

Edward Bickersteth who had become Bishop of Exeter in 1885 had held strong views on respecting the Lord's Day since his childhood at Watton Rectory. He spoke out in convocation against resolutions that he felt would weaken the cause that he held so dear.[80] He was quite prepared to sanction works of necessity, works

---

[75] Cited in ibid., p. 532.
[76] Battiscombe, *Shaftesbury. A Biography*, p. 253.
[77] *The Record*, 5 May 1834.
[78] Ibid.
[79] *Hansard*, Volume CLVIII, 14 May 1860, p. 1198.
[80] Algionby, *Edward Henry Bickersteth*, p. 67.

of mercy and works of piety, but was strongly opposed to other unnecessary work and recreational activities. In his *Expository Commentary on the New Testament* which was published in 1864, he wrote:

> How unlike are these things to the frivolous dissipation, the merely secular instruction, the pleasurable excursion, the unhallowed buying and selling which men legalise and defend! It is, indeed, surface study of this [Matthew 12:1–8] and other passages, which imagines that Scripture tends to, and countenances, the desecration of God's day.[81]

Bishop Ryle wrote extensively on Sunday observance. He did not, however, enlist the support of the Early Church Fathers in his argument, as Wilson had earlier done, but instead used the Bible exclusively. He was a strict sabbatarian in that he believed that the fourth commandment was enduring. He pointed out that 'the observance of a Sabbath Day is part of the eternal law of God. It is not a mere temporary Jewish ordinance.'[82] Again, he stressed, 'I cannot find a syllable' in the writings of the Apostles, 'which teaches that any one of the Ten Commandments is done away'.[83] Ryle was adamant that the coming of Christ's gospel 'did not alter the position of the Ten Commandments one hair's breadth'.[84] He professed himself unable to find 'clear evidence that the Old Testament Sabbath was intended by Moses to be more strictly kept than the Christian Sabbath'.[85] He spoke in uncompromising and specific terms about the desecration of Sunday:

> When I speak of public desecration of the Sabbath, I mean those many open, unblushing practices, which meet the eye on Sundays in the neighbourhood of large towns. I refer to the practice of keeping shops open, and buying and selling on Sundays. I refer especially to Sunday trains on railways, Sunday steamboats, and excursions to tea gardens and places of public amusement; and especially I refer to the daring efforts which many are making in the present day, to throw open such places as the British Museum, the National Gallery, and the Crystal Palace on Sundays, and to have bands playing in the public parks.

---

[81] Ibid., p. 131.
[82] Ryle, *Knots Untied*, p. 300.
[83] Ibid., p. 302.
[84] Ibid., p. 305.
[85] Ibid., p. 309.

On all these points I feel not the smallest doubt in my own mind. These ways of spending the Sabbath are all wrong, decidedly wrong. So long as the Bible is the Bible, and the Fourth Commandment the Fourth Commandment, I dare not come to any other conclusion. They are all wrong.[86]

Ryle was prepared to countenance works of necessity or works of mercy on a Sunday. But he wrote, 'To heal a sick person, or pull an ox or an ass out of a pit, is one thing: to travel in an excursion train, or visit picture galleries, is quite another.' 'What soul', he continued, 'was ever converted by tearing down to Brighton, or dashing down to Gravesend? What heart was ever softened or brought to repentance by gazing at Titians and Vandykes?'[87] Ryle did, however, countenance 'the employment of horses to take us to church on the Sabbath ... where it is a case of plain necessity and without the use of them the gospel cannot be heard'.[88]

The Rise and Fall of the Victorian Sunday

The popularity of sabbatarianism in mid-Victorian times was for a variety of reasons. It tapped into a long tradition of Sunday observance. It held particular appeal to a growing middle-class who were searching for stability and it fitted with the desire for an ordered life and a desire for respectability. Furthermore, it meshed with a straightforward and literal interpretation of the Old and New Testaments in a way that Evangelicals approved of and were familiar with. Many of their number were also motivated to campaign because they genuinely feared national and personal judgement if they allowed the British Sunday to lapse into the libertinism of continental Europe.

The peak of sabbatarian influence was probably the 1840s and 1850s. Significantly, this was also the high point of Evangelical influence. It was against this background that Dickens wrote his novel, *Little Dorrit*, which was published in 1855. His description of Sunday evenings in London represented them as depressing affairs:

---

[86] Ibid., p. 314.
[87] Ibid., p. 35.
[88] Ibid., p. 311.

Everything was bolted and barred that could by possibility furnish relief to an overworked people. No picture. No natural or artificial wonders of the ancient – all taboo ... Nothing to see but streets, streets, streets. Nothing to breathe but streets, streets, streets. Nothing for the spent toiler to do but to compare the monotony of his six days with the monotony of his seventh.[89]

There were a number of reasons for the decline of sabbatarianism in the later-Victorian years. The Rev James Augustus Hessey delivered the Bampton Lectures before the University of Oxford in 1880 and took as his subject 'Sunday: Its Origin, History and Present Obligation'. His approach, which was a non-legalistic, dominical theology, helped to loosen the stranglehold of conservative inter-pretation of Scripture. He taught that the legalistic approach to Sunday had been derived from the Roman Church, the Puritans and the Scottish Presbyterians. The Reformer, Martin Bucer, had asserted that thinking of work on Sunday as a sin was a denial of grace. Furthermore, the Government had a duty to promote, so far as it was able, the welfare of its people in conformity with Christian principles. Open spaces and parks should therefore be offered to the poor and public transport provided for them. Although Hessey did not want to see the religious character of Sunday disappear he was against the state trying to restrict Sunday leisure activities by legisla-tive means. In summary he quoted, 'Let no one judge us in respect of Sabbath days' (Colossians 2:16).[90]

Samuel Wilberforce, whose father had exhorted him when an undergraduate 'not to hold Sunday breakfast parties',[91] proved to be more liberal when he was Bishop of Oxford.[92] While he wanted to keep the religious atmosphere of Sunday, thinking it wise not to open museums and places of entertainment on that day, he worried less over rigorous attitudes which might cause a reaction which would loosen the influence of Sunday in a decisive way.

Liberal theologians and broad churchmen were much more concerned with Sunday as a day for rest, relaxation and as even, in some cases, a feast day. In 1852 Charles Kingsley wrote to George Grove that 'Sunday is a feast-day, so every Englishman should be

[89] C. Dickens, *Little Dorrit*, chapter 3.
[90] J.A. Hessey, *Sunday: Its Origin, History and Present Obligation*, pp. 243–8.
[91] Bradley, *Call to Seriousness*, p. 190.
[92] Wilberforce, *Life and Letters* Vol. 1, p. 378.

invited to refresh himself with the sight of the wonders of God's earth or men's art'.[93] Four years later he wrote to Frederick Denison Maurice, 'I feel with you that the only ground on which Sunday amusements can be defended is as a carrying over of the divineness of the Sabbath and not as a relaxation of it.'[94]

By the closing decades of the century both society and the church's attitude were changing. Working men now had the vote and the political parties could not afford to ignore their views on the matter, particularly in the large towns and cities. There were also changes in attitude among the churches. Early morning communion services in ritualist places of worship were leaving attendees with the whole day free. Wesleyan Methodism, driven by the influences of Hugh Price Hughes' Forward Movement, was becoming more socially concerned and more aware of the needs of the poor in the large towns and cities. Thus their support for the sabbatarian agenda was no longer what it had been in Jabez Bunting's day. The influence of the churches as a whole had begun to decline in the last quarter of the century. Evangelicals, and particularly Evangelical Anglicans, were beginning to withdraw from the political arena, predominantly as a result of the growing influence of holiness and Keswick spiritualities. Yet others were recognising that the working poor who laboured in confined conditions in the mine or on the factory floor needed open space, relaxation and entertainment on Sundays. These changes, coupled with the fact that the older generation of the LDOS supporters were either dead or aging, resulted in the decline of the once all pervading sabbatarian Sunday. Thus the Evangelical Handley Moule, who became Bishop of Durham in 1901, wrote in that year that 'the calming, deepening power of the well-kept Lord's Day is a waning thing in too many Evangelical families'.[95]

---

[93] F. Kingsley, *Charles Kingsley: His Letters and Memories of His Life* (popular edition), p. 139.
[94] F. Kingsley, *Charles Kingsley: His Letters and Memories of His Life* Vol. 1, pp. 277–8.
[95] Moule, *Evangelical School*, pp. 244f.

9

Culture and Evangelical Anglicans

There has been a good deal of scholarly interest in recent years in the relationship between Evangelicalism and the wider culture it emerged from. David Bebbington examined the impact of the Enlightenment, Romanticism and Modernism on the culture and theology of Evangelicals.[1] In *The Call to Seriousness* Ian Bradley addressed issues of leisure and lifestyle, and highlighted the other-worldly attitude to pleasure and pastimes adopted by many Victorian Evangelicals.[2] Doreen Rosman sought to compare the attitudes of Evangelicals and their contemporaries towards developments in the arts, amusements, fashions and thinking between 1790 and 1833.[3] John Wolffe, in a lengthy piece, examined the interaction of religion and culture. In particular, he illustrated what he termed as 'the seamless intermingling of religion, art and patriotism'.[4] Both Bebbington and Rosman sought to redress an earlier imbalance which had tended to portray Evangelicalism as 'philistine' and representing a rebellion against the major movements of nineteenth-century England.

What is Culture?

The term culture has been taken to designate many things. Among scholars there is no universal agreement as to its meaning. In *Culture*

---

[1] Bebbington, *Evangelicalism in Modern Britain*, pp. 57–8, 80–1, 84–5, 233–5, et passim.

[2] Bradley, *Call to Seriousness*, pp. 21–33, et passim.

[3] D. Rosman, *Evangelicals and Culture*.

[4] J. Wolffe, *God and Greater Britain: Religion and National Life in Britain and Ireland 1843–1945*, p. 187. See also pp. 159–212 where Wolffe discusses culture and belief.

and Society Raymond Williams traced the development of the word and noted that its literal meaning is 'tending to natural growth'.[5] From this it came by analogy to be used of 'a process of human training'.[6] This latter use then changed in the nineteenth century when culture came to be regarded as 'a thing in itself' rather than a process.[7] Williams charted this development in the following paragraph:

> It came to mean, first, 'a general state of the mind', having close relations with the idea of human perfection. Second, it came to mean 'the general state of intellectual development in a society as a whole'. Third, it came to mean 'the general body of the arts'. Fourth, later in the century, it came to mean 'a whole way of life, material, intellectual and spiritual'.[8]

For Williams culture was more than mere aesthetics or literary accomplishment; it embraced 'all sides of our humanity'.[9] Williams did not regard culture as an objective absolute. Rather it is an ongoing process. In this he followed the thinking of Matthew Arnold's (1822–1888) *Culture and Anarchy*, which was first published in 1869. Arnold wrote that culture is 'a pursuit of our total perfection by means of getting to know, on all matters which concern us, the best which has been thought and said in the world'.[10] For Arnold culture is the 'best self of men' but always emerging and developing, never reaching finality. His view of culture, which was essentially subjective, therefore contrasted with that of John Henry Newman who saw culture as containing 'an element of divine perfection'.[11]

Doreen Rosman offered a narrow and more confined understanding of culture. She regarded it as 'an umbrella term: its primary reference is to literary, aesthetic and intellectual interests, but it denotes too an inquisitive and affirmative attitude to life as a whole'.[12] Rosman's views resonate with what has sometimes been designated 'high culture'. One problem that this raises is that it is

---

[5] R. Williams, *Culture and Society*, p. xvi.

[6] Ibid., p. xvi.

[7] Ibid., p. xvi.

[8] Ibid., p. xvi.

[9] Ibid., p. 115.

[10] M. Arnold, *Culture and Anarchy* (1869), cited by Williams, *Culture and Society*, p. 115.

[11] Williams, *Culture and Society*, p. 127.

[12] Rosman, *Evangelicals and Culture*, p. 2.

value-laden and excludes working-class culture, which was by nature rarely devoted to the literary and intellectual. It was focused rather on a certain range of leisure and sporting activities. It also embraced the pubs, the penny papers and, in some cases, trade union philosophy, music, singing and aspects of folk religion.

This chapter attempts to adopt an understanding of culture which is more than mere middle and upper class intellectual, literary and artistic interests. It will also aim to embody something of the general social world of the nineteenth century and the way in which it interacted with Evangelical theology and lifestyle. It needs, of course, to be recognised that there were strong differences of opinion even among Evangelical Anglicans. Some, for example, held strongly to the view that this world was 'but the antechamber of the next'[13] and this caused them to seriously devalue secular activity. For example, Thomas Fowell Buxton wrote to a business acquaintance, 'the main purpose of our living here is to prepare for eternity'.[14] On the other hand, the missionary, Henry Martyn declared, 'Since I have known God in a saving manner, painting, poetry, and music have had charms unknown to me before. I have received what I suppose is a taste for them; for religion has refined my mind, and made it susceptible of impressions from the sublime and beautiful.'[15]

Clearly, therefore, there were often differences of opinion over particular issues when it came for example to Sunday activities or deciding what levels of nudity were acceptable in a particular painting or sculpture.

High Culture

Literature

Almost all the religious world, Evangelicals included, read poetry. Biographies make many references to Evangelicals who, even if they read little else, enjoyed poetry. However, at the heart of high culture, so-called, was the question of literature and the benefits or otherwise of reading novels. At the beginning of the nineteenth

---

[13] Ibid., p. 55.

[14] Buxton, *Memoirs*, p. 286, cited by Rosman, *Evangelicals and Culture*, p. 55.

[15] H. Martyn, *Diary*, cited by Russell, *Evangelical Movement*, p. 80.

century there was a frequently expressed hostility towards the novel in general. In 1800 the *Evangelical Magazine* placed 'love of novels' as 'among the most heinous of sins, more damning even than attendance at the theatre'.[16] In 1829 the *Eclectic Review* regarded novel reading as more damaging than poetry because 'the novelist relies more simply on the passion of curiosity for producing gratification, than the poet does who seeks to please by more refined means'.[17]

Early Evangelicals had a number of reasons against the reading of novels. Perhaps above all was the fact that many of them were written without any obvious moral aim. Some Evangelicals made the novels of Walter Scott the exception to their opposition, yet even he was criticised, on occasion, for a lack of morality.[18] William Wilberforce was among those Anglicans who did enjoy a good story. On one occasion he relaxed with a copy of *The Lady of the Lake*, but regretted that there was not 'much of a moral'.[19] Rosman makes the point that this criticism did not hold in the case of all Evangelicals and quotes magazines which deplored the pursuit of truth at any price while ignoring artistic impression. Among these, for example, were the *Christian Observer* whose editor reported on one occasion that he read *Roderick* with 'extraordinary pleasure' and that Southey was a 'true genius' who gave dignity and interest even to subject matter which was 'essentially and hopelessly fictitious'.[20]

Another reason for concern over novel reading was their light-hearted nature. The majority of Evangelicals were serious-minded and easy reading would, it was felt by some, detract from the possibility of more serious reading. This was doubtless in the back of William Wilberforce's mind when he wrote of *Peverill of the Peak*, 'this class of writing is too interesting: it makes other studies insipid, or rather light reading'.[21]

Evangelicals had further objections to novel reading. Among them were the plots and incidents and the way in which some of

---

[16] Rosman, *Evangelicals and Culture*, p. 183.
[17] *Eclectic Review* 1829, p. 162, cited by Rosman, *Evangelicals and Culture*, p. 185.
[18] Rosman, *Evangelicals and Culture*, p. 186.
[19] Ibid., p. 180.
[20] *Christian Observer* Volume IX, 1810, p. 367, and Volume XI, 1812, p. 384, cited by Rosman, *Evangelicals and Culture*, p. 180.
[21] R.I. Wilberforce and S. Wilberforce, *Life of William Wilberforce*, pp. 268–70, cited by Rosman, *Evangelicals and Culture*, p. 188.

them recounted the growth of religious doubt, particularly among the lower classes but also in the thinking of many clergy. Rosman investigated a number of Evangelical magazines to show that the Evangelical ideal was for a novel rather than for an involved and absorbing plot.

There were also a certain number of Evangelicals, Anglicans among them, who felt that there were better ways to be passing one's time. In short, this was no way for people who believed they would have to give account for every minute and every hour at the day of judgement to be spending their time. Too much living for pleasure meant that one's life would fail to be useful. The *Eclectic Review* wrote of the tradesmen and manufacturers, 'Their leisure hours are largely given to the maintenance of our philanthropic and religious societies ... they give their strength to business and public duties, not to books'.[22] Wilberforce once chided himself for giving his time to Scott's *Heart of Midlothian* which could have been better employed.[23] He believed Scott to be 'full of genius' but would have preferred to be found on judgement day reading Hannah More's little tract, *The Shepherd of Salisbury Plain*.

In the middle and later years of the nineteenth century some Evangelicals discouraged novel reading for the reasons that they began to give expression to the emergence of religious doubt. This was particularly so in the years after the publication of Charles Darwin's *Origin of Species* in 1859 and *Essays and Reviews* in 1860.

One of several Victorian novels that reflected the doubts felt by Evangelicals was Mrs Humphrey Ward's *Robert Elsmere*. The book was the most successful of its age. Published in 1888, 40,000 copies were sold in Britain and 100,000 in America within the space of a year. Elsmere is an Evangelical beset by doubt. Among his clerical neighbours is Mr Bickersteth, 'a gentle Evangelical, one of those men who help to ease the harshness of a cross-grained world, and to reconcile the cleverer or more impatient folk in it to the worries of living'.[24] Elsmere's doubts are compounded on account of Wendover, the squire of his parish, who had spent some time in Germany studying the works of Strauss, Baur and Ewald.[25] Among other things, Wendover is deeply sceptical concerning the historicity of Jesus' resurrection and of the events recounted in the prophecy of

---

[22] V. Cunningham, *Everywhere Spoken Against*, p. 54.
[23] Bradley, *Call to Seriousness*, p. 28.
[24] H. Ward, *Robert Elsmere*, chapter 17, p. 224.
[25] Ibid., chapter 14, p. 195.

Daniel.[26] Elsmere eventually returns to Oxford and discusses his growing anxieties and doubts with his former tutor.[27] In the end, Elsmere reaches the point where he can no longer accept the incarnation or the resurrection and 'miracle is a natural product of human feeling and imagination'.[28] All of this causes him to quit his parish and move to London where, among other projects, he set up a scientific Sunday school[29] and lectured to workingmen about 'the exquisite fable of the resurrection'.[30]

In Mrs Gaskell's *North and South*, which was first published in parts beginning in September 1854, Mr Hale, the Rector of Helstone, has doubts about the central tenets of the Christian faith. This causes him to recognise that 'he cannot conscientiously remain a priest of the Church of England and that he must give up Helstone'.[31] After twenty years of quiet parochial life the family move to Milton-Northern, a smoky manufacturing town. Here, not only do Hale's doubts continue to deepen, but he encounters widespread religious apathy on the part of the town's working classes. As one of their number expressed it to Hale,

> They're real folk. They don't believe I' the Bible – not they. They may say they do, for form's sake; but Lord, sir, d'ye think their first cri I' th' morning is, 'what shall i do to get hold on eternal life?' or 'what shall I do to fill my purse this blessed day? ... I ax your pardon, sir; yo'r a parson out o' work, I believe ... But I'll just ax yo' another question, sir ... If salvation, and life to come, and what not, was true – not in men's words, but in men's hearts' core – dun yo' not think they'd din us wi' it as they do wi' political 'conomy?[32]

George Eliot in *Scenes of Clerical Life*, which was first published in 1857, presents the reader with cameos of several Evangelical clergy. Amos Barton is a Simeonite who preaches extemporaneously at cottage meetings.[33] He is conscientious in his duties but not averse to pleasure. The story portrays his afflicted life, which includes an

---

[26] Ibid., chapter 24, p. 314.
[27] Ibid., chapter 27, p. 341.
[28] Ibid., chapter 28, p. 389.
[29] Ibid., chapter 38, p. 456.
[30] Ibid., chapter 40, p. 479.
[31] Mrs Gaskell, *North and South*, chapter 5, p. 78.
[32] Ibid., chapter 28, p. 289.
[33] G. Eliot, *Scenes of Clerical Life*, chapter 2, p. 25.

alleged scandal through to the death of his wife. The Rev Archibald Duke is represented as 'a very dyspeptic and evangelical man, who takes the gloomiest view of mankind and their prospects, and thinks the immense sale of the *Pickwick Papers*, recently completed, one of the strongest proofs of original sin'.[34] Later the book offers a more positive image of Evangelicalism in the account of Mr Tryan's powerful ministry at Milby.[35] Tryan is a teetotaller[36] with a heart for the poor who engages in social action as well as gospel preaching.[37] Yet he lives in a tasteless environment[38] with few luxuries and like many of his fellow Evangelicals he overworked.[39]

Among nineteenth-century novelists who present a harsher picture of Evangelicalism are Charlotte Brontë and Anthony Trollope. Charlotte and her literary sisters, Emily and Anne, were brought up at Haworth rectory. Their father, Patrick, was an austere Calvinist who found it hard to socialise. Their mother died while the children were still young with the result that they were brought up by their mother's sister, Aunt Branwell, who imposed her own strict and oppressive brand of Methodism on them. Aunt Branwell, it seems, succeeded in planting in the young, impressionable Charlotte a frightening sense of sin and dread of judgement, which may be reflected in her picture of Mr Brocklehurst as 'the dread judge'.[40] Charlotte's experience, along with her sisters, as a pupil in the Rev. William Carus Wilson's school for the daughters of clergy where she experienced hunger, hard discipline and a cruel environment led her to portray Mr Brocklehurst in a way that embodied all that she hated about the Evangelical religion of her day.

Brocklehurst was the vehicle which Charlotte used to expose the horrors of Evangelicalism. 'What a face he had', she wrote, 'what a great nose! And what a mouth! And what large prominent teeth!'[41] Following a misdemeanour, Brocklehurst asks Jane, 'Do you know where the wicked go after death?' 'They go to hell,' was her reply. 'And what is hell? Can you tell me that?' Jane's response was orthodox, 'A pit full of fire.' Brocklehurst went on to express his doubts

---

[34] Ibid., chapter 6, p. 46.
[35] Ibid., chapter 2, pp. 181–2.
[36] Ibid., chapter 3, p. 194.
[37] Ibid., chapter 10, p. 228.
[38] Ibid., chapter 11, p. 232.
[39] Ibid., chapter 11, p. 233.
[40] C. Brontë, *Jane Eyre*, chapter 7, p. 97.
[41] Ibid., chapter 4, p. 64.

as to whether Jane would go to heaven and he questioned her further about the regularity of her prayers and Bible reading.[42] Brocklehurst's utter hypocrisy is powerfully exposed when he commands Miss Temple to ensure that Julia Severn's curls are cut off. She protests that Julia's hair curls naturally to which he replied, 'Naturally, yes, but we are not to conform to nature'. Brocklehurst announces that he will send a barber tomorrow. Before their dialogue is completed the scene is disturbed by the arrival of three lady visitors and from under the brim of this graceful headdress of the two youngest there 'fell a profusion of light tresses, elaborately curled'. The elder lady was 'enveloped in a costly shawl' and she 'wore a false front of French curls'.[43] These ladies were deferentially received by Miss Temple, as Mrs and the Misses Brocklehurst. Charlotte Brontë's cameo of Brocklehurst is poignant. She describes him as 'this piece of architecture' and 'buttoned up in a surtout, and looking longer, narrower, and more rigid than ever'.[44] Elsewhere he is 'the black pillar'[45] and 'the black marble clergyman'.[46]

The portrait of St John Rivers at a later point in the book is less harsh and he emerges as a man in whom there is compassion and kindness despite his somewhat narrow horizons. Rivers is possibly a Simeonite since he has many friends in Cambridge.[47] He lives simply, conducts family prayers and is a devoted student of the Scriptures.

Clearly Brocklehurst is a crude characterisation and he cannot be made to represent the generality of Evangelical Anglican clergy. Doubtless there were some whose lives were harsh and judgemental, but there were many who were warm and compassionate and who gave themselves to the needs of their parishes and spent their lives in the service of the poor. One has only to think of men such as William Champneys, Montagu Villiers, Thomas Sutton, Lord Shaftesbury or Anthony Thorold to construct an altogether more favourable picture of Evangelical religion. That said, one can still readily understand why some critics were concerned that Charlotte's readers might be turned away from Evangelicalism. Charlotte's sister, Anne, whom she described as 'a very sincere and

---

[42] Ibid., chapter 4, p. 65.
[43] Ibid., chapter 7, p. 97.
[44] Ibid., chapter 7, p. 94.
[45] Ibid., chapter 4, p. 63.
[46] Ibid., chapter 7, p. 98.
[47] Ibid., chapter 34, p. 434.

practical Christian'[48] gives a warmer and more affectionate account of the Rev Weston in her novel *Agnes Grey*. 'The evangelical truth of his doctrine', as well as the 'earnest simplicity of his manner, and the clearness and force of his style were decidedly pleasing'.[49] Elsewhere he is depicted as a 'kindly visitor who impacted the lives of his parishioners in a very positive way'.[50]

Of all those novelists who were critical, indeed harsh in their picture of the Evangelical clergy of the state church, Anthony Trollope and, to a lesser extent, Frances, his mother, were the most severe. Anthony Trollope was a fairly high-ranking Post Office official, notable for having introduced the pillar box. He was a high churchman and was opposed to the Evangelical movement. The first chapter of *Barchester Towers* is a direct reference to the accession to power of Lord Palmerston and his appointment of nineteen English bishops, six Irish bishops and thirteen deans during his ten years premiership. In this, as has been noted, he was advised by Lord Shaftesbury.

Trollope was a prolific author and produced a total of forty-seven novels. Perhaps the most famous of these were the Barset series, which feature the city of Barchester with its bishop and Cathedral. Clergy also appear in his other books, sometimes as major characters, as for example in *The Vicar of Bullhampton* and *Dr Wortle's School* and sometimes as relatively minor ones, as for instance Mr Emilius in *Eustace Diamonds*. However, it is in the Barchester novels that Trollope's sharpest critique of the Evangelical world is most readily observable.

Here we are introduced to bishop and Mrs Proudie and the bishop's chaplain, Obadiah Slope. Dr Proudie is cast as mild, weak and ineffectual, and for those reasons his wife rules him. Her name is her mark in the sense that she is above all proud. She is also censorious, domineering, controlling, strict and a rigid sabbatarian. She possesses, in so far as Trollope understands it, not an ounce of Christian charity. Hers was a legalistic killjoy religion. In *The Last Chronicle of Barset*, Trollope caricatures her as follows:

Mrs Proudie always went to church on Sunday evenings, making a point of hearing three services and three sermons every Sunday of her life. On weekdays she seldom heard any, having an idea that weekday services

---

[48] C. Brontë, *Biographical Notice of Ellis and Acton Bell*, p. 55.
[49] A. Brontë, *Agnes Grey*, chapter 10, p. 139.
[50] See ibid., pp. 150–4.

were an invention of the high church enemy, and that they should therefore be discouraged. Services on saints' days she regarded as rank papacy, and had been known to accuse a clergyman's wife, to her face, of idolatry, because the poor lady had dated a letter, St John's Eve.[51]

Mrs Proudie's most fervent ally is Obadiah Slope. When he tries to assert his independence Slope is crushed by Mrs Proudie. Nevertheless, they share similar views, not least those concerning the Sabbath. But Slope is a hypocrite. At all times he tries to be smooth and to ingratiate himself particularly to those in positions of influence. In reality his religion is a sham. Slope pursues two women at the same time, Mrs Bold, the widowed daughter of the saintly Mr Harding, and 'Signora', the daughter of the Dean Dr Stanhope, whose marital status is uncertain, although thought to be one of estrangement. Trollope characterised Slope's religion in the harshest of terms:

> In doctrine, he, like his patron [Mrs Proudie], is tolerant of dissent, if so strict a mind can be tolerant of anything. With Wesleyan-Methodists he has something in common, but his soul trembles in agony at the iniquities of the Puseyites. His aversion is carried to things outward as well as inward. His gall rises at a new church with a high pitched roof; a full-breasted black silk waistcoat is with him a symbol of Satan; and a profane just-book would not, in his view, more foully desecrate the church of a Christian than a book of prayer printed with red letters, and ornamented with a cross on the back. Most active clergymen have their hobby, and Sunday observances are his. Sunday, however, is a word which never pollutes his mouth – it is always 'the Sabbath'.[52]

Clearly, Trollope presented the Victorian public with a very negative picture of Evangelical religion and one can well understand those members of the party who discouraged the reading of his novels for that reason. A.O.J. Cockshut was probably right in his assessment when he wrote:

> It would seem that he had three main objections to the practical working of the Evangelical creed. He was indignant at the attempt to deprive people of reasonable pleasures, he disliked people who would

---

51 A. Trollope, *The Last Chronicle of Barset*, chapter 17, p. 168.
52 A. Trollope, *Barchester Towers*, p. 29.

not be reticent about their feelings, and worst of all he resented the claim to guide people in every detail of their lives.[53]

It is difficult to leave Trollope without commenting on his mother, Frances Trollope, who clearly influenced his opinions. Frances was a parishioner of the Evangelical John Cunningham (1760–1861), Vicar of Harrow-on-the-Hill from 1811–1851, and a member of the Clapham Sect. Cunningham's first wife died in 1821. Six years later he married Mary Calvert, the daughter of General Sir Harry Calvert, Bart. She was twenty-one years his junior. She despised his low church Evangelicalism, and his use of 'inflated religious phraseology'.[54] Whilst Anthony did not share all his mother's views, like her he did not like cant or hypocrisy. Mrs Trollope went on in 1837 to write *The Vicar of Wrexhill*, which was a deliberate attempt to discredit Cunningham. As Samuel Wilberforce wrote to a friend the following year, '*The Vicar of Wrexhill* is meant, you know, for the Vicar of Harrow-on-the-Hill, Mr Cunningham. It is a most abominable personal attack.'[55] In the novel William Jacob Cartwright, the Vicar of Wrexhill, gains the affections of a wealthy widow whom he eventually marries. In this, as in many other matters, Cartwright's major concern is with power: 'To touch, to influence, to lead, to rule, to tyrannise over the hearts and souls of all he approaches, is the great object of his life.'[56] There is no doubt that Frances Trollope grossly misrepresented Cunningham and the Evangelicalism he stood for, since when one of her own sons asserted that she became obsessive about baiting the vicar, she 'conducted a crude and foolish vendetta against him'.[57]

Other novelists made passing references to Evangelical religion. William Makepeace Thackeray portrayed Evangelical clergymen and laity in a generally unfavourable manner. His mother was a convinced Evangelical but he turned away from her literalistic views to embrace the opinions of the higher critics. Thomas Hardy gave a not altogether favourable picture of Evangelical religion. Alec d'Urberville, the villain in *Tess of the d'Urbervilles*, was converted from a dissolute and amoral life, but when tested at a later point in

---

[53] A.O.J. Cockshut, *Anthony Trollope: A Critical Study*.
[54] V. Glendinning, *Trollope*, p. 19.
[55] Russell, *Evangelical Movement*, p. 117.
[56] F. Trollope, *The Vicar of Wrexhill* (1837) Vol. 3, p. 343, cited by Rosman, *Evangelicals and Culture*, p. 82.
[57] Rosman, *Evangelicals and Culture*, p. 82.

his life he backslides. In another story, *A Tragedy of Two Ambitions*, Hardy writes with less sympathy of two clerical brothers who embrace Evangelical religion not through inner conviction but rather as a means to furthering their careers.

The view that Evangelicals were hypocrites, rigid in their beliefs and disparaging of the good things of life, owed much to the port-rayals of the novelists we have considered. The fact of the matter was that there were elements of truth in their satires which they often exaggerated to powerful effect. For instance, many of their number were strict in their observance of Sunday and feared the rise of ritualism. Few of their number however were anything approaching a Mr Brocklehurst or an Obadiah Slope. Valentine Cunningham in *Everywhere Spoken Against* was of the view that Evangelicals have been 'grossly misrepresented by those who have relied on the testimony of novelists'.[58]

Notwithstanding the bad press the Evangelicals often received, reading novels became an increasingly popular leisure activity among them as the century progressed. It was a process that seems to have begun with small doses of Walter Scott. The process was further encouraged by the emergence of religious novels, such as Hannah More's *Coelebs in Search for a Wife*, which was first published in 1809. In it she tells the story of Coelebs, whose parents have died, seeking to find a wife who meets the standard of his parents. By 1842 Charles Mudie's Select Circulating Library had become the biggest and most popular of the Victorian circulating libraries reaching 25,000 subscribers by 1860. As an Evangelical, Mudie sought to provide books that were 'suitable' for his customers. The Methodist, W.H. Smith, also sold increasing numbers of carefully vetted books on his station bookstalls.

By the close of the Victorian era many Evangelical writers were producing novels, although few of them stood the test of time largely because they were frequently written with an evangelistic aim rather than as literature. Although writing for children had existed for many years it became more firmly established as the nineteenth century progressed. One of the earliest popular novels was Mary Sherwood's *History of the Fairchild Family*, which was produced in three parts in 1818, 1842 and 1847. In summary, it can be said that while in 1800 few Evangelicals read novels, by 1900 it was rare to find Evangelical opposition to such a pastime.

---

[58] Cunningham, *Everywhere Spoken Against*, cited by Rosman, *Evangelicals and Culture*, p. 6.

The theatre

It was not uncommon for Evangelicals to read plays in their homes. On the whole Evangelicals were well disposed to the works of Shakespeare, although some felt that even this was fraught with moral danger. They resorted to *Family Shakespeare* by Thomas Bowdler (1754–1825), which was published in 1818, and in which 'those words and expressions are omitted that cannot with propriety be read aloud in a family'.[59] By contrast, William Wilberforce maintained that to read Shakespeare was almost his 'greatest treat' and the *Eclectic Review* applauded Shakespeare's talent on several occasions. Their real objection to drama was focused on full performances in the playhouse. Attendance at stage production was one of the first activities which William Wilberforce felt he should lay to one side following his conversion.[60] On one occasion in 1817 a lady asked Simeon for direction on this same matter. Simeon felt so strongly that he even counselled her to disobey her husband to whom she had pledged her obedience.[61] George Russell recalled that the opera and the theatre 'were held in horror' by most Evangelicals.

A number of prominent Evangelical clergy took a strong stand against the theatre. Typical of their number were Francis Close, Henry Venn Elliott and William Champneys. Close was not at all happy about the influence of the stage and gave a public lecture entitled, 'The Stage Ancient and Modern'. He began by asserting, 'it is a matter of demonstration that the stage in all ages has proved itself to be a matter of immorality and vice'.[62] He went on to stress that the theatre was the source of much profaneness, many impure jokes and indelicate allusions.[63] One of his contemporaries said of Close, 'our manager of the theatre trembles at his form'.[64] On 3 May 1839 Cheltenham's Theatre Royal was burnt to the ground in the early morning; Close took it to be 'an act of God'. So strong was

---

[59] T. Bowdler, *A Memoir of John Bowdler* (1825), p. 230, cited by Bradley, *Call to Seriousness*, p. 98.

[60] Rosman, *Evangelicals and Culture*, p. 76.

[61] Carus, *Charles Simeon*, pp. 465f., cited by Rosman, *Evangelicals and Culture*, p. 76.

[62] F. Close, *The Stage Ancient and Modern its Tendencies on Morals and Religion. A Lecture by Francis Close, DD*, p. iii.

[63] Ibid., p. 46.

[64] W.E. Adams, *Memoirs of a Social Atom*, p. 14, cited by Ashton, 'Clerical Control', p. 137.

Close's influence against the theatre that there was not sufficient will to rebuild it until 1891, well after Close's death. In the view of W.E. Adams this was 'the most remarkable example of his authority in secular affairs'.[65]

Henry Venn Elliott wrote to a fellow clergyman on the subject of 'The Renunciation of Theatrical Entertainments Previous to Confirmation'. He regarded a visit to a theatre as to 'take delight in public exhibitions contrary to His [Christ's] commandments and opposed to His example, taking His name and His Father's name constantly in vain'.[66] Commenting on ballet, Elliott asserted that it promoted 'indecent exposure of the person, which would not be tolerated in a private room or in any respectable society'.[67]

William Champneys preached a sermon, entitled 'The Theatre: A Word to His Congregation', to his Oxford congregation in July 1836.[68] It was based on the text from 2 Corinthians 6, 'Come out from among them, and be ye separate'. 'Christians', Champneys declared, 'are to be a peculiar people' and this was to be seen not only in their avoiding evil 'but all appearance of it'.[69] Plays are evil, he continued, because 'they put forth false morality'.[70] In a later paragraph he was more specific: 'How few there are which have not woven with them some silly tale of sickly love falsely so called! It should be called by its right name, lust'.[71] The type of people attending theatre performances also troubled Champneys:

> But who are among the company that frequent such places? Who hang around the doors to ply their wretched trade? Is it not notorious, that the miserable prostitute is either, as in large cities, the constant attendant at the theatre, encouraged there to draw ... the idle, the giddy, the unguarded, who go thither, and who come out thence with hated minds and excited feelings, the ready victims of her snares?[72]

---

[65] Adams, *Memoirs of a Social Atom*, p. 14.

[66] H. Elliott, 'On the Renunciation of Theatrical Entertainments Previous to Confirmation', in Bateman, *Henry Venn Elliott*, p. 209.

[67] Ibid., p. 209.

[68] W.W. Champneys, *The Theatre: A Word to His Congregation in A Sermon Preached at St Ebbe's Church, Sunday Morning, July 3, 1836*.

[69] Ibid., p. 3.

[70] Ibid., p. 7.

[71] Ibid., p. 8.

[72] Ibid., p. 10.

Rosman makes the point convincingly that the fundamental Evangelical objection to the theatre and stage productions was that they portrayed life as they did not wish to see it.[73] Throughout the course of the nineteenth century there were substantial numbers of Evangelicals who avoided the theatre fearful lest they should be trapped by the lure of its fatal attractions.

Fine art

At the time of the Reformation and in the period of Puritan ascendancy in the mid-seventeenth century the earlier Evangelicals had been suspicious of religious art in churches believing it to detract from the true worship which was in Spirit and truth. By the eighteenth century, however, attitudes were changing and it became customary for Evangelicals from wealthier families to go on a grand tour, usually to Florence and Rome. Here they were able to contemplate the works of great painters and sculptors, such as Michelangelo and Bernini. In the same period it became fashionable for the aristocracy and the country gentry to have pictures hanging in their libraries and entrance halls. The nineteenth century therefore witnessed a considerable widening of this interest in painting with the opening of public art galleries and libraries, some of which had free entrance.

In the main, Evangelical periodicals, such as the *Eclectic Review*, appear to have taken the view that fine art enhanced life and that a genuine love for painting, architecture and sculpture could renew and sustain the human spirit. The *Evangelical Magazine*, for example, welcomed efforts that were made 'to improve the taste and to encourage fine arts'.[74] Predictably perhaps *The Record* was a little more guarded in its general approach to works of art but it was by no means hostile. Where it did take issue it was over issues of indecency or frivolity.[75] It objected, for example, to the displaying of Titian's painting of Venus[76] and three years later complained of 'the indelicacy of some pictures' on display in the Dulwich Picture Gallery.[77]

---

[73] *Evangelical Magazine*, series 2, Vol. 7 (1829), p. 495, cited by Rosman, *Evangelicals and Culture*, p. 152.

[74] Ibid., p. 152.

[75] See Rosman, *Evangelicals and Culture*, p. 152.

[76] *The Record*, 2 November 1828, cited by Rosman, *Evangelicals and Culture*, p. 152.

[77] *The Record*, 5 September 1833, cited by Rosman, *Evangelicals and Culture*, p. 152.

The *Eclectic Review* occasionally shared *The Record*'s disquiet on the matter, as was illustrated when one of its reviewers complained about 'naked statues' as a sin 'against national decorum and Christian morality'.[78] Shortly before the opening of the Crystal Palace at Sydenham in June 1854 there were similar complaints at the prospect of the nude statuary. Archbishop Sumner and his brother Charles together with various lords, including Lord Shaftesbury, felt it was their public duty to make a request for fig leaves. The directors agreed but expressed their doubts as to whether sufficient leaves could be found before the exhibition was due to open.[79]

For a brief period Evangelicals exerted pressure to have galleries and museums closed on Sundays,[80] which made it more difficult for the working classes to have the opportunity to see art. As the century progressed, however, Evangelicals came increasingly to appreciate the value of great paintings, particularly the work of emerging English artists, such as the Pre-Raphaelites, who worked on religious themes. John Everett Millais (1829–1896) completed his painting of 'Christ in the House of his Parents' in 1850 and Holman Hunt, although a non-church-goer, completed 'The Light of the World' in the same year. He also painted 'The Scapegoat' and 'In the Carpenter's Shop', both obvious biblical subjects which the Christian public could readily appreciate.[81]

Architecture

In the realm of architecture the main development was the emergence of Gothic revival that came as part of the Romantic Movement. This style, which was adopted soon after the ending of the War with France, was given impetus by the Act of Parliament in 1818 that pro-vided £1,000,000 for the building of churches in London and the provinces. Evangelicals, along with other sections of church, appreci-ated buildings of good quality, but they tended to be suspicious of ecclesiastical Gothic because it resonated with the ideals of the Tractarians. Indeed, Francis Close protested in a sermon that the

---

[78] *Eclectic Review* 6 (1806), p. 390 cited by Rosman, *Evangelicals and Culture*, p. 152.
[79] Chadwick, *Victorian Church* Part 1, pp. 463–4.
[80] Bradley, *Call to Seriousness*, p. 105.
[81] Wolffe, *God and Greater Britain*, p. 180.

restoration of churches in the Gothic style 'is the restoration of popery'.[82] For his part, Close rejoiced in the plain style of St Paul's Church, Cheltenham, a building for which he had been personally responsible. He spoke with affection of its lack of a receding chancel and praised 'its decent reading pew and pulpit from which the pure gospel sounded out'.[83] Notwithstanding the suspicions of Close and some of his fellow members of the Church Association, by the second half of the nineteenth century many Evangelicals seemed happy enough for their churches, schools and colleges to be in the Gothic style.

Music

Choral singing and classical music were particularly popular with the Victorian middle and upper classes. Consequently, hundreds of small choral societies and local orchestras were formed during the course of the nineteenth century. Typical among the many examples was the town of Nottingham, which had a long tradition of singing.[84] Another was the Newcastle and Gateshead Choral Society who gave occasional concerts in the 1840s.[85] John Berry, a Yorkshire woollen milliner, conducted Meltham Choral Society and founded the Meltham Philharmonic Orchestra. In larger towns and cities orchestras and choral societies often had big memberships and some had considerable success in crossing the class barriers.[86] Such were the Huddersfield Choral Society, the Leeds Philharmonic and the Bradford Festival Choral Society.[87] In the railway town of Crewe there was a Philharmonic Society, which sometimes had soloists from London and occasionally enjoyed performances from sections of the Hallé Orchestra.[88] Performances of Handel's *Messiah* were very popular. William Spark, the Leeds Borough organist, wrote that Handel's work, 'has done more to educate musical taste, unclasp the

[82] F. Close, *The Restoration of Churches is the Restoration of Popery: Proved and Illustrated from the Authenticated Publications of the Cambridge Camden Society: A Sermon Preached in the Parish Church of Cheltenham on Tuesday November 5th, 1844*, p. 7.

[83] Ibid., p. 4.

[84] J.K. Walton and J. Walvin (eds.), *Leisure in Britain 1780–1839*, p. 57.

[85] Ibid., p. 57.

[86] Ibid., p. 10.

[87] Ibid., p. 103.

[88] Ibid., p. 123.

hands of charity, and unfold the mind of God to man, than any other composition, save the Bible itself'.[89]

This growing popularity of choral singing in a non-church context gradually came to impact church worship. Evangelicals had brought popular hymns into Sunday worship in the early years of the century. By the end of the Victorian era it was becoming more customary to hear the responses sung in Evangelical churches. In 1891 the practice was introduced at Holy Trinity, Cambridge, Simeon's old church, for the first time.[90] Handley Moule noted in May of that year the first chanting of the responses, 'very sweet and very reverent'.[91]

Leisure and Pastimes

As has been noted, culture is a broad term and within the context of this chapter is taken to include a wide range of leisure activities and pastimes most of which straddled the class divide. The Clapham Sect in general had a more positive attitude to recreational pursuits than did some of the later Evangelical generations who succeeded them. 'There can be no dispute', wrote William Wilberforce, 'concerning the true end of recreations. They are intended to refresh our exhausted bodily or mental powers, and restore us with renewed vigour, to the more serious occupations of life.'[92] Along with Gisborne he maintained there was nothing amiss in a game of cards with sick or ageing relatives. The fact, however, that Wilberforce needed to make the point, as Rosman observed, was indicative that not all his fellow Evangelicals shared his opinion in the matter.[93] Isaac Milner, the Evangelical President of Queen's College, Cambridge, also played cards in his younger days but later gave it up on account of the time it wasted.[94] George Russell recorded how the

---

[89] W. Spark, *Musical Memories* (1888), p. 463. See R.H. Myers, *Handel's Messiah*, pp. 232–48, cited by Walton and Walvin (eds.), *Leisure in Britain*, p. 103.

[90] J.B. Harford and F.C. MacDonald, *Handley Carr Glyn Moule Bishop of Durham*, p. 136.

[91] Ibid., p. 136.

[92] Wilberforce and Wilberforce, *Life of William Wilberforce*, p. 453, cited by Rosman, *Evangelicals and Culture*, p. 121.

[93] Ibid., p. 71.

[94] Rosman, *Evangelicals and Culture*, p. 72.

Evangelicals banned card playing and made no distinction between good play and bad. 'Cards', he wrote, 'were labelled "the Devil's Prayer Book", and no good Christian could touch them.'[95] Hannah More recorded being present at an evening party in London and in one night 'the enormous sum of sixty thousand pounds was lost'. 'What a comfort for me', she continued, 'that none of my friends play at cards.'[96]

Most Evangelicals had few qualms about shooting, but hunting was widely condemned. According to the *Christian Observer* it caused exhaustion and incapacitated participants for serious reflection.[97] Foxhunting clergy, according to *The Record*, aided dissent since it lowered the respect in which such Church of England clergy were held.[98] Interestingly, George Russell's father, who was a staunch Evangelical, was also an inveterate hunter.[99]

Throughout the nineteenth century racing became increasingly popular, particularly with the working classes.[100] In certain big cities race meetings became almost exclusively working-class occasions. This was true of Manchester, Newcastle and Doncaster.[101] In other towns, such as Cheltenham, many middle and upper class people were attracted to the sport. For many Evangelicals it was the prospect of gambling and bad company that turned them against the races. *The Record* declared that for ministers of religion to attend race meetings was a prostitution of clerical character.[102]

Among those who had strong things to say against horse racing was Francis Close of Cheltenham. The early years of the nineteenth century drew between fifteen to twenty thousand people to Cheltenham's famous races. Many were attracted by the side events, shows and gambling. Close felt that Satan himself could not have suggested a course of action 'more ruinous to immortal souls, upon an extensive scale, than the annual festival of Race Week'.

---

[95] Russell, *Evangelical Movement*, pp. 74–5.
[96] Ibid., p. 75.
[97] *Christian Observer*, Vol. 24, 1824, p. 552, cited by Rosman, *Evangelicals and Culture*, p. 73.
[98] *The Record*, 17 June, 27 September and 4 October 1830, cited by Rosman, *Evangelicals and Culture*, p. 35.
[99] Russell, *Evangelical Movement*, pp. 134–5.
[100] P. Bailey, *Leisure and Class in Victorian Britain*, p. 23.
[101] Ibid., p. 23.
[102] *The Record*, 17 June 1830, cited by Rosman, *Evangelicals and Culture*, p. 74.

Close was particularly against the people who came to the races because they were

> ... dissolute persons who offer receptacles of gambling, drunkenness and lust ... and an ... influx of every species of nuisance; gamblers, rogues and dissolute persons follow races from place to place, as birds of prey hover over the rear of an advancing army to glut upon the bodies of the slain.[103]

Close launched his campaign from the pulpit with a sermon entitled 'The Evil Consequences of Attending the Race Course'. In it he lambasted Colonel Berkeley and his co-organisers who in addition to the activities of the racecourse brought undesirables and undesirable sports and pastimes into Cheltenham. Close aroused such indignation that he succeeded in getting the races closed down altogether and transferred to Tewkesbury from 1831 to 1835 in which year they returned to Cheltenham.

Evangelical clergy in Newmarket who shared Close's views succeeded in getting Sunday race meetings cancelled and the Rev Henry Moule was able to get the Dorchester races stopped altogether.[104] The Earl of Shaftesbury recorded how he experienced considerable emotional distress when Queen Victoria asked him to go with her to Ascot in 1841. He eventually decided he could not refuse and offered a prayer that his attendance at the racecourse 'may not be productive of any mischief to the slight influence I may have in the world for carrying forward measures and designs of good to mankind'.[105]

Closely allied to the races were local fairs. 'In most of our provincial cities and boroughs', the *Saturday Review* maintained in 1869, 'the fair and the race meeting are the two great festivals of the calendar, the two seasons from which the mass of people date forwards and backwards'. Fairs were known as places where liquor flowed freely and temporary brothels were erected. The London City Mission (LCM) and Evangelical churchmen mounted direct attacks on London's fairs.[106]

---

[103] Close, *Races*, p. 6.
[104] Bradley, *Call to Seriousness*, p. 101.
[105] Shaftesbury, *Diary* 8 June 1841, cited by Russell, *Evangelical Movement*, pp. 132–3.
[106] Lewis, *Lighten Their Darkness*, p. 67.

Most Evangelicals regarded dancing as particularly sinful and ball going was condemned. Sir Richard Hill, an Evangelical MP, reflected the views of many when he published an address to persons of fashion 'to demonstrate with the clearest of evidence that BALLS are entirely inconsistent with the Spirit of Christianity, and that it is not possible to be present at them without incurring great guilt'.[107] George Russell recalled that 'Ball-going was condemned; but certain palliatives were admitted.'[108] Nevertheless, there were differences of opinion. In some families square dances were allowed, while round dances were forbidden. In some families you were permitted to go to balls provided you came down to prayers at eight on the following morning.[109] In 1845 William Cowper, later well known as the author of the 'Cowper Temple Clause' and eventually as Lord Mount Temple, noted that members of LCM had felt insulted that he should have gone to the Queen's Fancy Ball on the same day as he had taken the chair at their anniversary meeting.[110] Among the clergy, Montagu Villiers warned young men of the dangers of the ballroom floor.[111] In contrast, William Thomson regularly held balls and parties at Bishopthorpe, and when the family went to London. John Ryle thought there was nothing wrong with dancing itself, although he was concerned at the long hours given to it as well as the vanity that resulted in dressing up for it.[112]

Despite the often quoted Victorian dictate 'little children should be seen and not heard' Evangelicals seem for the most part to have been happy for their children to enjoy playing and engaging in a wide range of leisure activities. Upper-class Evangelicals, such as the Clapham families, threw large parties for their children who enjoyed 'dressing up'.[113] Wealthier Evangelicals went on holidays together. Archbishop William Thomson enjoyed playing with his children in the nursery and rowed with his sons on the river Ouse.[114] Generally speaking, throughout the nineteenth century Evangelicals became growing advocates of creative play and sporting and leisure activities for children. Evangelicals such as

---

[107] Bradley, *Call to Seriousness*, p. 150.
[108] Russell, *Evangelical Movement*, p. 133.
[109] Ibid., p. 133.
[110] Ibid., p. 134.
[111] *The Times*, 10 August 1861.
[112] Kirk-Smith, *William Thomson*, pp. 170–1; Farley, *Ryle*, p. 28.
[113] Rosman, *Evangelicals and Culture*, p. 112.
[114] Kirk-Smith, *William Thomson*, p. 114.

Francis Close and William Wilson, who were promoters of primary education, were concerned to ensure that all schools were equipped with spacious playgrounds and that the pupils were provided with items such as tops and skipping ropes. James Walvin concluded his researches into nineteenth-century children's pleasures with the assertion that 'at the end of the century it was widely accepted that certain games played a crucial role in a child's education – and were also vital to the nation's future'.[115]

The view that physical recreation was good for the body, and certainly in the case of boys and men, became an unchallenged assumption in Victorian England. Gymnastic activities were promoted for both boys and girls. Among men and boys of all classes cricket and football were generally popular. Evangelicals fostered and promoted both. A number of their clergy were keen cricketers. John Sumner played for the Eton College first team and was one of the bowlers in the first match the school played against a local club side.[116] Ryle, who enjoyed watching cricket,[117] was a strong advocate of muscular Christianity: 'I see no harm in cricket, rowing, running, and other manly athletic recreations,' he said.[118] Ryle believed that two subjects were essential in education, games and English history.[119] Charles Studd and his two brothers, Kynaston and George, each captained the Cambridge University cricket team and Charles later went on to play for England. In 1882 he was a member of the team which beat the Australians at the Oval watched by a crowd of 20,000.[120] Charles' Christian faith and that of his brothers did much to raise the profile of cricket in the Evangelical world; the more so when Charles went out as a missionary to China.

With the growth of towns the game of football became more organised and confined. Instead of it being a village-wide affair playing fields were established in open spaces and clubs and leagues were formed. Churches played their part in this process. Bolton Wanderers were originally Christ Church Bolton Football Club which had been organised by the Rev J.F. Wright.[121] The leading

---

[115] J. Walvin, 'Children's Pleasures', in Walton and Walvin (eds.), *Leisure in Britain*, p. 228.

[116] Scotland, *John Bird Sumner*, p. 4.

[117] Farley, *Ryle*, p. 137.

[118] Ibid., p. 28.

[119] Ibid., p. 137.

[120] N.P. Grubb, *C.T. Studd: Cricketer and Pioneer*, p. 28.

[121] Bailey, *Leisure and Class*, p. 139.

influence behind the formation of Tottenham Hotspur was John Ripsher, a prominent member of All Hallows Parish Church and the YMCA.[122] Among the first rules were that 'all club members should attend Scripture classes at All Hallows Church on Wednesdays'.[123] Ripsher used the YMCA as the team's first base in 1883.[124] Other clubs had similar church origins, among them Everton and Southampton.[125] Wolverhampton Wanderers were originally the team of St Luke's Church School for Senior Boys, Wolverhampton. They were first organised by the Headmaster, Mr W.H. Barcroft, and played on Fallow Field before moving to Molineux.[126]

One thing is clear, even from this short chapter, and that is that nineteenth-century Anglican Evangelicals fully engaged with the culture of their day at almost every level. In the earlier years of the century some of their number, most notably those whose sympathies were with the Recordites, were hostile to the lifestyles of those they lived alongside. Apart from the Clapham Moderates, many adopted a world-denying stance towards pleasure and recreational activities. However, with the passing of the years, Evangelical theology changed from 'world-denying' to a 'world-affirming' stance. Along with this change there emerged a more positive attitude to the main aspects of culture. Evangelicals unashamedly read for pleasure, watched cricket matches and enjoyed music concerts and theatre performances. Much more than that, Evangelicals had to a large extent redeemed the culture. Their campaigning had helped to recall the nation back to what was regarded as morally decent. Vice and drunkenness had been reduced considerably, family life had been affirmed and reinforced. Children and children's welfare and the education of children had been greatly improved. It is the case that Evangelicals 'Christianised' much of nineteenth-century culture. This was more obviously visible in the upper echelons of society, but even the working poor had a knowledge of what was right – they probably had some link with a church or chapel, they knew some hymns and possibly sang some as they worked in the factory floor or in the

---

[122] P. Soar, *Tottenham Hotspur: The Official Illustrated History*, p. 11.
[123] Ibid., p. 13.
[124] Ibid., p. 13.
[125] Ibid., p. 13.
[126] Bailey, *Leisure and Class*, p. 139. See also *Log Book of St Luke's Church School*, Wolverhampton.

mines. Many had Bibles in their homes and, quite possibly, works by Bunyan and Watts.[127] Almost all knew that England was a Christian country.

---

[127] D. Vincent, 'Reading in the Working-Class Home', in Walton and Walvin (eds.), *Leisure in Britain*, p. 215.

10

Evangelicals and Education

Prior to the sixteenth century, education was always church education. There were a number of good grammar schools, many of
which were closely associated with the cathedrals and endowed by
merchants, guilds, nobles and the crown. The Reformation, whilst
cementing a new and closer relationship between the church and
state, had some important effects on education. At one end it
strengthened the range of grammar schools, a significant number of
which were built in the reign of Edward VI from the proceeds
of chantry money or from guild closures. At the other end, primary
education, which had been aided by the work of monks and friars,
suffered, as did women's education. In the seventeenth century
dissenters began to expand in numbers and many Particular
Baptists, Presbyterians, Congregationalists and Quakers prospered
with the result that they began to put money into education. Private individuals set up numerous small schools and academies.
The academies were largely for training men for the ministry.[1]
Gradually as a result poor children came to have the opportunity of
acquiring a rudimentary education.

By the latter part of the eighteenth century several different types
of elementary school existed. There were dame schools that could
be organised by any charitable woman who had been fortunate to
receive a rudimentary education and wanted to earn a small wage
teaching village children in her kitchen. The quality of education
offered in dame schools varied a good deal from place to place and
discipline was frequently harsh. At Risley Dame School in
Buckinghamshire for example, the girls were 'whacked across the
shoulders' as a punishment for laziness or poor work while the boys
were 'hung up to a beam by a chord under their arms'.[2]

---

[1] See H. McLachlan, *English Education under the Test Acts.*
[2] P.R.L. Horn, *Education in Rural England*, p. 24.

Alongside the dame schools, charity schools also developed in the eighteenth century. H.J. Burgess put the number at 'not less than 460'.[3] They were open to the poor and did not give the classical education which the grammar schools provided. The education that they provided was primarily 'a rescue operation' which aimed to produce children who would be hewers and drawers of water. Charity schools made a particular effort to provide religious instruction in an era when the church had for the most part ceased to catechise the children of the parish. By 1729 there were 1,400 charity schools in England educating 221,303 children. In the eighteenth century a number of religious societies, among them SPCK, were active in the formation of charity schools.

Of major significance were the Sunday schools. Among the first of such institutions to be opened was one in the city of Gloucester in 1780. It was sponsored and publicised by Robert Raikes (1735–1811), the Proprietor of the *Gloucester Chronicle*, but much of the organisational work and the curriculum was in the hands of the Rev Thomas Stock, the headmaster of the Cathedral School.[4] Although Raikes was largely motivated by his Evangelical faith, he did interest himself in the temporal welfare of at least some of the students, visiting them at home and talking to their parents about the general aims of the school, their children's progress and their involvement.[5] He later recalled:

> I am generally at church, and after the service they all come round me to make their bow; and, if any animosities have arisen, to make complaints. The great principle I inculcate, is, to be kind and good natured to each other; not to provoke one another; to be dutiful to their parents; not to offend God by cursing and swearing ... The going among them, doing them little kindnesses, distributing trifling rewards, and ingratiating myself with them ... have given me an ascendancy.[6]

The motives of Sunday school founders were a mixture of evangelistic concern and social control. Raikes made it clear that his aim was the reformation of society. This aim is well-illustrated by

---

[3] H.J. Burgess, *Enterprise in Education*.
[4] For Robert Raikes, see F.C. Booth, *Robert Raikes of Gloucester*.
[5] P.B. Cliff, *The Rise and Development of the Sunday School in England 1780–1980*, pp. 4, 67.
[6] *Gentleman's Magazine* Vol. 54, cited J.M. Goldstrom, *Education: Elementary Education 1700–1900*, pp. 17–18.

Thomas Noble, a Keighley blacksmith, who, in 1787, opened a Sabbath institution that aimed to have children 'taught in the gospel of Jesus Christ and the fear of God' in the hopes that 'it will put a stop to so much vice that is committed every Sabbath day'.[7] For the majority of sponsors and founders, however, it was the Evangelical belief in the overriding importance of the Bible that girded them into action. By 1801 there were 2,290 English Sunday schools of which 1,282 belonged to the Church of England. By 1851 over 2,000,000 pupils were enrolled in Sunday schools. This represented 75 per cent of working-class children between the ages of five and ten.[8] In 1907 there were 2,334,000 children in Church of England Sunday schools.[9]

The eighteenth-century grammar schools remained almost entirely in the hands of the Church of England and the bishop of the diocese concerned licensed the teachers.[10] By the end of the century, however, the church was beginning to lose its hold and the licence was not always required. In fact a number of grammar schools fell on bad times in areas where clergy were non-resident.

Education in the Nineteenth Century

At the beginning of the nineteenth century, only about one in twenty children received any education and much of that was of questionable value. One thing, however, remained clear as far as Evangelicals were concerned, the Bible must be the basis of all education. As William Dealtry, the chancellor of Winchester diocese, put it in a sermon in 1838, 'No child can be trained up in the way in which he should go, unless from early life he be made acquainted with the Bible.'[11]

Dame, charity and grammar schools all continued to play an active role in nineteenth-century English education, although some grammar schools were in decline until the reforms of the 1860s. The dame schools grew in numbers but probably declined in the quality of the education that they provided. In 1816 the government appointed Henry Brougham (1778–1868) to a committee 'to

---

[7] For Noble see T.W. Laqueur, *Religion and Respectability.*
[8] Gilley and Shiels, *Religion in Britain*, p. 312.
[9] A. Hastings, *A History of English Christianity 1920–1985*, p. 105.
[10] H.C. Barnard, *A History of English Education*, p. 14.
[11] W. Dealtry, *Charge*, p. 5.

inquire into the education of the lower ranks'.[12] According to their findings, 53,000 children were being 'educated or rather not educated' at dame schools.[13] The 1861 Newcastle Commission reported that 'Dame schools are very common both in the country and in the towns.' They were also declared in the same report to be 'generally very inefficient'.[14]

Substantial numbers of children continued to be educated in charity schools, almost all of which were under the control of the parochial clergy. They relied on legacies, endowments and voluntary contributions to cover their maintenance and basic running costs. Throughout the nineteenth century, until 1877, an annual service attended by charity school children from London was held in St Paul's Cathedral.

Sunday schools continued to be of great value throughout the nineteenth century, although after about 1840 they were beginning to outlive some of their usefulness because day school provision was increasing rapidly. However, the numbers in Sunday schools did not drop although many of them moved away from reading, writing and arithmetic. In 1803 a Sunday school union was formed with a committee that was composed of half churchmen and half dissenters. The Sunday School Union's most important work was in publishing and distributing textbooks, learning aids and magazines for students and teachers. For example, the Union's spelling book sold 5,000,000 copies between 1811 and 1850. In that year there were reckoned to be 7,125 Sunday schools with 844,728 pupils.[15] Sunday schools came increasingly to promote a basic education in reading, writing and arithmetic for those children who were not able to attend schools on weekdays for one reason or another.

Sunday schools were particularly effective in providing at least a rudimentary education for the very poor. By 1850 it was calculated that three quarters of the age five to fifteen working-class population of England was attending Sunday school. Prominent among early Evangelicals who supported Sunday schools were William Wilberforce and other members of the Clapham Sect. With Wilberforce's support, Hannah and Martha More devoted ten years of their lives to establishing Sunday schools in the Mendip Hills of Somerset. Their work, which was always done in connection with

---

[12] Barnard, *English Education*, p. 66.
[13] Ibid., p. 66.
[14] *Report of the Newcastle Commission*, 1861, Vol. 1, pp. 28–9.
[15] Burgess, *Enterprise in Education*, p. 10.

local clergy, transformed the entire neighbourhood in and around Cheddar. The two sisters worked among the miners giving them instruction in the Scriptures and setting up adult classes, including one in Bristol. The main criticism levelled at Hannah More is that her work was too paternalistic and in consequence socially controlling. In a letter penned in 1801 to the Bishop of Bath and Wells, Dr Richard Beadon, she wrote:

> My plan of instruction is extremely simple and limited. They learn, on weekdays, such coarse works as may fit them for servants. I allow no writing for the poor. My object is not to make them fanatics, but to train up the lower classes in habits of industry and piety. I know no way of teaching morals but by teaching principles or inculcating Christian principles without imparting a good knowledge of the Scriptures.[16]

A major controversy among Evangelical Sunday schools was the question of the teaching of writing on the Sabbath. Those who had a more rigid view of Sunday observance felt that it was in breach of the commandment and therefore refused to sanction it. Robert Raikes, it should be noted, taught both reading and writing in his Sunday schools. By the second half of the century, when Evangelicals came to have a more moderate view of the Sabbath, there was much less general opposition to writing.

Sunday schools had many positive effects on nineteenth-century English society. Importantly, they opened up opportunities for laymen and women as teachers. They also paved the way for popular education by propounding the concept that all children ought to receive a free education. Sunday schools became a vehicle through which the working classes developed self-respect and were motivated to self-improvement, discipline and progress. This was recognised by the *Morning Chronicle* in an article published in 1848:

> Long before Education Committees of the Privy Council and British and Foreign societies were heard of, long previous to the era of Institutes and Athenaeums, the Sunday Schools were sedulously at work impregnating the people with the rudiments of an Education which, though always rude and often narrow and fanatical in its teachings, was yet preserving a glow of moral and religious sentiment, and keeping alive a degree of popular intelligence which otherwise would assuredly

---

[16] R.B. Johnson, *The Letters of Hannah More*, pp. 179–88.

have perished in the rush and clatter with which a vast manufacturing population came surging up upon the land.[17]

Enrolment peaked about 1885; certainly figures never again attained the same level after that year. In 1880 Lord Shaftesbury who had been a keen supporter of Sunday schools took the central part in the Raikes Centenary celebrations in Gloucester unveiling a monument in the Cathedral on 27 June. A little later, on his return to London, he took part in the unveiling of a monster statue of Raikes on the Thames Embankment.[18] Clearly, as Edward Royle observed, 'Sunday schools were the major distinctive contribution of Evangelicals to popular education.'[19]

A nineteenth-century development in the education of the poor was the emergence of the ragged schools, the first of which appeared in 1820. Evangelicals gave these institutions considerable support. The man generally credited with this institution was John Pounds, who came from Portsmouth, although Thomas Cranfield of Camberwell was said to be caring for children who were unsuitable for Sunday school before this. Pounds fed and clothed the children, and instructed them. His particular concern was to prevent such children from returning to living on the streets. Many ragged schools arose out of the work of Evangelically-inspired London City Missions.

A Ragged School Union (RSU) was formed in 1844 with the object of drawing the various ragged schools together. Among its aims was a concern to give 'permanence, regularity and vigour to existing ragged schools and to promote new ones'.[20] Lord Shaftesbury, who had already been actively involved with the running of Field Lane Ragged School at Saffron Hill,[21] was its chairman and R.L.C. Beaven its treasurer. Edwin Hodder wrote that 'From the time that Lord Ashley joined the movement, the Ragged School Union grew in importance and usefulness, and for over forty years his love for and zeal in the cause never knew abatement or change.'[22] Among the RSU's committee members were several

---

[17] *Morning Chronicle*, 15 November 1848.
[18] Hodder, *Life and Work of Lord Shaftesbury*, pp. 717–18.
[19] E. Royle, 'Evangelicals and Education', in Wolffe (ed.), *Evangelicals and Public Zeal*, pp. 120–1.
[20] Heasman, *Evangelicals in Action*, p. 72.
[21] Hodder, *Life and Work of Lord Shaftesbury*, pp. 259–60.
[22] Ibid., p. 349.

leading Evangelicals, including the Rev Baptist Noel, who was closely connected with LCM, Lord Kinnaird and the Rev James Sharman of Surrey Chapel. Bishop John Pelham of Norwich was the only bishop who was ever seen on a ragged school platform.[23] Sixteen schools joined the RSU when it was formed and by 1851 the number had risen to 132 with 23,643 children.[24] By 1867 there were 226 ragged Sunday schools, 204 weekday schools and 207 evening schools in London alone, with some 26,000 pupils.[25] Among other prominent Evangelical Anglicans who gave their energies and support to the ragged schools were Archbishop John Bird Sumner, General Gordon and Quinton Hogg.[26]

Despite the efforts made there was still an enormous amount of work to be done. The Report of the Select Committee on the Education of Destitute Children of 1861 stated that 'there exists in many of our great cities and towns a class of children whom the system of national education supported by Parliament ... does not reach'. It continued:

> This class consists partly of the children of the very poor persons, many of them actually paupers in receipt of parochial relief ... who are unable to spare the fees charged in the National and British schools, or provide the children with the dress suitable to those schools ... We have collected no precise statistics as to the extent of this class of children, but we have evidence to show that it is considerable.[27]

In 1876 Dr Barnardo estimated that there were still about 30,000 neglected children living rough on the streets of London.[28] Thomas Barnado (1845–1905), who left the Brethren movement and eventually became a lay reader in the Church of England,[29] came to appreciate the huge numbers of destitute children through his work as a ragged schoolteacher in London's East End. Barnardo taught at Ernest Street School, which was in the Mile End Road area. Here he reported that ' upward of a hundred persons' crowded into 'a low,

---

[23] Ibid., p. 350.
[24] Royle, 'Evangelicals and Education', p. 122.
[25] Ibid., p. 122.
[26] Bready, *England*, p. 359.
[27] *The Report of the Select Committee on the Education of Destitute Children*, 1861.
[28] For Barnardo, see Wagner, *Barnardo*, pp. 70–85.
[29] Ibid., pp. 169, 264–5.

narrow, and badly ventilated room, which contains sittings for only eighty-six' and becomes 'especially in summer, very unpleasant if not impossible'.[30] Education became a key aspect of Barnardo's work and he founded free ragged schools in Copperfield Road.[31] A report from Her Majesty's Inspector of the Privy Council of Education in 1881 proved how effective Barnardo's schemes had become. It showed that 452 children had been presented for examination and that 376 had been successful.[32]

Partly arising from Barnardo's work, a concern emerged that many of the children were unable to learn because they had so little to eat. This led to the founding of the Destitute Children's Dinner Society, with Lord Shaftesbury again as president. The organisation gave free meals to hungry children at ragged schools and Christian missions. By 1888 there were sixty-four dining rooms serving 17,000 dinners a week. This was in fact a forerunner of what was later incorporated into the Education Provision of Meals Act of 1906.

The demise of the ragged schools came with the passing of the Forster Education Act of 1870. Many of them were attacked on account of their inefficiency and the majority of their children were soon incorporated into the new board schools. In 1870 ragged schools had 32,309 children on their books, but just two years later this had reduced to a mere 9,347.[33] Despite this somewhat ignominious ending Royle has rightly observed that though the Evangelicals had limited objectives they offered the poor more than those conservatives who thought it dangerous to provide them with any knowledge at all.[34]

Of all the societies operating in the nineteenth century for the teaching of young children, the two biggest and the most influential were British and Foreign Bible Society, which was controlled by Nonconformists, and the National Society for the Promotion of Education of the Poor in the Principles of the Established Church. Both societies arose out of the work of two earlier pioneers in the field of education, Joseph Lancaster (1778–1832), a Quaker schoolmaster, and Andrew Bell (1753–1832). Both of these men independently from each other created what was known as the monitorial system,

---

[30] Ibid., p. 25.
[31] Ibid., p. 85.
[32] Ibid., p. 85.
[33] Bentley, *Transformation of the Evangelical Party*, p. 82.
[34] Royle, 'Evangelicals and Education', p. 119.

whereby older pupils in a school taught the younger children. This was an attractive system because it was economical and at the same time introduced poor children to the concepts of discipline, responsibility and corporate school life.

Andrew Bell was a Scottish Anglican who graduated from St Andrews University in 1769 and then taught for a while in Virginia. On his return home in 1781 he worked as a private tutor and then was ordained by Bishop Shute Barrington of Salisbury, who was a warm supporter of elementary education for the poorer classes. In 1787 Bell went out to Madras as superintendent of the Military Male Asylum. It was there seeing a native teacher instructing local children that he began his experiment of using pupils to instruct their fellows. He selected an eight-year-old boy, John Fricksen, and set him to teach the lowest class. The experiment proved to be so successful that Fricksen was put in formal charge. Bell returned to England and in 1797 he published an account of his work in Madras under the title, *An Experiment in Education*. The book ran through five editions, the last of which was in 1814 and was considerably enlarged. The extent to which Bell had enabled the Church of England to wake to its responsibilities can be gauged by the fact that in the twenty years between the formation of the National Society and his funeral, in Westminster Abbey, nearly 1,000 national schools had been formed.[35] By 1878 the figure had grown considerably to 10,910.[36]

The members of SPCK established the National Society on the 16 October 1811. Charles Simeon and Lord Teignmouth were among the society's first members. Its aim was quite simply to provide primary school education for the nation in association with the established church. It took over the existing charity schools and soon began to attract considerable support. The universities of Oxford and Cambridge each gave £500. In order to receive support and sponsorship from the National Society a school had to follow the monitorial system as laid down by Bell, to give pupils instruction in the liturgy and catechisms of the Church of England, and to take them to church on Sundays. At the same time, there was a conscience clause in the trust deeds of some schools that allowed children to be withdrawn from religious instruction.

---

[35] E.P. Cubberley, *The History of Education*, p. 632. Bell lived for a time in Cheltenham and worshipped at St John's Church.
[36] Chadwick, *Victorian Church* Part 2, p. 304.

For almost all of the nineteenth century the education of young children revolved around the rivalry between the Nonconformist British and Foreign Schools Society and the Church of England's National Society. In this struggle the National Society had a number of advantages. They had influential backing from Joshua Watson and members of the Hackney Phalanx, an energetic group of high churchmen who had financial resourses and a deep concern for social issues. Additionally, they attracted support from influential bishops, such as Shute Barrington. Among Evangelicals, William Wilberforce and Zachary Macaulay of the Clapham Sect, gave active public support to the founding of national schools.[37] In 1828 Joseph Cotton Wigram, the Evangelical incumbent of St Luke's, Berwick Street, London, was also appointed secretary of the National Society, a position that he held until 1839.[38] As the century progressed a number of Evangelical bishops worked in association with the National Society among them Henry Ryder, John Bird Sumner and Anthony Thorold. While Ryder was Dean of Wells, he established two national schools and by 1813 was planning a third. On his consecration to the See of Gloucester the following year, Ryder continued to give enthusiastic support to the new society.[39]

Sumner having himself been a schoolmaster was a strong supporter of education. During his time as Bishop of Chester more than 700 schools were opened in the diocese. Sumner, it should be noted, saw school buildings not just as places where children were able to obtain a rudimentary education but also as centres where Christian meetings and other forms of instruction could take place.[40] Later, following his translation to Canterbury, he continued to promote school building albeit on a less grandiose scale. He urged his clergy to take a strong lead influencing the life and work of their parochial schools.[41] As primate, Sumner also served as chairman of the National Society. Thorold had supported the National Society since his time as incumbent of St Pancras, London. Soon after his arrival he converted the old ragged school buildings into national schools at a cost of £6,536, giving £550 of his own money

---

[37] Howse, *Saints in Politics*, p. 98, n. 16.
[38] See *Seventh Report of the National Society*, 1828, and *National Society General Committee Minutes*, 8 May 1839. Joseph Wigram later became Bishop of Rochester.
[39] Soloway, *Prelates and People*, p. 374.
[40] Scotland, *John Bird Sumner*, p. 155.
[41] Ibid., p. 155.

to the project. Later, when Bishop of Winchester, he emerged as a staunch defender of voluntary schools, and so strongly did he put the case for them in a public address in 1892 that the Council of the National Society printed his address as a pamphlet and circulated it the length and breadth of the country.[42]

Several of the Evangelical bishops appointed by Lord Palmerston were very committed to building schools in their dioceses. Charles Baring, for instance, during his time at Durham, saw no fewer than 183 elementary schools erected or enlarged during his episcopate. Robert Bickersteth was heartened to discover in 1870 that there were only thirty-five benefices in his diocese in which there were no church schools. Following the passing of the Forster Act in that same year, he urged the clergy of those parishes to make swift efforts to provide a school where distinctive religious teaching and the catechism could be an established part of the curriculum.[43] Francis Jeune was pleased to report that only in one out every twelve parishes in his Peterborough diocese was there no school, and in most of those there was a school within easy walking distance.[44]

Both the National Society and the British and Foreign Schools Society proved successful in their work and organisation, but still they only managed to reach a small percentage of the country's children. Accurate figures are almost impossible to obtain, but Llewellyn Woodward estimated that in 1833 in a number of large towns only between one third and a half of all working-class children received schooling of any kind. In that year the Government made its first ever grant of £20,000 to be divided equally between the two societies. However, in subsequent years this annual figure was divided between the two bodies in proportion to the amount that they themselves raised. Since members of the Church of England were, generally speaking, richer, the resources of the National Society increased at the expense of their rival. This meant that of £100,000 paid out by the government over a five-year period the National Society secured £70,000.

By 1831 the National Society had 2,002 schools; the British and Foreign Society had only 191.[45] The number of young children receiving education continued to rise and more buildings and teachers were

[42] Simpkinson, *Bishop Thorold*, pp. 52, 349–51.
[43] M.C. Bickersteth, *Robert Bickersteth*, p. 230.
[44] Jeune, *Charge, Peterborough*, p. 11.
[45] Cubberley, *History of Education*, p. 632.

needed. The government became increasingly concerned and in 1839 a special Committee of the Privy Council was set up. Its brief was 'the consideration of all matters affecting the education of the people ... to superintend the application of any sums voted by Parliament for the purpose of promoting public education'.[46] In order to see how well the money was being spent, the Committee proposed a system of inspection and, further, put forward a plan to establish a non-denominational normal school for the training of teachers. Both of these proposals met with opposition from the church and eventually the teacher training idea was dropped. The projected plan for inspection was grudgingly accepted after a compromise was found. Many churchmen felt that Government inspectors might be unfavourable to the ethos of church schools. After a brief struggle it was agreed that the archbishop of the province might veto the appointment of all inspectors in connection with the National Society.

Until the 1840s Anglican Evangelicals played a part, though not a particularly prominent one, in day and Sunday school education. Among a number of prominent parochial clergy who actively supported Evangelically-controlled education for the poor were Hugh McNeile of Liverpool and Hugh Stowell (1799–1865) of Salford. Both men publicly challenged the local municipal authorities that were set on establishing purely secular education in their respective areas. Both were successful in establishing church-based primary school education within the cities in which they ministered.[47] William Pennefather who had prospered at Barnet began his ministry at St Jude's Mildmay Park in 1864. Almost his first action was to raise funds for a new school for the poor of the parish.[48] Two years later, in a letter to a friend who had helped him to raise much of the needed money, he wrote, 'You will rejoice with me that we have already upwards of 300 additional scholars in our new schools.'[49]

Teacher Training

In the first three decades of the nineteenth century both the British and Foreign Schools Society and the National Society continued to

---

[46] Burgess, *Enterprise in Education*, p. 68.
[47] Hylson-Smith, *Evangelicals in the Church of England*, pp. 147–50.
[48] Braithwaite, *William Pennefather*, pp. 391–2.
[49] Ibid., p. 403.

use the monitoring system. However, by the later 1830s there was widespread dissatisfaction with it.

With the availability of state aid from 1833 there was a demand for an increased number of qualified teachers. The Government's own plan to establish a training college had crumbled in the face of opposition from the church.[50] The money was therefore made available instead through the National Society and the newly formed Diocesan Boards of Education. By this means several training colleges were founded in 1839 and 1840, among them Chester, Exeter, Oxford, Chichester and Norwich. Gloucester followed in 1853. Much of the energy that led to the founding of these institutions had come from high church pressure groups. In addition, the National Society established three colleges of its own at Chelsea, Whitelands and Battersea. By 1846 there were fourteen male training colleges and about half as many for women. Some of these were very small but Chester, which had been established by Sumner and his Evangelical chancellor, Henry Raikes, had a capacity for seventy men. Its sister college in Warrington had provision for thirty-five women. Several Evangelical bishops gave particular attention and support to the teacher training institutions in their dioceses. John Pelham was proud to relate that 'our diocesan training institution has continued to maintain its high character' and that its examination results were amongst the best in the country.[51]

In the years before 1846 no college could exist without the financial backing of a society or diocesan board. The result of this was that the only college outside of the National Society's control was the Home and Colonial Society's institution in Gray's Inn Road, London, which had been founded in 1836 by a group of Evangelical churchmen and dissenters. Its primary concern was in any case the training of mistresses for infant schools.

By this time, Francis Close, the incumbent of Cheltenham, who had for some years played an active role in national educational matters, became increasingly alarmed at the growing Tractarian influence within the National Society in whose affairs he had also been much involved. He came to see the crucial importance of training school teachers who had definite convictions. For some years he had been involved in training teachers in Cheltenham's national schools and in 1845 had asserted that 'over 250 teachers in

---

[50] Burgess, *Enterprise in Education*, p. 109.
[51] Pelham, *Charge, Norwich*, p. 19.

schools in different parts of the country had been trained in the national and infant schools in the town'.[52]

As Close saw it, none of the existing training colleges were run on Evangelical principles and the reformed religion of the Church of England. In 1845 he became chairman of a newly formed Church of England Training Society, which had as its object the establishment of an Evangelical Protestant Training College to counteract the Tractarian tendencies of the existing colleges. When, therefore, Samuel Codner (1776–1858),[53] an Evangelical merchant with an interest in education was supportive, Close called a meeting on 23 September 1845 at which it was resolved that 'an institution for the training of pious masters and mistresses upon scriptural and Evangelical principles, in connection with the Church of England, is urgently called for at the present time'.[54] The first building, which housed up to a hundred students, the principal, vice-principal and one master, was opened on 8 April 1850.[55] At the same time as the Cheltenham College was being developed, another Evangelical institution, Highbury College in London, was being opened between 1849 and 1850.[56] Highbury subsequently experienced recruitment problems and was forced to close. The money realised from the sale of its buildings was used to build St Mary's Hall for women students in Cheltenham, which was opened in 1869.[57]

Robert Bickersteth was instrumental in founding and raising money for the building of the Ripon Diocesan Training College and laid the foundation stone on 1 February 1860.[58] He later expressed his thankfulness for the Female Training School, which

---

[52] A. Platts and G.A. Hainton, *Education in Gloucestershire*, p. 70.

[53] Samuel Codner who was born in Teignmouth, Devon, on 5 August 1776 was a fish merchant engaged in Newfoundland. In 1823 with Prime-ministerial support he founded The Society for the Education of the Poor in Newfoundland. He did this because he feared that the poor in Newfoundland would be sucked into the Roman Catholic Church. With the help of the governor he established forty-five schools with some 12,000 pupils. Plain Christian charity, anti-Catholicism and British Imperialism activated Codner's activities.

[54] *First Annual Report of the Church of England Training Schools at Cheltenham* 1847, p. 15.

[55] C. More, *The Training of Teachers 1847–1947 A History of the Church Colleges at Cheltenham*, p. 12.

[56] Ibid., p. 9.

[57] Ibid., p. 32.

[58] M.C. Bickersteth, *Robert Bickersteth*, p. 218.

was opened in August 1862.[59] Bickersteth was a frequent visitor to the college and often sat and talked to the students. His son later wrote that 'to the end of his life his interest in the college never flagged. He made a point of being present at the meetings of the Committee of Management'.[60] Joseph Wigram extolled the excellence of the diocesan training institution at Hockerill: 'The qualifications of its teachers', he declared, 'have been acknowledged throughout the country'.[61]

Infant Education

Evangelicals were to the fore in the matter of infant education, probably on account of their belief in child conversion. Infant schools were seen by many of their number as nurturing grounds for the Christian faith. Joseph Wilson, a member of the Clapham Sect, had been so impressed by the infant school opened in London by the teacher of Robert Owen's school at New Lanark in Scotland that he established a similar venture at Spitalfields in London in 1819. The task of running the new institution was given to the then unknown Samuel Wilderspin (1792–1866)[62] who left his position as a clerk in a merchant's office to take up the work. Wilderspin was not the originator of the infant school system, the credit for which is usually given to two people, Frederick Oberlin, the pastor of Waldebach in the Alsace region of France, and Robert Owen, in Britain. Wilderspin was, nevertheless, to become the dominant influence in the promotion of infant school education in nineteenth-century England. In 1852 he wrote:

> Upwards of twenty five thousand children have now been under my own care, in various parts of the United Kingdom, whose age has not exceeded six years: myself, my daughter, and my agents, have organised many schools, and thus I have had opportunities for studying the infant mind and heart, such as none of my contemporaries have ever possessed.[63]

---

[59] R. Bickersteth, *Charge, Triennial Visitation*, pp. 25–6.
[60] M.C. Bickersteth, *Robert Bickersteth*, p. 219.
[61] Wigram, *A Charge 1864*, p. 12.
[62] Wilderspin was a Swedenborgian.
[63] S. Wilderspin, *The Infant System for Developing the Intellectual and Moral Powers of All Children*, p. iii.

With the passing of the years, Wilderspin developed a distinct philosophy for the instruction of the very young. His own early childhood experiences had been harsh. He later recalled, 'I often had the raps with the cane across the shoulders, and on the hand, and I found it was mainly for not learning what the teacher had forgotten to teach me.'[64] In the light of this he resolved to ensure that infant schools were happy and secure places which were free from an environment of fear. He regarded 'teaching through the senses' as crucially important for young children. To facilitate this there should amusements, singing, exercise, play, pictures and object boards. Each school should have no more than 200 pupils and should be well lit and have plenty of ventilation. Wilderspin felt the school playground to be particularly important, not merely for exercise but as an integral part of learning. Ideally, it should be equipped with rotary swings, spinning tops and wood bricks with which the children could build castles and other structures. Wilderspin advocated that a master should live on the school premises in a small but adequate house containing three or four rooms.

Religion played an important part in Wilderspin's infant teaching. He wrote, 'Perhaps in nothing has that simplicity of teaching so requisite for the young, and so earnestly contended for by me throughout, been so much disregarded, neglected, and perverted as in the matter of religion.'[65] In 1852 he expressed the great hope that the time would come 'when the distinct precepts of Christ ... will be faithfully regarded. The religion for infants should be a simple trust in the love and kindness of God our Saviour'.[66] This must, he later reflected, 'be the wish of all true Christians' that infant school-age children be taught the fundamental truths of the everlasting gospel.[67] In so far as content was concerned, Wilderspin was of the view that simple stories and parables were the most suitable teaching material. He also felt that the Church of England liturgy had an important part to play:

Many beautiful and simple prayers are to be found in the Church of England[68] *Prayer Book* which I think cannot be mended, and which

---

[64] Ibid., p. 4.
[65] Ibid., p. 17.
[66] Ibid., p. 17.
[67] Ibid., p. 94.
[68] S. Wilderspin, *Early Discipline Illustrated or the Infant System Progressing and Successful*, p. 20.

I have found quite suitable to the infant mind. Several of the Collects, for simplicity of language and rich fullness of divine truth cannot be surpassed.[69]

In addition to writing extensively about his system, Wilderspin toured the country lecturing and encouraging the opening of new infant schools. Among those who were convinced by his scheme were two prominent Evangelical clergy, William Wilson (1791–1867) of Walthamstow, the brother of Joseph Wilson, and Francis Close of Cheltenham. Wilson visited one of Wilderspin's infant schools and was convinced of their value. As a result, he asked Wilderspin to carry out a survey of his parish to see if an infant school was a feasible project. Eventually, an infant school was established in a barn belonging to Wilson. No expense was spared and one of Wilderspin's associates spent five to six weeks at Walthamstow in order to ensure that the new institution was properly managed.

In a short space of time William Wilson became a strong advocate of infant schools and following in the footsteps of Wilderspin he began to both write and preach on the matter. In his first book he emphasised that 'the education of the hearts of young children' is crucial. By the heart Wilson meant 'the seat or fountain of the passions and desires'.[70]

When Close opened his Sunday school at Alstone, on the outskirts of Cheltenham, he received a grant from William Wilson and his brother Joseph. As a condition, they prescribed that the premises be used during the week as an infant school. Close was happy to comply with this requirement and early in 1826 the building was opened by Samuel Wilderspin with 100 pupils and two women teachers.[71] The experiment proved so successful that plans were put in place for another similar institution in the centre of town. A site was selected for this purpose at St James Square. Although Close was adamant that the Bible was the *sine qua non* of education at all levels,[72] he was by no means closed to new ideas about infant

---

[69] Ibid., p. 95.

[70] W. Wilson, *The System of Infants' Schools by William Wilson AM Vicar of Walthamstow*, second edition, p. 37.

[71] Hart, *History of Cheltenham*, pp. 211f. See also Wilderspin, *Early Discipline*, p. 94.

[72] See his speech at the Annual General Meeting of the Cheltenham National and Sunday Schools, *Cheltenham Journal*, 15 August 1842.

education emanating from Wilson and Wilderspin, such as learning through play. This is suggested by the description of the new school in a contemporary guide to Cheltenham:

> The New Infant School room is a neat edifice sixty feet long, thirty feet wide and twenty feet high and will hold 300 children. It is airy and has a gallery 20 feet wide and a playground attached to it is spacious and secure. Swings and various gymnastic exercises were provided for the children; these are calculated to invigorate the frame, to quicken the intellect and to enliven the spirit.[73]

One master and his wife, and a daughter assisting in the teaching, staffed the school. Close's enthusiasm for the education of younger children soon caught the town as a whole so that by 1848 there were six schools in the parish of Cheltenham, the others being Naunton School in Exmouth Street (opened in 1834), Waterloo School in Tewkesbury Road (opened in 1836), Fairview School in Sherborne Street (opened in 1840) and St Paul's School in Brunswick Street (opened in 1848).

So many infant schools began to appear that in 1836 Evangelical churchmen, in co-operation with Nonconformists, founded The Home and Colonial Infant School Society for 'the improvement and general extension of the Infant School System on Christian principles as are set forth and embodied in the doctrine and articles of the Church of England'.[74] The founders felt that these objectives could only be achieved by special training for teachers of infant schools, and therefore established the Home and Colonial Training College in Gray's Inn Road. With the passing of time the National Society were prodded into action in 1836 and began formally to support parochial infant schools. They started to use Tufton Street Parochial Infant School for infant school training purposes.

Strife in the National Society

By the middle years of the nineteenth century, Close, along with a number of other Evangelical clergy, was becoming increasingly concerned at the rising Tractarian influence in the National Society. In particular, there was a growing insistence that the

---

[73] J. Lee, *A New Guide to Cheltenham and Its Environs*, p. 140.
[74] *Quarterly Education Magazine of the Home and Colonial School Society*, 1844, p. 44, cited by Burgess, *Enterprise in Education*, p. 66.

clergyman should control the school and ensure that children attended Church of England worship and that the catechism was properly taught. This, together with the growing tide of ritualism, antagonised Nonconformists and made Anglican Evangelicals increasingly suspicious.

In his early years, Close had been a strong advocate of the National Society, because he was, at that time, convinced that secular education led only to radicalism and, perhaps, insurrection and violence. Speaking as chairman at the 1842 Annual Meeting of Cheltenham National and Sunday Schools he said, 'I unhesitatingly assert that mere secular education without religion is worse than no education at all: better that the peasant should remain as the dull lump of clay he cultivates than that religion should be dispensed with, and religious instruction prohibited.'[75]

Close went on in the same address to maintain that if 'the spiritual wants' of the masses had been met through the Sabbath, national, infant and Sunday schools, the 1840s would not have witnessed the scenes of violence and bloodshed they had done.[76] Because of his deeply-held convictions, when proposals were first mooted for a national Government scheme of education to supersede the two main denominational societies, Close was vehement against them. He believed that in the end the Christian influence would be totally lost in the English schools. In a publication entitled *National Education and Lord Brougham's Bill Considered*, Close thundered: 'The people do not desire it, the members of the Church of England do not wish it.'[77] He was not happy, as he put it in the document, to leave national education 'to the unruly wills of sinful men'.[78] In Close's view, as long as there was a national church 'no consistent churchmen' could be happy about weakening the regulations by putting national education in the hands of secular government. Close also felt the stubbornness of Gloucestershire folk would be a problem if it came to compelling people to send their children to a particular school; 'They might as well try to get a Gloucestershire ox to drink when it is not thirsty, as to try to drive the Gloucestershire peasant to a school against his will'.[79]

---

[75] *Cheltenham Journal*, 15 August 1842.

[76] Ibid.

[77] F. Close, *National Education and Lord Brougham's Bill Considered*, p. 47.

[78] Ibid., p. 47.

[79] *Cheltenham Journal*, 8 February 1838.

However, despite Close's vehement views against state education, events took place that caused him to radically alter his thinking on the matter. The Anglo-Catholic caucus, led by George Denison (1805–1896), were increasingly taking control of affairs and Close, among others, was of the view that the National Society could no longer be trusted. The teacher training institutions at Westminster, Battersea and Chelsea were frequently assailed for their Tractarian tendencies, and it was put about that the purpose of the National Society who ran them was 'to send into our villages and hamlets, as well as mining districts, schoolmasters initiated into all the ecclesiastical millinery and ceremonies of Puseyism'.[80] Close gave public vent to his concern in October 1845:

> For years gone by I have advocated the principle that the Church of the people ought to educate the people, that the National Church should be the medium of national instruction but when I see day after day the defection and apostasy of the Church of England clergy I cannot feel the same repose were the Christian education of the people exclusively committed to the Church of England.[81]

Three years later Close again sided with the Government in their dispute with the National Society over the management clause which, among other things, proposed the appointment of lay managers to supervise the running of the schools. He asserted:

> I cordially support the present Government Scheme because I think it not only hits the via media of honest union of Church and State and the fair and equitable adjustment of lay and clerical influence in the details and because I see in it a machinery well adapted to counteract the high priestly notions with which Mr Denison and those he represents would rivet the country.[82]

In the same year, Close published *Co-operation with the Committee of the Council on Education Vindicated and Recommended by the Rev Francis Close AM Incumbent of Cheltenham*. In it he stated that the assistance offered by the Government to the churches was calculated 'to secure a system of Education adapted

---

[80] *Cheltenham Journal*, 27 October 1845.
[81] Ibid.
[82] *Cheltenham Journal*, 13 November 1848.

to the great necessities of the land both in quality and extent'.[83] In contrast to the high churchmen who resented any kind of state interference in their church or school, Close gave his total backing to the Government scheme of inspection which he held 'to be so fair, so open, so popular, that it is utterly impossible that any inspector, could either act in an unfair manner, or make his office subservient to the propagation of his views'.[84] Close again praised the system of Government inspection in a pamphlet published in 1852 in which he attacked the Manchester Bill. This was an ecumenical scheme by the city's churches to put the city's schools on the local rates. As Close saw the proposal, it would dry up church giving and ultimately the schools would find themselves in secular hands.[85]

Matters finally came to a head in 1853 when Close and two or three hundred others walked out of the National Society Annual General Meeting in London because there was not enough Evangelical support. He asserted that the society 'had forfeited all claim to the confidence of the Protestant portion of the Church of England'.[86] Together in a nearby coffee house some of those who had left founded The Church of England Education Society. The new organisation had among its vice-presidents the Earls of Effingham, Shaftesbury and Cavan, Lord Charles Russell and the Bishops of Manchester, Sydney and Mauritius. Its committee included most of the Evangelical leaders and a number of MPs. The Church of England Education Society made it clear that in schools that were the recipients of its aid, 'The holy Scriptures are the basis of education' and that 'the religious teaching is in accordance with the Articles and formularies of the Church of England'.[87]

Francis Close gave one of his reasons for leaving the National Society in order to help found the new society the refusal to relax the terms of union in favour of dissenters.[88] Edward Girdlestone

---

[83] F. Close, *Co-operation with the Committee of the Council on Education Vindicated and Recommended by the Rev Francis Close AM Incumbent of Cheltenham*, p. iii.

[84] Ibid., p. 44.

[85] F. Close, *The Secular System The Manchester Bill and the Government Scheme Contrasted by the Revd Francis Close AM*, pp. 36f.

[86] Berwick, *Life of Francis Close*, pp. 13–14.

[87] See Church of England Education Society, *Annual Report* 1869, p. 8, cited by Bentley, *Transformation of the Evangelical Party*, p. 56.

[88] *Cheltenham Journal*, 18 November 1854.

(1805–1884),[89] another Evangelical who later gave strong support to the National Agricultural Labourers' Union, underlined the moral dangers of 'being so bigoted as to shut the door in the face of the Dissenters' of working class origin 'and thus exposing them to ignorance and vice just because they would not repeat every word of the Church catechism'.[90]

From its inception the new society developed a very different emphasis from the National Society. It made its main concern the maintenance of schools rather than the construction of new school premises. The committee of the new society soon found there was an ever-widening need for the provision of salary grants for teachers, book funds to schools and provision of fees to training-college candidates. The society made one of its priorities the recruitment and maintenance of teachers during their training. Some scholarships were offered at one of the three Evangelical colleges to particular categories of unqualified teachers.[91] H.J. Burgess commented that the Society 'proved to be a useful supplement to the older Society's work'.[92]

Despite its internal struggles the National Society proved to be the major player in primary school education in nineteenth-century England. In 1869 it was able to claim that of 14,709 ecclesiastical districts in England and Wales, only 338 were completely destitute of Anglican day schools in the near vicinity, if not in the parish itself.[93]

By the 1860s it was clear that the state was making a steadily increasing contribution to the cost of running primary schools. In the light of this fact, many on the Privy Council's Committee for Education were of the view that the state should have a role in their management. As far as Denison and those in the National Society were concerned such a proposal was an unconstitutional involvement in an area that was solely the church's domain. The state then further realised that the existing management clauses were insufficient to safeguard the rights of those Nonconformists who rejected Anglican teaching, not to mention those who wanted a purely secular education for their children. For this reason, Robert Lowe

---

[89] For Girdlestone, see Reynolds, *Evangelicals at Oxford*, p. 92 See also his entry in the *D.N.B.* Vol. 7, p. 1274.

[90] Burgess, *Enterprise in Education*, p. 160.

[91] Ibid., p. 143.

[92] Ibid., p. 142. See also pp. 160, 172f., 189.

[93] National Society, *Annual Report* 1869, p. 8, cited by Bentley, *Transformation of the Evangelical Party*, p. 57.

put forward a Code, which the Government felt would satisfactorily resolve the issue.

With the pressing need for economy hanging over the whole education system a Royal Commission headed by the Duke of Newcastle was set up in 1861 'to enquire into the present state of popular education'.[94] In effect, the Commission endorsed the provision of support for the church's work in education but made it clear that it would have to be based on results. Robert Lowe, who was vice-president of the Committee of the Council, asserted that 'the object of the government was to make education effective, not religious!' Inevitably, he was sharply attacked by Evangelical churchmen. Dr Charles H. Bromby, the forthright and outspoken principal of the Cheltenham Normal College, attacked the proposed cutbacks on teacher education as 'a deadly blow'.[95] He was also vehement that to make grants dependent on successful reading, writing and arithmetic would not only undermine the status of religious education but also disadvantage the poor from educational opportunity. Unfortunately, the Church of England did not speak with one voice in the matter. The Evangelical Home and Colonial Society unanimously condemned the Code, whereas some high churchmen supported it maintaining that the children of labourers should only be instructed in those subjects 'which really befit their station'.[96]

The truth of the matter was that Robert Lowe was a decided secularist who worked hard and with skill to undermine the church-based religious education in schools. One of the most crippling of the measures in his Code was the provision that Government grants to individual schools would be reduced by the amount of any endowments which they possessed. *The Times* supported Lowe's campaigns, which caused the redoubtable Bromby to complain that 'A single recommendation to the effect that special encouragement be given to the three elementary subjects is tortured into an evidence that these subjects are neglected, and that there resides no remedy for the existing system'.[97]

The 1870 Act was a significant milestone in the history of English education. 'Its object', said William Forster the Bill's sponsor, 'is to

---

[94] Burgess, *Enterprise in Education*, p. 173.
[95] Ibid., p. 175.
[96] Ibid., p. 177.
[97] C.H. Bromby, *Letter to the Rt Hon. R Lowe* (1861), p. 23, cited by Burgess, *Enterprise in Education*, p. 184.

complete the present system, to fill in the gaps.'[98] Denominational schools were allowed to continue independently if they were already effective, and their grants were increased. The idea of financing schools by means of levying a local rate was decisively rejected much to the relief of the majority of the clergy, and of the Anglo-Catholics and the National Society in particular. Evangelicals, such as the Seventh Earl of Shaftesbury, were greatly relieved at this step. Shaftesbury had earlier commented, 'I dread, sadly dread, these schemes of national education ... such a plan is a death warrant to the teaching of Evangelical religion.' It had better be called 'a water rate to extinguish religious fire among the people'.[99]

Two other Evangelicals, Charles Buxton and Francis Close, shared Shaftesbury's convictions. Buxton was of the view that rate support would put an end to voluntary donations and that the management of schools would ultimately fall into the hands of committees of rate payers, who would not be interested in the character of education given.[100] Close was more emphatic and spoke of the 'crushing evidence against an Education rate' which, in his view, would have 'dried up all the sources of voluntary effort, and ultimately would have handed all the schools of the country to the secularists'.[101]

The Act also laid down that where local school provision was insufficient, the denominational societies were to make good the deficiency. If they were unable to come forward with proposals to do so within the prescribed time of six months, then a local board school would be established, financed by the state.

In the matter of religious education the Act laid down two important regulations. In all schools that received state grants from public funds, parents were given the right to withdraw their children from religious education. In the new board schools 'no catechism or religious formulary which is distinctive of any particular denomination shall be taught'.[102] William Thomson, the Evangelical Archbishop of York, spoke of the Act as 'an honest measure and likely to be "worthy" of the church's support'. It had been 'framed with great care and certainly in no hostile spirit towards religious

---

[98] T. Jarman, [Add details. This book not previously cited. Not in Bibliog] p. 265.
[99] Hammond and Hammond, *Shaftesbury*, p. 257.
[100] Burgess, *Enterprise in Education*, p. 189.
[101] Ibid., p. 190.
[102] Ibid., p. 197.

education'.[103] *The Record* felt that the Act was 'better than our fears if not as good as our hopes'.[104]

In the few months immediately following the Forster Act, the National Society, prompted by many of the diocesan bishops, made a huge effort to close the gaps with church schools before the new school boards could establish secular ones. The society was able to make 1,114 grants to new schools all but 140 of which were able to secure Government aid.[105] Robert Bickersteth, the Bishop of Ripon, was heartened to discover in 1870 that there were only thirty-five benefices in his diocese in which there was no church school. He immediately pressed the clergy of those parishes to make prompt efforts to provide a school 'where distinctive religious teaching and the catechism could be an established part of the curriculum'.[106]

Where school boards were found to be necessary the church aimed to secure a dominant influence. In a number of areas in London 'churchmen' and dissenters combined on a platform of religious education in board schools. In the first election to the boards in London, the supporters of religion in schools, gained thirty-six of the forty-nine seats. There were several prominent Evangelicals among them including Charles Buxton, John Miller, Vicar of Greenwich, and Anthony Thorold, Vicar of St Pancras. By the 1870s a significant number of Evangelical clergy were urging the importance of greater co-operation with school boards. At the Church Congress of 1875, William Cadman, Rector of St George's Southwark, advised churchmen against adopting a hostile stance towards the boards, but at the same time he urged them not to give up their schools unless circumstances forced them to do so.[107]

Despite the anxieties which had been entertained by many Evangelical clergy *The Record* felt confident that the Forster Education Act would not after all result in the demise of the voluntary schools. Their numbers had risen from 8,281 to 14,181 since the Act and the number of transfers to the boards had not been particularly great,[108]

---

[103] *The Times*, 22 October 1870.

[104] *The Record*, cited by Bentley, *Transformation of the Evangelical Party*, p. 60.

[105] National Society, *Annual Report* 1871, pp. 11–12, cited by Burgess, *Enterprise in Education*, p. 212.

[106] M.C. Bickersteth, *Robert Bickersteth*, p. 230.

[107] *The Record*, 21 March 1884, cited by Bentley, *Transformation of the Evangelical Party*, p. 84.

[108] *The Record*, 5 September 1881, cited by Bentley, *Transformation of the Evangelical Party*, p. 86.

In 1890 the Church of England was still the major educator of the population with church schools accounting for 11,922 of the total of 14,784.[109]

Public Schools

In 1861 Nathaniel Woodard famed on account of his own Woodard schools convened a large public meeting at the Sheldonian Theatre in Oxford to promote his new scheme of establishing boarding schools for the middle classes. Two prominent Evangelicals, Francis Jeune and Joseph Wigram, both agreed to take part in the meeting. Jeune, who warmly supported Woodard's proposals, agreed to take the chair and Wigram consented to second the main speech that was to be made by William Gladstone. As those who had been invited to the meeting entered the theatre they were given handbills that denounced Woodard's scheme as popery. At the time Jeune took little notice, but in the weeks following it became clear that there was more than a little truth in what had been written in them. Wigram eventually wrote to Jeune after he had been informed that Romish practices, including in particular confession, were taking place at St Nicholas College, Herstmonceux, of which Woodard was provost. Although Woodard was subsequently exonerated it emerged that doctrines that ran counter to Protestantism were being taught in the school. This led Wigram to adopt a position of hostility. It also led Evangelicals to redouble their efforts to found boarding school institutions with a distinctively Evangelical ethos.

Francis Close had earlier been a member of the board that founded Cheltenham College in 1840, as a school which would adhere strictly to what he described as 'the plain, honest, Protestant Evangelical religion of the written Church of England'.[110] To Close's great disappointment, the College subsequently departed from his original vision. This further convinced him to throw in his lot with those who now sought to regain the initiative for the Evangelicals. Clifton College was opened in 1861 in a 'Simeonite' parish because Bristol Grammar School did not take boarders. Other Evangelical schools were founded by local endeavour and had as their main objective, 'to wean away the professional and trading classes from Anglo-Catholicism or irreligion'.[111] Some of these institutions were

---

[109] Bentley, *Transformation of the Evangelical Party*, p. 89.
[110] *Cheltenham Journal*, 26 June 1843.
[111] Royle, 'Evangelicals and Education', p. 126.

founded by clerical and lay associations which came into being as regional organisations from 1858 onwards.[112] These associations stood for 'a sincere and loyal attachment to the principles of the English Reformed Church as distinguished, on the one hand, from the doctrines and practices of a Romanising tendency and from the rationalistic free handling of Revelation, on the other'.[113] In 1885 eighteen such associations came together to form a central union which included an objective of promoting education on Evangelical principles. Among the schools established were Trent College at Long Eaton in 1866; Monkton Combe, near Bath, which was founded by the local vicar, the Rev Francis Pocock, in 1868, Weymouth College, founded in 1879; and St Lawrence College, Ramsgate, which was founded in the same year by the South Eastern Clerical and Lay Association.

Following the death of Francis Close in 1882, the Western Clerical and Lay Association decided to follow the example of Ramsgate and found an Evangelical day school in Cheltenham. The project had the support of the Central Committee of the Clerical and Lay Association in London whose general appeal received widespread support.[114] This enabled the purchase of a substantial acreage of land fronting the Shelburne Road in the immediate proximity of the Banbury railway line. The school, which was originally called The Dean Close Memorial School, was opened in 1886.[115] The opening ceremony was preceded by a special service at the parish church of St Mark where the Rev Canon Edward Hoare (1812–1894) gave the address. He referred to Francis Close as 'one of the most useful men in our church, and as having great foresight'.[116] Canon Brooke who chaired the luncheon gathering spoke of Dean Close as 'one of the best organisers that ever lived'. He went on to say that 'he did not think that any other way of perpetuating the memory of Dean Close, could have been found ... than that which had been followed, education – the education of the upper-middle classes, the education of the poor, the training of teachers, the whole was dear to his heart'.[117]

---

[112] See Balleine, *History of the Evangelical Party*, p. 273.
[113] Royle, 'Evangelicals and Education', p. 126.
[114] *Cheltenham Examiner*, 19 May 1886.
[115] See *Cheltenham Free Press*, 15 May 1886, and *The Decanian*, Vol. 1, 1892.
[116] *Cheltenham Examiner*, 19 May 1886.
[117] Ibid.

Education of the Clergy

One of the reasons why the Evangelicals were effective in the parishes was because they devoted a good deal of time and energy to training and stimulating the clergy. The largest and most influential conference was the Islington clerical meeting, which began in 1827 when Daniel Wilson invited a group of twelve friends to study the subject of prayer. One criticism that could be levelled at some of their early discussion topics was that they tended to be somewhat introverted in nature. For example, subjects included 'The validity of the ministry with reference to the theories of the Plymouth Brethren' and 'What rules are to be adopted in interpreting the pro-phetic Scriptures?' Nevertheless, these discussions paved the way for the founding of theological colleges.

One of the earliest Evangelicals to give serious consideration to theological colleges was Bishop John Sumner of Chester. He took a keen interest in the College at St Bees in Cumberland, founded in 1816 by Bishop G.H. Law of Carlisle to educate clergy for the remote areas that could not attract university men.[118] St Bees was largely devoid of Evangelical influence apart from a brief spell from 1840–1846 when Robert Pedder Buddicom was the principal.[119] Sumner was also involved in the founding of St Aidan's College, Birkenhead, in 1846 where he gave much encouragement to its first principal and founder, Joseph Baylee (1808–1883).[120] Both institu-tions had been set up with the specific object of assisting men who could not afford a university education.[121] Baylee established the college on firm Evangelical lines. This continued when William Saumerez Smith took over as principal in 1869.[122] By the mid-point of the century Evangelicals were becoming concerned that some-thing more needed to be done.

In 1857 Canon John Miller of St Martin's, Birmingham, spoke for many when he addressed the University of Oxford in a sermon entitled 'The Defective Ministerial Training of our Universities a Main Hindrance to the Efficiency of the Church of England'. Miller

---

[118] See T. Park, *St Bees College 1816–1895*.
[119] D.W. Dowland, *Nineteenth-Century Anglican Theological Training*, p. 4.
[120] Ibid., p. 67.
[121] Scotland, *John Bird Sumner*, p. 52.
[122] Dowland, *Anglican Theological Training*, p. 67. Smith was principal from 1869 to 1890 and Bishop of Sydney from 1890 to 1899.

bemoaned the fact that in most cases only a very short period elapses between Oxford life and ordination. 'This interval,' he pointed out, 'was rarely given over to any defined course of study'.[123] Miller went on to point out that students in medicine, law and music are required to take added training and such ought to be the case for candidates for holy orders. In particular, he cited the necessity for practical pulpit training for clergy.[124] Miller was not overly sold on theological colleges being situated either in small towns nor in their attachment to a diocese where their theological complexion will bear the impress of the bishop.

The first theological colleges for graduates opened at Chichester in 1839, Wells in 1840 and Cuddesdon near Oxford in 1854. All were high church and still there was no similar Evangelical college. Litton Hall was founded in 1855, with help from Lord Shaftesbury, for both Anglican and Nonconformist Evangelicals. It proved unsuccessful and closed in 1860. Three year later, however, the London College of Divinity proved to be much more successful. It was started with funds donated by Alfred Peache (1818–1900), the wealthy Vicar of Mangotsfield in Gloucestershire. Located initially at Kilburn it moved to Highbury in 1865. Its first principal was Thomas P. Boultbee (1818–1884) who had earlier been the most significant of Francis Close's curates in Cheltenham and theological tutor at Cheltenham College. At this stage Evangelicals were still suspicious of theological training outside the universities, believing that they were likely to fall into the hands of the Tractarians.

When, however, Oxbridge Universities were stripped of most of their Anglican monopolies, by virtue of the Universities Tests Act of 1871, undergraduate degrees in theology were instituted in both institutions. This led Evangelicals to open graduate halls in which to ensure the soundness of the teaching the students received. Wycliffe Hall was opened at Oxford in 1877, followed by Ridley Hall at Cambridge in 1881. Wycliffe Hall opened under the principalship of Robert Girdlestone (1836–1923) and Ridley Hall was placed in the charge of Handley Moule.[125] Both Halls offered relatively inexpensive accommodation and some lecture courses for graduate

---

[123] J.C. Miller, *The Defective Ministerial Training of our Universities a Main Hindrance to the Efficiency of the Church of England: A Sermon Preached before the University of Oxford*, p. 28.

[124] Ibid., p. 33.

[125] For Ridley Hall, see F.W.B. Bullock, *The History of Ridley Hall, Cambridge* 3 Vols.

ordinands who continued in their attachment to their old colleges. Most students stayed in residence for only one year. Girdlestone wrote in a brief account of Wycliffe Hall that its teaching 'is designed to be practical and devotional, not controversial, and to be supplementary to – not a substitute for – the work of the Divinity Professors'.[126]

Higher Education

Since early times Evangelical influence was apparent at both Oxford and Cambridge, and this inevitably meant that there were always a number of fellows and professors whose convictions were Evangelical. In the nineteenth century Evangelical influence was markedly more pronounced in Cambridge. In large measure, this was due to the influence of Charles Simeon who was both Fellow of King's College and incumbent of Holy Trinity Church. Among Simeon's close associates were James Scholefield, who became Regius Professor of Greek, and Francis Wollaston and William Farish, who were both Jacksonian Professors of Natural and Experimental Philosophy, the latter succeeding the former. Joseph Jowett was Regius Professor of Civil Law from 1872 to 1813. Isaac Milner, the President of Queens' College, was, for a period, Professor of Mathematics and University Vice-chancellor.[127]

Hardman has chronicled some of the key Evangelicals who impacted the University of Cambridge in the middle and later years of the nineteenth century. Among them were Edwin Guest, who was Master of Caius College from 1852–1880. Hardman commented, 'It can hardly be doubted that Guest's presence at the head of Caius must itself have been an attraction to Evangelical parents.'[128] The three Perowne brothers were also responsible for drawing the sons of Evangelicals to Corpus Christi College. They were 'a remarkable trio', the sons of John Perowne, a CMS missionary in India. T.T. Perowne was 'the firmest Evangelical' and contributed in the greatest measure to promote Evangelical views among the student body.[129]

---

[126] R.B. Girdlestone, *Wycliffe Hall, Oxford; Its Nature and Object*, p. 2.
[127] Hylson-Smith, *Evangelicals in the Church of England*, pp. 104–5.
[128] Hardman, *Evangelical Party*.
[129] Ibid., p. 406.

At Oxford, Isaac Crouch (c. 1765–1835) has been credited as 'the father of Evangelicalism'.[130] His lectures in the Greek Testament and church history were highly valued, and on Sunday evenings he held reading parties of a religious character. Crouch became vice-principal of St Edmund Hall in 1783 and held the position until 1806. During his time in office he set the college on the map as an Evangelical institution and in time men were attracted to Oxford by its reputation. Crouch was succeeded by Daniel Wilson who held office from 1807–1812 and then by John Hill, who was vice-principal from 1812–1851.

Dr John MacBride became vice-principal of Magdalen Hall in 1813. He was the first Evangelical to be appointed as head of an Oxford College. According to Reynolds, Magdalen 'in some ways tended to succeed St Edmund Hall as a home for Evangelical undergraduates'.[131] Reynolds provides convincing evidence to counter J.H. Overton's criticism that Evangelicals at Oxford 'made no marks in the schools'.[132] He points out that 'there was a total of twenty three "firsts" among undoubted champions of the Evangelical cause, including five "double firsts", over thirty years, in days of short class lists'.[133]

From 1858–1862, the Evangelical, Francis Jeune, was vice-chancellor of the university. Reynolds suggests that it was during this period that 'the Evangelicals at Oxford were at the height of their influence'.[134] He also points out that a significant number of very able Evangelical clergy and lay people graduated from the university during 1845–1871.[135] Included among them were Bishops Shirley, Baring, Oxenden, Pelham, Villiers, Smith, Anderson, Ryle and Waldegrave, and a number of notable parish clergy. Among the prominent laymen were Sir Robert Inglis, the Second and Third Earls of Harrowby and Sir George Grey. J.I. Packer points out that Evangelical theologians made their weightiest contributions in dogmatics, historical theology and certain fields of church history. The work of Edward Arthur Litton and in particular his *Introduction to Dogmatic Theology* 'towers above all the rest'.[136] Packer also cites

---

[130] Reynolds, *Evangelicals at Oxford*, p. 59.
[131] Ibid., p. 86.
[132] Overton, *English Church*, p. 86.
[133] Ibid., p. 86.
[134] Reynolds, *Evangelicals at Oxford*, p. 119.
[135] Ibid., p. 157.
[136] J.I. Packer, 'The Oxford Evangelicals in Theology', in Reynolds, *Evangelicals at Oxford*, p. 86.

Robert Girdlestone, Principal of Wycliffe Hall from 1877–1889, whose *Dies Irae: The Final Judgement and Future Prospects* (1869) put a strong case against universalism and annihilationism. Reynolds concludes with the assertion that the Evangelical movement at Oxford continued with 'considerable vigour' during the last decades of the nineteenth century.[137]

When all this is put together, it is clear that the Evangelicals of the established church had deep concern for education at all levels. In the parishes they devoted time and energy to the building and running of primary schools. Through the energetic labours of men such as Francis Close, Robert Bickersteth, Joseph Wigram and the Sumner brothers, they were active in the promotion of teacher education and the building of teacher training colleges. In the education of clergy and the development of theological colleges Evangelicals were to the fore. In both the universities of Oxford and Cambridge there was a significant Evangelical presence, both in terms of students and scholarship.

---

[137] Reynolds, *Evangelicals at Oxford*, p. 97.

11

Revivalism and the Keswick Convention

Revival and Revivalism

From the mid-eighteenth century onwards both English and American Christianity were profoundly influenced by revivals of religion. The Anglican and Calvinist, George Whitefield (1714–1770) had a major impact on the 'Great Awakening' in New England and the Eastern Colonies in the 1740s. John Wesley (1703–1791) sent a cluster of dynamic preachers to America who played a significant role in the revivals of the early nineteenth century. Their impact was also reciprocated by a number of preachers and teachers of revival who came to hold special meetings in the British Isles. Among them were Lorenzo Dow (1777–1834), who helped to birth Primitive Methodism; James Caughey (1810–1891) and Charles Finney (1792–1875) who were active mid-century and, later in the century, Phoebe Palmer (1807–1874) assisted by her husband Walter, Dwight L. Moody (1837–1899) and Robert (1827–1899) and Hannah Smith (1832–1899). Of these, it was really only Moody and the Pearsall Smiths who impacted the Church of England to any significant degree.

There have been a number of studies of 'revival' and its impact on Christianity on both sides of the Atlantic.[1] Few of them however have attempted to define what is meant by the terms 'revival' and 'revivalism'.[2] Generally speaking, revivals have been periods of 'intense religious interest' in a single church or community. Revival,

---

[1] S. O'Brien, 'Eighteenth Century Publishing Networks in the First Years of Transatlantic "Evangelicalism"', in M. Noll et al. (eds.), *Evangelicalism: Comparative Studies of Popular Protestantism in North America 1700–1900*, pp. 38–57.

[2] G.M. Ditchfield, *The Evangelical Revival*.

as opposed to revivalism, has been regarded, not as something Christians do for God, but rather a work that God does for men and women. Revival was held to be a 'sovereign work of God' or to use Jonathan Edwards' words, a 'surprising' occurrence. In his celebrated *Lectures on Revivals of Religion*, William B. Sprague stated that 'in all ordinary cases in which revival takes place, it would be no difficult thing to mark a distinct providential agency preparatory to it'.[3] In a recent study of revival, Stuart Piggin made the point that revivals will always be 'a repeat of what happens in the Book of Acts'.[4] Any definition of revival which encompasses the Great Awakening and the Wesleyan movement in England would necessarily include an enduring renewal of church and society which magnifies Christ and releases the gift and fruits of the Holy Spirit in people's lives.

Since the ministy of Finney there have been those who have distinguished between revival and revivalism. J. Edwin Orr pointed out that the term revivalism was first used in the 1820s following the Second Great Awakening.[5] A number of the leaders who were at the centre of this frontier revival in Kentucky and Tennessee preached an Arminian gospel in which they stressed that men and women could of their own free will repent of their wicked ways and turn back to God. Some of them introduced novel ideas in an effort to induce repentance. For Iain Murray and a number of scholars herein lies the difference between revival and revivalism. 'The term implied', Murray wrote, 'that there were certain men capable of producing emotion and excitement which ... was the essence of revival.'[6] Such men, he continued, could not see the distinction in the assertion of Gardiner Spring (1785–1873) that 'Revivals are always spurious when they are got up by man's device and not brought down by the Spirit.'[7] The 'means' used by many of the revivalists of the Second Great Awakening, and those who followed them in the subsequent years of the century, included protracted meetings, camp meetings, exhortations and the anxious bench or penitent form.

---

[3] W. Sprague, *Lectures on Revivals of Religion*, p. 93.

[4] S. Piggin, *Firestorm of the Lord: The History and Prospects for Revival in the Church and the World*, p. 102.

[5] J.E. Orr, *The Re-Study of Revival and Revivalism*.

[6] I. Murray, *Revival and Revivalism: The Making and Marring of American Revivalism*, p. 201.

[7] G. Spring, *Personal Reminiscences* Vol. 1, pp. 217–18, cited in Murray, *Revival and Revivalism*, p. 201.

The eighteenth-century Wesleyan revival had left a concern for revival in its wake and the early-nineteenth century witnessed the emergence of a number of revivalistic Methodist offshoots. Among them were the Primitive Methodists who emerged in 1811 with the coming together of Hugh Bourne's revivalistic Camp Meeting Methodists and the followers of William Clowes.[8] A little later in 1815 a further group emerged taking the name Bible Christians. One of their number, Billy Bray, was to be influential in the life of the Tractarian incumbent of the parish of Baldhu in Cornwall. Further outbursts of revivalism followed with the formation of the Leeds Protestant Methodists and the later Wesleyan Reformers. These and other similar groups kept alive a concern for holiness and a desire for the renewing witness of the Spirit among Evangelicals of all denominations.

American Influences

During the course of the nineteenth century, a number of American revivalists came to the British Isles and held series of special meetings. Almost all of them had different perceptions of revival and utilised different 'means' in effort to achieve it. Those who came in the earlier decades had little or no direct influence on Anglican clergy or churches. They included Lorenzo Dow, James Caughey, Charles Finney, and Walter and Phoebe Palmer. Dow came to England twice, once from December 1805 to June 1807 accompanied by his wife Peggy, and a second time alone from June 1818 to June 1819. On both occasions, his labours were largely focused among the Methodists, and he played a significant part in the origin and early development of the revivalistic followers of Hugh Bourne whom he enthused with the great utility of camp meetings. James Caughey, who was a Methodist episcopal preacher, laboured in England from 1840 to 1847. His preaching for the most part took place in the industrial towns and cities of central and northern England. He operated almost entirely within the Methodist circuits which embraced those places.

Charles Finney made two visits to England. The first took place from 1849 to 1851, just after his second marriage to Elizabeth Atkinson in November 1848, and the second followed between

---

[8] H.B. Kendall, *The Origin and History of Primitive Methodism* Vol. 1, pp. 31f.

January 1859 and August 1860. During the initial occasion, Finney laboured at Houghton and then in Birmingham, where the meetings were full on weekdays and so crowded on Sundays that hundreds went away for want of room. He then moved to London where he reported 'a great number of most interesting cases of conversion', and recorded that 'I preached a great deal on confession and restitution'.[9] On his second visit, Finney was in Scotland, Manchester and Bolton where 'three thousand and more were packing the hall every meeting' and 'where the anxious came forward in great numbers'.[10]

Phoebe and Walter Palmer were staunch Methodists. They emphasised entire sanctification. Theirs was an altar theology in which participants in their meetings were invited to fully surrender their lives to God. In practice this meant that those who came to their services were invited to come to the altar at the front of the building and offer their whole lives to God. This included their time, money, possessions and ambitions. In 1859 the Palmers landed in England for what proved to be a four-year series of meetings. During their campaigning in the British Isles most of their time was spent in Wesleyan Methodist churches and circuits in more than fifty major towns and cities. On their return to America, Phoebe Palmer published an account of their labours entitled *Four Years in the Old World*.[11] Although the Palmers did not have a great deal of direct involvement with Church of England clergy, Phoebe's books on revival topics were becoming well-known in Europe and were doubtless read by clergy of the Anglican establishment.

Church Armies

Through the Palmers' holiness meetings William and Catherine Booth came into 'entire sanctification', an experience which transformed their lives and the work of their Salvation Army.[12] Their brand of revivalistic militarism in turn impacted a number of Evangelical clergy who began to experiment with Anglicanised versions of the organisation. Among them were Evan Hopkins and Wilson Carlisle. Evan Hopkins who was incumbent of Holy Trinity, Richmond, was dissatisfied with his own home mission work. This led in

---

[9] R.A.G. Dupuis and G.N. Rosell, *The Memoirs of Charles G. Finney*, p. 515.
[10] Ibid., p. 515.
[11] P. Palmer, *Four Years in the Old World*.
[12] J. Kent, *Holding the Fort*.

1881 to his parishioners visiting Booth at Whitechapel. In conse-
quence, he started a similar work in his parish called the Church
Gospel Army.[13] Two years later, in the autumn of 1883, Wilson
Carlisle, another Evangelical Anglican, founded the Church Army.[14]
Carlisle was an Evangelical who had trained for the ministry at the
London College of Divinity in 1878 and served a curacy under Dr
Glynn Carr in Kensington. His Church Army became one of the
Church of England's most enduring Home Missionary Societies.
The Palmers had a further indirect impact on Evangelical Anglicans
through Dr Thomas Upham. He was an influential teacher in the
early years of the Keswick Convention and had received entire sanc-
tification at one of the Tuesday meetings held in the Palmers' home.

The Palmers, Robert Aitken and William Haslam

1859, the year in which the Palmers had set foot in England, proved
to be a significant one. By that time, the Great Awakening, which
had begun in New York and elsewhere in America in 1857, had
spread across the Atlantic to Ulster and into Scotland.[15] In England
in the years immediately following 1859, according to Edwin Orr,
both the free churches and the established church were impacted,
the latter with an increase in membership of 250,000.[16] Despite the
fact that the extent of the awakening in England has been
questioned by some,[17] there is little doubt that American revivalism
had been and would continue to influence the Victorian Church.

By the 1850s there was a return to open-air preaching and a
renewed emphasis on special services. Evangelistic preachers,
such as the Liverpool solicitor, Reginald Radcliffe (1825–1895),[18]
were travelling to different parts of the country. In Cornwall the
Rev Robert Aitken (1800–1873), 'England's premier evangelist',[19]

---

[13] A. Smellie, *Evan Henry Hopkins*, pp. 40–4.
[14] E. Rowan, *Wilson Carlisle and the Church Army*, pp. 136–8; *The Record*, 13 October 1882.
[15] Bentley, *Transformation of the Evangelical Party*.
[16] J.E. Orr, *The Second Evangelical Awakening*.
[17] Bentley, *Transformation of the Evangelical Party*, p. 343.
[18] For Radcliffe see Kent, *Holding the Fort*, pp. 96–8, 112–13. Radcliffe's revivalistic style and lengthy sermons did not appeal to the majority of Evangelical Anglicans.
[19] J.I. Packer, 'Robert Aitken', in D. Lewis (ed.), *Blackwell Dictionary of Evangelical Biography 1730–1860* Vol. 1, p. 6.

journeyed across the country and saw thousands of 'Aitkenite' converts. He became incumbent of Pendeen, near Lands End, from where he periodically emerged to lead revival missions in other towns and cities. In Aitken's parish there were sporadic revivals. In October 1854 he reported, 'We had a bit of a shower last night. The parsonage was full of penitents in every room, and in the passages too.'[20] A year later he wrote:

> We are in a state of wild religious excitement. Blessed be God, it is better than spiritual death. Last week I was sent for to the east of Cornwall some fifty miles distant. The vicar has found God. He is the brother of the High Sheriff of the county, a most lovely and superior soul, of the Extreme High Church School, and the parish belongs to his brother. On my return on Monday I found my whole parish in a flame under Knott and Fenton. There had been some eight or ten conversions before I left, which made me most unwilling to leave, but they now number upwards of a hundred. You see it never rains in Cornwall but it pours. In short we had a downright Cornish revival at Old Pendeen. Penitents are praying and rejoicing around me in the different rooms. My voice is quite gone, and I have been praying with penitents almost since I returned. I mean, night and day we have work.[21]

Another cleric to whom Aitken had also given assistance was William Haslam (1817–1905) who was incumbent of the mining parish of Baldhu. Many of his congregation had been converted through attending revivalistic Methodist gatherings in the neighbourhood. As a result, he had sought Aitken's advice and the latter had impressed on him the absolute necessity of salvation. Shortly afterwards, whilst expounding the gospel for the day during a Holy Communion service, Haslam was overwhelmed by the presence of God giving him assurance of salvation. This caused a Methodist local preacher by the name of Billy Bray, who happened to be in the congregation, to call out, 'the parson be converted'.[22] Haslam remained at Baldhu for another nine years and then after spells at Bath, Buckenham in Norfolk and Curzon Chapel in Mayfair he worked with the Church Parochial Mission Society.[23]

---

[20] Woods, *Canon Hay Aitken*, p. 69.
[21] Ibid., p. 68.
[22] W. Haslam, *From Death unto Life*, p. 48.
[23] See the entry for 'W. Haslam', in Lewis (ed.), *Blackwell Dictionary of Evangelical Biography* Vol. 1. p. 529.

Another American who impacted English Christianity was W.E. Boardman whose book *The Higher Christian Life* was first published in 1858. A further edition was brought out in London in 1860 when revival excitement was at a high level. Its message helped commend full salvation to Christians who came from the Reformed tradition. Boardman himself conveyed his message to the Mildmay Conference of 1869. Along with Asa Mahan, Boardman played a significant role in 'extending holiness teaching in Britain in the run up to the first Keswick Convention'.[24]

The Pearsall Smiths

Two American revivalists who were destined to make a significant impact on the Church of England's Evangelicals were Robert Pearsall Smith and his wife, Hannah Whitall Smith. They were a Quaker couple, whose teaching on the 'Higher Life' was to have a remarkable influence and be instrumental in the founding of the Keswick Convention. Both Robert and Hannah were accomplished writers and Hannah's book, *The Christian's Secret of a Happy Life*, became a major best-seller. Both were from notable Quaker families; the Smiths were publishers and the Whitalls were glass manufacturers. Their upbringing gave them a secure basis and additionally provided sufficient financial backing to enable them to travel. Both were converted through contacts with American Methodists and were baptised by immersion in 1858. Hannah also associated with the Brethren for a time and received much from their biblical teaching. Through attending camp meetings, Robert and Hannah received the second blessing or baptism of the Holy Spirit, although Robert's experience of it was much more emotional than Hannah's. Hannah later wrote that 'from head to toe he had been shaken with what seemed like a magnetic thrill of heavenly delight and floods of glory seemed to pour through him'.[25]

In essence, the Pearsall Smiths' teaching was that a higher Christian life is possible. In a series of articles in *The Christian's Pathway of Power*, a journal started by her husband, Hannah taught that the higher life is simply 'letting the Lord carry our burdens and manage our affairs, instead of trying to do it ourselves'.[26] It results in a sweet

---

[24] Bebbington, *Evangelicalism in Modern Britain*.
[25] H.W. Smith, *The Unselfishness of God: A Spiritual Autobiography*, pp. 288–9.
[26] *The Christian's Pathway of Power* Vol. 2, 2 March 1874, p. 38.

rest. 'The Higher Christian Life', she explained, is entered by faith and involved 'consecration' or a willingness on the part of a believer 'to commit your case to him in absolute abandonment'.[27] Both Robert and Hannah set out this teaching in books: Robert in *Holiness Through Faith* (1870) and Hannah in *The Christian's Secret of a Happy Life*, in which she wrote, 'The Higher Life [is characterised by] an entire surrender to the Lord, and a perfect trust in Him, resulting in victory over sin and inward rest of soul.'[28] Hannah in fact developed an altar theology which had strong echoes of Phoebe Palmer's teaching.

Following a relentless round of speaking engagements and the death of his son, Frank, a promising undergraduate student at Princeton University, Robert suffered a nervous breakdown. By Christmas 1872 his position was somewhat improved and his physicians recommended a trip abroad where he would be free from speaking engagements. Robert duly set out for Europe intending only to make a brief stop in England en route. As things turned out, he attended the Mildmay Conference and became involved in teaching and exhorting on the higher life. He appeared to have made a full recovery and two years of very active ministry followed, which included breakfast meetings[29] and major conference gatherings.

Hannah, who was somewhat bemused by this turn of events, joined him with some of their children in January 1874. Together they were active speakers and leaders in a series of meetings that led directly to the founding of the Keswick Convention in the summer of 1875. In February, Robert was one of several speakers at a three day series of 'Meetings for Consecration and Power for Service' held at the Hanover Square Rooms. He spoke of 'the mighty movement sweeping over the churches where the grace of God had been truly preached, drawing the people of God near to Christ and to each other'.[30]

---

[27] *The Christian's Pathway of Power* Vol. 2, 1 April 1874.
[28] H.W. Smith, *The Christian's Secret of a Happy Life*, p. 37.
[29] *Guide to Holiness*, February 1874, reported on such a breakfast meeting in London on 5 December 1873.
[30] *The Christian's Pathway of Power*, 1 April 1874, p. 57.

Meetings and Conferences

The Mildmay Conferences

The Mildmay Conference, which Robert Pearsall Smith attended, was one of a series which had been started in 1856 by William Pennefather (1816–1873) when incumbent of Christ Church, Barnet. They continued and further developed when Pennefather moved to St Jude's, Mildmay Park, in 1864. After his death the chairmanship passed to Stevenson Blackwood and the meetings continued on an annual basis well into the twentieth century. William Pennefather often spoke of the object of the meetings as 'fourfold' – manifested unity, social communion, increased personal holiness and enlarged interest in the promotion of Christ's kingdom throughout the world.[31] The invitations to the first conference at Barnet stated that the object was 'to promote holiness, brotherly love, and increased interest in the work of the Lord'.[32] Meetings held in the evening focused on home and foreign missions, personal holiness and the 'Lord's coming', a topic that was always close to Pennefather's heart.

The ethos of the first conferences at Barnet was set by Pennefather; he chose the speakers and members of his congregation organised the hospitality and stewarding of the meetings. Pennefather's view of holiness was rooted in the notion of separation from the world and from worldly influences. He felt 'self-control' and 'self-denial' to be very important aspects of Christian character.[33]

One of the things that had drawn Pennefather to Barnet was the presence of Captain Trotter of whom he wrote in a letter, 'He and his wife are serving the Lord fully, and are very *separate* from the world.'[34] Some years later, one of his friends recalled a sermon he preached against conformity to the world. It was at a time when very small bonnets were in fashion and seeing numbers of young women in his congregation wearing them, he felt compelled to speak out and demanded, 'Where is the shamefacedness of our daughters?'[35] Pennefather did not articulate a specific method of achieving

---

[31] Braithwaite, *William Pennefather*, pp. 247–98.
[32] Ibid., p. 305.
[33] Ibid., p. 256.
[34] Ibid., p. 267.
[35] Ibid., p. 379.

holiness, such as was the case at Keswick where those attending the conference were taught that full-surrender and faith were necessary prerequisites. Pennefather did, however, lay particular emphasis on receiving the power of the Holy Spirit. In a letter, dated 5 December 1851, he urged the need 'to look for the power of the Holy Ghost'.[36]

Mildmay continued to grow and a special conference hall was erected in 1870. Although Mildmay never achieved attendance levels comparable to Keswick, there was at least one year when the numbers attending reached 3,000.[37] Mildmay added to the growing desire for holiness on both sides of the Atlantic and gave a platform to men such as Reginald Radcliffe, George Muller, Dwight L. Moody, the Rev William Aitken and, shortly afterwards, the Pearsall Smiths who were to impact meetings at Oxford, Brighton, and Keswick. One of William Pennefather's close friends, the gentleman-Evangelist, Admiral E.G. Fishbourne, became one of Robert Pearsall Smith's supporters during 1875. Barnet and Mildmay paved the way for convention Christianity in a variety of places in the British Isles, including Bath, Bristol, Dover and Aberdeen.[38]

Conferences at Broadlands, Oxford and Brighton

The meeting that really launched the Pearsall Smiths into the English Evangelical world was the conference organised in July 1874 by Mr and Mrs Cowper Temple, later Lord and Lady Mount Temple, in their beautiful home at Broadlands. About two hundred people attended, with some fifty staying in the mansion itself. A number of undergraduates camped in the extensive grounds, while others rented rooms in nearby villages. Those who were present included Canon Wilberforce, George Macdonald, Theodore Monod, Sholto Douglas, Evan Hopkins, the Earl of Chichester, Samuel Morley MP and Arthur Blackwood who was then chief of the Postal Service in England. The purpose of the conference was 'to have a few days of quiet prayer and meditation upon the Scriptural possibilities of the Christian life, as to maintained communion with the Lord and victory over all known sin'.[39] During the six-day conference Hannah's

---

[36] Ibid., p. 261.
[37] Bebbington, *Evangelicalism in Modern Britain*, p. 160.
[38] Ibid., p. 161.
[39] Anon, *Account of the Union Meeting for the Promotion of Scriptural Holiness Held at Oxford August 29 to September 7, 1874*, pp. 19–29.

preaching, as well as Robert's, was much admired. *The Christian's Pathway of Power* reported that 'no description could convey the wonderful sense of the presence and power of God which attended those six days of waiting upon the Lord'.[40] Describing the events at Broadlands, Robert Pearsall Smith, who acted as Chairman, wrote:

> We began with the negative side, renunciation of discerned evil, and even of doubtful things which are not faith, and therefore sin. For some days the company was held under the searching light of God, to see and to remove any obstacles to a divine communion, aught that frustrated the grace of God.[41]

There was evidently a good deal of confession and 'self-renunciation' with Smith reporting that 'many secret sins ... were here brought up and put away in the presence of the Lord'.[42] A number of the meetings were held beside the quiet flowing river under the shade of some large beech trees. At 10 o'clock there were conversation meetings with Bible in hand and prayer with singing at 11 o'clock. At one o'clock Mrs Smith held a ladies meeting. There were Bible readings after tea and a regular evening meeting. Here 'the provisions in the indwelling Holy Ghost, the exceeding great promises of the Word, the separating power of the cross, the risen Saviour, the life more abundant', were then set before the assembled company.[43] Notwithstanding, the emphasis was more on 'seeking to realise, in living personal apprehension, the truths of the Word already known and taught by those present' than on teaching.[44]

The Broadlands gathering had proved to be an uplifting occasion in which many ministers and others had experienced 'something of what it is "to be filled with the Spirit"' and been given a desire to walk in the way of holiness.[45] It was therefore inevitable that the possibility of holding a further conference open to a much larger number of people was discussed on the last day. When Arthur Blackwood proposed that such a conference be held at Oxford at the earliest opportunity, there was unanimous agreement.[46]

---

[40] *The Christian's Pathway of Power*, 1 August 1874, p. 124.
[41] Anon, *Account of the Union Meeting at Oxford*, p. 21.
[42] Ibid., pp. 21–2.
[43] Ibid., pp. 21–4.
[44] Ibid., pp. 19–20.
[45] *The Christian's Pathway of Power*, 1 August 1874, p. 124.
[46] E.H. Madden, *Freedom and Grace: the Life of Asa Mahan*, p. 197.

The Oxford Union Meeting

This Convention was held in Oxford from 29 August to 7 September 1874 during the University vacation. Despite the fact that there were a mere three weeks between the announcement and the start of the conference, a large number of clergymen and lay people came from all parts of the British Isles and some from the continent. The invitation announced that it was to be a 'Union meeting for the Promotion of Scriptural Holiness'.[47] It opened with the following statement:

> In every part of Christendom the God of all grace has given to many of His children a feeling of deep dissatisfaction with their present spiritual state, and a strong conviction that the truths they believe, might and should exercise a power over their hearts and lives, altogether beyond anything they have as yet experienced.[48]

Robert Pearsall Smith in a promotional article announced that most of Oxford's hotels were offering generous reductions and that lodgings could be had for between 9s and 12s a week. He gave a list of clergy who intended to be present – they included Hay Aitken, Alfred Christopher, James Fleming, Evan Hopkins and William Haslam – and urged would be attendees to book in for 'the whole Pentecostal period of days'.[49] Robert Pearsall Smith was once again the prime mover and principal speaker. He was assisted by his wife, Hannah, whose Bible readings proved very popular, and about a dozen others, including Evan Hopkins, Canon T.D. Harford Battersby from England, Theodore Monod from Paris, and Asa Mahan[50] and W.E. Boardman from the United States. The number who attended was estimated at between 1,200 to 1,500.[51] Printed

---

[47] *The Christian's Pathway of Power*, 1 September 1874, p. 160.
[48] Ibid., p. 160.
[49] Ibid., p. 160.
[50] After the death of his first wife, Asa Mahan, the first president of Oberlin College, married Mary E. Chase at Adrian on 22 May 1866. They arrived in England soon after to press his wife's claim to a share in the Townley-Chase estate in Lancashire. Shortly after their arrival Mahan became active in holiness circles in London. They decided to stay and established their first home at 14 Bedford Place, London. Madden, *Freedom and Grace*, pp. 192, 195. For W.E. Boardman, see Mrs W.E. Boardman, *The Life and Labours of the Rev W.E. Boardman*.
[51] *The Christian's Pathway of Power*, October 1874, p. 161.

cards were handed out to the delegates on their arrival offering a number of suggestions including, 'come in a receptive spirit, submit yourself wholly to the teaching of the Holy Spirit' and 'Eat moderately, dress simply, retire to rest early'. Two themes ran through the teaching given at Oxford: (i) learning to trust in Christ for the strength to live holy lives and not depending on 'fleshly resolutions and efforts of their own'; and (ii) 'full surrender' or 'definitely handing over ALL to God'.[52]

A striking aspect of the Oxford Conference was the fact that many middle-aged and elderly clergymen acknowledged that the meeting 'formed the next great epoch of their spiritual life after their conversion'.[53] Alfred Christopher of St Aldate's later wrote:

> That which above all things fills my heart with deep thankfulness in relation to the recent Conference at Oxford for the promotion of Scriptural Holiness, is that the POWER OF GOD was so signally manifested at it, that I felt as if I had never witnessed this power in visible operation on Christians before. The calmness and simplicity of the addresses, and the absence of excitement, made it all the more clear that the remarkable results given were the fruit of God's power, not the effects of man's influence.[54]

Christopher went on in the same article to cite the case of one Evangelical clergyman who had read a paper at a clerical meeting against Robert Pearsall Smith's teaching but who was now 'in his new joy and strength writing a book to promote a full trust in Christ from the heart, and for power for holiness and for the diligent and effective service of God.'[55]

The Brighton Convention

At a meeting of Church of England and Nonconformist ministers held during the Oxford Conference it was resolved 'to seek a repetition of similar meetings everywhere among Christians'.[56] Within nine months of the Oxford Convention a still larger series of meetings was organised at Brighton. Robert Pearsall Smith returned from

---

[52] Anon, *Account of the Union Meeting at Oxford*, pp. 69, 71.
[53] *The Christian's Pathway of Power*, October 1874, p. 161.
[54] Ibid., p. 177.
[55] Ibid., p. 177.
[56] *The Christian's Pathway of Power*, 2 November 1874, p. 199.

America in the spring of 1875 and a committee was established consisting of Stevenson Blackwood, Admiral Fishbourne, Donald Matheson and T.B. Smithies. Robert Pearsall Smith served as chairman.[57] The Brighton Corporation generously gave free use of the Dome, Pavilion, Corn Exchange and Town Hall. It was estimated that about 8,000 delegates participated, with over 200 coming from the continent, Germany, France and Switzerland in particular. In all, twenty-three different countries were represented. A large number of those present were from the Nonconformist churches.[58]

During the time of the Brighton Convention, D.L. Moody was bringing his great campaign in London's Covent Garden to a close. On the opening day of the Convention he said to his audience, 'Let us lift up our hearts to seek earnestly a blessing on the great Convention that is now being held in Brighton, perhaps the most important meeting ever gathered.' He sent a telegram which read: 'Moody and 8,000 at the closing meeting at the Opera House have specially prayed for the Convention, that great results may follow'.[59] In response, Robert Pearsall Smith, the Brighton chairman, said, 'Let us ask an answering blessing upon our beloved brother, Mr Moody, a man who walks with God.'[60]

Although some of the Brighton buildings could seat several thousand individuals, none of them could accommodate all those who came to the Convention. Meetings were therefore held simultaneously at the different venues. The early morning prayer gatherings at seven o'clock attracted about 3,000 people and on most days overflow meetings had to be held in a separate building. The Pearsall Smiths were the main speakers, but Theodore Monod, a French pastor, played an important part and often presided over the evening meetings in the Dome while Robert Pearsall Smith was speaking in the Corn Exchange. Other important speakers included Stevenson A. Blackwood, Evan H. Hopkins, Henry Varley, Hanmer Webb-Peploe and Dr Asa Mahan.

The pattern of the meetings and the content of the teaching at the Brighton Convention were much the same as at Oxford. However, serious questions were raised regarding some of Robert Pearsall Smith's utterances. During the course of one of his addresses he

---

[57] Anon, *Record of the Convention for the Promotion of Scriptural Holiness held at Brighton 29 May – 7 June 1875*, p. 7.
[58] *The Christian*, 17 June 1875.
[59] W.B. Sloan, *These Sixty Years*, p. 19.
[60] J.B. Figgis, *Keswick from Within*, p. 34.

distressed his hearers with remarks that were clearly antinomian in character. He said things that unmistakenly implied that those who are 'in Christ' are no longer subject to the letter of the law as the rule of their conduct. They are 'lifted up to a higher sphere of life, and thus walk in a freedom unknown to those who are strangers to the exalted adventure of the new and better life'.[61] During the course of this address, Dr Mahan exclaimed 'Horrible!' in a whisper to the Rev G.A. Rogers, the Vicar of Christ Church, Dover, who responded, 'What are we coming to?'[62]

Worse was to follow when what was regarded as a scandalous incident involving Robert took place. The exact details of what happened were never entirely clear. In substance, however, Miss Hattie Hamilton requested a private interview with Robert in his hotel bedroom. He was somewhat reluctant but found her in uncontrollable hysterics, shaking and saying that she did not feel accepted by Jesus as his child. He apparently sat beside her on the bed and put his arm around her, during which time he explained to her the unwise and unorthodox teaching which Dr Foster had shared with him during his recovery from breakdown in 1872. This was that 'Christ wanted us to feel thrills [akin to sexual thrills] up and down our bodies because this would make us feel closer to Him.'[63] The following morning Miss Hamilton went to Mr Stevenson Blackwood, Robert's Brighton sponsor, and related what he had said and that he had tried to make love to her. Blackwood summoned Robert to his office and made it clear that he accepted Hamilton's version of events and recommended that he halt his ministry immediately. In a letter written after the event to Lord Mount Temple, Robert stated:

> I blame myself greatly yet I can say before God, my intentions were as free from the wish for adultery as it were my own child, I put my arm about her ... I do not defend or extenuate these thoughtless things – I condemn them without limit. Nothing beyond this was laid to my charge in the course of my hearing – But it *was* in my room and my door was locked – and I did desire the dear heartbroken child should find full rest in the manifested love of her Lord. I do not think my intentions could have been more pure to my own daughter.[64]

[61] Madden, *Freedom and Grace*, p. 201.
[62] Ibid., p. 201. See also *Banner of Holiness*, 16 December 1875.
[63] M. Henry, *The Secret Life of Hannah Whitall Smith*, p. 81.
[64] Robert Pearsall Smith to Lord Mount Temple, *Mount Temple Collection*, Hampshire Record Office.

Needless to say, what had transpired was eagerly reported in the press. *The Brighton Weekly* headlined the event as, 'Famous Evangelist Found in Bedroom of Adoring Female Follower'.[65] The 'Council of Eight' did their best to recover the situation and issued a statement that 'the individual referred to' 'had in private conversation', inculcated 'most unscriptural and dangerous doctrines'.[66] There had also been questionable behaviour which, though 'free from evil intention', necessitated action on their part. They had therefore insisted that he put aside all public work and that the return of his nervous illness had made this imperative.[67] Robert was deeply shocked over what had happened. He suffered nausea and lost twenty pounds in weight. When he was sufficiently recovered he returned to America together with Hannah and the family. *The Record* newspaper published a series of articles on 'The collapse of Pearsall Smithism' in which it virtually said 'I told you so' and pointed out the 'discrepancy between the reports of the Brighton Convention and the facts which now emerged'.[68]

The Keswick Convention

One of those who had received great blessing at the Oxford Convention was the Rev Thomas Harford Battersby (1822–1883). A decade after the event he described his experience as 'a revelation of Christ to my soul'.[69] Nearer the event itself, while still resident in Oxford, he wrote, 'Christ was revealed to me so powerfully and sweetly as the present Saviour in His all-sufficiency.'[70]

Battersby was a cultured Balliol man who numbered Matthew Arnold, Lord Coleridge and Frederick Temple, later to be Archbishop of Canterbury, among his contemporaries. While up at Oxford Battersby came for a while under the influence of John Henry Newman and adopted his Tractarian views. After receiving his degree he served a curacy in an Anglo-Catholic parish at Gosport. He soon found that he was not suited to a high church environment and after only two years he moved north to Keswick to

---

[65] Henry, *Hannah Whitall Smith*, p. 82.
[66] *The Freeman*, 17 December 1875.
[67] Ibid.
[68] *The Record*, 22, 24, 27 December 1875, cited by Bentley, *Transformation of the Evangelical Party*, p. 410.
[69] C. Price and I. Randall, *Transforming Keswick*, p. 26.
[70] Ibid., p. 26.

work with the Rev Frederick Myers, a broad churchman and author of *Catholic Thoughts*. Initially, Battersby felt that in Myers he had found 'a guide and a prophet'[71] but after only a short period he became dissatisfied and turned back to his earlier Evangelical convictions. Within two years of his settling in Keswick, Myers died and Thomas Harford Battersby succeeded him as incumbent of St John's Church.

Despite the fact that he was a diligent pastor to his people and a leading and respected Evangelical in the diocese of Carlisle, he still felt that his Christian life was lacking. In 1873 he wrote in his diary,

> At this moment I am feeling much inward struggle and questioning about this 'higher Christian life' which is so much talked of and written about ... What I have been reading of the experience of others, Mr R.P. Smith and his excellent wife and their wonderful boy, Frank, has made me utterly dissatisfied with myself and my state. I feel that I am dishonouring God and am wretched myself by living as I do; and that I must either go backwards or forwards, reaching out towards the light and the glory which my blessed Saviour holds out to me, or falling back more and more into worldliness and sin.[72]

At the Brighton Convention Thomas Harford Battersby and his friend Mr Robert Wilson, a Quaker businessman from Broughton Grange, Cockermouth, decided to hold a similar gathering at Keswick. Wilson had also been particularly blessed at Oxford and the two were keen to share what now meant so much to them. Accordingly, they gave invitations to several of the leading Brighton speakers, among them Robert and Hannah Pearsall Smith. Robert agreed to preside and the meetings were scheduled to begin three weeks after the close of the Brighton Convention on the 29 June.

Just days before the Convention was due to begin the news broke that all of Robert Pearsall Smith's engagements were cancelled and that he was returning to America. No explanation was given and inevitably rumours abounded that the real reason was his erroneous teaching and immoral conduct. The former certainly seems to have been the case. As John Kent pointed out in *Holiness Through Faith*, Robert Pearsall Smith had written that the Christian was cleansed 'not only from the stain of sin, but from sin itself'.[73] On the second

---

[71] Anon (two of his sons), *Memoir of T.D. Harford Battersby*, p. 58.
[72] Ibid., p. 15.
[73] Kent, *Holding the Fort*, p. 354.

matter, Price and Randall stated that the facts as they eventually emerged would hardly 'raise an eyebrow today'.[74] Indeed, Kent's view was that Smith's indiscretion was less remarkable than the reaction of William Cowper-Temple, Lord Radstock and Stevenson Blackwood who extracted a written confession which forced him to return with his family to America.[75] Robert Pearsall Smith's career as an Evangelist was finished and he lost his faith altogether by the end of his life.

Some of the chosen speakers withdrew but Battersby managed to persuade others to come in their place. The meetings were held in a tent with about 300 to 400 attending. The speakers included the Rev H. Webb-Peploe, the Rev George N. Thornton, the Rev T. Phillips, Mr H.F. Bowker, Mr T.M. Croome and Mr Murray Shipley. Battersby occupied the chair at all the meetings.

When the Convention was over, Harford Battersby wrote to *The Record* of the blessing that had been received by those who had attended from all parts of the United Kingdom. He also acknowledged the debt which he and thousands more owed to Robert Pearsall Smith and added, 'The Lord has been showing us, in a wonderful way, that if he chooses to lay aside one instrument, he can and will find others to testify of His truth, and to carry on His work.'[76] The inevitable consequence was that the whole movement was subjected to violent criticism and opposition from the Evangelical leadership. Battersby wrote:

> I fully see now that my espousing still the 'higher life' teaching will be to expose myself to still warmer and fiercer hostility from those 'who seem to be pillars in the Evangelical camp', and to separation from their company, it may be. If I make a mistake as to this, my whole future influence in the church and ministry will be compromised.[77]

He felt it necessary to carefully review his position before committing himself to organising another convention at Keswick. 'There must', he wrote, 'be a thorough sifting of my motives, opinions and conduct before God.'[78] In the Spring of 1876 he and Wilson took the

---

[74] Price and Randall, *Transforming Keswick*, p. 30.
[75] Kent, *Holding the Fort*, p. 355.
[76] Sloan, *These Sixty Years*, p. 22.
[77] Anon, *Memoir of T.D. Harford Battersby*, p. 176.
[78] Price and Randall, *Transforming Keswick*, p. 32; and Sloan, *These Sixty Years*, p. 23.

decision to hold a further convention. For this second occasion they changed the wording of their publicity slightly to read, 'Meetings for the Promotion of Scriptural Holiness'. After the success of their second gathering there was never any doubt that Keswick should be held yearly.

Throughout the last quarter of the nineteenth century the Convention grew steadily. In 1878 between 400 to 500 were reckoned to be present at the early morning prayer meetings. In 1882, 1,200 were reported to have attended meetings and 2,000 in 1886. *The Christian* calculated that 4,000 had come to one or other of the meetings in 1891, nearly three quarters of whom had stayed for the whole convention.[79]

Charles Price and Ian Randall have helpfully summarised the character of Keswick teaching as Bible-based, Christ-centred, Holy Spirit enabled, practical and mission orientated.[80] The Scripture was always given full and final authority in all the teaching and preaching. While giving a Bible reading at the Convention in 1894 Webb-Peploe said, 'There is not one person present, I imagine, who would deny that this Book contains the revelation of God; that it is the Word of God, and the only Word whereby the world may live and Christ may be glorified in the earth.'[81] All the meetings had a strong Christological focus and every exposition was 'ultimately an exposition of Christ'.[82] Closely related to this was Keswick's emphasis on the Holy Spirit. Indeed, Price and Randall state, 'For decades it was at Keswick that people would hear sermons on the fullness of the power of the Spirit that were otherwise rare in Evangelical Christianity.'[83] The practical was seen in the applied nature of what was taught. People who came to the Convention wanted to find out where their lives were failing and how they might, to use a frequent Keswick term, walk in 'victory'.[84] Keswick came to have a growing missionary impetus which extended hugely in its extent in the twentieth century.

Although there was a strong emphasis on Christian unity and church order was not debated, Church of England Evangelicals

---

[79] Bentley, *Transformation of the Evangelical Party*, p. 415, citing *The Christian*, 30 July 1891.
[80] Price and Randall, *Transforming Keswick*, pp. 35–6.
[81] Ibid., pp. 35–6.
[82] Ibid., p. 35.
[83] *The Keswick Week*, 1894.
[84] Ibid., p. 36.

continued to play a significant role at Keswick down to the close of the nineteenth century and beyond. Among the nucleus of frequent speakers were Hanmer Webb-Peploe, incumbent of St Paul's Onslow Square, Evan Hopkins of Holy Trinity, Richmond, and Charles Fox, who gave a number of stirring addresses. There were several prominent free churchmen who shared the Keswick platform. Included in their number were John Figgis of the Countess of Huntingdon's Connection in Brighton, the Baptist, the Rev Frederick B. Meyer and Dr James Elder Cumming, a Church of Scotland minister in Glasgow. Nevertheless, the Anglicans held the dominant position and Webb-Peploe in particular jealously guarded his reputation as a churchman.[85] The recruitment in 1886 to the Keswick platform of Handley Moule, who was then principal of Ridley Hall and later Bishop of Durham, further enhanced both the influence of the Church of England and the Keswick movement as a whole.

Some of the teaching given at Keswick by Victorian Anglicans showed strong traces of the influence of the Pearsall Smiths. Webb-Peploe and Evan Hopkins, for example, both taught a form of sanctification by faith. Speaking in 1883 Webb-Peploe urged, 'There is nothing between us and the realisation of the fullness of blessing except our unwillingness to believe God's Word.'[86] At the 1899 Convention Hopkins stated that before we can experience sanctification as a process, 'we must receive it as a gift'.[87] Both Webb-Peploe and William Haslam gave teaching that was reminiscent of the Pearsall Smiths' altar theology[88] in which they urged the importance of full-surrender on the part of all believers. In 1892 Haslam spoke on 'The Debt of the Redeemed' and stressed, 'There is every reason to make a full, loving sacrifice of ourselves to Him.'[89]

It was Evan Hopkins who emerged as the significant influence and theologian at Keswick. He was only thirty-eight years old at the time of the first Convention and that year he took over Pearsall Smith's *Pathway of Power*, changing the title to *Life of Faith* in 1883 and remaining editor in chief until 1913. Hopkins taught a two-stage Christian life. Sanctification was a second stage that began with an initial act of faith and consecration and then

---

[85] Bentley, *Transformation of the Evangelical Party*, p. 417.
[86] *The Life of Faith*, 1 March 1883.
[87] *The Keswick Week*, 1899, pp. 79–80.
[88] See E.H. Hopkins, *The Holy Life*, pp. 69–70, cited by Bentley, *Transformation of the Evangelical Party*, p. 420.
[89] Bentley, *Transformation of the Evangelical Party*, p. 420.

continued as a process. Hopkins was adamant that no one could claim to be free of sin in this life but that union with Christ gave a conquering and sustaining power.

The majority of Evangelical Anglicans continued to stand aloof from Keswick. Canon Alfred Christopher was one of the few prominent representatives who gave the Convention his active support. By 1877, Dean Francis Close had warmed towards Harford Battersby.[90] However, that same year, John Charles Ryle published what was in fact a veiled attack on the Keswick teaching. Although he studiously avoided any reference to the Convention's leaders, Ryle's criticism was hardly disguised. As he saw it, they were confusing justification and sanctification, the former achieved by faith alone, but the latter being a process in which the individual must watch, fight and pray.[91] Furthermore, it seemed as though they were teaching that the old sinful nature was not changed or improved but *replaced* by the Spirit of Christ. For Ryle the natural person remains corrupt in nature, although by the help of the Holy Spirit is able to resist its pull towards evil.[92] Ryle therefore steadfastly asserted the sinfulness of man.

The quest for holiness during the first decades of the convention's existence led to intense earnestness and to heightened expectations of experience. In the 1890s there were those who spoke at Keswick who wanted to identify sanctification with the baptism of the Spirit. However, by this time the influence of Handley Moule was beginning to have a steadying hand on the Convention, which had grown in both spirituality and missionary concern.

Moody and Sankey

Another expression of revivalism that was to have a major impact on Victorian England was that represented by Dwight L. Moody (1837–1899). Moody hailed from Chicago and had first visited England briefly in the summer of 1867 largely to hear and learn from Charles Spurgeon and George Muller. During that time he met with Henry Moorhouse and was subsequently influenced by his preaching the love of God. He was back again in the summer of 1872 and spent the bulk of his time preaching in Nonconformist

---

[90] Anon, *Memoir of T.D. Harford Battersby*, pp. 207–8.
[91] J.C. Ryle, *Holiness*, p. 1.
[92] Price and Randall, *Transforming Keswick*, p. 213.

chapels in London. During that visit he gave an address at the Mildmay Conference and this brought him into contact with a number of Evangelical Anglican clergy. As a consequence, he was invited to return for an evangelistic tour by William Pennefather and Cuthbert Bainbridge, a wealthy Methodist layman from Newcastle-upon-Tyne, the latter promising him funding. Moody assumed that the two men had done the necessary organisation and without actually confirming the arrangements set out for England with his wife and children together with his singing soloist, Ira Sankey (1840–1908).

On his arrival, Moody was somewhat nonplussed to learn that both men who had invited him to return had died. However, he went to York at the invitation of a Baptist minister, the Rev Frederick Brotherton Meyer (1847–1929). The meetings got off to a slow start but by the end of his time there audiences were reaching 1,000. It was, however, at Edinburgh and London that Moody was most successful. At the close of the Edinburgh campaign it was reported that 1,400 people had professed conversion.[93] During the course of 1874 Moody held services at a number of major cities in the north of England, including Manchester, Liverpool, Sheffield and Birmingham, where he held audiences of 3,000 to 4,000 in rapt attention.

From February through to 12 July 1875 Moody and Sankey began their mission to London, making use of four preaching places: the Agricultural Hall at Islington, which seated 13,700, with standing room for 4,000 to 5,000 more; Bow Road Hall in the East End, with 10,000 seats; the Royal Opera House in the West End and the Victoria Theatre in the South. William R. Moody wrote of his father's campaigning in London, 'Nothing is clearer than that London has been remarkably stirred by the labours of these two evangelists.'[94] A total of 285 meetings were held and attended by 2,530,000 people.[95] George Davis estimated that 100,000 souls were won for Christ during this two-year campaign.[96]

There were a number of reasons for the appeal of Moody's campaigns, particularly to the middle-classes and those with some sort of church connection. Sankey's music evoked a powerful response and created a fresh outburst of enthusiasm for Christian singing. London errand boys whistled Sankey's tunes, and barrel

[93] W.R. Moody, *The Life of Dwight L. Moody*, p. 190.
[94] Ibid., p. 211.
[95] Ibid., p. 211.
[96] G.T.B. Davis, *Dwight L. Moody: The Man and His Mission*.

organs instead of 'Pop goes the Weasel', ground out 'Hold the Fort'. Penny copies of some of Sankey's songs sold throughout the United Kingdom at an estimated 250,000 copies a month. Both Moody and Sankey were gracious, well-dressed, middle-class individuals with 'business tact' who resonated with Victorian ideals. Moody as a layman who operated without ecclesiastical garb held a particular appeal both to the Nonconformists and to those Anglicans who were suspicious of ritualism and clericalism. The informality of Moody and Sankey was in keeping with the growingly democratic influences in British society. Moody had succeeded in putting his endeavours on a business-like footing. In North London, for example, the Rev R.C. Billing had planned and executed an intensive visitation scheme prior to Moody's arrival and a strategic follow up in which 2,000 visits were made to those who had professed conversion.[97]

Moody and Sankey had endeared themselves to all classes of society. In particular, Moody had gained an unexpected popularity among the upper classes. His afternoon Bible readings at the Queen's Opera House in the Haymarket drew the wealthy and influential in large numbers. A witness reported that the roads out-side the building were 'literally blocked with the carriages of the aristocratic and plutocratic of the land'.[98] However, W.H. Daniel who knew Moody personally reported his impact on shipyard workers in Glasgow and noted that in Birmingham 'artisans in the manufactories crowded to the meetings in large numbers'.[99]

So the friendly, if cautious, welcome which Moody and Sankey had received at the Islington Clerical Conference in January 1874 was extended to one of enthusiastic acclaim. In May 1875 even Archibald Tait, the Archbishop of Canterbury, published a letter in which he expressed the deep interest that all the bishops and parochial clergy felt in the movement and prayed that it might be blessed. At the same time he made it clear that his words were not to be taken as an official endorsement.[100] The London Mission came to an end on Sunday 11 July 1875 and a farewell meeting was held at Mildmay on the afternoon of the Monday following. Among the ministers who were present there were 188 Anglican clergymen,

---

[97] Bentley, *Transformation of the Evangelical Party*, p. 233.

[98] J.C. Pollock, *Moody Without Sankey: A New Biographical Portrait*, p. 143.

[99] W.H. Daniel, *D.L. Moody and His Work*, p. 343.

[100] *The Record*, 24 May 1875, cited by Bentley, *Transformation of the Evangelical Party*, p. 360.

154 Congregationalists, 85 Baptists and 81 Wesleyans.[101] Lord Shaftesbury read out letters that demonstrated the enormous demand for religious tracts on the part of the working classes, and all subscribed to his view that Moody and Sankey had 'conferred an inestimable blessing on Great Britain'.[102]

Moody returned to England in 1881, and again briefly from November 1891 to November 1892, but it was the visit of 1873–1875 which had made him an international figure. One significant aspect of the next campaign was his visit to Cambridge for eight days in November 1882. During the opening meeting Moody preached on 'Daniel in the Lions' den'. Every time he said the word Daniel, which he pronounced 'Dan'l', he was mimicked and hooted at by unruly undergraduates.[103] Moody appeared unperturbed and took it all in good humour, with the result that Gerald Lander, who had led the disruptive element, apologised to him. He agreed to demonstrate the genuineness of his change of heart by quiet attendance at the next meeting. News of this spread and attendances grew rapidly, such that on the Sunday night the 12 November nearly 2,000 university men came to hear Moody preach from Luke on 'Good Tidings of great joy ... A Saviour'. After the choir had sung, 'Just as I am without one plea', Moody prayed and asked all who had received a blessing to stand. Two hundred rose.

Moody's visit to Cambridge had a significant impact on overseas missionary work. Lander became a missionary bishop and a number of other converts and helpers offered themselves for service on the foreign field. Among them were Charles Studd (1862–1931), the Cambridge and England cricket captain. A group including Studd who became known as 'the Cambridge Seven' toured British universities stirring students to faith and commitment. They held one final great meeting in London on 4 February 1885 before sailing for China.[104]

There is no doubt that Moody and Sankey had made a significant impact among the middle classes in particular. However, among the

---

[101] *Narrative of Messrs Moody and Sankey's Labours in Great Britain and Ireland*, Supplementary Issue 44, cited by Bentley, *Transformation of the Evangelical Party*, p. 364.

[102] *Narrative of Messrs Moody and Sankey's Labours in Great Britain and Ireland*, Supplementary Issue 59, cited by Bentley, *Transformation of the Evangelical Party*, p. 365.

[103] Pollock, *Moody Without Sankey*, p. 202.

[104] Ibid., p. 208.

poorer elements of society they were less effective. Towards the end of April 1875 *The Record* noted that Moody and Sankey had not touched the deep mass of practical heathenism of the lower classes.[105] James Findlay has pointed out that Moody himself 'was disappointed at the effectiveness of his revival in London to reach the unchurched poor'.[106]

Moody's last visit to the United Kingdom, which lasted from November 1891 to November 1892, was far less publicised and attracted much less attention. It was perhaps an indication that by the closing years of the century revivalism was being seen as a last means of reaching the unchurched and of rejuvenating Christian believers. Sections of the mainstream churches were turning away from the old, old gospel story to engage with liberal critical theology and social reform. That said, many from the Evangelical party in the Church of England had stood solidly behind the Moody and Sankey campaigns.[107] They included Handley Moule, Principal of Ridley Hall, R.B. Girdlestone, Principal of Wycliffe Hall and Bishops John Charles Ryle of Liverpool and Anthony Thorold of Rochester.[108]

---

[105] *The Record*, 14 July 1875, cited by Bentley, *Transformation of the Evangelical Party*, p. 369.

[106] J.F. Findlay, *Dwight L. Moody American Evangelist 1837–1899*, p. 174.

[107] *The Christian*, 24 November 1892.

[108] Bishop Anthony Thorold was very supportive of Moody. See Moody, *Life of Dwight L. Moody*, pp. 269–71.

12

Overseas Missions

Britain's Missionary Activity Before 1800

British Christians did not exhibit a significant concern for overseas missionary activity in the years before 1800. The Society for the Propagation of the Gospel (SPG) had been founded in 1701, but it was not strictly speaking a missionary society, since its main objective was to provide pastoral and spiritual care for British settlers abroad. It was particularly focused on those who had taken up residence in the American colonies. One of its early chaplains was John Wesley, who went out to Georgia in 1736.

The Society for the Promotion of Christian Knowledge (SPCK) was established in 1698, but, as its name suggests, it was mainly concerned with the distribution of Christian literature. The society did, for a brief period, give support to a small group of Lutheran missionaries in Sierra Leone (prior to it being an English territory) and organise a mission to Madras in 1726.[1] Several of the most important missionary societies were not formed until the last decade of the eighteenth century and the beginning of the nineteenth century, a period that generally marks the origins of the modern missionary movement.

The largest Anglican missionary society operating in the nineteenth century was the Church Missionary Society (CMS), which was formed at a meeting on 12 April 1799,[2] with John Venn, the Rector of Clapham, declaring that it should be based on 'the Church-principle, not the high-church principle'.[3] CMS's stance was strongly Protestant and its membership almost entirely Evangelical

---

[1] F.W. Cornish, *A History of the English Church in the Nineteenth Century* Part 2, p. 381.

[2] The Society was originally called The Society for Missions in Africa and the East.

[3] Murray, *Proclaim the Good News*, p. 7.

clerics and laymen and women. It was to be the major vehicle by which Evangelical Anglicanism was fostered on all the world's major continents.

Motivational factors

There were a number of factors that prompted British missionary endeavour in the nineteenth century.[4] Perhaps the most significant of these was the Methodist revival that impacted Anglican clergy and people with a desire to go into the entire world and preach the gospel. Jocelyn Murray described the Wesley brothers and Whitefield as 'apostles of a new movement in the land'.[5] John Wesley not only left perhaps as many as 100,000 men and women of Evangelical convictions in his own societies, he had also revived other major religious denominations, including the established Church of England. Most notably, he was seen as a father figure to the Evangelical party which clustered around the leadership of Charles Simeon at Cambridge, William Wilberforce and the members of the Clapham Sect.

The nineteenth century would not have been a great epoch of overseas missionary endeavour if it had not been for this large up-surge of new spiritual vigour within the British Isles. Those who went abroad did so motivated by the desire to save as many of the heathen as possible from the everlasting damnation which other-wise would have been their destiny.[6] The spiritual awakening in England stirred many hundreds of men and women to leave their home shores and venture out into the furthest corners of the British Empire and beyond.

Among English Christians there was a growing desire to see the gospel proclaimed in the areas of the world where no preachers or missionaries had ever set foot. There were strong feelings of mille-narian expectancy and many believed that the revival might truly usher in the 1,000-year period of bliss on earth, as foretold in the Apocalypse of St John. It was a longing which found expression in some of the great hymns of the period such as Isaac Watts' 'Jesus Shall Reign where ere the sun doth his successive journeys run' and De Young's 'Nearer and nearer draws the time, the time that shall surely be, when the earth shall be filled with the glory of God as the waters cover the sea'.

---

[4] C.P. Williams, 'British Religion and the Wider World: Mission and Empire 1800–1940' in Gilley and Shiels, *Religion in Britain*, p. 381.

[5] Murray, *Proclaim the Good News*, p. 2.

[6] Vidler, *Age of Revolution*, p. 252.

Charles Simeon made a major contribution to nineteenth-century Evangelical Anglican overseas missionary work. Several of his distinguished curates, among them Henry Martyn and Claudius Buchanan, served with distinction as chaplains of the East India Company in the Middle and Far East.[7] Many undergraduates who attended Simeon's Holy Trinity Church in Cambridge were challenged and inspired with the ideal of overseas service. Simeon, along with others of the Clapham Sect, was influential in the affairs of the BFBS,[8] which had been founded in 1804.

Later in the nineteenth century there was a second spring of revivalistic activity sometimes referred to as the '1859 Revival' although, strictly speaking, it lasted until 1865. It began in the United States and was born of intensive prayer, which then impacted the British Isles.[9] In this period of six years more than half-a-million people were converted to Christianity in the United Kingdom. The majority joined the Methodist, Baptist and Congregational churches, but also in its wake came the Moody and Sankey missions, the Keswick Convention and the founding of college Christian Unions, all of which impacted the Church of England. Eugene Stock observed that the 1859 Revival provoked intensive seasons of prayer in various sections of the foreign mission field. CMS periodicals contained notices of gatherings as far east as Shanghai and as far west as Red River.[10] Sober and thoughtful missionaries 'testified to the depth and reality of the work' and there was 'a work of the Spirit' among the English soldiers in India.[11] The revival also ushered in several new missionary societies, among them the China Inland Mission (CIM), which was founded by James Hudson Taylor (1832–1905) in 1865.[12]

On 25 June 1865 Hudson Taylor found himself in a concourse of several hundred or more British believers but 'unable to bear the sight of a congregation of a thousand or more Christian people rejoicing in their own security while millions were perishing for lack of knowledge'. He left and wandered the sands alone and 'surrendered myself to God for this service'. In addition he asked 'for twenty-four fellow

---

[7] Murray, *Proclaim the Good News*, p. 26; see also Stock, *Church Missionary Society* Vol. 1, pp. 97–8, 101, 216, 222, 232.

[8] H.G.C. Moule, *Charles Simeon*, p. 96.

[9] See J.E. Orr, *The Light of the Nations*, pp. 101–10, 126–45.

[10] Stock, *Church Missionary Society* Vol. 2, p. 33.

[11] Ibid. Vol. 2, p. 34.

[12] For Hudson-Taylor see H. Taylor, *Hudson Taylor and the China Inland Mission*; for Charles Studd see Grubb, *Studd*.

workers'.[13] The mission was accordingly established and Taylor sailed on 26 May 1866 with fifteen missionary companions, six men and nine women.[14]

Commerce

Another factor that helped to open up the way for missionary societies was commerce. Early inroads had been made into India for trading purposes and the East India Company was granted a Royal Charter on 31 December 1600.[15] This meant that quite large numbers of British citizens went out and settled in India. Initially, little attention was paid to their spiritual needs[16] and it was eighty years before a church was built. In 1698, however, a new charter was issued by William III which required the Company to provide a chaplain in every garrison and principal factory. It further required the chaplains to learn the native languages.

In the eighteenth century, missionary work began and continued in Southern India. In 1758, after his victories had laid the foundation for British Supremacy, Robert Clive (1725–1774), who was later to become Governor of Bengal, invited missionaries to the north. Later in the century, Charles Grant, who had risen to the rank of senior merchant in the East India Company, returned to England in 1790 and urged Wilberforce and others in the Clapham Sect to seriously consider plans for the evangelisation of India.[17] Three years later, Sir John Shore, a man with strong Evangelical convictions, was made Governor General. After four years in post he returned to England, became Lord Teignmouth and joined the Clapham Sect. He wrote, *Considerations on Communicating the Knowledge of Christianity to the Natives of India*, which was a moderate and reasoned argument for Christian missionary activities among the Indian peoples. Prompted by Shore's influence, the Saints began to see the possibilities of Church of England missionary concern focused not merely on the settlers but extended beyond to the native peoples.

However, it was not until the East India Act of 1813 was passed that the church could plan ahead with a proper strategy. The basic problem at that point was simply that missionaries were only

---

[13] Stock, *Church Missionary Society* Vol. 2, p. 580.
[14] Ibid. Vol. 2, p. 581.
[15] Ibid. Vol. 1, p. 51.
[16] Ibid. Vol. 1, p. 52.
[17] Ibid. Vol. 1, p. 54.

allowed to work in those places where CMS was already operating. The Act provided for the appointment of a bishop and three arch-deacons for India. This widened the door of opportunity for sharing the faith.

It should be noted at this point that Anglican Evangelicals had also played a part in the formation of the London Missionary Society (LMS), which came into being in 1795 and sent out many mission-aries to India. Two of its founder members were Dr Haweis, Rector of Aldwinkle, and Mr Pentycross, the Vicar of Wallingford.[18]

In a number of other countries, notably in West and Central Africa and China, trading links paved the way for missionary work. When Samuel Marsden (1764–1838) had persuaded CMS to take a mission to New Zealand in 1808 they agreed to his suggestion that the missionaries should comprise a carpenter, a smith and a twine spinner.[19] In 1850 Henry Venn, the general secretary of CMS, sent cotton gins to Henry Townsend, one of his missionaries who served in Abeokuta.[20] Venn also requested information on which varieties of cotton were best suited to the West-African soils and climate. In 1859 Venn wrote, 'There are now 200 or 300 gins at work at Abeokuta, and five or six presses in the hands of natives.'[21] Thomas Clegg, a Manchester industrialist and cotton-merchant, helped Venn with this project.[22] Venn's purpose in the venture was clear: it was 'to benefit the natives, and to secure no more profit to himself than a bare commission on the transaction'.[23]

In his celebrated public address at the Senate House of the University of Cambridge on 4 December 1857, David Livingstone said:

I beg to direct your attention to Africa – I know that in a few years I shall be cut off in that country, which is now open; do not let it be shut again! I go back to Africa to try to make an open path for commerce and Chris-tianity; do you carry out the work I have begun. I leave it with you![24]

[18] Ibid. Vol. 1, p. 60; see Overton, *English Church*, pp. 256–7.
[19] Stock, *Church Missionary Society* Vol. 1, p. 206.
[20] Ibid. Vol. 2, p. 110.
[21] Ibid. Vol. 2, p. 111.
[22] Ibid. Vol 2, p. 110.
[23] H. Venn, *Private Journal*, 15 November 1856, cited by Stock, *Church Missionary Society* Vol. 2, p. 111; see also Hennell, *Sons of the Prophets*, p. 82.
[24] W. Monk, *Dr Livingstone's Cambridge Lectures*, p. 24, cited by Stanley, *Bible and the Flag*, p. 70.

Clearly, Christian missionaries increasingly benefited from the growing commercial links between England and other parts of the world. However, it needs to be stressed that this relationship was never total or uncritical.

Transportation

The developments in transportation associated with the Industrial Revolution proved favourable to missionary enterprise. In particular, rail and shipping links made missionary travel a great deal easier, especially in the last quarter of the nineteenth century. Fast sailing ships and then steam ships, as William Jacob has shown, made it possible for bishops from overseas to visit England from time to time.[25] For several of the early bishops of Calcutta their appointment was something akin to an exile as no plans were made for their return until the end of their fifteen-year term of office. Stephen Neill wrote that the acquisition of steam and, later, electricity 'sent Europe out conquering and to conquer with a new sense of self-confidence, and ... a new sense of mission to the world'.[26] David Edwards wrote similarly, 'The number of missionaries going to Africa grew along with the invention of the steamship.' There was, he continued, 'no shortage of Englishmen eager to convert the Kingdoms of West Africa'.[27]

Colonial expansion

There can be no doubt that colonial expansion aided the origin and spread of Christian missionary work. Colonialism has been defined as 'that form of imperialism in which the imperial power imposes governmental control on a territory without resort to large-scale human settlement'.[28] Colonialism is therefore generally seen as distinct from Colonisation where the dominant group settles large numbers of its people in the subjugated territory. Such was the case in Southern Rhodesia and Kenya, which became colonies with a substantial white population. One of the striking phenomena during the reign of Queen Victoria was the immense increase in the number of British people living in British colonies. At the beginning

---

[25] Jacob, *Making*, p. 155.
[26] S. Neill, *A History of Christian Missions*, p. 246.
[27] D.L. Edwards, *Christian England* Vol. 3, p. 327.
[28] D.K. Fieldhouse, *Colonialism 1870–1945*, pp. 4–6, cited by Stanley, *Bible and the Flag*, p. 34.

of the reign it had been a mere 4,000,000 including all dependencies. By 1900 it had multiplied fourfold.[29]

The ending of the French Wars in 1815 brought an extended period of peace in Europe. This meant that the British Government was able to give its attention to maintaining peace within its colonies. Just as the Pax Romana had aided the spread of Christianity in the first century, so now in the nineteenth century the British Empire, on which it is said 'the sun never set', aided Christian mission. As new lands were opened up to trade with western nations and to the influence of western culture, so new ways of entry were opened up to missionaries as never before. Clearly, those who went out in the wake of the flag felt that there was always the possibility that they could look to the British Government and colonial rule for protection.

Generally speaking, successive British Governments did not directly support Christian missions, but they did support Christian schools. This was not because they were Christian, but simply because they provided a basic education which resulted in a more civilised and stable society. This in turn helped to generate greater economic prosperity. Similarly, mission hospitals and medical work enabled British colonialism to display a humanitarian concern at minimum cost. This relationship between missionaries and the Government was inevitably ambivalent. In the early years of the century, for example, missionaries had been influential in the fight against slavery. They stood out against policies of brutality and exploitation, and were opposed to imperialism and national self-aggrandizement. On the other hand, many missionaries were happy to endorse Gladstone's opinion of the empire as a sacred trust. Many were of the view that benevolent British rule was in God's providence and in the best interests of the indigenous populations. Peter Williams summed the matter up by stating that 'the picture is of qualified missionary support for imperialism'.[30]

Other factors

There were doubtless other motivational factors which prompted some nineteenth-century English men and women to missionary service. There were certain individuals who offered their services to the great societies out of a sense of duty[31] and there were doubtless a

---

[29] L.E. Elliott-Binns, *Religion in the Victorian Era*, p. 394.
[30] Williams, 'British Religion', p. 398.
[31] See S. Piggin, *Making Evangelical Missionaries 1789–1858*, pp. 147–8.

few who joined CMS as a way to ordination, with the hope of returning to England and obtaining a living in the established church. Stuart Piggin has also charted a number of other issues which prompted individuals to enter missionary service. These included the quest for economic security, the desire for greater respectability and eschatological motives.[32]

Missionary Strategy and Attitudes

As the Evangelical missionary societies established themselves they developed a variety of strategies for reaching the various people groups and nations with the Christian message. Implicit in these strategies were values and attitudes, some of which were severely scrutinised both by their contemporaries and by subsequent historians.

Hostility to the native cultures

We have noted that the major impetus to missionary service was an evangelistic one. Missionaries went out to foreign lands to rescue as many as possible of 'the heathen' from the everlasting damnation that otherwise awaited them. This was a powerful motivation, but it often led to a condemnatory assessment of the value of other religions and of the cultures which had been shaped by those religions. In its most extreme form non-Christian religions and their cultures were seen as evil. 'The heathen in his blindness was bowed down to wood and stone' and that was the sum of it. Something of this condemnatory attitude was reflected in some of the missionary hymns. For example, verse 6 of L. Hensley's 'Thy Kingdom Come O God' (1867) read as follows:

> O'er heathen lands afar
> *Thick darkness* broodeth yet
> Arise, O morning star
> Arise and never set.[33]

In 1867 K.G. Pfander, a CMS missionary, expressed a similar kind of hostility in his apologetic entitled, *Balance of Truth*. In it he contrasted the early spread of Christianity and early spread of

---

[32] Ibid., pp. 124–49.
[33] Hymn 217, *Hymns Ancient and Modern*.

Islam; the one by preaching and the other by the sword: 'The fact that Mohammedanism was propagated by the sword is conclusive proof that it is not of God.'[34]

One of the counter-productive aspects of this approach was that the native peoples sometimes became very hostile to the missionary. Joseph Thompson was one of their early critics. He commented that 'arriving among brutal and degraded savages, they at once adopt an aggressive attitude; they preach a crusade and declare that they have come to change all the old customs. Natives naturally become alarmed and suspicious.'[35] Although it could be said that the CMS committee, under the guidance of Henry Venn, adopted what Jacob described as 'a more gradualist approach recommending that polygamous wives might be baptised',[36] it was not until the closing years of the nineteenth century that significant numbers of missionaries began to take a more sympathetic view of local culture and to find in it points for dialogue. Others began to take the view that if other world faiths were better understood they could be more easily combated.[37]

Superimposing western culture

The concomitant of a hostile attitude to native culture was clearly visible in the frequently employed strategy of superimposing western culture on the local populations. Such objectives are well displayed in some missionary hymns. For instance, the following verse from Bishop Reginald Heber's hymn, 'From Greenland's Icy Mountains', contains the tacit assumption of the superiority of white western European culture:

> From Greenland's icy mountains
> From India's coral strand
> Where Afric's sunny fountains
> Roll down their golden sand,
> From many an ancient river
> From many a palmy plain
> They call us to deliver
> Their land from error's chain

---

[34] K.G. Pfander, *Balance of Truth*, p. 130.
[35] M. Warren, *Social History of Christian Mission*, p. 76.
[36] Jacob, *Making*, p. 202.
[37] Williams, 'British Religion', p. 386.

The majority of nineteenth-century missionaries, particularly in the early decades, had no doubt in their minds as to the supremacy of western culture. They therefore felt it incumbent upon them to transport Christianity in all its western forms to the new lands that they had gone out to serve. Hence, Gothic-style churches were built in some African countries and in the East, as well as in Australia and New Zealand. Native priests were dressed up like European clergy and some overseas bishops even came to wear the riding attire of eighteenth-century English prelates. For example, Bishop Samuel Crowther of Sierra Leone, the first black bishop, wore English clerical collars and vestments.

Sierra Leone also witnessed the spectacle of some local chiefs in the region of Abeokuta becoming interested in the architecture of the mission compounds and schools. Some of their number not only sent their children to mission schools, they even started to build their own houses with English style windows.

Although this happened, it needs to be recognised that not all missionaries wanted it to. Some of their number genuinely wanted to see an African ethos reflected in church architecture and worship, but the power of Victorian England was such that it tended to overrun the local culture.[38] This whole attitude was well expressed in Sir Harry Johnston's message for the Basoga people deep in Africa where he was a British Colonial administrator. 'We were', he wrote, 'like you, going about naked ... with our war paint on, but when we learned Christianity from the Romans we changed and became great. We want you to learn Christianity and follow our steps and you too will be great.'[39] This patronising attitude in no way impugns the sincerity and intelligence of many very fine men and women who ventured out to take the Christian message to foreign parts. It does however reflect the attitude and opinions of the greater majority of nineteenth-century English missionaries, both Evangelical and high church.

To establish denominational Christianity

When LMS was founded in 1795 it declared its intention 'to preach the pure gospel without tying it to any western form or organisation

---

[38] See C.P. Williams, 'Grand and Capacious Gothic Churches', *Tyndale Bulletin* 43.1 (1992), pp. 33–52.

[39] R. Oliver, *Sir Harry Johnston and the Scramble for Africa*, p. 297; for Johnston, also see Stanley, *Bible and the Flag*, pp. 125–6, and Stock, *Church Missionary Society* Vol. 3, pp. 359, 472.

or policy'.[40] The organisation's constitution stated, 'It is a fundamental principle not to send Presbyterian, Independency, Episcopacy or any other form of church order or government about which there may be differences of opinion among serious persons, but the glorious gospel of the blessed God to the heathen'.[41] Despite having such high ideals, wrote Bishop Stephen Neill, 'they usually ended by producing a copy, faithful down to the minutest detail, of that form of Christian faith to which they themselves were accustomed in their own country'.[42]

Evangelical Anglicans, and particularly those who were affiliated with CMS, were no exception. They carried with them to the far-flung corners of the Empire the particular brand of low-church Protestantism in which they had been nurtured in their homeland. Indeed, there were a number of quite sharp disputes on parts of the mission field between Evangelical Anglican missionaries and high-church bishops whose loyalties were tied to the SPG or some form of Catholic churchmanship.

One major instance occurred in Ceylon in 1876 between the bishops and the Rev W. Clark, the senior CMS missionary who was in charge of the Tamil Coolie Mission. For the most part, the services for the coolies were held in the coffee stores or in schoolrooms, but in a few places in the small towns there were churches with chaplains in charge. In some of these buildings ecclesiastical ornaments began to appear and Clark sent instructions to the catechists not to use these venues; they should, instead, only worship in buildings belonging to CMS. Bishop Copleston asserted that Clark's action was a breach of church unity and gave a counter-instruction. For his part, Clark asserted that the bishop had no direct authority over the catechist but only through him as the clergyman in charge.[43] The bishop then required the missionaries to dissociate themselves from Clark's action[44] and on their declining to do so he withdrew their licences. A lengthy struggle ensued which lasted until March 1880 when Archbishop Tait was finally able to mediate and find an acceptable way forward.

The outcome was in several ways favourable to CMS. Regarding lay agents such as the catechists of the Tamil Coolie Mission, Tait,

[40] Neill, *History of Christian Missions*, p. 258.
[41] Edwards, *Christian England* Vol. 3, p. 110.
[42] Neill, *History of Christian Missions*, pp. 258–9.
[43] Stock, *Church Missionary Society* Vol. 3, p. 205.
[44] Ibid. Vol. 3, p. 206.

together with the Archbishop of York and the Bishops of London, Durham and Winchester, ruled that 'a bishop's direct control should only be over such as in the absence of the clergyman, were virtually doing a clergyman's work'.[45] At the same time, the prelates were strongly of the view that the missionaries 'could not be justified in declining to associate themselves with their bishop in the highest act of Christian worship', 'so long as they were required to do nothing contrary to the declared law of the Church'.[46]

Struggles and disputes of the kind that had occurred in Ceylon clearly caused tension and difficulty on foreign fields. It failed to unify new Christian believers and often meant that missionary churches were divided. Alec Vidler commented, 'When one considers how in country after country the Christian missionary movement thus belied its own credentials, it is amazing that it made as much progress as it did.'[47] It was the greater scandal of a divided denominational front on the mission field which led to the beginnings of the ecumenical movement. The objective of its first leaders was to establish one undivided expression of the Christian church.

Civilisation

A number of missionary societies, but by no means all, took the view that native peoples needed first to be civilised as a precursor to their being able to embrace the Christian faith. Henry Venn believed that 'civilisation was an advantage but not a necessity'.[48] In the early days of CMS, Samuel Marsden was of the opinion that the Maoris who had such a fearful reputation must first be 'civilised' before they could be evangelised. Marsden himself wrote:

> Nothing in my opinion can pave the way for the introduction of the Gospel but civilisation – and that can only be accomplished among the heathen by the arts ... The arts and religion should go together. The attention of the heathen can be gained, and their habits corrected, by the arts. Till their attention is gained, and moral and industrious habits are induced, little or no progress can be made in teaching them the

---

[45] Ibid. Vol. 3, p. 214.
[46] Ibid. Vol. 3, p. 214.
[47] Vidler, *Age of Revolution*, p. 254.
[48] Williams, 'British Religion', p. 23.

Gospel ... To preach the gospel without the aid of the arts will never succeed among the heathen for any time.[49]

An inexperienced CMS committee instructed the members of Marsden's party 'to introduce amongst the Natives the knowledge of Christ; and in order to this, the Arts of Civilised Life'.[50]

Many missionary strategists were of the view that this was also the way to make Africa Christian. Thomas Fowell Buxton was of the view that the way to break the West African slave-trade and to civilise the native people was through a civilising strategy. In a letter to Lord Melbourne he wrote, 'It is the Bible and the Plough that must regenerate Africa.'[51] He believed that as local inhabitants began to engage in better agriculture and to develop industries there would be sufficient money to build churches, schools and to provide education. This, in turn, would create a people more open and ready to receive the Christian message.

Much of the early work done by CMS in West Africa, particularly in the region of Freetown and Regent village, was focussed on education. In many of the mission settlements a church and school were erected beside each other on the same compound and both regarded as vitally important. Later in the century, CMS even built an English-style grammar school in Freetown and by 1849 a girls' grammar school had also been erected in the town. CMS missionaries valued education. For example, they committed themselves to producing grammatical structures and vocabularies of Niger languages in order that the local people would be able to read the Bible, hymns and Prayer Book in their own language.[52]

A number of societies with which Evangelical Anglicans were involved saw the establishment of colleges of higher education as crucially important. In 1827 Fourah Bay College was established under the direction of the Rev C.L.F. Hansel who had been ordained by the Bishop of London. It provided education for many African clergy and leading laity.[53] In 1838 the Rev Joseph Henry Gray, who had gained high honours at Trinity College, Dublin, was sent to Madras to establish the Madras Divinity College.[54]

---

[49] Stock, *Church Missionary Society* Vol. 1, p. 206.
[50] Ibid. Vol. 1, p. 206.
[51] Ibid. Vol. 1, p. 451.
[52] Jacob, *Making*, p. 203.
[53] Stock, *Church Missionary Society* Vol. 1, p. 336.
[54] Ibid. Vol. 1, pp. 326–7.

CMS also established other institutions of higher learning, including Calcutta Divinity School,[55] St John's College Agra,[56] Lahore Divinity College,[57] and Poona Divinity School.[58]

Churches with local leadership

In the early days of the East India Company a pattern had been established whereby chaplains were sent out to organise church life for British settlers. From this base, some chaplains had begun to reach out to the native peoples in their locality. Subsequent generations of English missionaries seem to have supposed that British Imperial power would last forever. For this reason many of them developed strategies which involved setting up a compound with church school and mission houses staffed by white English missionaries.

This situation began to change when Henry Venn became secretary of CMS in 1841. Venn was forward thinking and he articulated a policy which aimed to establish 'self-governing, self-supporting and self-propagating churches'.[59] Nowhere did Venn state this ideal more forcibly than in his brief to missionaries who set out for Madagascar in 1863. The great aim of a mission, he declared, was 'the raising up of a Native Church – self-supporting, self-gathering, self-extending. The Mission is the scaffolding; the Native Church is the edifice. The removal of the scaffolding is the proof that the building is completed.'[60] In Venn's opinion the work of pastoring churches was not the work of missionaries. His aim was that this should be the work of local pastors. For this reason endeavours were made between 1877 and 1888 to appoint indigenous bishops in India, Ceylon and Africa. As has been noted, theological institutions and divinity colleges were set up to train local clergy. Missionaries, as Venn saw it, were there to do the work of an Evangelist. Missionaries were there to train native pastors in the use of the Bible. Venn was strongly of the view that missionaries should not settle down as pastors of local congregations.[61] Missionaries who

---

[55] Ibid. Vol. 3, pp. 132, 134.
[56] Ibid. Vol. 2, pp. 168, 531.
[57] Ibid. Vol. 2, pp. 400, 576–8.
[58] Ibid. Vol. 3, p. 472.
[59] For Venn's strategy see W.R. Shenk, *Henry Venn – Missionary Statesman*, ch. 4, 'Venn as Strategist', pp. 39–47.
[60] Ibid., p. 46.
[61] Ibid., p. 40.

did this would cause harm by holding back the native churches from self-expression and self-autonomy. In earlier times, Venn was among those who had little enthusiasm for medical missionaries, possibly for the reason that they might be more likely to establish themselves in a settled location. As late as 1864 Venn reported that CMS had 'a uniformly unsuccessful experience with medical missionaries.'[62] Venn stated that CMS regarded preachers as its responsibility rather than doctors.[63] In a document entitled, *The Native Pastorate and Organisation of Native Churches*, issued in 1851, Venn gave clear direction that missionaries were not to become settled pastors:

> Whilst the work of a missionary may involve for a time the pastoral care of newly baptised converts, it is important that, as soon as settled congregations are formed, such pastoral care should be devolved upon native teachers, under the missionary's superintendence.[64]

Despite Venn's enlightened policy, it was not until much later in the nineteenth century that Christian communities founded by the missionaries began, even in a limited way, to be seen as independent churches rather than the overseas work of English missionary societies, such as CMS or CIM. The fact was that the high imperialism of the later Victorian years generated policies of control in all aspects of colonial life and this inevitably impacted the church. It was not until a much later point in the twentieth century that missionaries began to see themselves as going out to serve under native church leadership.

Missionary Recruits

Many of those who went out to the overseas mission field in the first part of the nineteenth century seem to have been skilled journeymen and skilled artisans. It was this which led Sydney Smith to jibe that missionary endeavour was in the hands of 'consecrated cobblers'. Despite Smith's malicious criticism the fact was that men with a trade or practical skill were much more suited to the pioneer phase of a mission. In the early years of the nineteenth century there was a high

---

[62] Ibid., p. 40.
[63] Ibid., p. 40.
[64] H. Venn, *Native Pastorate*, paragraph 2.

death rate among missionaries and this also helped to deter middle-
class professionals.[65] S. Piggin gives a list of 148 missionaries sent out
by CMS to India between 1815 and 1848. Of these, thirty-four could
be categorised as having a trade.[66] Among those who went out to
Africa with CMS before 1874 only one was a university graduate.

In India the situation was perceived as being different, because
the culture was taken to be more developed. Instead of primal and
tribal religion there were developed major world faiths such as
Hinduism, Islam and Sikhism. Sanskrit was held to be a language
worthy of serious study and there was an unspoken opinion by
those at CMS headquarters that high-caste Hindus and a more
sophisticated culture called for men and women who had a higher
level of academic attainment.

After 1815 the pattern of recruitment changed following
the consecration of the Evangelical Henry Ryder as Bishop of
Gloucester. Stock noted that Ryder along with Bishop Bathurst
'ordained men at the Committee's request, accepting as a title the
committee's agreement to employ them'.[67] Things were made a
great deal more easy when in 1819 the Colonial Service Act gave
the Archbishops of Canterbury and York and the Bishop of
London power to ordain men for 'His Majesty's Colonies and
Foreign Possessions'.[68] These developments made more men
willing to go since they had the possibility of obtaining a Church of
England incumbency on their return.

The last quarter of the nineteenth century saw recruitment to
Evangelical missionary societies reach a peak. By the beginning of
the twentieth century CMS had more than 700 missionaries in the
field. The LMS had reached its high point twelve years earlier.

A further development was the growing number of single
women who went out to the foreign fields in the closing years of
Queen Victoria's reign. A number of factors contributed to this.
Role models such as Florence Nightingale, Josephine Butler and
Catherine Booth inspired Evangelical women. More graduates
were needed, particularly in translation work, while the need for
skilled craftsmen was much less urgent. Others were stirred by the
campaigns of Moody and Sankey, particularly the evangelistic
meetings which they held in the universities of Cambridge and

---

[65] See Murray, *Proclaim the Good News*, pp. 21–2.
[66] See Piggin, *Making Evangelical Missionaries*, pp. 267–74.
[67] Stock, *Church Missionary Society* Vol. 1, p. 245.
[68] Ibid., p. 245.

Oxford. Several Cambridge graduates, including Charles Studd, the former university and England cricket captain, were drawn to China partly as a result of Moody's message.[69] The Keswick Convention (see the previous chapter) laid great stress on full-surrender teaching[70] and mission,[71] and challenged many, both men and women, to offer themselves for overseas service.

In May 1840 Bishop Blomfield addressed a letter to the Archbishop of Canterbury urging that a fund be established for endowing colonial bishoprics. In response, a meeting was held on 27 April 1841 at which the fund was formally incorporated.[72] This meant a more developed church-life, which, in turn, needed more personnel to staff and administer the new diocesan organisations.

Some Significant Achievements

Africa

The early focus of Evangelical Anglican missionary endeavour was in West Africa with CMS establishing its Sierra Leone mission in 1816. Edward Bickersteth, who later became general secretary of CMS, was sent out to assess the situation before any missionaries were commissioned.[73] The first missionaries were William Johnson and a German, Henry Düring. Shortly after landing on 14 July 1816, Johnson soon met with success and many native hearts were 'touched' as a result of his inviting them to his hut for singing and prayer.[74]

In this early period, Sierra Leone was known as 'the white man's grave' because many missionaries died of tropical diseases. 1823 proved to be a terrible year. Six missionaries died and also the chaplain and his wife and several officials. Among the dead were Johnson, Düring and his wife.[75] Over twenty new missionaries arrived in 1830, among them Henry Townsend who was later to lead the Niger Mission.

---

[69] See J.C. Pollock, *The Cambridge Seven*, pp. 77f.
[70] See S. Barabas, *So Great Salvation*, pp. 108–27.
[71] Ibid., pp. 148–55.
[72] Stock, *Church Missionary Society* Vol. 1, p. 408. See also Cornish, *History of the English Church* Part 2, p. 411.
[73] Stock, *Church Missionary Society* Vol. 1, p. 159.
[74] Ibid. Vol. 1, p. 160.
[75] Murray, *Proclaim the Good News*, p. 20.

The first Bishop of West Africa was Owen Emeric Vidal, a Sussex rector with a real gift for languages. He was a compelling preacher who captivated the Sierra Leonians. Vidal died onboard a ship which was returning home to England in December 1854.[76]

Those who felt the future demanded an indigenous local ministry were encouraged by the consecration of Samuel Crowther, an ex-slave, as Bishop of the Niger territories in 1864. By 1842 there were some 7,000 regular attendees at public worship in Sierra Leone of whom over 1,500 were communicants.[77] There were also fifty schools with 6,000 pupils.[78]

In Southern Africa the major figure was the high-church bishop, Robert Gray (1809–1872) whose sympathies were strongly those of the SPG. In fact, he stumped the country denouncing CMS for its 'stinginess' in not granting his application for £1,000 a year to assist in developing his Zulu Mission. The diocese of Cape Town was formed in 1847 and Gray was consecrated as its first bishop.[79] When Gray first went to Cape Town there were only thirteen English clergymen in the whole of South Africa. By the end of the period there were nine bishops and more than 400 clergy.

Among these bishops was the Evangelical, Henry Cotterill who, after having been CMS secretary in Madras, was consecrated by Archbishop Sumner to succeed John Armstrong as Bishop of Grahamstown.[80] Bishop Gray was not consulted and was furious at the appointment. It was felt that Sumner had either acted on the advice of Lord Shaftesbury or been persuaded by a dissident congregation in Port Elizabeth.[81] As things turned out, however, Bishop Gray found in Cotterill 'a wise and sympathetic colleague' who moved his diocese away from Erastian policies towards self-government by forming his own synod in 1858.[82]

David Livingstone's expeditions into central Africa and H.M. Stanley's travels opened up the continent's interior and paved the way for the CMS mission to Uganda and stimulated further

[76] Stock, *Church Missionary Society* Vol. 2, p. 121.

[77] Ibid. Vol. 2, p. 236.

[78] Ibid. Vol. 2, p. 336.

[79] Cornish, *History of the English Church* Part 2, p. 392.

[80] H.P. Thompson, *Into All Lands: The History of the Society for the Propagation of the Gospel in Foreign Parts 1701–1950*, p. 116.

[81] P. Hinchliff, *The Anglican Church in South Africa: An Account of the History and Development of the Church of the Province of South Africa*, pp. 58–61.

[82] Ibid., pp. 58–61.

concern for Madagascar. Evangelical work in Madagascar was largely in the hands of LMS though CMS sent two missionaries to the island in 1864.[83]

In 1875 Stanley wrote to the *Daily Telegraph* challenging the churches to do something for Central Africa. One of those who responded was James Hannington (1847–1885), curate of the proprietary chapel of St George, Hurstpierpoint. He offered himself to CMS and went out to Zanzibar. After a year his health failed and he returned home to England. By 1884 he was fit and well and was consecrated Bishop of Eastern Equatorial Africa. As he reached the borders of Uganda, King Mwanga believing him to be the forerunner of a conquest, had him imprisoned and ordered him to be put to death. The entries in his diary end on 29 October 1885 and it seems most probable that he was murdered either on that day or the day following.[84] He left behind him in England a wife and children. Among his last recorded words was the sentence, 'I am about to die for the Buganda, and have purchased the road to them with my life.'[85] His biographer wrote that 'he has given to the Mission in East Africa an impulse of which we may confidently expect that it will not lose the momentum'.[86]

Work in East Africa was further extended when Alfred Tucker, curate of St Nicholas, Durham, was appointed Bishop of Equatorial Africa in 1890.[87] He set foot in Buganda when tension with the natives was still running high. Sensing that there could very well be more Protestant martyrdoms, he persuaded CMS to underwrite the task of retaining the services of the small British force which had been put in place to protect The Imperial British East Africa Company. Tucker shared Henry Venn's concern to establish a local ministry and by 1899 there were twenty-one African clergy in Uganda.[88] In addition, there were two hundred native teachers and Evangelists scattered over the country, entirely supported by the Church of Uganda itself.[89]

---

[83] Cornish, *History of the English Church* Part 2, p. 399.

[84] E.C. Dawson, *James Hannington First Bishop of Eastern Equatorial Africa*, p. 442.

[85] Ibid., p. 447.

[86] Ibid., p. 450.

[87] See Jacob, *Making*, pp. 220–1, and Stock, *Church Missionary Society* Vol. 3, pp. 365, 434.

[88] Jacob, *Making*, p. 220.

[89] Stock, *Church Missionary Society* Vol. 3, p. 738.

India

In India CMS work had grown and developed from the earlier endeavours of the East India chaplains and the inspiring foundation laid by William Carey's Baptist Missionary Society (BMS). The first CMS agent in India was a native convert called Abdul Masch. He began work in 1813.[90] In the same year, the East India Act was passed, and among other things, it provided for the appointment of a bishop and three archdeacons for each of the three 'capitals' of Calcutta, Madras and Bombay.[91] The first bishop, a high churchman, Dr T.F. Middleton (d. 1822), had been Vicar of St Pancras. Reginald Heber, who ordained the first native deacon in 1823, succeeded him. In 1832 the See passed to Daniel Wilson (1778–1858), a staunch Evangelical, who held the family living of Islington from 1824 to 1832. He commenced the building of Calcutta Cathedral, established local churches and visited Madras, Bombay, Ceylon and even Borneo. He became a close friend of the Governor-General, Lord William Bentinck, a man with deep Christian convictions, who had abolished a number of abuses, including the practice of suttee, in which widows were burnt alive on their husband's funeral pyres. Wilson, who was a strong opponent of the caste system, died in office aged eighty on 2 January 1858.[92]

Wilson's successor at Calcutta was George Cotton who had been a schoolmaster at Marlborough. As an educationalist, he gave much time and energy to the affairs of Calcutta University as well as to the training of native clergy. Cotton was drowned in the Ganges in October 1866 when he lost his footing while boarding a steamer at night. His death marked the ending of an important epoch in the history of Anglicanism in India.[93] Of the twelve men who had been appointed to Indian Sees up to that time six had been 'decided Evangelicals'.[94] But Lord Palmerston had now died and was replaced by Lord Derby whose sympathies were with high churchmen. Among the Evangelicals were Thomas Carr, first Bishop of Bombay, and his successor in 1861 Bishop John Harding, and Bishop Dealtry (d. 1861) of Madras who was succeeded by Frederick Gell.

---

[90] Ibid. Vol. 1, p. 183.
[91] Ibid. Vol. 1, p. 293.
[92] Ibid. Vol. 2, p. 225.
[93] Ibid. Vol. 2, p. 495.
[94] Ibid. Vol. 2, p. 160.

The Evangelical Anglican influence in India continued to grow steadily through the century. In 1871 there were 102 ordained CMS missionaries in India and by 1890 the figure had risen to 146. In 1890 there were also 147 native ordained clergy and 1,605 lay agents. In 1890 CMS had 28,216 communicants whilst SPG had 24,078. In the same year CMS had 56,578 scholars in its schools whilst SPG had 22,572.[95] Commenting on the state of missions in Ceylon at the close of the nineteenth century, Eugene Stock noted that the number of Singhalese and Tamil Christians in the Church of England 'will be so numerous as practically to dominate the Church'.[96]

Australia and New Zealand

Australia was first visited in 1770 by Captain James Cook and received its first shipment of convicts from England in 1788. No chaplain or schoolmaster was sent with them. In 1794 Samuel Marsden (1764–1838), an intimate of Charles Simeon, who was later to become the first missionary and 'apostle' to New Zealand, was sent out to Botany Bay as chaplain on the recommendation of William Wilberforce. In 1825 he established an auxiliary CMS as a base from which to evangelise the aborigines of Australia.

In 1829 William Grant Broughton (1788–1853) was sent to Australia as Archdeacon of New South Wales, his diocesan being the Bishop of Calcutta. Seven years later the diocese of Australia, which included the whole of the South Seas, was founded. Broughton was consecrated its first bishop. He was generous and very mission orientated, and for a considerable period of his episcopate he gave a quarter of his income towards the founding of new dioceses. Gradually his hopes were realised with formation of Melbourne, Newcastle and Adelaide in 1847.[97] Broughton's own metropolitan diocese took the name of Sydney.[98] By the close of the century there were three provinces of Sydney (New South Wales), Melbourne (Victoria) and Brisbane (Queensland), each corresponding with a State of the Commonwealth and containing four or more dioceses.

When Bishop Broughton died in 1853, the Duke of Newcastle who was colonial secretary and a Tractarian could find no Tractarian

---

[95] See statistical tables ibid. Vol. 3, p. 509.
[96] Ibid. Vol. 3, p. 557.
[97] Cornish, *History of the English Church* Part 2, p. 405.
[98] Ibid., p. 405.

or high churchman who was willing to go to Sydney. With the advent of the Crimean War, Newcastle moved to the War Office and the task of colonial secretary devolved to Sir George Grey. He turned to Archbishop Sumner for a candidate for the vacant See and he put forward Frederick Barker who had been vicar of Edgehill, Liverpool, which was in Sumner's previous diocese of Chester. Having worked in both Ireland and Liverpool Barker was hostile to both Roman Catholics and high churchmen, which led him to concentrate on recruiting Evangelical clergy in his diocese.[99]

Among the Evangelical bishops, Charles Perry (1807–1891) who was consecrated Bishop of Melbourne in 1847 proved to be outstanding.[100] He was incumbent of St Paul's Church, Cambridge, and a close friend and disciple of Charles Simeon, whose strong Evangelical convictions he shared. In 1854 the Victorian Legislature gave power to the church of that colony to manage its own affairs. Bishop Perry achieved the honour of having organised and presided over the first synod of the colonial church with the power to pass Acts which would have the force of law.[101] In contrast, the Evangelical Bishops of Sydney, Bathurst and Goulburn were reticent to break the relationship with the British Crown, which they felt might result from Bishop Perry's action.[102] Saumarez Smith who was curate of St Paul's, Cambridge, from 1859 to 1861 was later sent out as Bishop of Sydney (1890–1897). He won high academic honours. He was the Tyrwhitt scholar in 1860 and in 1864 was awarded the Seatonian Prize. His career after leaving Cambridge was largely spent as principal of St Aidan's College, Birkenhead.

During the 1850s there was sharp churchmanship tension between bishops Perry of Melbourne and Barker of Sydney, and those bishops who aligned themselves with the high church. As a consequence, many Evangelicals moved into the diocese of Sydney. By the end of the century the Church of England in Australia and Tasmania had become self-supporting and virtually independent except in matters of ritual and the *Prayer Book*.[103]

In 1814 when only a few Christian mechanics were settled in New Zealand the Evangelical, Samuel Marsden, made the first of seven visits to the territory. Henry Williams (1792–1861), another

[99] Jacob, *Making*, p. 139.
[100] See B.E. Hardman, *The Evangelical Party in the Church of England 1855–1865*, pp. 378f.
[101] Stock, *Church Missionary Society* Vol. 2, p. 91.
[102] Jacob, *Making*, p. 141.
[103] Ibid., p. 139.

CMS missionary, followed him in 1822. It was through his influence and that of his brother that the Maori tribes submitted to the sovereignty of Queen Victoria in 1840.

In the same year, New Zealand became a British colony and moves were made to establish a bishopric. George Selwyn (1809–1878) of St John's College, Cambridge, was appointed to the See. Although not an Evangelical he established good relations with CMS before leaving England. On his arrival Selwyn was full of praise for the CMS mission that he found in place with 400 communicants and zealous and capable clergy.[104] Warre Cornish observed that 'the Church Missionary Society had indeed gone far in converting and civilising the Maori nation'.[105] Selwyn founded St John's College in Auckland but was slow to ordain Maoris to the diaconate and priesthood.[106] In 1853 Selwyn returned to England to persuade the British Government to allow the New Zealand Church, within certain limits, to frame its own laws. Additionally, Selwyn pressed for his territory to become a separate Province with four additional dioceses.

Although several of the new bishops, who were largely Selwyn's appointees, were high church in their sympathies,[107] William Williams, who with his brother, Henry, had evangelised the Maoris for thirty-four years, was consecrated Bishop of Waiapu on 3 April 1859. Selwyn wrote of him, 'He is an episcopally minded man, and it would give me great pleasure to divide my diocese with him. Yea, let him take it all, as I cannot pretend to equal his piety or maturity of wisdom.'[108] In the last quarter of the century the Anglican Church in New Zealand was able to resource itself and the CMS committee was gradually withdrawing the level of its financial support in order to fund other unevangelised countries. Evangelicals had played a very significant role in both the founding of and the subsequent development of the Anglican Church in New Zealand.

Canada and the Far East

Before concluding this brief examination of Evangelical influence on some key areas of overseas missions and the colonial church, mention should be made of Canada, the Far East, Europe and South

---

[104] Cornish, *History of the English Church* Part 2, pp. 412–13.
[105] Ibid., p. 413.
[106] Stock, *Church Missionary Society* Vol. 2, p. 93.
[107] Ibid. Vol. 2, p. 96.
[108] Ibid. Vol. 2, pp. 92–3.

America. Canada contained the oldest colonial bishoprics, those of Nova Scotia, which was founded in 1787, and Quebec in 1793. In 1791 an Act of the British Parliament divided the country into two, Upper Canada (Quebec) and Lower Canada (Ontario). Here the main missionary thrust was in the hands of the SPG – which was revitalised by the giving and concern of the Hackney Phalanx, a high church group of clergy and laity. John Jacob Mountain (1749–1825) was consecrated Bishop of Quebec in 1793 and organised the building of what became the cathedral church at Quebec in 1801. His son, George Jehoshaphat Mountain (1789–1863), was consecrated coadjutor Bishop of Monteal in the diocese of Quebec in 1836. When Montreal was divided in 1850 he elected to take the poorer See of Quebec. He was committed to education and the development of grammar schools. He also founded Bishop's College of Lennoxville for the training of clergy. As the church extended westward, other dioceses were formed, including Toronto in 1839, Huron in 1857 and Ontario in 1861.

CMS and Evangelical influence was stronger in western Canada. Here the society established the North-West America Mission and, a little later, The North Pacific Mission in 1819. CMS was influential in Winnipeg and the development of the diocese and University of Manitoba. The earlier mission centred around the Rev John West who went out to Rupert's Land in 1820 as a chaplain to the Hudson's Bay Company. He was adopted by CMS in 1822 but served the society for only one year.[109] CMS then sent out others to continue the work he started.[110] In 1844 Bishop George Jehoshaphat Mountain made a 2,000-mile journey from Montreal to visit the area and was astonished at what he found. He confirmed 846 candidates, including a large number of Indians, delivered sixteen addresses and conducted an ordination.[111] As a result of his visit, he urged the need for a bishopric and in 1849 David Anderson went out as first Bishop of Rupert's Land. Archbishop Sumner, who solicited Anderson's appointment, told Earl Grey that Anderson 'was for many years in my Diocese of Chester and is a person whom I can confidently recommend'.[112] Anderson, 'a highly esteemed Evangelical clergyman', was consecrated in Canterbury Cathedral and 'proved to be a

---

[109] Murray, *Proclaim the Good News*, p. 85.
[110] Thompson, *Into All Lands*, pp. 255–6.
[111] Stock, *Church Missionary Society* Vol. 2, p. 364, and J.T. Sweeny, *A Short History of The Diocese of Quebec 1793–1993*, p. 16.
[112] J.B. Sumner, to Third Earl Grey, 10 May 1850.

great traveller and encourager under whose leadership new mission stations were opened up and the Bible translated into Native American languages.'[113] Anderson served until 1864 and in that period seventeen men were sent out or adopted as CMS missionaries. The work expanded among various Indian groups and northwards to the Hudson Bay among the Eskimo peoples. Eugene Stock in his end of century summary of the work in Canada made it clear that it was particularly in the western part of the dominion that Evangelical and CMS's influence was at its strongest.[114]

In China and Japan the main missionary work was in the hands of non-episcopal missions, a number of which were based in the United States of America. In China the chief missionary work was done by CIM, which was founded in 1865[115] by Hudson Taylor who had grown up among the Methodists.[116] Taylor, who was essentially a revivalist, described how the apathy of so many English Christians provoked him to engage in overseas evangelism.[117] His public address, on the needs of China resulted in seven Cambridge students, including Charles Studd[118] the English cricket captain, leaving England in February 1885 to work with the CIM. One of their number, William Cassels, was consecrated Bishop of the new diocese of Western China whilst in England on his first furlough in 1895.[119]

Japan opened up for Christian mission in the last quarter of the century. In 1887 Anglicans and members of other denominations founded the 'Japan Church' on Anglican principles. In 1887 its synod adopted the *English Prayer Book* with some changes. Arthur Pool (d. 1885) was consecrated first bishop of Japan in October 1883.[120] His successor was Edward Bickersteth, the grandson of the former CMS general secretary.[121] It was estimated that between 1883 and 1900 the number of Anglican Christians in Japan grew from 500 to 10,000.[122]

---

[113] Stock, *Church Missionary Society* Vol. 2, p. 312.
[114] Ibid. Vol. 3, p. 810.
[115] Taylor, *Hudson Taylor*, pp. 33–47.
[116] H. Taylor, *Hudson Taylor in Early Years*, pp. 50–1, 75–80.
[117] Taylor, *Hudson Taylor*, pp. 31–3.
[118] Grubb, *Studd*.
[119] Pollock, *Cambridge Seven*, p. 107.
[120] Stock, *Church Missionary Society* Vol. 3, p. 592.
[121] Ibid. Vol. 3, p. 592.
[122] Cornish, *History of the English Church* Part 2, p. 389.

Throughout the century Evangelical Anglican Missionary concern was also focused on Europe. As has already been noted,[123] the Recordites among them developed a growing interest in the Jewish people and in particular in their return to Palestine.[124] A number of branches of the BFBS were set up from 1804 onwards in various German towns and cities in which there were Jewish communities.[125] The Jerusalem bishopric, which was discussed at length in the earlier chapter of this book on theology, was founded in 1841 as joint Anglo-German venture. For many Evangelical Anglicans it was seen as a major step in the evangelisation of the Jewish nation.

South America was something of a neglected continent but was promoted by the South American Missionary Society. It began amid tragic circumstances surrounding its pioneer missionary, Allen Gardiner (1794–1840) who died of starvation with six fellow workers in Tierra del Fuego. A second party was sent out in 1859 most of whom were murdered.[126] By the end of the century the impact of Evangelical Christianity in South America was, in the words of Stephen Neill, 'still the day of small things'.[127] As late as 1914 he estimated that there were probably not more than 500,000 Protestants in the entire sub-continent.[128]

By the end of the nineteenth century the Anglican Communion had witnessed an enormous expansion. In 1860 there were no more than thirty-five Anglican bishoprics, but by the end of the century there were 107.[129] Besides those there were a number of other missionary bishops who were subject to the primacy of the Archbishop of Canterbury.[130] In all of this development, Evangelicals had played a prominent role. They had provided the greater part of the missionary candidates. In CMS they had the largest Church of England organisation. In Henry Venn they had a very forward thinking and able mission strategist whose policies had fostered the growth of indigenous self-governing Anglican churches which were no longer dependent on the mother church. In Archbishop John

---

[123] See chapter 7.
[124] Railton, *No North Sea*, p. 207.
[125] Ibid., pp. 76, 115.
[126] See P. Thompson, *An Unquenchable Flame: The Story of Captain Allen Gardiner.*
[127] Neill, *History of Christian Missions*, p. 391.
[128] Ibid., p. 391.
[129] Cornish, *History of the English Church* Part 2, p. 423.
[130] Ibid., p. 424.

Bird Sumner they had a primate who made a significant contribution to the colonial church and its episcopate.[131] Not only were a number of his appointments Evangelicals whom he had known personally, for the most part they proved to be judicious administrators and effective pastors who fostered ongoing mission. Evangelical Anglicans unlike their high church counterparts also served in inter-denominational societies such as LMS and the CIM.

---

[131] Scotland, *John Bird Sumner*, pp. 147–8.

13

Ritual Controversies

The Emergence of Ritualism in Nineteenth-Century England

English church worship in the era before the Reformation was characterised by ritual centred on the mass and the sacramental system. The sixteenth-century Protestant Reformers eradicated most of this heritage of colour, symbol, procession and ritual. They regarded it as superstitious and out of keeping with the simpler home-based church practices recounted in the pages of the New Testament. Thus, for the most part, from the sixteenth century down to the middle years of the nineteenth century the worship of the Church of England remained plain and unadorned.

In the early Victorian period, however, a series of events and movements combined to create a renewed desire to revive medieval ritual in the Church of England. In July 1833 John Keble preached his celebrated Assize Sermon in the University Church of St Mary the Virgin, Oxford. Although it was intended that he should address the assembled judiciary he departed from the purpose of the occasion and spoke out in the most forthright tones against the country's 'national apostasy'. Thus the Oxford Movement began with the overarching aim of re-establishing universal respect for the Church of England as the national church. As has been noted, they sought to achieve this end by means of the doctrine of apostolic succession and the contention that the Church of England was a branch of the one catholic and apostolic church.[1] They also aimed to assert the authority of the established church by promoting architecture, worship and art.

In May 1839 John Mason Neatle (1818–1866), a Ritualist clergyman, formed the Cambridge Camden Society to facilitate this latter

---

[1] See chapter 7.

aspect. The society aimed 'to promote the study of Gothic Architecture and Ritual Arts and the Restoration of Mutilated architectural remains.'[2] It sought to ensure that all new churches were erected in the Gothic style and that all restorations were carried out after the pattern of medieval buildings. The society kept lists of specially approved architects. Among them were Sir Gilbert Scott (1811–1878), William Butterfield (1814–1900) and Augustus Pugin (1812–1852). Pugin had such an enthusiasm for Gothic that on one occasion his friends presented him with a Gothic pudding.[3]

The Camdenians promoted the construction of lofty Gothic-style buildings that dominated their surrounding landscape and so raised the profile of the church. They also promoted worship which they felt would cause people to fear, respect and honour God. It was this that led to their elevating and separating the chancel from the people by rood screens. They replaced the communion tables with altars that were often raised on three steps. Clergy were encouraged to wear colourful vestments to make them appear more prominent and respected. Organs, robed chairs, choral singing and process-ionals were all advocated as further means of achieving dignity and reverence. Many of these ideas were set out in the *Tracts for the Times* which was commenced in 1833. This desire for colour and movement was further reinforced by the Romantic Movement which looked back with warm esteem to 'merrie England' of the medieval period. The Romantic ideal was in some ways a reaction to the grow-ing emphasis on rationalism, scientific discovery and logic.

Ritualism also arose partly out of a desire to reach the poor with the Christian message. The lives of most working-class people were spent in the dull and dreary atmosphere of slum alleys and streets. Many could neither read nor write so there was little to cheer them. In such circumstances, it was felt that the unemotional, arid services of low-church Protestantism would never touch the poor. Indeed, Bishop Blomfield described the average church service of the 1850s

---

[2] B.F.L. Clarke, *Church Builders in the Nineteenth Century*, p. 75.
[3] Butterfield was the first advocate of the Gothic style which he argued for in his book, *Contrasts or A Parallel between Noble Edifices of the Four-teenth and Fifteenth Centuries, and Similar Buildings of the Present Day: Showing the Present Decay of Taste* (1836). It was not until 1847 that the society organised its ideas on restoration and the result was a tract entitled *Principles of Church Restoration* by E.A. Freeman. Later, in 1850, Gilbert Scott published *A Plea for the Faithful Restoration of Ancient Churches*.

as being 'blank, dismal, oppressive and dreary'. 'Matins and the litany', he continued, 'with a sermon lasting the best part of an hour, in a cold gloomy church was not the kind of worship to appeal to a man or woman with no education or little imagination.'[4] The Tractarians therefore determined to reach the people for whom dull, grey buildings had little appeal with 'mystery, movement, colour and ceremonial'.

As the Tractarians turned again to the *Prayer Book* they discovered that the ornaments rubric gave support to their cause. The rubric stated that 'such ornaments of the Church, and the ministers thereof, at all times of their ministration shall be retained and be in use, as were in the Church of England, by authority of Parliament in the second year of the reign of King Edward VI'.[5] On this basis the Ritualists were able to maintain that they were simply adhering to the original regulation and that it was perfectly legal to wear 'a white albe plain with vestment or cope and to celebrate', not at the north side of the table but 'afore the midst of the altar' as specified in the *Book of Common Prayer* immediately before the prayer of consecration.

In the early days it was therefore quite hard to argue legally against the Ritualists. However, following the trial of John Purchas for ritualistic innovations in 1870 the use of this rubric to justify the use of Eucharistic vestments was brought to an end. This was done on the basis of the Act of Uniformity that, whilst it sanctioned the use of vestments, also added the words 'until other order shall be therein taken by authority of the Queen's Majesty'. 'Such order,' it was argued, had been taken in 1566 when Archbishop Matthew Parker had issued advertisements which condemned all vestments but the surplice. Although Elizabeth I did not sign the bill, she clearly assented to its provisions because the use of vestments at Holy Communion services entirely disappeared.

The Ritualists provoked widespread hostility at every level from the monarchy down to the working classes of the East End of London. Queen Victoria wrote: 'It is clear that … the liberties taken and the deference shown by the clergy of the high church and Ritualist party, is so great that something must be done to check it, and prevent its continuation.'[6]

---

[4] J.R.H. Moorman, *History of the Church of England*, p. 367.
[5] 'An Act for the Uniformity of Common Prayer, and Service in the Church, and Administration of the Sacraments', *The Book of Common Prayer*, p. v.
[6] P.T. Marsh, *The Victorian Church in Decline*, pp. 101–2.

Evangelical Anglican Opposition to Ritualism

There were a number of aspects of Victorian ritualism to which Anglican Evangelicals took particular exception. Prominent among them were the doctrine of the real presence in the Eucharist, the use of wafer bread, mixing water and wine in the chalice during the service, reservation, adoration, benediction, the eastward position of the celebrant, the wearing of vestments, including albes, chasubles and coloured stoles. Priestly absolution, and in particular making the sign of the cross during it, the use of confessionals and bowing at the name of Jesus were all particularly offensive to Evangelicals. This chapter considers some of these actions in more specific detail and identifies the nature and reasons for Evangelical opposition to them.

The real presence

The Tractarians found the Eucharist a largely neglected ordinance in 1833. In fact, it was almost an optional adjunct to normal Anglican worship. In the early nineteenth-century, many congregations celebrated Holy Communion only four times a year. As Newman and the leaders of the Oxford Movement studied the Early Church Fathers of the undivided Catholic Church, however, they found the Eucharist to have had a much more central place in their worship. They discovered also a clear doctrine of a 'real presence' taught by Cyril of Jerusalem in his *Catechetical Lectures*. In a celebrated sermon, entitled 'The Holy Eucharist A Comfort to the Penitent', which was preached in 1843, Pusey spoke of 'that bread which is his flesh' and 'of touching with our lips the cleansing blood'.[7]

This doctrine that Pusey had proclaimed was clearly taught in *Hymns Ancient and Modern*, an avowedly Anglo-Catholic collection, which was first published in 1861 under the editorial direction of John Mason Neale. Significantly, out of a total of 273 hymns in the first edition, 187 were, according to the Church Association, taken from Roman Catholic Breviaries, Missals and other Roman Catholic sources. Hymn 309 clearly taught the real presence of Christ in the sacrament:

---

[7] E.B. Pusey, *The Holy Eucharist A Comfort to the Penitent. A Sermon Preached before the University in the Cathedral Church, in Oxford on the Fourth Sunday After Easter*, pp. 21–3.

That last night, at supper lying,
'Mid the Twelve, His chosen band,
JESUS, with the law complying,
Keeps the feast its rites demand;
Then, more precious food supplying,
GIVES HIMSELF with His own hand.

Word made flesh TRUE BREAD HE MAKETH
By his word His Flesh TO BE;
Wine, His Blood; which whoso taketh
Must from carnal thoughts be free;
Faith alone, though sign forsaketh,
Shows true hearts the mystery.

Therefore we, before Him bending,
This great sacrament revere;
Types and shadows have their ending,
For the newer rite is here,
Faith, our outward sense befriending
Makes our inward vision clear.

Commenting on the hymn, the Rev James Ormiston, the Vicar of
Old Hill, near Dudley, wrote:

> Is not its presence as a communion hymn ... conclusive evidence that
> the hymnal includes the great central error of the great apostasy. Our
> Church having plainly protested in Article 28 against the figment of any
> change in the bread and wine, it is inexplicable how this contravention
> of its authority should be allowed.[8]

Anglican Evangelicals took their stand against the real presence on
the argument set out by Cranmer in the *Book of Common Prayer*
that Christ's local bodily presence is not on earth but in heaven. In
The Nature of Christ's Presence William Goode made two points
against the Tractarian doctrine of the real presence:

1. The doctrine in question is opposed to the testimony of Scripture as
   to Christ's departure from the world, ascension, and session at the
   right hand of the Father until the end of the world.
2. That Christ's body, being a human body, cannot be present in more
   than one place at the same time.

---

[8] J. Ormiston, *Hymns Ancient and Modern and Their Romanising
Teaching* Tract 21, p. 11.

Goode's conclusion on the matter of the presence was that 'the Fathers, generally, did not hold, that the risen Body and Blood of Christ in any form, are so joined to the consecrated bread and wine, or so exist under their forms, that they are received into the mouths of the communicants'.[9]

Robert Bickersteth, Bishop of Ripon, declared that the doctrine of the real presence is 'not maintained in the Articles or formularies of the Church of England, nor can it be held consistently with these standards of belief'.[10] In his *Bampton Lectures*, William Thomson declared that 'the sacraments confer the grace of God, they do not contain it; they are channels, not fountains. Nor are they the sole or the peculiar means of conveying to believers the effects of our Lord's incarnation'.[11] Bishop John Ryle also took a strong stand against the doctrine of the 'real presence'. In his address to the seventh Liverpool Diocesan Conference in November 1898 he declared:

> Our Reformers found the doctrine of a real corporal presence in our Church, and laid down their lives to oppose it. They would not even allow the expression 'real presence' a place in our Prayer Book. They distinctly repudiated alike both Romish transubstantiation and Lutheran consubstantiation. They declared in their 29th Article that faithless communicants are 'in no wise (*nullo modo*) partakers of Christ?' The extreme Ritualists have reintroduced the doctrine, and too often honour the consecrated elements in the Lord's Supper as if Christ's natural body and blood were in them.[12]

Reservation and adoration

The second-generation Tractarians reintroduced reservation and adoration or the custom of retaining and storing some of the bread from the Holy Communion service. Reservation was a common practice in medieval times but was halted by Cranmer and the Protestant Reformers. This is made clear by the sixth rubric at the end of the 1662 Prayer Book Service which stated categorically, 'if any [of the consecrated elements] remain of that which was consecrated … the priest and such other of the Communicants as he shall then call unto him, shall, immediately after the Blessing, reverently eat and drink the same.'

---

[9] W. Goode, *The Nature of Christ's Presence* Vol. 1, p. 201.
[10] M.C. Bickersteth, *Robert Bickersteth*, p. 211.
[11] W. Thomson, *The Atoning Work of Christ*, p. 227.
[12] Ryle, *Charges and Addresses*, p. 360.

Some Ritualists first argued the need for reservation during the great cholera epidemics. When people were dying suddenly in large numbers it was not possible, given the immediate need, so it was said, to consecrate bread and wine for each person who needed it. Instead, sufficient quantities would be set aside after the church service for the use of the sick and dying in the coming week. Notwithstanding this fact, reservation was viewed with disfavour because it could readily lead on to the concomitant practices of adoration and benediction.

Adoration involved placing some of the reserved bread in a pyx and allowing people to come to worship Christ who was believed to the locally present in the consecrated element. In later Victorian years, tabernacles, which were placed on the altar, began to supersede the use of the pyx.[13] One of the first Ritualists to take up the practice was George Dennison, Archdeacon of Taunton and Vicar of East Brent. He preached a series of sermons in 1853 in which he asserted that the body and blood of Christ, although present naturally in heaven, are nevertheless really, supernaturally and invisibly present in the Lord's Supper under the elements by virtue of the prayer of consecration. He further declared that worship was due to the body and blood of Christ present under the form of bread and wine. Backed by the EA, Joseph Ditcher, the incumbent of the adjoining parish, made a formal complaint to Archbishop Sumner. The eventual outcome was that Sumner held an ecclesiastical court at Bath on 25 July 1855 with Dr Lushington as his assessor. Lushington's judgement was that certain passages taken from the sermons were contrary to the teaching of the Church of England. Denison refused to retract and was in consequence deprived of all his preferments.[14] However, the decision was reversed the following year on a technicality.

Notwithstanding this judgement, services of adoration and devotion became an increasingly popular aspect of ritualistic spirituality. It featured in the worship of some sisterhoods that were established in the 1850s and 1860s. The Sisterhood of Margaret Community of Nuns, founded at East Grinstead by John Mason Neale, was the first Church of England order to have permanent reservation. For the

---

[13] For a detailed study of reservation and adoration in the Victorian church, see C.E. Pocknee, 'Reservation in the Church of England and the Anglican Communion since 1549 until the Present Century', in A.A. King, *Eucharistic Reservation in the Western Church*, pp. 229–52.

[14] See Scotland, *John Bird Sumner*, pp. 116–17.

purpose of devotion, reservation was usually in one kind (the bread only). The practice of benediction represented a further extension of adoration. A consecrated wafer was placed in a glass-fronted container known as a monstrance. The priest then stood before the altar and worshippers came forward and were blessed with the sacred host.[15]

As far as Evangelicals saw it, adoration was nothing short of idolatry. They held the practice to be explicitly condemned by Article 25 which stated that 'the sacraments were not ordained by Christ to be gazed upon, or to be carried about, but that we should duly use them'. Joseph Bardsley, in a forthright piece entitled *Ritualism: Its Origin, Tendency and Antidotes*, cited *The Little Book, Intended Chiefly for Beginners in Devotion*. It advised the following:

> At the words, 'This is My Body, This is My Blood', you must believe that the bread and wine become the Real Body and Blood, with soul and Godhead, of Jesus Christ: bow down your heart and body in deepest adoration when the priest says these awful words, and worship your Saviour then verily and indeed present on His altar.[16]

Bardsley's apposite comment was that these words 'maintain that the nature of Christ's presence is an objective presence – not a presence to the heart by faith'.[17] In response to the Ritualist suggestion that 'when the bread and wine have been consecrated, you are to worship your Saviour there bodily present on His altar', Bardsley reminded his readers that the practice was not supported by the rubric at the end of the Holy Communion service in the *Book of Common Prayer*:

> It is hereby declared, that thereby no adoration is intended, or ought to be done, either unto the Sacramental Bread or Wine there bodily received, or unto any Corporal Presence of Christ's natural flesh and Blood. For the Sacramental Bread and Wine remain still in their very natural substances, and therefore may not be adored; (for that were idolatry, to be abhorred by all faithful Christians).[18]

---

[15] G. Rowell, *The Vision Glorious*, p. 114.

[16] J. Bardsley, 'Ritualism: Its Origin, Tendency and Antidotes', in *Truth for the Times*, p. 84.

[17] Ibid. p. 84.

[18] Ibid. p. 90.

Bardsley also pointed out that 'until the last thirty or forty years' the practice of early communion had hardly been known since the days of the Reformation. It should be noted however that some Evangelicals both valued and introduced early Communion services.

In 1867 the Rev James William Bennett, the Vicar of Frome Selwood in Somerset, published a paper in which he spoke of the Holy Communion as 'the great sacrifice'. The year following he published *A Plea for Toleration in the Church of England* in which, among other things, he spoke of 'the real, actual, and visible presence of our Lord upon the altars of our churches', and continued, 'who myself adore, and teach the people to adore, the consecrated elements, believing Christ to be in them'.[19] As a result the Church Association decided to proceed against Bennett for publishing unsound doctrine. Bennett then made some alterations to the wording of his pamphlets on the recommendation of Pusey, with the result that when his case was heard the Court of Arches ruled that he had not transgressed the liberty allowed by the law. The Privy Council upheld this decision. The Evangelical Archbishop of York afterwards spoke of the judgement as having been 'a miscarriage of justice'.[20]

Vestments and the eastward position of the celebrant

The eastward position of the celebrant at Holy Communion and the use of Roman Catholic mass vestments, including the albe, chasuble and stoles, were further prominent aspects of ritualism. Many Ritualists adopted the custom of standing at the east side of the communion table or altar with their back to the people. In such a position, the priest was held to be adopting a mediatorial role between the people and the altar. This was taken to imply that the Eucharist was in some senses a sacrificial act. As has been noted, Ritualists attempted to justify the eastward position on the basis of the rubric immediately preceding the prayer of consecration. However, this understanding was in contradiction of the fourth rubric at the beginning of the service, which enjoined the priest to stand at the north side of the table.

In a sermon, entitled the 'Restoration of Churches is the Restoration of Popery', which was preached in 1844, Francis Close was critical of those officiating ministers who 'stand not "at the north side of the table", as directed by the rubric, but at a distance of some

---

[19] Proby, *Annals* Vol. 2, p. 230.
[20] Ibid. Vol. 2, pp. 281–2.

feet from it – North West.' He also condemned 'the profanation' of those who repeatedly 'adore or bow towards the altar' and 'read the Epistle and Gospel on the Eastern side of the rood-screen'.[21] Anthony Thorold, when Bishop of Rochester, wrote to one clergyman in his diocese who had declined the position of rural dean for the reason that he took the eastward position when celebrating Holy Communion. Thorold assured him that though he disagreed over the matter, 'I know your loyalty well-enough to be well assured that I am safe in your hands.'[22]

Vestments, including the albe, chasuble and stole, began to appear in the 1850s. The Rev Brian King first used them in 1857 at St George's Mission, in London's dockland area, when a group of his parishioners offered him a gift of two silk chasubles. Liturgical colours to indicate the changing seasons and festivals of the Church's year became a growing feature. One observer reported seeing 'green and golden priests' at St Alban's Holborn.

Evangelicals expressed their disquiet at the wearing of vestments in a variety of ways. Charles Baring, when Bishop of Durham, for example, suspended the Rev Francis Grey, Rector of Morpeth, from the office of Rural Dean because he had worn a black stole with three crosses embroidered on it.[23] In March 1867 Lord Shaftesbury introduced a clerical vestments Bill into the House of Lords 'for better enforcing uniformity in clerical vestments and ornaments to be worn by ministers of the united Church of England and Ireland in the performance of public worship'.[24] The Bill enjoined the surplice and hood or tippet for use in saying public prayers and ministering sacraments and other rites of the church, but left the use of the black gown in the pulpit untouched. The second reading was moved on 13 May but was lost.

The removal of the surplice before the minister entered the pulpit had been a long-standing tradition among Evangelical clergy. By the 1870s, however, it was becoming a matter of indifference. In the spring of 1872 the recently formed Clerical and Lay Union considered the matter at a meeting in the Exeter Hall. A circular had

---

[21] F. Close, *The Restoration of Churches is the Restoration of Popery: Proved and Illustrated from the Authenticated Publications of the Cambridge Camden Society: A Sermon Preached in the Parish Church of Cheltenham on Tuesday November 5th, 1844*, p. 7.

[22] Simpkinson, *Bishop Thorold*, p. 86.

[23] Proby, *Annals* Vol. 2, p. 230.

[24] Ibid., p. 228.

been sent to 1,250 Evangelical clergy, the majority of whom appear to have been members of the Church Association. Of 406 who responded fifty-four were in favour of the immediate adoption of the surplice, and a further ninety-two recommended that legal opinion be sought.[25]

Significantly, in 1876 Ryle, while on holiday in the Lake District, caused offence to the three Protestant tourists who attended a service in Crossthwaite Church because he preached in a surplice. The visitors subsequently wrote a letter of protest to the editor of *The Rock* who declared that the surplice, in itself innocent, was detestable as a first step on the road to Rome. Many who subsequently wrote to the paper condemned Ryle's action. Francis Close, however, wrote strongly in Ryle's defence, condemning those who quibbled over trivialities. Close had preached wearing a surplice, which he much preferred, for twenty years.[26]

A celebrated case involving the introduction of vestments concerned the Rev John Edwards who became Vicar of Prestbury in Gloucestershire. He arrived in the parish on 25 October 1860. He was a model Tractarian who restored the church along Camden lines and introduced a daily celebration of the Eucharist. At Christmas 1860 there were thirty-nine communicants but at Easter 1869, the first occasion when communion was celebrated after the church had been restored, there were 215. The rapidly-developing ritual, including the use of stoles, albes and chasubles, at Prestbury Church eventually attracted the attention of the Cheltenham branch of the Church Association. On Good Friday, 11 April 1873, Charles Combe (a local tailor) and another person, who seems to have been Baron de Ferriers,[27] sent a protest to Charles Ellicott, the Bishop of Gloucester. Although Combe was not a parishioner and had never received communion in Prestbury Parish Church, the bishop accepted the protest lodged in his name. Combe's case was heard in the Court of Arches on 23 January 1875, but no decision was reached for the reason that Combe was not a parishioner and was in fact renting a pew in a Cheltenham dissenting place of worship.[28]

Edwards was, however, subsequently required to appear again before the Court of Arches on several counts and he was suspended

---

[25] Bentley, *Transformation of the Evangelical Party*, p. 161.
[26] *The Rock* 15 and 22 September 1876, *The Record* 18 and 27 September 1876, cited by Bentley, *Transformation of the Evangelical Party*, p. 162.
[27] Proby, *Annals* Vol. 2, p. 303.
[28] Ibid. Vol. 2, p. 303.

from his ministry for six months by the bishop shortly before Easter 1878. Although the bishop appointed Charles Lyne, another priest, to take his duty, Edwards insisted on doing it himself, with the result that he was deprived of his incumbency altogether by Lord Penzance in the spring of 1880.[29]

Earlier, Bishop Samuel Waldegrave had described wearing the surplice in the pulpit as 'in many cases but the first of a series of Romeward movements'.[30] Bishop Bickersteth of Ripon wrote in 1876 to a clergyman who had adopted vestments that 'they are almost inseparably associated with the tendencies to Romish error and superstition'. He continued by stating that he did 'not believe it possible for you or any other clergyman who makes such innovations to acquit himself in the judgment of the Church at large'.[31]

Francis Close was angered at the way in which the Tractarians 'all conspire to one result, The Superstitions and unscriptural Exaltation of the Priesthood'.[32] He fulminated against 'the duty of confession to a priest, the elevation of the altar and its adoring priests'.[33] Like many Evangelicals, Close felt an intense dislike for the new styles of clerical dress which 'transform the Church's ministering servants into Popish or Jewish, sacrificing and interceding priests'.[34] Preaching in Cheltenham Parish Church he thundered:

> I protest against those who would take from her (the Church of England) the simple garments in which she has ministered for three hundred years, and cover her again with the meretricious decorations which she then renounced … who would again rivet the chains of her priestly tyranny on the hands of the lady.[35]

In a later sermon Close said: 'It is a pitiable sight to see a clergyman of decidedly Evangelical principles walking in a procession among

---

[29] Ibid. Vol. 2, p. 374.
[30] S. Waldegrave to Rev G.H. Ainger, 23 August 1867, Carlisle Record Office.
[31] M.C. Bickersteth, *Robert Bickersteth*, p. 214.
[32] F. Close, *Priestly Usurpation its Cause and Consequence: A Sermon Preached in the Parish Church of Cheltenham on Sunday March 30th, 1845*, p. 16.
[33] Ibid., p. 16.
[34] Ibid. p. 18.
[35] Ibid. p. 18.

Catholics decked out in fancy dresses of all colours, who rejoice in his involuntary conformity to medieval fashion.'[36]

There were other aspects of ritualism that gave offence to Victorian Evangelicals. These included the use of incense in worship, the singing of the *Agnus Dei* or 'Lamb of God' during the reception of the bread and wine at communion, and bowing at the name of Jesus. In the summer of 1869 a member of the Church Association complained to Charles Sumner about the ritualistic practices of the Rev Richard Wix, who was Vicar of Swanmore on the Isle of Wight. Sumner ordered him to cease using both lighted candles and incense during the performance of divine service.[37]

In fact, Charles Sumner was a consistent opponent of ritualism during his long episcopate. As early as January 1843 he had written to one of his incumbents requesting that he remove a statue of the Virgin Mary with nimbus and a lily. Sumner regarded the statue as 'inadmissible' and suggested the introduction in its place of 'a central figure of our Lord'.[38] In his charge to the diocese of Winchester in 1845 he warned against excessive 'decoration of our places of our worship'. 'Men's minds', he continued, 'are apt to run riot in externals'[39] and 'We must not be forgetful of realities in the midst of the enticements of architecture.'[40]

The confessional and priestly absolution

Nothing provoked a stronger reaction on the part of Evangelicals than the introduction of the confessional and the practice of priestly absolution.

Pusey's use of the confessional, with Keble as his ear, began on 1 December 1846 and set a pattern for what followed. In 1846 Pusey preached a sermon entitled 'Entire Absolution of the Penitent' in which he pressed for the use of sacramental confession. He made reference to the *Prayer Book* order for the 'visitation of the sick' as a moment for personalised confession and absolution.

In his charge of 1853 to the clergy of his Canterbury diocese, Archbishop John Sumner turned to the question of the confessional

[36] Close, *Catholic Revival*, p. 26.
[37] Proby, *Annals* Vol. 2, p. 274.
[38] G.H. Sumner, *Life of Charles Richard Sumner*, pp. 286–7.
[39] Letter dated 15 January 1843, in G.H. Sumner, *Life of Charles Richard Sumner*, p. 287.
[40] G.H. Sumner, *Life of Charles Richard Sumner*, p. 297.

or 'the perversion of certain of his own clergy'[41] as he termed it. In a lengthy discourse, Sumner pointed out that the sacrament of penance had no warrant in Scripture. He observed:

> It is remarkable, further, that the Apostles themselves have left no example of the exercise of this special absolution. Peter used his power of the keys in a very different manner, when he opened the door of the kingdom to them, saying, repent, and be baptised in the name of the Lord Jesus Christ for the remission of sins ... We hear nothing of absolution. St Paul's forgiveness of the Corinthians offered no sentence of absolution.[42]

In his charge of 1858 to the clergy of Carlisle, Bishop Montagu Villiers said, 'I am thankful that we appear to be clear of the filthiness of the confessional, as well as free, in nearly every parish from the more harmless puerilities connected with the Church of Rome.'[43] In the same year, Hugh Stowell preached a sermon on the subject of confession in his church, Christ Church, Salford. He referred to auricular confession as 'a wretched attempt to set up a minister of Christ as a kind of God upon earth'. He spoke of the practice as being akin to 'drawing out with a thumbscrew' the deep things of the heart and the conscience. For any man to attempt this, he asserted, 'is a near approach to blasphemy, it is taking the place of the great High Priest'.[44]

The antagonism against confessional further increased on account of its use by some of the 'slum-Ritualist' priests during the Anglo-Catholic missions of the later 1860s. In a sermon entitled 'Priestly Usurpation its Cause and Consequence' Close denounced ' "the duty of confession" as one of the particular links in the great chain of corrupt doctrine that was forged in this (the Papal) foundry of error'.[45]

The issue of the confessional came to a point of heightened tension in 1867 when the Rev James Ormiston, a London clergy-man, engaged in what was described as an act of 'aggressive

---

[41] J.B. Sumner, *The Charge of John Bird Lord Archbishop of Canterbury to the Clergy of the Diocese at His Visitation 1853*, p. 297.
[42] Ibid., pp. 37–9.
[43] H.M. Villiers, *A Charge Delivered to the Clergy of the Diocese of Carlisle at the First Visitation of the Hon. Montagu Villiers, DD, Lord Bishop of Carlisle 1858*, p. 12.
[44] Rowell, *Vision Glorious*, p. 135.
[45] Close, *Priestly Usurpation*, p. 15.

Protestantism'.[46] He went incognito to the vestry of St Alban's Church, Holborn, and joined the queue of those waiting to make their confession to the Rev Alexander MacKonochie. When his turn came, instead of expressing contrition for his sinful estate he read out a protest against Catholic and ritualistic practices. Ormiston was subsequently required by the bishop to make an apology. At least one Evangelical, the Rev Daniel Wilson, also expressed his disapproval of Ormiston's conduct.[47]

In March of the same year, John C. Miller, the Vicar of Greenwich, gave a Church Association lecture on the confessional in St James Hall, Piccadilly. He described the confessional as 'the chief engine of sacerdotal power of the Church of Rome'.[48] He pointed out that the priest who hears confession will be polluted: 'The heart of a man into whose ear is poured all the moral and spiritual filth of his parish must indeed be a wonderful heart if it escapes the direst pollution.'[49] Towards the close of his lecture, Miller cited, with obvious approval, some lines from J.W. Burgon's *The Pastoral Office*: 'to the whole system of auricular confession, whether constant or periodical, the Church of England stands utterly opposed'.[50] Miller emphasised the fact that:

> If some hapless Evangelical had written this passage, what a howl there would be against him as a Low Churchman, as one unfaithful to the doctrines of his church. But it is written by an admirable clergyman of another section – one of whose learning, labours, and character any party may be proud.[51]

In 1867 Samuel Waldegrave preached a sermon, which was subsequently published, entitled 'The Apostolic Commission on Auricular Confession and Priestly Absolution'. He began by defining what he understood as confession, which was not 'that general and open confession' nor 'that exceptional confession of the sick or dying penitent'. What he meant was 'that minute, that prolonged, that exhaustive confession of every thought, every word, every deed of ill, which needs to be drawn forth by questioning, detailed and

---

[46] Proby, *Annals* Vol. 2, p. 230.
[47] Ibid., p. 230.
[48] J.C. Miller, *The Confessional: A Lecture at St James Hall, Piccadilly*, London, 12 March 1867, p. 4.
[49] Ibid., p. 13.
[50] Ibid., p. 28.
[51] Ibid., p. 28.

often necessarily polluting, from the inmost recesses of memory and conscience'. Waldegrave continued: 'The whole scheme is a fond thing, vainly invented and hath no warranty of Holy Scripture.' His advice to those who felt drawn to make a confession was 'resist the very beginning of this evil'.[52]

Waldegrave took up the matter again later in the same year in his charge to the diocese. He warned against the practice of auricular confession that 'invests you with power over the maidens and matrons of your flock'.[53] He continued, 'its noxious influence, places human society itself at your feet'.[54]

William Thomson was unequivocal in his condemnation of the use of the confessional. In a speech to Convocation in 1878 he objected that 'it would sap the family life of this country, sow discord between husband and wife, diminish the legitimate authority of the parent over the child, and put the priest who has much slighter responsibility in the place of those whom God has placed full responsibility'.[55] Thomson added a further argument against confession. 'It was not good', he declared, 'that when sins have been committed, that the priest should have to bear the weight of them alone on his mind.'[56]

Francis Jeune, the Evangelical Bishop of Peterborough, joined the fray. He reminded his clergy that it was only after the Fourth Lateran Decree (1215) had 'rendered auricular confession obligatory upon all members of the Western Church, that it was used'. 'By what means is forgiveness to be obtained by believers?' Jeune asked. 'By confession of sins to Him who forgives.' 'Other absolution', he declared, 'we need not.'[57] Alarm bells continued to sound

---

[52] S. Waldegrave, *The Apostolic Commission on Auricular Confession and Priestly Absolution*, p. 20.

[53] S. Waldegrave, *The Christian Ministry not Sacerdotal but Evangelistic. The Charge Delivered in September 1867 at his Third Episcopal Visitation by the Hon And Right Rev Samuel Waldegrave DD*, p. 49.

[54] Ibid., p. 49.

[55] *The York Journal of Convocation* 1878, p. 101, cited in K.S. Smith, *William Thomson Archbishop of York, His Life and Times*, p. 33. For a further explanation of Thomson's view on confession see his letter to a fellow bishop in 1878 in E.H. Thomson, *The Life and Letters of William Thomson Archbishop of York*, pp. 186–8.

[56] Ibid. p. 101.

[57] F. Jeune, *The Throne of Grace. Not the Confessional. A Sermon Preached Before the University of Oxford on Sunday 18th October 1846*, p. 46.

particularly over the issue of confession when in 1873 over 400 priests in favour of the 'selection of trained confessors' presented a petition to the Upper House of Convocation.[58]

Anthony Thorold was 'a pronounced low churchman' in whose diocese of Rochester there were several churches with 'the most advanced ritual in London'.[59] Inevitably, he soon ran into conflict with some of his clergy over the question of confession. The opportunity to express his views on the matter came when the Rev R.R. Bristow, of St Stephen's, Lewisham, sent him a copy of a sermon entitled 'Liberty of Confession in the Church of England'.[60] Thorold was forthright in his response which came in a letter dated 14 August 1877:

> I solemnly protest against the continuance of the practice of hearing confessions in St Stephen's Church; as your brother in the ministry, with all kindness and goodwill, desiring to persuade you out of it ... as what more than anything else embitters the dissensions in our Church, hurts and scandalises grave good men of all schools ... is inconsistent with the practice and teaching of the Apostles, and dishonours the priesthood of Christ ... I also ask you to tell me if your curates, as well as yourself, are in the habit of receiving confessions.[61]

Thorold later had an interview with Bristow on 12 September and recorded that he 'liked him very much' and found 'he was very reasonable about confession'.[62] Thorold subsequently assured Bristow that he had no objection to his offering his parishioners religious counsel provided he 'declared a full and free forgiveness through the blood of Christ' and was careful 'not to thrust himself into the holy place of the Divine Mediator, and to pronounce absolution not in a form taken out of another service, but by "the ministry of the word" '.[63]

Of all the aspects of ritualism, confession seems to have provoked the most united opposition on the part of Evangelicals. In particular, it undermined Christ's atonement and gave the

---

[58] *Chronicle of Convocation*, 9 May 1873, cited by Hardman, *Evangelical Party*, p. 180.

[59] Simpkinson, *Bishop Thorold*, p. 77.

[60] Ibid., p. 78.

[61] Ibid., p. 79.

[62] Ibid., p. 80.

[63] Ibid., p. 82.

clergyman a priestly mediatorial role which ran counter to the Reformation ordinal. Additionally, it raised a number of sensitive moral and emotional issues both for the priest and the penitent. For these reasons Evangelical bishops were strongly united in their opposition to the practice.

Further Evangelical Opposition to Ritualism

Since the reign of James II the cry of 'no popery' had been strong in England. In fact, suspicion of anything Roman had been burned into the nation's consciousness. During the course of the nineteenth century, Protestantism became less a personal faith and increasingly a public sentiment. Particularly after the restoration of the Roman Catholic hierarchy there was a suspicion and hatred of anything that even resembled popery. It was this which led to outbreaks of violence, the worst of which was seen in the East End of London.

Trouble began in 1856 when the Rev Bryan King introduced Eucharistic vestments at St George's-in-the-East. He then caused further tension by circulating 'Romish' tracts which urged that children as young as seven years of age should go to confession and that 'the bread and wine become the body and blood of Christ'.[64] Matters came to a high-tension point when the congregation elected the Rev Hugh Allen, a distinguished 'no Popery' preacher, as Parish Lecturer, with the right to use the pulpit from time to time. It was only a short time before numbers of Allen's afternoon congregation began to attend the other main Sunday services in the church. Week after week there was rioting, disorder and buffoonery; books and kneelers were hurled from the galleries and anti-Ritualist rent-a-mobs shouted down King as he tried to read the liturgy. At one evening service in January 1860 there were three thousand in the church, including 1,000 boys in the galleries. Some of those present tried to break up the altar and the cross on it. They barracked King, Lowder and the twelve white-robed choristers who were trying to lead the worship. It took an inspector and a dozen policemen to clear the church, with assistance of some sixty to eighty gentlemen who attended the service.[65]

---

[64] Davidson and Benham, *Tait* Vol. 1, p. 233.

[65] *The Times*, 30 January 1860, cited by Bowen, *Idea of the Victorian Church*, p. 294.

Questions were asked in the House of Lords of Tait, as Bishop of London, about this lawless behaviour in his diocese. The problem, he observed in his response, 'was identifying who the disturbers were'.[66] Some weeks later he was able to report to the House of Lords that a Sunday evening service at St George's had 'passed off quietly', though he added that sixty policemen had been stationed inside the building. Tait blamed 'foolish vestments' as the major root cause of the disorders, and in another speech to the House of Lords he urged clergy 'not to irritate the feelings of the protestant congregations who were placed under their charge'.[67] When further instances of disorder occurred later in the summer, Tait was quick to defend the Rev Hugh Allen to members of the upper chamber. He was an able preacher commended both by Archbishop Sumner and the Bishop of Cashel, who spoke of his 'zeal and efficiency'.[68]

Hugh Allen was by no means the only Evangelical who spoke out in forthright terms against the Ritualists. Among others who did so was Francis Close. According to Pakenham, some of Close's annual anti-papal diatribes stirred Cheltenham's Protestants to fever pitch.[69] In 1850, when the Roman Catholic hierarchy had been restored, a disorderly mob tore down the railings surrounding the Roman Catholic Church and tried to set fire to the building. Their efforts having failed, the mob turned their energies to smashing the windows of Catholic-owned shops and made an unsuccessful attempt to burn an effigy of the Pope.[70] Like other churchmen whose faith was deeply rooted in the Protestant Reformation, Close favoured worship that was plain and unadorned. Commenting on the Eucharist, Close maintained:

> The distinguishing characteristic of this ordinance as related in Scripture is extreme simplicity and the total absence of all pomp, ceremony or splendour: so that the Holy Supper as instituted by its founder, differs as widely from the pompous imitation of it in the Romish Church, as it does from the redundant ceremonial of Judaism.[71]

---

66 *Hansard* Vol. 156, 7 February 1860.
67 *Hansard* Vol. 156, 1860, p. 914.
68 *Hansard* Vol. 158, 1860, and 22 May 1860, p. 1599.
69 See S. Pakenham, *Cheltenham*.
70 Hart, *History of Cheltenham*, p. 220.
71 Close, *Restoration of Churches*, p. 7.

Close was vehement in his denunciations of the Camden Society with its twin aims of ensuring that all new churches should be built in the gothic style and that all restorations should be more of the same. He recognised only too clearly that large Gothic-style buildings were conducive to ritualistic Roman worship and not to Protestant worship. He condemned the Camdenians for fitting out interiors with sacred furnishings by which the Tractarians could carry out their principles. In short, he protested 'that the Restoration of churches is the Restoration of Popery'.[72] In a forceful outburst Close denounced the Camden Society's ideal churches:

> What are these model churches built for? The orgies of superstition! For long processions of priests repeating dirges ... for the solemnisation masses and elevations of the Host: where blind priests might perform superstitious, idolatrous services to and for the dead in an unknown tongue; such churches are palpably unfit for all circumstances of modern worship.[73]

The nub of the whole matter was, as Close saw it, that Tractarianism was a 'Lying Spirit' of 'fraud and deception'.[74] How was what Close regarded as the corrupting influence of ritualism to be counteracted? He had two remedies. First, Christians must play an active and urgent role in promoting education and religious education in which the Bible was central. Secondly, Christians must stand uncompromisingly on the foundation of the canonical Scriptures of the Old and New Testament.[75]

The Church Association

In addition to writing, preaching and demonstrating against ritualism, Evangelical Anglicans formed the Church Association in November 1865. It was a riposte to the earlier founding in 1860 of The English Church Union which aimed 'to defend and maintain unimpaired the doctrine, discipline and ritual of the Church of

---

[72] Ibid., p. 11.
[73] Ibid., p. 17.
[74] F. Close, *The Roman Antichrist, 'A Lying Spirit': Being the substance of a Sermon Preached in the Parish Church of Cheltenham, November 5th, 1846*, p. 11.
[75] Ibid., p. 27.

England against Erastianism, Rationalism and Puritanism, and to afford counsel and protection to all persons, lay and clerical, suffering unjust aggression or hindrance in spiritual matters'.[76]

The Church Association had the avowed aim of fighting ritualism in the courts by means of legal action. Many, such as Lord Shaftesbury, who had tried to introduce various Bills into Parliament to curb ritualism, were growing frustrated at their inability to do anything effective. The Church Association had a number of influential members, including the Rev Dr William Wilson, brother-in-law to the Bishop of Winchester. Canon William Champneys who was made Dean of Lichfield was an original member of the Association, and the Rev Hugh McNeill, DD, Dean of Ripon, was also a member.[77] By 1870 the association had 8,000 members and 138 branch associations.[78]

The purpose of the association was:

to uphold the doctrines, principles, and order of the united Church of England and Ireland, and to counteract the efforts now being made to pervert her teaching on essential points of Christian faith, or to assimilate the services to those of the church of Rome, and to further encourage concerted action for the advancement and progress of spiritual religion.[79]

Many meetings and publications supported this objective in an effort to secure episcopal and other authoritative suppression of ceremonies, vestment and ornament that departed from the church at the time of the Reformation.

A typical instance of a Church Association tract was that entitled 'Address to the Lay Members of the Council of the Church Association to the People of England'. It gave advice on how to recognise whether your parish clergyman is a Ritualist or has Ritualist sympathies:

The test by which the laity may detect such a man is easily applied. If the clergyman calls himself a priest [a note here indicated that by priest is meant a sacrificing] if he tells his people that by his priestly power he can absolve them from sin; if he says that by his priestly act he can turn

---

[76] Stock, *Church Missionary Society* Vol. 2, p. 348.
[77] Proby, *Annals*, p. 250.
[78] Bentley, *Transformation of the Evangelical Party*, p. 125.
[79] Proby, *Annals*, p. 223, Stock, *Church Missionary Society* Vol. 2, p. 348.

the bread and wine of the Lord's Supper into the body and blood of Christ – the case is clear, we can see what he is; he is not a pastor of the Reformed Church of England; he is a priest of the Church of Rome.

The pamphlet continued: 'He must be treated as such ... such persons must be treated as men having the plague. They must be put in quarantine, lest they infect us.'[80]

A major aspect of the Church Association's campaign was the attempt to take Ritualist clergymen to the church courts. There were a number of celebrated cases and some of the later ones after the Public Worship Regulation Act resulted in clergy serving time in prison. In 1867, for example, the Church Association lodged a protest against Alexander MacKonochie for his ritualistic practices at St Alban's, Holborn. He was accused of a number of illegal practices, including 'the elevation of the host, the use of lighted candles and the mixed chalice together with incense, chasubles of coloured silk, confessionals, stations of the cross and other popish toys'.[81] The Court of Arches pronounced against most of these items. MacKonochie then appealed the Judicial Committee of the Privy Seal, a secular court, and this resulted in a three months suspension from his ministry. Two years later, the Church Association moved against John Purchas, perpetual curate of St James, Brighton. He was arraigned on thirty-five counts, including 'the hanging of a stuffed dove over the altar'. The Court of Arches ruled against Purchas on most points. Purchas' subsequent appeal to the Privy Council if anything worsened the situation.

By 1865 Evangelicals were working in close concert with A.C. Tait and anyone else who would join with them in the struggle against the Ritualists. Henry Law (1797–1884), the Dean of Gloucester, wrote to Tait offering his support to 'obtain a Commission to consider the rubrics with a view to greater uniformity, or at least to repress extravagant excess'.[82] Eventually, in 1867 a Royal Commission on Ritual was established headed by the Archbishops of Canterbury and Armagh. Membership of the commission was weighted against the Evangelicals, although Henry Venn, Canon Payne Smith, Lords Harrowby and Ebury and Sir Joseph Napier

---

[80] Proby, *Annals*, p. 234.

[81] F.W. Cornish, *A History of the English Church in the Nineteenth Century* Part 2, p. 137.

[82] *Tait Correspondence* Vol. 80, No. 53–6, cited by Bentley, *Transformation of the Evangelical Party*, p. 221.

were included.[83] They discussed vestments and other issues, but proved in the end to be ineffectual insofar as stemming the tide of ritualistic practice was concerned.

As months dragged by it was recognised that the commission was a delaying tactic. This failure led to the passing of the Public Worship Regulation Act in 1874. Archbishop Tait introduced the Bill. He made it clear that 'it is our desire that the laws of this Reformed Church of England should be observed, and therefore what we request of your Lordships is to give us greater facilities in the administration of those laws.'[84] Tait's original proposal was that in the first instance a complaint about ritualistic practice should be heard by the bishop and three assessors with the right of appeal to the archbishop.[85] However, in the committee stage Lord Shaftesbury proposed that a single lay judge, appointed by the archbishops, should replace the two existing provincial judges, and would hear all representations under the Act without the intervention of diocesan courts or the preliminary Commission of Inquiry. Because of the general support for Shaftesbury in the Lords, Tait and Thomson reluctantly agreed to his amendment. The significance of this legislation was that clergy now had to recognise the right of secular courts to pronounce on spiritual matters.

In the various struggles that the Church Association continued to promote, six points became crucial: vestments, the eastward position of the celebrant, wafer bread, incense, altar lights and the mixed chalice. In the prosecutions that followed in the last quarter of the nineteenth century, four clergymen were sent to prison, which, more than anything else, made the British public sympathetic to the Ritualists. Furthermore, in the process of this controversy, the Evangelical Anglicans began to lose sight of the fact that Protestantism had originally emerged as a 'protest for' the Reformed biblical faith and not a 'protest against' Romanism. Evangelical Anglicans thus began to some extent to lose the support of both the church and society in general.

In 1888 the Church Association turned on Bishop Edward King of Lincoln for observing the most advanced form of liturgy. This

---

[83] See Moule, *Evangelical School*, p. 70; Bentley, *Transformation of the Evangelical Party*, p. 137.

[84] *Hansard* Vol. 218, 20 April 1874, p. 786.

[85] Ibid. Vol. 218, 20 April, 1874, p. 790.

included the eastward position, lighted candles on the altar, mixing water with wine, allowing 'O Lamb of God' to be sung, using the sign of the cross at the absolution and blessing, and cleansing the vessels during the service. This resulted in a prosecution that was upheld on some counts. The matter however backfired in that King was widely known for his saintly living and the sympathies of many people began to move to the Ritualists. From this point on, the impact of the Church Association began to wane. Only the Protestant Truth Society, which was founded in 1890 by John Kensit, sustained a campaign, often taking direct action to disrupt obnoxious services. At All Saints, East Clevedon, for instance, the Ritualist vicar issued brass knuckle-dusters so that members of his congregation could resist the Kensitites.[86]

Ritualism emerged within the Church of England as a steadily growing phenomenon and an integral part of the second phase of the Oxford Movement, which was led by Pusey and Keble. The papal aggression and the restoration of the Roman Catholic hierarchy in 1850 in England and Wales, with Nicholas Cardinal Wiseman as first Archbishop of Westminster, heightened the conflict between Evangelicals and the Ritualists. This led many Evangelicals to the view that ritualism was in reality Romanism in disguise.

Francis Close of Cheltenham epitomised this opinion in the anti-papal sermons that he preached every Guy Fawkes Day. It was his opinion that 'Tractarianism within the bosom of our Church, is a kindred spirit to the Roman Anti-Christ – and that it bears the great family likeness to the "Lying spirit" – fraud and deception.'[87] Close and others like him found they were able to tap support from a residual English folk religion which was strongly Protestant in character. It revealed itself in the rent-a-mobs who disrupted ritualistic worship in the East End of London and engaged in acts of sporadic violence in Cheltenham and elsewhere.

The 1874 Public Worship Regulation Act represented the high point of the Evangelical crusade against ritualism. But the prosecutions and imprisonments which followed in its wake began to turn public and church opinion in favour of the Ritualists. Bishop Anthony Thorold had wisely warned that 'if you want to rally the masses to the side of the Ritualists, make martyrs of them'.[88] His words seem

---

[86] Bebbington, *Evangelicalism in Modern Britain*, p. 147.

[87] Close, *Roman Antichrist*, p. 27.

[88] A.W. Thorold, *A Pastoral Letter to the Diocese of Rochester*, p. 53, cited by Bentley, *Transformation of the Evangelical Party*, p. 153.

to have gone largely unheeded by the Church Association who tested the law and established that it upheld the Evangelical convictions on forty-four points of ritual. However, the association did not slow down the advances of ritualism. In fact they appeared to have contributed to its popularity.[89]

Part of the problem lay in the fact that in the 1840s and 1850s Protestant opposition to all things Roman had become very aggressive and had strongly politicised. John Wolffe has shown how Hugh McNeile and Hugh Stowell formed Protestant Operative Associations in Liverpool and Salford respectively, dividing their towns into districts and assigning a Protestant watchman to each.[90] There were similar Protestant Operative Associations in some of the London suburbs.[91] Wolffe commented that 'these movements, though clumsy, appear to have struck into lower class consciousness'.[92]

If the Public Worship Regulation Act represented a high point in the Evangelical fight over ritualistic practice, the prosecution of Edward King was a significant low point. In delivering his judgement Archbishop Benson condemned the sign of the cross at blessing and absolution, mixing the wine with water during the service and so standing as to hide the manual acts. But the administration of a previously mixed chalice, the *Agnus Dei* and the absolution after the service were allowed. In addition, the use of lighted candles and the eastward position were acceptable provided the manual acts were visible. These were declared to have no doctrinal significance. In his judgement, Benson protested against the procuring of witnesses to spy on ritualistic worship.

The Church Association, and indeed many Evangelicals, felt there was now an anomaly over these matters between the secular courts and the church court. They therefore protested to the Judicial Committee of the Privy Council who confirmed the Archbishop's judgement on 2 August 1892.[93] This was a resounding triumph for the Ritualists who could now claim the support of the highest ecclesiastical court for their ritualistic practices. Evangelicals were despondent and there was talk in some circles of secession but Bishop Ryle urged against despair. Although accepting the judgement as

---

[88] C.A. Burg, *The Church Association*, pp. 20–4, cited by Bentley, *Transformation of the Evangelical Party*, p. 130.

[89] J. Wolffe, *The Protestant Crusade in Great Britain 1829–1860*, p. 172.

[90] Ibid., p. 175.

[91] Ibid., p. 174.

[93] A.C. Benson, *The Life of Edward White Benson* Vol. 2, pp. 374–5.

'a law abiding Englishman and a believer in the Royal Supremacy',[94] he declared, 'There is no reason for panic and despair.'[95]

With the coming of the First World War, the Ritualists were able to argue the need for reservation in order to give the sacrament to the dying in the trenches and on the field of battle. Perhaps the biggest deficit for Evangelicals in their fight with the Ritualists was that it turned them in on themselves. They became introverted and neglected what Samuel Garratt called 'its old crusade against public evils'.[96]

---

[94] Ryle, *Charges and Addresses*, p. 248.

[95] Ibid., p. 252.

[96] S. Garratt, *What Shall We Do? Or, True Evangelical Policy*, p. 24; cited by Bebbington, *Evangelicalism in Modern Britain*, p. 147.

14

Evangelical Anglican Spirituality

There has been a divergence of opinion regarding the meaning and scope of the term 'spirituality'. James Gordon, for example, noted that the word is most often taken to describe 'those attitudes, beliefs and practices which animate people's lives and help them to reach out towards super-sensible realities'.[1] Focusing more specifically on Christian spirituality, Gordon emphasised that it concerns both 'the interior life of the inward person' and 'the implementation of the commandments of Christ, to love God and our neighbour'.[2] In its original usage 'spirituality' referred to the clergy, as opposed to secular authorities', and it was only at a later point that it came through writers such as Madam Guyon to mean piety or devotion.[3] Most contemporary writers have therefore come to understand spirituality to embrace both devotion and the ways in which it worked out in terms of daily living. Linda Wilson in her pioneering study of nineteenth-century English female spirituality urges that 'spirituality can be both the way in which a person develops his or her relationship with God, and the outworking of that in his or her life, both public and private'.[4] This is the way spirituality is understood in this chapter.

---

[1] Gordon, *Evangelical Spirituality*, p. vii, citing G. Wakefield (ed.), 'Spirituality', in *A Dictionary of Evangelical Spirituality*, pp. 361–3.

[2] Ibid., p. vii.

[3] O. Chadwick, 'Indifference and Morality', in P. Brooks (ed.), *Christian Spirituality: Essays in Honour of Gordon Rupp*, p. 205.

[4] L. Wilson, *Constrained by Zeal: Female Spirituality Amongst Nonconformists, 1825–1875*, p. 4.

The Devotional Aspect

The heart of nineteenth-century Evangelicalism was the individual's devotional life. As David Bebbington and others have pointed out, Evangelical spirituality was distinctive enough to mark its adherents off from other Christians.[5] There was a significant and fundamental difference between Evangelical and high church piety. For the Evangelical, conversion was crucial and it was this which gave assurance and the certainty that he or she was fairly and squarely on the road to the heavenly city. In contrast, the Anglo-Catholics and Ritualists saw the Christian faith as a journey which they hoped, by the help of the church and her sacraments, would carry them safely into the final estate of the righteous. For this reason Evangelicals emphasised their conversion experience as the basis and beginning of their spirituality. As David Bebbington noted, for most of the nineteenth century, and still at its end for most Evangelical Anglicans, 'a sense of having made a definite entry on the way to holiness was de rigeur'.[6] Robert Bickersteth, for example, did not insist on a sudden conversion but he was always ready to stress that 'a conscious turning from sin to God was the crisis of the religious life and the only true foundation of future peace and progress'.[7] John Ryle, in outlining the leading features of Evangelical religion, stated, 'We hold that an experimental knowledge of Christ crucified and interceding, is the very essence of Christianity, and that in teaching men the Christian religion we can never dwell too much on Christ Himself ... and the simplicity of the salvation there is in Him for every one that believes.'[8]

It was for this reason that much Evangelical devotion focused on the cross. This was true both of their hymnology and their meditation. Prayer books and other literature often stressed human sinfulness in order to evoke a continuing sense of dependency on Christ and his redemption. In the late eighteenth-century, for example, Augustus Toplady calculated that everyone who lived to the age of eighty committed 2,522,880,000 sins or one every second.[9] About 100 years later Bishop Ryle used a different and more credible

---

[5] See D.W. Bebbington, *Holiness in Nineteenth-Century England*, p. 50, et passim.
[6] Ibid., p. 38.
[7] M.C. Bickersteth, *Robert Bickersteth*, p. 48.
[8] Ryle, *Knots Untied*, pp. 5–6.
[9] R.E. Davies, *Methodism*, p. 88.

formula for the same purpose. Assuming a waking day of fifteen hours and two sins per hour, a person would amass 210 sins a week, 10,080 per year and over 100,000 in each decade.[10] The accuracy of the arithmetic was, of course, not important, the point was to emphasise that all men and women regardless of their station in life were in a fallen state. In fact, the upper classes might well be less aware of their perilous condition than the lower orders. Thus William Wilberforce had felt compelled to provide in his best-selling publication, *A Practical View*, a critique of 'the prevailing religious system of professed Christians in the Upper and Middle Classes of this country contrasted with real Christianity'.[11] Nominal Christians, Wilberforce pointed out, 'rest their eternal hopes on a vague general persuasion of the unqualified mercy of the Supreme Being' or more erroneously still 'they rely in the main on their own negative or positive merits'.[12]

Prayer, reading and quiet

Anglican Evangelicals, like their Nonconformist counterparts, were early risers. John Wesley regularly awoke at an early hour and it was Simeon's custom to do the same. On one occasion, a guest who stayed at Simeon's rooms in Cambridge recorded, 'Mr Simeon invariably rose every morning, though it was the winter session, at four o'clock; and after lighting his fire, he devoted the first four hours of the day to private prayer, and the devotional study of Scripture.'[13] Warmth was important to Simeon because it enabled him to read without being distracted by the cold. He sometimes made the acceptance of a preaching engagement conditional on being given a tolerably warm room. 'A tinder box, a little wood to kindle a fire speedily, a few roundish coals', he noted on one occasion, 'are but small matters in themselves; but to one who rises early, and longs to serve his God without distraction, they are of some importance',[14]

All of the Clapham fraternity were noted early risers who awoke to meet their Lord through Bible study and prayer. Michael Hennell asserted that by this they 'were enabled by God to bring to bear on

---

[10] J.C. Ryle, *Old Paths*, cited by Gordon, *Evangelical Spirituality*, p. 220.
[11] Wilberforce, *Practical View*, p. 47.
[12] Ibid., p. 47.
[13] Carus, *Charles Simeon*, p. 67.
[14] Ibid., p. 233, cited by Gordon, *Evangelical Spirituality*, p. 102.

this age "the powers of the world to come" '.[15] When John Bird Sumner was elevated to the See of Canterbury he still continued to live in the lifestyle of a quiet frugal country clergyman. He rose at dawn to pray and lit his own fire.[16] In his time as principal of Ridley Hall when his life was 'very full' Handley Moule began his day on the stroke of 7.00 a.m. Before 8.30 a.m. chapel he always had a time of prayer.[17] Hannah More, whose educational and social work changed the face of the Mendips, was convinced that the success of a day's work was dependent on such a time of regular devotion being set aside. 'The hour of prayer or meditation', she wrote, 'is a consecration of the hours employed ... In those hours we may lay in a stock of grace, which if faithfully improved, will shed its odour on every portion of the day.'[18]

For Evangelicals, the Bible was the inspired Word of God and it was read and treated with great reverence. It was highly regarded because it was viewed as providing both an account of humankind's redemption and also practical guidance for daily living. Wilberforce once told a friend, 'My judgement rests altogether on the Word of God'[19] and counselled a naval officer that 'if he read the Scriptures with earnest prayer ... and a sincere desire for discovering the truth and obeying it when known, I cannot doubt of your attaining it'.[20] To one who was once earnest about the condition of his soul but had since declined, Simeon's prescription was, 'Be much in reading the Holy Scriptures and in heavenly meditations; be much in prayer to God through Christ; read the promises and rely upon them, and cast yourself entirely on Christ as able and willing to save you to the uttermost.'[21] Simeon believed that God could speak directly from the Scriptures. On one occasion when he had been ridiculed for his beliefs at the University of Cambridge, he opened the New Testament at random and read the story of Simon of Cyrene being compelled to carry Jesus' cross. What seems to have been a sort of association of ideas led him to the conviction that it was his (Simeon being the same as Simon) task to bear for the Lord the cross

---

[15] Hennell, *John Venn and the Clapham Sect*, p. 208.
[16] Scotland, *John Bird Sumner*, p. 158.
[17] Harford and MacDonald, *Handley Carr Glyn Moule*, p. 311.
[18] J. Collingwood and M. Collingwood, *Hannah More*, p. 133, cited by Gordon, *Evangelical Spirituality*, p. 5.
[19] J.C. Pollock, *Wilberforce*, p. 145.
[20] Ibid., p. 146.
[21] Moule, *Charles Simeon*, p. 84.

of ridicule. He commented, 'I henceforth bound persecution as a wreath of glory round my brow.'[22] For Hannah More's devotions Bible reading and prayer went together. Read in an attitude of prayer the Bible could be 'nutriment to the heart' and 'oil to the lamp of prayer'.[23]

Evangelical clergy constantly urged the members of their congregations to grow in their knowledge of the Scriptures. As a young incumbent William Marsh felt that the way to achieve this end was 'by reading about four chapters every day, which will carry you through the Old and New Testaments within a year'.[24] However for the purpose of 'real devotion' he had further recommendations:

> Whatever chapter you may read, at the end of it ask some such questions as these – What doctrine does it contain? Do I believe it, and see its practical tendency? What promise does it contain? Do I feel my need of it? Do I pray that it may be fulfilled in my experience? What precept does it contain? Do I humbly implore God's Holy Spirit to write it on my heart, and to enable me to reduce it to practice?[25]

For Bishop Ryle, the Bible was the source book of Evangelical truth. He declared that it was 'the grand instrument' by which souls are converted and then established in the Christian faith.[26] It was 'God's written word'[27] and Evangelical religion categorically denied 'that there is any other guide for man's soul, co-equal or co-ordinate with the Bible'.[28] In a piece entitled 'Private Judgement', Ryle wrote, 'Let us read our Bibles regularly, and become familiar with their contents.' He continued:

> A little knowledge of the Bible will not suffice. A man must know his Bible well, if he is to prove religion by it; and he must read it regularly, if he would know it well … There must be patient, daily, systematic reading of the Book, or the Book will not be known [29]

---

[22] Carus, *Charles Simeon*, p. 676, cited by Gordon, *Evangelical Spirituality*, p. 97.

[23] Gordon, *Evangelical Spirituality*, p. 113.

[24] C. Marsh, *The Life of the Reverend William Marsh*, p. 32.

[25] Ibid., p. 32.

[26] Gordon, *Evangelical Spirituality*, p. 223.

[27] Ryle, *Knots Untied*, p. 4.

[28] Ibid., p. 4.

[29] Ibid., p. 59.

As far as Ryle was concerned, 'the man who has the Bible and the Holy Spirit in his heart has everything which is absolutely necessary to make him spiritually wise'.[30] The Bible, he wrote, contains 'the unchanging mind of the King of Kings'[31] and a regular reading of its pages moulds and shapes the mind and produces character and strength of purpose.

During the later 1850s Ryle produced his well-known *Expository Thoughts on the Gospels* – Matthew was published in 1856, Mark in 1857, Luke in 1858 and, a little later, John, in three volumes. They were written for use in families. A small section of the text would be read and this was followed by practical comments which aimed to apply it to daily living. These books proved exceptionally popular and they were sold widely.

John Bird Sumner had earlier produced similar volumes on the gospels and some of the epistles when he was Bishop of Chester. His *Practical Exposition of the Gospel According to John*,[32] for example, was 'intended to assist the practice of domestic instruction and devotion'.[33] Inevitably, even in devotional reading difficulties of interpretation or meaning would arise, but most were probably content to follow Lord Shaftesbury's practice of leaving those passages to one side and concentrating on the many 'thousands as brilliant as day'.[34]

Alongside Bible reading, Evangelicals were serious about the matter of private prayer. The study of the Scriptures provided the fuel that led on to prayer. Hannah More spoke of prayer as 'the application of want to Him who alone can relieve it, the voice of sin to Him who alone can pardon it'.[35] Ryle regarded private prayer as 'the pith, marrow and back bone' of practical piety.[36] Ryle was so certain in his mind about this that he asserted that 'converted people always pray'.[37] In so far as private prayer was concerned, he was

---

[30] J.C. Ryle, *Practical Religion*, cited by Gordon, *Evangelical Spirituality*, p. 223.

[31] J.C. Ryle, *The True Christian*, p. 120, cited by Gordon, *Evangelical Spirituality*, p. 223.

[32] J.B. Sumner, *A Practical Exposition of the Gospel According to St John*, 2 Vols.

[33] Ibid. Vol. 1, title page.

[34] Hodder, *Life and Work of Lord Shaftesbury*, p. 733.

[35] H. More, *Works*, pp. 8, 74, 109, cited by Gordon, *Evangelical Spirituality*, p. 113.

[36] Gordon, *Evangelical Spirituality*, p. 223.

[37] Ryle, *Practical Religion*, p. 66, cited by Gordon, *Evangelical Spirituality*, p. 224.

averse to praying out of a book. He regarded prayer as intimate conversation with God and as such it did not require a script.[38]

A number of Evangelicals found it helpful to pray aloud during their private devotions. Granville Sharpe of the Clapham Sect would sing out loud in his private devotions so that those who were passing by in the street below would sometimes stop 'to listen to the not unpleasing cadence, though the voice was broken by age, and the language was to them an unknown tongue'.[39] Edward Bickersteth when Rector of Watton spent part of his time 'in a retired walk above the garden, engaged in his devotions'.[40] Handley Moule found he was able to concentrate better when he prayed out loud. Canon Lillingston recalled among early impressions, in 1887, at Ridley Hall, 'the sight of Mr Moule walking in his garden every morning from 7.00 to 7.30 a.m. with eyes closed, and a shawl on his shoulders, saying his prayers'.[41] He found, according to his joint biographers, that he could pray best speaking aloud as he walked.

Edward Bickersteth produced several devotional works and his *A Treatise on Prayer* (1818) found a steady market in Evangelical households. The book arose out of a series of twelve sermons which he preached at Wheler Chapel. It was designed to help Christian people to pray and it included sections on the theology of prayer, the practice of private prayer and the problems of distraction. Bickersteth also considered the various aspects of prayer, such as confession, petition and thanksgiving in detail.

It was customary in many Evangelical households for there to be family prayers. Horton Davies wrote, 'There is no institution which more clearly reveals the stamp of the Evangelicals on the Victorian age than that of family prayers.'[42] It is at this point that we see a clear link between the Victorian Evangelicals and the Puritans of the sixteenth and seventeenth centuries. Family devotions were not exclusively an Evangelical preserve, but high-church family worship was usually liturgical and sometimes involved reading an edifying book other than the Bible. According to G.W.E. Russell, the use of Thornton's *Family Prayers* was a distinctive sign of Evangelicalism.[43] Such occasions could involve the whole household and

---

[38] Ibid., p. 224.
[39] Stephen, *Essays in Ecclesiastical Biography*, p. 543.
[40] Algionby, *Edward Henry Bickersteth*, p. 6.
[41] Harford and MacDonald, *Handley Carr Glyn Moule*, p. 311.
[42] H. Davies, *Worship and Theology in England* Vol. 3, p. 219.
[43] Bradley, *Call to Seriousness*, p. 180.

sometimes last up to an hour. Wilberforce made an entry in his private journal in November 1785, shortly after his conversion, 'began this night constant family prayer, and resolved to have it every morning and evening'.[44] A visitor to the Wilberforce household recalled how the whole family, and seven women and six men servants, gathered in the drawing room at a quarter before ten. When the assembly was complete they all knelt down by a chair or sofa while Wilberforce knelt at a table in the middle of the room and began to read a prayer in 'a solemnly awful voice'.[45]

Edward Henry, the only son of Edward Bickersteth, recalled how 'the whole household at Watton rectory assembled at 8.00 a.m. for breakfast, and there followed at 8.30 a.m. family prayers, with a hymn, a reading and exposition of Holy Scripture, the whole being concluded by 9 o'clock, when all dispersed to their several occupations'.[46] George W.E. Russell later recalled:

> We had family prayers both morning and evening. My father read a chapter, very much as the fancy took him, or where the Bible opened itself; and he read without note or comment. I remember a very distinct impression on my infant mind that the portions of the Bible which were read at Prayers had no meaning, and that the public reading of the words, without reference to the sense, was an act of piety. After the chapter, my father read a prayer from a book – William Wilberforce's or Henry Thornton's or Bishop Ashton Oxenden's.[47]

Books of prayer and devotion

The early nineteenth-century Evangelical Anglicans were warmly attached to the *Book of Common Prayer*, not just as the centrepiece of public worship but also as a handbook for private devotion. This development owed a good deal to the influence of Charles Simeon who viewed the *Prayer Book* more highly than any other book

---

[44] Wilberforce and Wilberforce, *Life of William Wilberforce* Vol. 1, p. 91, cited by Bradley, *Call to Seriousness*, p. 180.

[45] C.H. Smyth, *Simeon and Church Order*, p. 22, cited by Bradley, *Call to Seriousness*, p. 180; and Davies, *Worship*, p. 220.

[46] Algionby, *Edward Henry Bickersteth*, p. 6.

[47] Russell, *Evangelical Movement*, p. 142. Bishop Ashton Oxenden was made deacon in 1823 and ordained priest in 1824. He was Bishop of Montreal from 1869 to 1878 and Assistant Bishop of Canterbury from 1979.

apart from the Bible. He regarded it as thoroughly scriptural and 'adapted in every respect to the wants and desires of all who would worship God in spirit and truth'.[48] He also wrote, 'If all men could pray at all times as some men can sometimes, then indeed we might prefer extempore to pre-composed prayer.'[49]

The most popular manual for family devotion in Evangelical households was Henry Thornton's *Family Prayers*, which first appeared in 1834 and passed through thirty editions in the next two years. It was found to be particularly valuable by those who felt uncomfortable with extempore prayers. Edward Bickersteth's book on prayer[50] included a chapter on 'Family Worship', which he suggested, in a footnote, 'may perhaps be read with advantage by the master of a family, when first beginning to attend to this duty'.[51] The last chapter sets out forms of prayer suitable for use both by individuals and in a family context. Bickersteth later expanded the last two chapters into *Family Prayers*, which was published in 1842 and provided a course lasting eight weeks with additional prayers suited for a variety of occasions.[52] They included moving to a new home, choosing a school, and servants coming to join the household or leaving for new positions. There was a prayer for 5 November which thanked God for 'our deliverance from the papal conspiracy of the gunpowder plot'.[53] The prayer for servants reflected Bickersteth's convictions regarding the divinely established nature of the social hierarchy, 'We desire to welcome into our household another member of our family, entreating thee, who has appointed the various stations of life, for grace to fulfil the several duties of our stations to thy glory.'[54]

Among other Evangelical works on family prayer and devotion was Joseph Wigram's *The Cottager's Family Prayers*, which was published in 1862 while he was Bishop of Rochester.[55] In the introduction he wrote, 'I know nothing, among domestic duties, so calculated to bring the blessing of God Almighty upon you and

---

[48] Davies, *Worship*, p. 218.

[49] Ibid., p. 218.

[50] E. Bickersteth, *A Treatise on Prayer*.

[51] Ibid., p. 145, cited Hennell, *Sons of the Prophets*, p. 39.

[52] E. Bickersteth, *Family Prayers*, cited by Hennell, *Sons of the Prophets*, p. 39.

[53] Ibid., p. 39.

[54] Based on Hennell, *Sons of the Prophets*, pp. 39–40.

[55] J.C. Wigram, *The Cottager's Family Prayers*.

yours as that of Family Prayer.'[56] Wigram went on to advocate that there should be a fixed time, every day, morning and evening when every person in the house should assemble together. During that time they should 'all kneel upon their knees, that one of them should read a proper form of prayer, and all the others follow him'.[57] Following this, they should all repeat the Lord's Prayer aloud together and close with the blessing.[58]

Wigram's prayers are arranged thematically. So, for example, on Tuesday nights, the focus is 'Fruits of the Spirit' and prayer is made 'that we may be delivered from vain and bad desires, from sinful words and unholy thoughts'. A further prayer invokes 'the Spirit of Thy Son so that the fruits of the Spirit appear in our lives'.[59] Other themes included 'Peace in Believing' on Wednesdays[60] and 'self-denial' on Fridays.[61]

A number of other devotional books were widely read in Evangelical homes. Thomas Gisborne's (1758–1846) writings, which aimed to promote Evangelical morality, were popular in the early years of the century. 'Gisborne', wrote Henry Thornton, 'is the man of almost all others whom I could wish you implicitly to follow'.[62] The moderate Evangelical, Edward Goulburn's (1818–1897) *Thoughts on Personal Religion* was also popular in Victorian England.[63] Many Evangelicals valued the devotional writings of Edward Henry Bickersteth (1825–1906), the Bishop of Exeter (1885–1900). Edward Henry shared his father's love of music and poetry. His earliest prose composition was *Water From the Wellspring*, which was published in 1852, a complete course of morning and evening meditations for every Sunday in the year.[64] Twenty years later, Bickersteth published *The Master's Home Call: A Memoir of Alice Frances Bickersteth*.[65] It was basically a sermon

---

[56] Ibid., introductory page.

[57] Ibid., introductory page.

[58] Ibid., introductory page.

[59] Ibid., p. 13.

[60] Ibid., p. 15.

[61] Ibid., p. 19.

[62] Overton, *English Church*, p. 75.

[63] Edward Meyrick Goulbourn (1818–1897), Dean of Norwich, later became a high churchman.

[64] E.H. Bickersteth, *Water From the Wellspring: Meditation*.

[65] E.H. Bickersteth, *The Master's Home Call: A Memoir of Alice Frances Bickersteth*.

preached in Christ Church, Hampstead, after her death, with a postscript that gave a straightforward account of her life, illness and death. About 27,000 copies were printed. William Gladstone was among those deeply affected by reading the book and he sent copies of it to his friends.[66] *The Reef and Other Parables* came out in 1873 as a book intended for young people. This book was not a success since the parables were found to be too elaborate for most children.[67] The book to which Edward Henry devoted most of his time was his *Practical and Expository Commentary on the New Testament*. He began writing in 1860 and completed it in 1864. Its stated object was 'to provide such brief remarks from Holy Scripture as the educated classes of the day might read to their families at morning or evening worship, "that golden-girdle" of family life'.[68] He aimed to be practical as can be instanced from his comments on Matthew 12:1–8 where he pointed out that 'Christ sanctioned (1) works of necessity as leading an ox or ass to watering, (2) works of mercy as lifting the sheep from the pit into which it had fallen, (3) works of piety'.[69]

In the later years of the nineteenth century many valued the spiritual writings of Handley Moule.[70] Along with numerous other publications, he brought out several volumes of his sermons[71] which were read devotionally by a wide circle of people. His *Secret Prayer* 1890 'helped thousands to pray'[72] but it was his *Christian Sanctity* and its companion booklets which helped many to experience the reality of life in Christ.[73] Bishop Moule was a fertile author and continued to publish devotional books, papers and tracts almost to the time of his death. His spirituality was essentially a passive one in which he emphasised the need for a second crisis of grace and total surrender to the will of Christ.

---

[66] Algionby, *Edward Henry Bickersteth*, pp. 125–7.
[67] Ibid., p. 127.
[68] Ibid., p. 130.
[69] Ibid., p. 131.
[70] Harford, and MacDonald, *Handley Carr Glyn Moule*, pp. 176–7.
[71] See for example *Fordington Sermons, Life in Christ and For Christ, The Consummation of Love, The Devotional Study of Holy Scripture, Thoughts on Union with Christ, Thoughts on Secret Prayer* and *Prayers for the Home*.
[72] Harford and MacDonald, *Handley Carr Glyn Moule*, p. 177.
[73] Ibid., p. 177.

Holy Communion

The developing focus that Holy Communion played in nineteenth-century Evangelical Anglican spirituality has not always been recognised. Whilst it is true that John Wesley had a high view of the sacrament, the fact was that at the beginning of the nineteenth century it was largely a forgotten ordinance. In the public worship of many churches it was not unusual for celebrations of the Lord's Supper to take place only once a quarter.[74] Nevertheless, Charles Simeon and members of the Clapham Sect and Edward Bickersteth were among those who attached great importance to Holy Communion. In 1806 the Rev Leigh Richmond introduced a monthly celebration at Turvey which was preceded by a monthly communicant class on the Saturday evening. Richmond treated preparation for the sacrament with great seriousness.[75] Evangelicals made a particular effort to hold communion services at a time when it was more convenient for the working classes to attend. In many of the larger towns this led to the practice of holding evening communions. The custom was observed in Birmingham and Leeds in 1852. Its popularity was such that by 1869 sixty-five London churches had adopted it.[76] It was Lord Shaftesbury's habit to look at virtually every issue from the standpoint of the poor. When this question of evening communion was under the consideration of the Evangelical clergy he said:

> We must consider what has long been the condition of these people, and have some regard to their wants, habits, customs and feelings, and we must remember that vast numbers of them, especially the women, have not a moment's leisure from domestic duties till the evening; and the rectors and vicars of large parishes tell me that, for one poor man or woman who has attended morning communion, fourteen or fifteen have attended evening communion.[77]

On another occasion, Shaftesbury was adamant that if the clergy refused to bend to this need for evening communion services the poor will stay away from the churches altogether.[78]

---

[74] In 1800 in his second charge to the clergy of the diocese of Rochester, their high church bishop, Dr Horsley, insisted on four celebrations a year.

[75] Overton, *English Church*, citing *Life of Leigh Richmond*, p. 131.

[76] Balleine, *History of the Evangelical Party*, p. 244.

[77] Hodder, *Life and Work of Lord Shaftesbury*, p. 743.

[78] Ibid., p. 743.

In the middle years of the century, several of the Evangelical bishops appointed by Lord Palmerston urged the clergy of their dioceses to hold more frequent sacramental services. Montagu Villiers, for example, felt that the practice of holding only three or four communion services a year was 'a most injurious tendency'.[79] He expressed the hope that it would be kept as a monthly ordinance.[80] Charles Baring reflected that there had been some improvement in the number of churches in the Gloucester diocese holding more frequent Holy Communion services. There was, however, still much room for improvement.[81] At his visitation of 1865 John Pelham rejoiced 'to find throughout the diocese a more frequent ministration of the Lord's Supper'. Services were held monthly and on principal festivals in 302 churches. In 109 churches Holy Communion was held from eight to twelve times a year and in 304 churches six to eight. Nevertheless, Pelham bemoaned the fact that in 287 churches the rite was celebrated on only three occasions. His opinion was that the clergyman should 'aim at leading his flock, however gradually, to attend this blessed ordinance at least once every month and on great festivals'.[82] In 1864 Robert Bickersteth urged his clergy who did not hold Holy Communion services for their people at least once a month to reconsider their practice. In his view, such infrequency was 'to deny them a privilege which it is our duty to afford'.[83]

Bickersteth's episcopal colleague, Joseph Wigram, was also an advocate of more frequent Holy Communion services. Shortly after his consecration as bishop he expressed his disapproval of the fact that there were some 270 churches in the diocese in which the sacrament was observed on less than twelve occasions in the year.[84] William Thomson also made it clear that 'too many clergy are neglecting to give sufficient opportunity to their people to attend

---

[79] H.M. Villiers, *A Charge Delivered to the Clergy of the Diocese of Carlisle at the First Visitation of the Hon H. Montagu Villiers DD, Lord Bishop of Carlisle 1858*, pp. 31–2.

[80] Ibid., p. 32.

[81] C. Baring, *A Charge Delivered to the Clergy of the Diocese of Gloucester and Bristol at His Triennial Visitation in October 1860*, p. 23.

[82] Pelham, *Charge, Norwich*, p. 23.

[83] R. Bickersteth, *A Charge Delivered to the Clergy of the Diocese of Ripon at his Triennial Visitation, April 1864 by Robert Lord Bishop of Ripon*, pp. 13–14.

[84] Bishop of Rochester's Visitation of the Chelmsford Archdeaconry, *Essex Weekly News*, 4 November 1864.

Holy Communion'.[85] When Anthony Thorold arrived at Rochester he found that exactly one hundred churches out of a total of 291 held an evening communion service.[86] At the same time, he observed that the number of churches offering evening communion in London as a whole had risen from 65 in 1869 to 267 in 1880.[87]

The writings of many nineteenth-century Evangelical Anglicans testify to the way in which Holy Communion was a significant aspect of their spirituality. William Wilberforce wrote on 1 January 1812, 'I have been detained long at Church, according to a custom which I have observed for twenty-six or twenty-seven years, of devoting the New Year to God by public worship in a Sacrament on 1 January'.[88] A staunch Evangelical, Henry Hutton (1808–1863) who eventually became Rector of St Paul's, Covent Garden, wrote as follows on the eve of his ordination to the priesthood:

> I hope and trust that the FATHER of mercies will give ear to our united prayers, and that He will vouchsafe to me a more abundant supply of His Holy Spirit to make me more faithful and diligent to execute the sacred office of Priest to a congregation of His people. It will be a source of unmixed gratification to me, if I am spared to administer the Holy Sacrament of the Body and Blood of our Blessed Saviour to the many devout and faithful worshippers who are wont to approach the Lord.[89]

This aspiration, which could almost have been written by a high churchman, illustrates the fact that for most Evangelicals the Eucharist was not a mere memorial but also a communicating ordinance. Charles Simeon in a sermon on the Lord's Supper asserted that the ordinance was not 'merely commemorative'. Rather, he continued, 'We must apply it, every one of us, to ourselves. We must feed upon it, and by so doing declare our affiance in it. We must ... have our souls nourished by means of union and communion with our blessed and adorable Redeemer.'[90] At a later point in this same address Simeon remarked that it was 'the experience of many' that the Saviour has 'again and again, in more abundant measure, made himself known in the breaking of bread'.[91]

---

[85] Thomson, *Charge, York*, p. 24.
[86] Simpkinson, *Bishop Thorold*, p. 139.
[87] Ibid., p. 139.
[88] Russell, *Evangelical Movement*, pp. 33–5.
[89] Ibid., p. 20.
[90] Pollard, *Let Wisdom Judge*, p. 176.
[91] Ibid., p. 178.

Bishop Ryle was clear that there is 'a spiritual presence of Christ in the Lord's Supper to every faithful communicant, but no local corporal presence in the bread and wine to any communicant'. This, he went on to assert, 'is evidently the uniform doctrine of the Church of England'.[92] Ryle was quite specific as to the meaning of 'a spiritual presence'. He spelt it out as follows: 'But we by the real spiritual presence of Christ do understand Christ to be present, as the Spirit of God is present, in the hearts of the faithful by blessing and grace; and this is all which we mean'.[93] In another piece entitled 'The Real Presence' Ryle wrote:

> There is a real 'presence' of Christ with the hearts of all true-hearted communicants in the Lord's Supper ... I can never doubt that the great ordinance appointed by Christ has a special peculiar blessing attached to it. That blessing, I believe, consists in a special and peculiar presence of Christ, vouchsafed to the heart of every believing communicant ... In a word, there is a special spiritual 'presence' of Christ in the Lord's Supper, which they only know who are faithful communicants, and which they who are not communicants miss altogether.[94]

Handley Moule revered Holy Communion and encouraged evening communion services.[95] He also allowed reservation of the sacrament provided it was for special use and not for the purpose of adoration.[96] In 1895 he was awarded a DD for his scholarly edition of Bishop Ridley's work *On the Lord's Supper*. His work included an account of the book that Ratramnus wrote against Paschasius in the ninth century, from which Ridley drew much of his information.[97] Along with Ryle, Moule firmly believed that the bread and wine were 'not bare signs, mere occasions of reminiscence, however tender'.[98] They are, he declared, 'personally given Warrants and Witnesses of eternal realities'.[99] For Moule, the hour of communion was 'indeed an hour with God, with the Son of God' in which 'He speaks to us, and as it were sensibly

---

[92] J.C. Ryle, 'The Lord Supper', in *Knots Untied*, pp. 173–4.
[93] Ibid., p. 175.
[94] Ibid., p. 198–9.
[95] Harford and MacDonald, *Handley Carr Glyn Moule*, p. 216.
[96] Ibid., p. 220.
[97] Ibid., p. 171.
[98] Moule, *Outlines of Christian Doctrine*, p. 242.
[99] Ibid., p. 242.

touches us.'[100] The believer 'goes forth refreshed' from communion 'bearing its innumerable benefits'.[101]

The Evangelical understanding of Holy Communion remained substantially unchanged throughout the nineteenth century. It was seen as both a remembrance and a receiving of a spiritual presence. Most were of the view that there were spiritual benefits available to worthy communicants that were not available to others. Evangelical discussions centred on the nature of the presence of Christ in the sacrament and what feeding on the body and blood of Christ meant. The Evangelical view was that as the bread and wine feed the physical body, the body and blood nourish the soul but only in a heavenly and spiritual manner.

Hymns

Another important aspect of Evangelical spirituality was the singing of hymns. Such singing took place not only in public worship on a Sunday but in the homes and in many instances in the work place.[102] Perhaps the greatest change that Evangelicals made to the church service was the introduction of the singing of hymns.[103] Many high churchmen held fast to the notion that only the psalms should be sung in church. They regarded the use of hymns as sectarian nonconformity. The psalms were often badly chanted and there were complaints that many congregations sat down when they were sung.[104] In 1819 Reginald Heber, later to be Bishop of Calcutta, compiled a collection of hymns for his parishioners at Hodnet but even he had 'some high church scruples about using it'.[105]

A major influence in this was, of course, Charles Wesley who published more than six thousand hymns.[106] Among them were some of the very best in the English language such as 'Love Divine, all loves excelling', 'Rejoice the Lord is King' and 'Hark the Herald Angels Sing'. Wesley saw hymns as a vehicle for communicating truth, particularly to those who were unable to read. Such people could memorise key doctrines as they sang the words to simple

---

[100] Ibid., p. 242.
[101] Ibid., p. 242.
[102] Overton, *English Church*, p. 192.
[103] Elliott-Binns, *Early Evangelicals*, p. 373.
[104] Overton, *English Church*, p. 134.
[105] Balleine, *History of the Evangelical Party*, p. 137.
[106] Ibid., p. 36.

joyous melodies. When John Wesley published *Wesley's Hymns*[107] he described them as 'a little body of practical divinity'.[108] He claimed that the hymns contained 'no doggerel, nothing put in to patch up the rhyme, no feeble expletives, no cant expressions'.[109]

Other hymn writers began to emerge at the same time, among them Augustus Toplady who is remembered for 'Rock of Ages', John Newton author of 'How Sweet the Name of Jesus sounds' and 'Glorious things of Thee are spoken' and William Cowper who wrote among others, 'O for a closer walk with God' and 'Jesus, where'er Thy people meet'.[110]

During the nineteenth century a number of collections of hymns were published. Among the most popular was Edward Bickersteth's *Christian Psalmody*, which first appeared in 1833 and soon reached a hundred and fifty thousand copies.[111] Later in the century, his son, Edward Henry Bickersteth, edited a replacement volume for his father's compilation, entitled *Hymnal Companion to the Book of Common Prayer*.[112] He wrote:

> If I might humbly take up, though with most unequal hands, the mantle which fell from my beloved father ... if it might be permitted me in any way to advance a cause which he had so much at heart, and which is so intimately bound up with the spiritual life of the church, I should esteem it one of the greatest mercies of my ministry.[113]

Within a very short space of time the book had replaced a large number of private compilations that had been in use in many Evangelical parishes of England. Despite the publication of *Hymns Ancient and Modern* in 1866, which appealed to high churchmen, Evangelicals adopted Bickersteth's collection 'almost without exception' and its circulation was 'very large'.[114] Even at the close of the century it was still the most used book in the Evangelical parishes of England.[115]

---

[107] J. Wesley, *A Collection of Hymns for the People called Methodists*, p. iv.
[108] Ibid., p. iv.
[109] Ibid., p. iv.
[110] Ibid., p. 109.
[111] Overton, *English Church*, p. 133.
[112] Balleine, *History of the Evangelical Party*, p. 282.
[113] Algionby, *Edward Henry Bickersteth*, p. 113.
[114] Ibid., p. 114.
[115] Ibid., p. 114.

Hymn singing became increasingly more popular among Evangelical Anglicans following the visits of Moody and Sankey and the immensely popular *Sacred Songs and Solos*.[116] The Keswick Convention added further to the popularity and importance of hymns as a significant aspect of Evangelical spirituality.[117] The hymns of Frances Ridley Havergal (1836–1879) proved immensely popular at the Keswick meetings. Havergal was the daughter of a Church of England clergyman. She experienced entire consecration in 1873 near the end of her short life. 'I saw it', she related, 'as a flash of electric light'.[118] Her best known hymns were, 'I am trusting Thee, Lord Jesus' (1874), 'Take my Life and let it be consecrated Lord, to Thee' (1874), and 'Who is on the Lord's Side?' (1877). She wrote in the region of fifty hymns, some of which were included, much to her delight, in the first revision of *Hymns Ancient and Modern*. The Keswick Convention's first hymnbook, *Hymns of Consecration and Faith*, was produced by James Mountain and published in 1875.[119] In 1890 the volume was updated and revised by Isabella Hopkins, the wife of Evan Hopkins, resulting in a much larger collection. These hymns naturally conveyed the Keswick message of full salvation through consecration. Numbers of them also speak of entering into God's perfect peace and of resting in God. Keswick hymns expressed a mood of confidence and happiness in God.

Not all Victorian Evangelicals, it should be said, endorsed the more revivalistic hymns. Henry Venn Elliott, for example, saw them as 'an evident attempt at too much excitement'.[120] 'I cannot think,' he wrote in reply to a correspondent, 'that souls get to heaven by exciting or marching music'.[121]

Diaries and self-examination

Although Evangelicals knew themselves to be numbered among the redeemed many of them kept diaries, which reveal that they were anxious about the state of their souls.[122] In his times of prayer and

---

[116] See chapter 11.

[117] Price and Randall, *Transforming Keswick*, p. 85.

[118] Ibid., p. 85; also see M.V.G. Havergal, *Memorials of Frances Ridley Havergal*, p. 101.

[119] Sloan, *These Sixty Years*, p. 38.

[120] Bateman, *Henry Venn Elliott*, p. 204.

[121] Ibid., p. 205.

[122] Bradley, *Call to Seriousness*, pp. 23–4.

self-examination, Wilberforce would check his spiritual progress against a list that he kept of his 'chief besetting sins', which seem mostly to have been excesses of food and drink.[123] In the early days after her conversion, Hannah More bemoaned 'a weak faith' and 'little progress in the divine life'.[124] After a further three years she was still troubled at her spiritual state and wrote, 'there must be something amiss in my heart which I do not know of ... because I have little sensible joy ... I have a stronger sense of sin than of pardon and acceptance'.[125] There is an entry in her diary of 1789, when she was fifty-three, in which she appears deeply disturbed by the poverty of her own spiritual condition. 'I will confess my sins', she recorded, 'repent of them – plead the atonement – resolve to love God and Christ – implore the aid of the Spirit for light – be humbled for my failures – watch and pray'.[126] James Gordon commented that in an age of exaggerated flattery Hannah More's attitude to praise became ambivalent.[127] He notes that her severe self-criticism marred the joy of her communion with God. Additionally, she was unreasonably hard on herself, on one occasion rebuking herself for not meditating during a migraine.[128]

Henry Thornton, another member of the Clapham circle, also kept a diary. It was his custom to open it at the beginning of each year with a brief summary of his main faults. One year the list ran as follows:

> First, I lie idly in bed often and even generally longer than I need. 2. I am not steady and punctual enough in reading the Scriptures. 3. In my prayers I am idle. 4. In my secret thoughts and imaginations I am far from having learnt self-denial. 5. I am not self-denying in my business.[129]

Lord Shaftesbury also kept up a diary throughout most of his life. Interestingly, for the most part, the comments he makes about his achievements and his standing before God are quite positive[130] and

---

[123] Pollock, *Wilberforce*, p. 45.

[124] Gordon, *Evangelical Spirituality*, p. 107.

[125] Roberts, *Memoirs* Vol. 2, p. 277, cited by Gordon, *Evangelical Spirituality*, p. 277.

[126] Ibid., p. 107.

[127] Gordon, *Evangelical Spirituality*, p. 107.

[128] Ibid., p. 111.

[129] Bradley, *Call to Seriousness*, p. 23.

[130] See, for example, Shaftesbury, *Diary*, 9 and 11 October 1839.

exude an air of confidence and thanksgiving. Only on a few occasions does he appear overly self-critical. On 19 March 1853 he recorded that he 'Felt dull, incompetent, and confused in my speech ... It dispirits me, for, old as I am, I am full of projects.'[131] Much later, in December 1871, Shaftesbury noted that he was, in earlier years, 'intellectually, not strong; over anxious for success, over-fearful of failure, easily exalted, as easily depressed; with a good deal of ambition, and no real self-confidence.'[132]

The major concern among Evangelicals, and not just those who kept spiritual journals, was that they might be accountable to God for the way in which they spent their lives. In his searing critique of Evangelical religion, E.P. Thompson forcibly reminds us that, 'God was the most vigilant over-looker of all'[133] and even above the chimney breast there hung the text, 'Thou God see-est me'.[134] It was for this reason that Henry Thornton once voted against William Pitt. On being questioned by the latter as to why he had done so, he replied, 'I voted today so that if my master had come again at that moment I might have been able to give an account of my stewardship.'[135] Bishop Ryle pointed out that if Christian growth is to take place, watchfulness over our conduct and in the small details of everyday life is essential.[136] Life, he emphasised, is made up of 'the little things of every hour' and 'we must aim to have a Christianity which, like the sap of a tree, runs through every twig and leaf of our character, and sanctified all'.[137]

This requirement to follow one's conscience and to strive towards a greater and more costly obedience was strengthened by the teachings of Keswick in the later Victorian years. The emphasis of this Keswick holiness doctrine was entire surrender to God's will in every aspect of living. Yet, it was not perceived as merely a matter of determined self-will. As Handley Moule pointed out, Christians have the help of the Holy Spirit. It is possible, he maintained, to become strongest even at our weakest point by 'unreserved resort to divine power'.[138]

---

[131] Shaftesbury, *Diary*, 19 March 1853, cited by Hodder, *Life and Work of Lord Shaftesbury*, p. 469.
[132] Shaftesbury, *Diary*, 31 December 1871.
[133] Thompson, *English Working Class*, p. 406.
[134] Ibid., p. 406.
[135] Hennell, *John Venn and the Clapham Sect*, p. 207.
[136] Birks, *Memoir* Vol. 1, pp. 9–10.
[137] Ryle, *Holiness*, p. 93.
[138] Ibid., p. 93.

Work

Evangelicals' work and the way in which they conducted their duties became a key ingredient in their spirituality because they were deeply concerned that every aspect of their lives should be answerable to God. For this reason, Thomas Gisborne wrote a volume entitled *An Enquiry into the Duties of Men*. It had chapters that addressed the responsibilities of those in politics, the civil service, the armed forces, the law, medicine, the church, trade and business. Although Evangelicals professed to be justified apart from good deeds, they regarded their daily round as a divine calling and most worked excessively hard and often for very long hours.

Shortly after her conversion, Hannah More became deeply committed to the campaign to abolish the slave trade. On principle she refused to use any West Indian sugar. She carried with her, whenever possible, a plan of a slave ship with which she ruined many a social evening. Between 1788 and 1805 Hannah gave herself unstintingly to a programme of writing. During the 1790s she began a programme of rudimentary education for the children of farm labourers and miners of Cheddar. Eventually, her scheme included the building of more than twenty schools in parishes spread over a wide area of the Mendip Hills.

Edward Bickersteth also felt bound before God to make the fullest possible use of his every waking moment. As a young man he wrote, 'I have lived twenty-two years, that is near two hundred thousand hours and twelve million minutes; for the employment of everyone of those minutes I am accountable to God. In every minute it was my duty to love God with my whole heart and strength.'[139]

Lord Shaftesbury exhibited similar tendencies towards workaholism. In his diary entry for 28 March 1857, he remarked 'have now, at least, a hundred letters unanswered'. He went on to state that he had not had leisure to do 'one stitch of private business' or to enjoy barely an hour of private recreation and that two books he had wanted to read were still unopened.[140]

Evangelical clergy were little different from their laity regarding their long hours of work. When Simeon came to the end of a holiday in Scotland he calculated that he had given seventy-five addresses to

---

[139] H.C.G. Moule, *Thoughts on Christian Sanctity*, cited by Gordon, *Evangelical Spirituality*, p. 207.

[140] Shaftesbury, *Diary*, 28 March 1857, cited by Hodder, *Life and Work of Lord Shaftesbury*, pp. 550–1.

87,310 people in three months![141] Simeon was also a prolific letter writer and stated that he had 7,000 copies of his letters, which he retained in case anyone should attempt to misrepresent him. For Simeon as for many Evangelicals, letter writing was not merely an art; it was a very real part of his spirituality. In correspondence he encouraged those on the mission field, congratulated people on their appointments, consoled the bereaved, advised younger and misguided clergy and gave advice on anything from domestic to doctrinal matters. Simeon carried a substantial pastoral workload and held weekly informal conversation parties for students of the university. In addition, he gave of his time to the CMS and was a life-long supporter of the BFBS. On top of all of this Simeon wrote 2,536 sermons and outlines, collected in 1833 under the title *Horae Homileticae*, literally 'hours of sermons'.[142] One of many clerics who followed in Simeon's steps was Spencer Thornton, Rector of Wendover. Each week he gave seven evening lectures, two afternoon readings and taught four Bible classes.[143]

At the episcopal level the picture was little different. Charles Sumner when at Winchester followed a very strict routine. He took a quarter of an hour's stroll after breakfast and then went to his study, where he stayed until lunch which was at 1 p.m. In 1867, the year before he resigned the See, the bishop wrote upwards of 3,500 letters on matters of business.[144] Many of these, according to son and biographer, required a great deal of thought.[145] In addition to family and diocesan letters, Sumner's position as visitor to Winchester College and no fewer than five colleges at Oxford occasionally required much correspondence.[146] Bishop Robert Bickersteth of Ripon was in very much the same mould and surprised many by his wish to preach several times each Sunday in the churches of his diocese.[147] In addition to his very heavy schedule, Bickersteth took on the semi-parochial charge of North Leys, a small village about a mile from his residence.[148]

---

[141] Hopkins, *Charles Simeon of Cambridge*, p. 140.
[142] Pollard, *Let Wisdom Judge*, p. 13.
[143] Bebbington, *Evangelicalism in Modern Britain*, p. 11.
[144] G.H. Sumner, *Life of Charles Richard Sumner*, p. 212.
[145] Ibid., p. 212.
[146] Ibid., p. 213.
[147] Bebbington, *Evangelicalism in Modern Britain*, p. 11; Scotland, *Good and Proper Men*, p. 189.
[148] M.C. Bickersteth, *Robert Bickersteth*, pp. 123–4.

An aspect of this issue that has yet to receive the attention it demands is that of female spirituality. Linda Wilson has recently broken new ground with her book on female spirituality amongst Nonconformists between 1825 and 1875.[149] We await something similar for Anglican women. One thing is clear, the majority of middle-class Evangelical Anglicans were of the opinion that middle- and upper-class women were called to exercise their spirituality in the home or domestic sphere. This view was more strongly held in the earlier years of the century, but even then there were exceptions. Simeon recalled going to a meeting of the Eclectic Society in April 1807 where a group of clergy discussed the question, how may pious women best sub-serve the interests of religion? Simeon recalled that the majority seemed to think they did their best by remaining at home and minding their own business. He commented that 'my ideas did not perfectly coincide with theirs'.[150] Hannah More and her sisters were further earlier exceptions.

In contrast, Francis Close, the ebullient incumbent of Cheltenham, was of the view that the women's place was in the home. When the female Chartists presented themselves in the town's parish church on 25 August 1839 as part of a national publicity campaign, Close roundly rebuked them. He warned that they were in danger of becoming like their sisters in the French Revolution who 'glutted themselves with blood and danced like maniacs amidst the most fearful scenes of the Reign of Terror!'[151] 'Your place, the fountain of all your influence', Close declared to the women of Cheltenham, 'is your home – your own fireside ... there you are born to shine, there you may diffuse the best graces of Christianity'.[152]

Towards the end of the century, however, attitudes began to change. David Bebbington pointed out that Evangelical religion was more important than feminism in enlarging the sphere of work open to women.[153] Single, and some married, Evangelical women were employed on the mission field, as nurses, domestic visitors and teachers.

---

[149] Wilson, *Constrained by Zeal*.

[150] Carus, *Charles Simeon*, p. 224, cited by Gordon, *Evangelical Spirituality*, p. 105.

[151] F. Close, *The Female Chartists' Visit to the Parish Church. A Sermon Addressed to the Female Chartists of Cheltenham, Sunday August 25th 1839*, p. 18.

[152] Ibid., p. 18.

[153] Bebbington, *Evangelicalism in Modern Britain*, p. 129.

Sean Gill has detailed some of the contributions made by Evangelical women in the nineteenth century.[154] Mary Paley Marshall was one of the first five students to attend Newnham College, Cambridge in October 1871. She was the daughter of a strict Evangelical clergyman. Her father had taught her Latin and Hebrew and introduced her to English classical literature.[155] Emily Davies, the first principal of Girton College, was also the daughter of an Evangelical clergyman. From an early age Constance Maynard received instruction from her Evangelical mother. In 1882, Constance became the first principal of Westfield College. Her faith led her to ensure that Christianity was central to the life of the college and she began a course of divinity lectures in the college in 1901.[156]

Gill also noted the impact of William Pennefather's training scheme for home mission women;[157] the women's section of the Church Army, which was opened in 1889 under the direction of Marie, Wilson Carlisle's sister; and the growing overseas opportunities for women provided by CMS.[158] In fact, Gill made the point that the wives of CMS missionaries played significant roles on the mission field from the beginning of the century.

In addition to the points which Gill made, there can be no doubt that pioneering women such as Ellen Ranyard, Josephine Butler and Florence Nightingale were role models. Their work helped to reinforce the change. And, as we have noted earlier in this chapter, women also made other contributions to Evangelical spirituality, particularly in the area of hymnology, singing and devotional writing.

Evangelical Anglicans saw their spirituality as not merely the nurturing of their souls but involving their minds and their daily work commitments. Many exercised great dedication in their private devotions rising at an early hour to read, study and pray. Others, such as the Clapham Sect, broke off from their work during the day to engage in prayer and meditation. It was the depth of their personal devotions that gave Evangelicals moral strength and the tenacity of purpose that sustained their campaigns for social and

---

[154] S. Gill, *Women in the Church of England*.
[155] Ibid., p. 115.
[156] Ibid., p. 118.
[157] Ibid., p. 165.
[158] Ibid., p. 179.

political reform. It was this which generated a spirit of dedicated preaching and pastoral work in their parishes.

If there is a criticism to be levelled at Evangelical Anglican spirituality it is perhaps that in some instances it had a tendency to be overly introspective and denying of some worldly pleasures, such as the theatre and sporting activities, which succeeding generations came to regard as wholesome and even healthful. It was not for nothing, however, that Henry Parry Liddon asserted that Evangelical religion was deep and fervid.[159]

---

[159] Liddon, *Pusey* Vol. 1, p. 255.

15

Parish Life

Stretching back to the times of Archbishop Theodore, the Church of England ideal had always been the parish church. Each parochial area was seen in terms of a family knit together by the Christian faith and under a spiritual father. The parish system was dear to churchmen because it gave them status and they were seen to hold a special position in relation to other Nonconformist ministers. At the beginning of the nineteenth century, the parish influenced almost every aspect of the lives of those who dwelt within its bounds. The rector or vicar was responsible for baptising their children, conducting their marriages and burying their dead. In addition, the incumbent probably collected tithes and, together with the wardens and the vestry meeting, he was responsible for fixing the annual church rate and for distributing charity and dispensing the Poor Law relief. As likely as not, the only schools were also under the parish clergyman's control or influence.

The parish community belonged essentially to the rural areas of pre-industrial England. It was in the hierarchical society of the countryside that the parish church had a status and an importance that it rarely achieved in towns or cities. However, by the beginning of the nineteenth century the parish system was failing both in the countryside, because of laxness and non-residence, and in the towns due to the rapid increase in population, which meant clergy often found themselves single-handedly attempting to minister to the needs of 10,000 to 15,000 inhabitants. Birmingham, for instance, was a single parish of 120,000 in the early 1820s as were Sheffield and Manchester. When William Wilberforce visited Hannah More at her Somerset home, he made an expedition to the Mendip Hills. What he discovered horrified him. The Vicar of Cheddar lived at Oxford and the Curate at Wells and the thirteen neighbouring parishes were without a resident clergy.[1] In 1823 a certain Richard

---

[1] Balleine, *History of the Evangelical Party*, p.154.

Yates had compiled tables to show that over 5,300 of the estimated 12,000 beneficed clergymen in England and Wales did not ordinarily reside in their parishes.[2] When Bishop Bathurst died in 1827, the diocese of Norwich contained 900 parishes. His confirmations were septennial. An inhabitant of the cathedral city noted, 'In 1837 I saw from my window nine parishes, of which only one contained a resident clergyman.'[3] In another deanery that was composed of twenty-eight parishes only five had two services every Sunday.[4]

Against this background a number of Evangelicals had begun to exercise a real measure of dedication and concern for the spiritual welfare of their parishioners. Among them were Thomas Robinson (1749–1813) who began forty years of ministry at St Martin's, Leicester, in 1774, John Newton (1725–1807), who ministered first at Olney and then in the City of London at St Mary Woolnoth, and Charles Simeon, who served as incumbent of Holy Trinity, Cambridge, from 1782 to 1836. These men, together with others, such as Thomas Gisborne (1758–1846) and Henry Blunt (1794–1843), influenced many of their contemporaries to become conscientious pastors and preachers, and to work their parishes with dedication and commitment.

Thomas Robinson was a scholarly man having been a Fellow of Trinity College, Cambridge, but he became a dedicated pastor whose sermons attracted large numbers of people. He paid particular attention to pastoral visiting and was a welcome visitor in many homes.[5] John Newton was a devoted pastor. He estimated that his church at Olney, which could hold almost 2,000 people, was 'well filled'.[6] He carefully prepared people for the Holy Communion, often by preaching a special sermon on a Friday before sacrament Sunday.[7] Sometimes more than 200 children attended his catechism classes and he reported to Lord Dartmouth that 'about hundred of them come constantly to church and sit in a body before the pulpit'.[8] Newton was a dedicated visitor and made a daily round of calls to the 'sick and sorrowful'. Later, when at St Mary Woolnoth,

---

[2] E.R. Norman, *Church and Society in England 1770–1970*, p. 69, citing R. Yates, *Patronage of the Church of England*, p. 61.
[3] Carpenter, *Church and People 1789–1889*, p. 55.
[4] Ibid., p. 55.
[5] Balleine, *History of the Evangelical Party*, pp. 120–1.
[6] Hindmarsh, *John Newton*, p. 187.
[7] Ibid., p. 191.
[8] Ibid., p. 197.

he took some of the needy under his own roof and visited prisoners at Newgate.[9]

Charles Simeon, despite his immense influence over the town and gown of Cambridge, also devoted his attentions to the pastoral care of his parish. Early in his ministry he divided his territory into a number of districts, each with a male and female visitor. It was their task to see that the needs of the poor in their allotted areas were met. Simeon preached an annual sermon in aid of their efforts.[10] He also gathered the ordinary folk of his parish together on a regular basis in a hired room and there expounded the Scripture and prayed with them.[11] Thomas Gisborne who lived at Yoxhall Lodge in Needwood Forest undertook the charge of the populous village of Barton. Here he laboured conscientiously among the poor.[12] Henry Blunt, having spent his early years in Cambridge, took the curacy of St Luke's Chelsea in 1824 and in 1830 succeeded to the living of the new church of Holy Trinity, upper Chelsea. He was described by Overton as 'a good parish priest' who drew around him the most influential congregation in London or its neighbourhood. Commoners, tradesmen and the poor all hung on his discourses.[13]

These men, and several dozen others[14] whose ministries began in the eighteenth century, set an example of conscientious concern for their parochial charges. Like the earlier Puritans to whom some of them looked back with affection, their ideal clergyman was a faithful pastor and a good preacher. In his celebrated article on 'Church Parties' in *The Edinburgh Review* of October 1853 W.J. Conybeare noted that Evangelical clergy were observed to be good pastors:

> Such pastors may not perhaps be men of the most comprehensive understanding; not the fittest teachers for inquiring minds, nor qualified to refute the learned infidelity of Strauss or Newman. But upon the middle and lower ranks of their parishioners, they often have a stronger influence than their more intellectual brethren.[15]

---

[9] Ibid., p. 309.
[10] Moule, *Charles Simeon*, p. 49.
[11] Ibid., p. 47.
[12] Overton, *English Church*, pp. 74f.
[13] Ibid., p. 84.
[14] Overton, *English Church*.
[15] Conybeare, 'Church Parties', p. 281.

The Inadequacy of the Parish System

Alan Gilbert in his study of religion and society in Industrial England described the period 1740 to 1830 as 'a disaster for the Church of England'. Upholding the social fabric, he observed, had been a popular enough function while the pressures upon it were relatively unstrained.[16] However, once industrialisation began to develop apace in the early years of the nineteenth century it was clear that the parochial system was insufficient to cope with either its social and charitable or its spiritual roles. By the last quarter of the century successive governments had found it necessary to make other and additional arrangements for the registration of births and deaths, the solemnisation of marriages and the administration of the Poor Law. David Smith observed that:

> the traditional parish system, which had evolved in quite different social conditions, was an obstacle to urban evangelisation. What was needed was for city churches to form 'a real working Evangelical Alliance' so that they might act together in confronting the situation as it existed in 'the dark and destitute districts of the city'.[17]

Many Evangelical clergy worked conscientiously in their parishes and on the surface some were quite successful but most of their number failed to recognise that the parochial system was too confining. In fact, Charles Sumner was one of the very few Evangelicals who saw the problem with clarity. As he surveyed the London end of his diocese he was acutely aware of the problems that confronted the nine ministers in the parish of Southwark who had to minister to a population of 91,500. There were similar percentages of clergy to laity in both Lambeth and at Portsea. In another Surrey parish there were free seats for only 150 out of a total of 14,000 parishioners. As Sumner so clearly saw, 'The Shepherd, in too many instances, is so far from being able to know his sheep, that he can scarcely count them ... He is disabled by the magnitude of his charge.' The result, he continued, 'is a neglected population, and an uneducated community without check or religious restraint ...'[18] A little later Lord

---

[16] A.D. Gilbert, *Religion and Society in Industrial England: Church, Chapel and Social Change 1740–1914*, p. 77.

[17] Smith, *Transforming the World?*, p. 46.

[18] C.R. Sumner, *A Charge Delivered to the Clergy of the Diocese of Winchester in October 1833*, pp. 16–18, cited by K.S. Inglis, *Churches and the Working Classes in Victorian England*, p. 300.

Shaftesbury saw the issue in much the same way. 'The parochial system', he observed during the course of a Parliamentary debate, 'is no doubt, a beautiful thing in theory, and is of great value in small rural districts; but in the large towns it is a mere shadow of a name'.[19]

In 1851 Joseph Wigram, Archdeacon of Winchester, drew up a report on 'The Spiritual Necessities of Portsea' in which he stated that 'the deficiency in the spiritual provision of Portsea has long excited painful feelings in the minds of those to whom its real state was known'.[20] He noted that 'for the population of the parish of Portsea, now containing about 50,000 souls ... there are not more than ten clergy, inadequately remunerated',[21] and that the island of Portsea contained 596 drinking houses with accommodation for 24,000 'while in Churches and Chapels together it does not much exceed that for 12,000'.[22] His suggested solution to this problem that four new churches costing £3,000 each should be built[23] seems inadequate, to say the least.

Later in the century Evangelicals were still acutely aware of the inadequacy of the parochial system to grapple with the huge influx of population who were moving into the towns and cities. Anthony Thorold wrote in 1874, 'In our large towns, if the parochial system is not supplemented by missionary enterprise, whether occasional or permanent, it must hopelessly and ignominiously fail.'[24]

Bishop Ryle was strongly of the view that the parochial system was not sacrosanct. In 1883 he declared:

> The Church of England has made an idol of her parochial system and has forgotten that it has weak points as well as strong ones, defects as well as advantages. To hear some men talk, you might fancy the parochial system came down from heaven, like the pattern of a Mosaic tabernacle, and that to attempt another sort of ministry but a parochial one was

---

[19] *Hansard* CXXXIX, p. 500, cited by Inglis, *Churches and Working Classes*, p. 25.

[20] J.C. Wigram, *A Letter on the Spiritual Necessities of Portsea Within and Without the Walls Addressed to the Principal Inhabitants of the Town and its Vicinity*, p. 11.

[21] Ibid., p. 11.

[22] Ibid., pp. 12–13.

[23] Ibid., p. 14.

[24] A.W. Thorold, *Parochial Missions*, p. 5.

a heresy and a sin. It is high time that we should change our tune and humbly acknowledge our mistake.[25]

One of Ryle's particular criticisms of the parochial system was that where the minister of the parish is ignorant of the gospel, 'it is absurd to expect the head of a family to endanger the souls of his children, as well as his own, for the sake of parochial order'.[26] He concluded, 'There is no mention of parishes in the Bible, and we have no right to require men to live and die in ignorance, in order that they may be able to say at last, "I always attended my parish church".'[27] At the close of the century, the Vicar of Selhurst noted in his visitation return that 'parochial boundaries are little recognised or even observed by many, all over Croydon, except as regards the very poor and that mainly for relief purposes, the congregational system has superseded the parochial.'[28]

The tragedy of the situation was that the only class for whom the parochial system had by that time any meaning at all, namely the urban poor, were alienated from the established church. In the countryside the poor had for the most part rebelled against the oppression of the squire and farmers. In the towns and cities, the sheer numbers of people who crowded into the parishes meant that, for the vast majority, there was scant hope of any contact with the parish clergyman.[29] There can be little doubt that though many Evangelical clergy worked with great dedication, their uncritical acceptance of the parochial system was a significant factor in their failure to make a more significant Christian impact among the poor.

District Churches and Proprietary Chapels

In the densely populated urban areas Evangelicals tried a number of methods to supplement the inadequacy of the worship of the parish church. These included district churches, proprietary chapels, mission halls and the licensing of schoolrooms for public worship.

---

[25] Ryle, *Can They be Brought In?*, p. 28, cited by Farley, *Ryle*, p. 110.
[26] Ryle, *Knots Untied*, p. 375.
[27] Ibid., pp. 375–6.
[28] J. Morris, *Religion in Urban Croydon 1840–1914*, pp. 49f.
[29] For the problems of an urban parish in Victorian England see Wickham, *Church and People in An Industrial City*.

The advantage of the schoolroom and the mission hall was that the Church of England liturgy could be adapted or omitted altogether.

Until 1843 no new Church of England parish could be established without an Act of Parliament. This meant that to subdivide large industrial parishes into smaller ones was often a slow and lengthy process. Most incumbents therefore sought to circumvent the difficulty by building district churches and appointing a clergyman to be responsible for organising the worship and for pastoring and caring for the people in his area. Some of these district churches were financed by the Church Building Act of 1818, which made a grant of £1,000,000 available for the building of new churches. After twelve years, 134 new churches had been built. The eventual total exceeded 300 new places of worship.[30]

Thomas Sutton, who was a strong Evangelical churchman and Rector of Sheffield, was one of a number of prominent Evangelical clergy who supervised the building of district churches within the bounds of his parish. The 1821 decennial census gave the population of the parish of Sheffield as 65,275. At that time there were three Church of England churches which between them had only 300 seats for the poor. Feelings of great hostility were expressed against the pew holders who, according to a complainant at the vestry meeting in 1819, 'have excluded the rest of the parishioners from the use of the church and claim an absolute right to their pews'.[31] Four 'million churches'[32] were built within the parish of Sheffield; St George's in 1825 with 2, 240 sittings, of which 1,000 were free, Christ Church, Attercliffe, in 1826 with 1,304 sittings, of which 448 were free, St Philip's in 1828 with 1,755 sittings, of which 629 were free, and St Mary's in 1830 with 2,000 sittings, of which 800 were free. Sutton appointed clergy who shared his theological outlook and this endeared them to the many Nonconformists in the town and prevented a good deal of rivalry. Their salaries were paid for by the income raised from pew rents.

The Church of England went on to make a remarkable recovery in Sheffield under Sutton's leadership. By 1851 there were twenty-three places of worship with a total attendance of 14,881. However, it should be said that the great majority of this number were

---

[30] Soloway, *Prelates and People*, p. 291.
[31] Cited by Wickham, *Church and People in An Industrial City*, p. 71.
[32] Churches which were built with funds made available from £1,000,000 grant by the Church Building Act of 1818 were often referred to as 'million churches'.

drawn from ranks of the more prosperous elements of society. 'Criticus', a journalist with the *Sheffield Post*, made a number of visits to Church of England places of worship in the town between 1869 and 1875. The reader gets the impression from his comments that the established church in Sheffield was largely middle class in orientation. On a Sunday at the parish church in 1869, Criticus found about 600 people besides children. 'The congregation', he observed were 'highly respectable' and 'comprised many of the best families'.[33] At St Paul's in the centre of town '800 were present in the morning and 1,200 at night, almost solidly middle-class.'[34]

Part of the reason for the absence of the poor, it was suggested by J.C. Symons, was that they felt out of place in the elegant Gothic-style buildings that had only recently been erected. Symons, one of the district church clergy, wrote, 'The grandeur of our churches and the free sittings being in the aisles, made many feel more than they otherwise would do, the shabbiness of their clothes as a hindrance'.[35] John Livesy, the clergyman in charge of St Phillips Church, gave further illustration of the reasons for the alienation of the lower classes. In a letter to Sir Robert Peel, Livesy stated that 'subordination of ranks is a divine institution and should be observed in church'.[36]

The provision of district churches and the subdivision of a large parish church, as had taken place in Sheffield, was replicated in many other places. The large parish of Birmingham was subdivided on the arrival of the new young rector, the Rev Thomas Moseley. One of those who became an assistant minister to Moseley was the Rev William Marsh, who took charge of the newly consecrated church of St Thomas where to the Chartists and other radicals he became known as 'millennial Marsh'.[37] He acquired this name on account of his strongly expressed belief in the coming millennium, which the uninstructed radicals and Chartists of the area took to be the 'golden age' that they had been led to expect. In 1827 Joseph Wigram went to work in the parish of St James, Piccadilly, as the

---

[33] Wickham, *Church and People in An Industrial City*, p. 144.

[34] Ibid., p. 144.

[35] Ibid., p. 90.

[36] John Livesy, Letter to Sir Robert Peel, *Local Pamphlets* Vol. 103. Sheffield Library, in Wickham, *Church and People in An Industrial City*, p. 87.

[37] Marsh, *William Marsh*, pp. 143–66.

clergyman in charge of the district church of St Luke, Berwick Street.[38] In a visitation sermon preached some years later, Wigram described in some detail how the parish was divided into six districts, under as many resident clergymen; and, again, these districts into rather more than sixty parts for visiting the poor. 'The division of the work was', according to Wigram, 'the secret of such strength as we had.'[39]

Proprietary chapels were another popular means by which Evangelicals sought to cope with the increase of population. John Overton observed that proprietary chapels were 'strongholds of the Evangelicals'.[40] Although they were to all intents and purposes virtually private chapels, bishops were for the most part content to allow them to be built as a way of coping with the rapidly-expanding population at a time when the law made it very difficult to form new parishes. Proprietary chapels were not consecrated and they had no parochial districts attached to them. Their clergy were not permitted to perform baptisms, marriages and burials. The lay proprietors were allowed to appoint their own minister, although a later Act directed that after forty years the patronage devolved back to the incumbent of the parish in which the chapel was situated. The majority of proprietary chapels were erected in the populous parishes in the larger towns and cities. In London a considerable number of proprietary chapels were built, most of them in the later years of the eighteenth century and the first quarter of the nineteenth century. According to the *New Picture of London* there were fifty-nine in London in 1824.[41] W.H. Proby suggested that at the highest point there were more than 200 in the country as a whole. By the second half of the nineteenth century the majority of proprietary chapels had either become parish churches or been granted a conventional district.

Among the more prominent proprietary chapels in London were St John's Bedford Row, which became well-known under the ministry of Richard Cecil (1780–1808), and Bentinck Chapel

---

[38] For details of his ministry at St Luke's Berwick Street, see J.C. Wigram, *Ministerial Watchfulness: A Sermon Preached at the Visitation of the Rt Rev The Lord Bishop of Winchester in the Parish Church of Alton on Friday 17th October 1845*.

[39] Ibid., p. 27.

[40] Overton, *English Church*, p. 148.

[41] *New Picture of London*, cited by Baring-Gould, *Evangelical Revival*, p. 319.

close to the Edgware Road, where Basil Woodd (1785–1831)[42] encouraged his wealthy congregation to give generously to worthy causes.[43] Lock Hospital chapel, which admitted both seat holders and patients, had been founded by the Evangelical, Martin Madan, who also ministered there for a number of years before being succeeded by Thomas Scott, Newton's spiritual son, and then by Thomas Haweis (1734–1820).

Where proprietary chapels were well managed – as, for example, St Mary's, Brighton, where Henry Venn Elliott (1792–1865) was incumbent from 1827 until his death in 1865 – the system worked well. However, in many instances, Evangelical clergy were not always fully aware of the weaknesses of the system. For example, speculative clergy who hoped to attract a paying congregation erected some chapels. The *Christian Remembrancer* of November 1842 reported on one proprietary chapel that after paying all expenses cleared the minister £400 a year.[44] Such chapels often had the effect of drawing people away from their local parish church. The majority, however, were built by lay speculators, such as Sherrick, the wine merchant, who had his cellars under the chapel.[45] Members who enjoyed the ministry of the chaplain were supposed to purchase their liquor from Sherrick![46]

Another weakness of proprietary chapels was that they depended to a large extent on income from pew rents. This inevitably meant that there was little chance of ministering to the poor in any significant numbers. Had the attendees at proprietary chapels given their money and time to their parish churches, there would have been much greater support to supplying the wants of the parochial clergy. Proprietary chapels also had the effect of drawing out of the parochial ministry some of the more able clergy. Many Evangelicals were shocked to find that the proprietary system was condemned by their own periodical, the *Christian Observer*, in 1829. 'The proprietary chapel system', it declared, 'is utterly at variance with clerical efficiency and parochial instruction.'[47]

---

[42] For Basil Woodd see S.C. Wilks, 'Memoir of the Rev Basil Woodd, late Rector of Drayton Beauchamp and Minister of Bentinck Chapel', *The Christian Observer*, 1831.

[43] Balleine, *History of the Evangelical Party*, p. 61.

[44] Baring-Gould, *Evangelical Revival*, p. 319.

[45] Ibid., p. 319.

[46] Ibid., p. 319.

[47] Overton, *English Church*, p. 148.

Evangelical clergy also sought to supplement the work of their parish by promoting mission halls. Some of these buildings were erected in connection with major inter-denominational mission organisations, such as the LCM. Others were independent or specifically Anglican. At the end of the nineteenth century, Charles Booth noted in his social survey of the nation's capital, 'We find London dotted over with buildings devoted to this work. In the poorer parts especially, in almost every street, there is a mission; they are more numerous than schools or churches, and only less numerous than public houses.'[48] Anglican Evangelicals also actively supported a number of the inter-denominational missions. For example, the Seventh Earl of Shaftesbury was an active supporter of the LCM[49] and the Rev William Pennefather laboured on behalf of several mission societies.[50] Agnes Weston developed sailors' rest homes where young sailors were welcomed into hostel accommodation and encouraged to take temperance pledges.[51] Anthony Thorold, when he was Rector of the parish of St Giles in London, had several Anglican mission rooms, the largest of which had 200 worshippers.[52] Typical of many others, Francis Close established a mission church at the lower end of the High Street in the parish of Cheltenham, specifically to cater for the needs of the poor. Bishop Ryle was a strong advocate of mission rooms in the diocese of Liverpool. They could, he pointed out, be built at a quarter of the cost of a church and had the advantage that non-liturgical services could be held in them. 'The amount of work done from these shabby centres', wrote Charles Booth, 'is, however, in the aggregate enormous.'[53]

The mission halls that Evangelical Anglican clergy either supported or set up were an important means of missionary outreach. Additionally, many missions were effective agents of moral and philanthropic work. One positive outcome from their endeavours was the growing use of laymen and women. The layman could read part

---

[48] C. Booth, *Life and Labour of the People in London* Vol. 7, p. 270, cited by Lewis, *Lighten Their Darkness*, p. 275, and by Heasman, *Evangelicals in Action*, p. 30.

[49] Hodder, *Life and Work of Lord Shaftesbury*, p. 686.

[50] Heasman, *Evangelicals in Action*, pp. 38, 116, 260.

[51] See D. Gulliver, *Dame Agnes Weston*; see also E.A. Weston, *My Life Among the Blue Jackets*.

[52] Simpkinson, *Bishop Thorold*, p. 38.

[53] Booth, *Life and Labour*, p. 273.

of the Anglican liturgy or, in the case of an inter-denominational mission hall, be given free rein to preach and lead an entire service. On the negative side, the mission-hall movement was, as Donald Lewis pointed out, an admission that the churches were themselves the preserve of the middle classes.[54]

A number of forward-thinking Evangelicals also recognised the value of the school as a place of worship. John Bird Sumner anticipated the later nineteenth-century Roman Catholics because he recognised that a school building was often of greater value since it could meet the needs of both worship and education. Sumner impressed upon his Chester clergy the importance of this latter function: 'It [a schoolroom] is sometimes hardly inferior to a church. The stranger to the church is more likely to enter it than a church. The poor who are unwilling to exhibit their poverty and rags in a church might well enter a schoolroom.'[55]

The Use of Laity in the Parish

One of the things which the Evangelical clergy had learned from John Wesley and the Methodists was the great value of utilising lay-men and laywomen to assist in pastoral visiting, Scripture reading and evangelism. Following the lead given by John and Charles Sumner, Evangelical bishops urged their clergy in the matter and Evangelical societies, such as the CPAS, the LCM and the Church Army, raised money to train, support and organise full-time workers in the parishes.

In addition to being impressed by the impact of Methodist local preachers, John Sumner would undoubtedly have witnessed the powerful oratory of many of the Chartist and Owenite speakers who were active in parts of his diocese. If laymen could prove so effective in the cause of radicalism, they could undoubtedly be harnessed in the service of Christ. Sumner was also impressed with Thomas Chalmers' use of lay-helpers in the work of his Glasgow parish. He also drew the attention of his clergy to the 'large and populous town of Brighton'. 'This', he pointed out, 'had for some years been divided into six districts ... and has visitors regularly appointed ... some males but chiefly females.'[56] Sumner first

[54] Lewis, *Lighten Their Darkness*, p. 275.
[55] J.B. Sumner, *A Charge 1838*, p. 32.
[56] J.B. Sumner, *A Charge 1829*, p. 32.

mooted the possibility of lay-helpers and visitors in his episcopal charge of 1829. Having remarked on the very large size of parishes, Sumner declared it was not for the strength of activity of the clergy alone to provide what was necessary. He went on to remind them that in the early church there were those who were not commissioned to preach as apostles, but who were, nevertheless, associated in that task. Sumner came to the point by applying this situation to the Chester diocese:

> Let the minister of a populous district, using careful discrimination of character, select such as 'are worthy' and 'of good report', and assign them their several employments under his direction: they may lessen his own labour by visiting and examining the schools, by reading and praying with the infirm and aged, by consoling the fatherless and widows in their affliction.[57]

Sumner established the Chester Visiting Society, which provided visitors who would bring care to the needy and read and explain the Scriptures. In many ways, Sumner was a forward-thinking bishop and in this matter he anticipated the two great home missionary societies, the CPAS and the LCM.

David Nasmith and two friends who met with him in his small house in Canning Terrace established the LCM on 16 May 1835. Nasmith later recorded, 'After prayer we three founded LCM, adopted our constitution, assigned offices to each other, and after laying the infant mission before the Lord, desiring that He would nurse and bless it, and make it a blessing to tens of thousands, we adjourned.'[58]

Fortuitously, Nasmith's initiative coincided with the publication of an influential pamphlet by the Rev Baptist Noel, then a leading London Evangelical clergyman. Entitled *The State of the Metropolis Considered*, it made a rigorous plea for hard hitting means to be used in the efforts to evangelise the poor.[59] Noel proposed a whole range of measures which included rigorous house to house visitation, the subdivision of large parishes, the building of proprietary chapels, Episcopal approval for services in unlicensed rooms, greater use of the laity and open-air preaching.

---

[57] Ibid., p. 21.
[58] Hodder, *Life and Work of Lord Shaftesbury*, p. 61.
[59] Lewis, *Lighten Their Darkness*, p. 49.

LCM struggled in the early years of its existence, but managed to survive thanks to the support of Evangelical churchmen.[60] Prominent among them were Baptist Noel, Thomas Fowell Buxton and the Rev John Garwood, who became secretary of the society. Lord Ashley was also involved with the society from its early days.[61] The society divided London into districts each of which had a superintendent whose role was to be responsible for the missionaries in his area. Those selected and trained were working-class men. Often they were assigned to a certain number of streets or to particular groups of people such as cabmen, postmen, or policemen.

Generally speaking, Evangelical Anglican clergy were reluctant to give their wholehearted support to LCM, though a number of Recordite laymen did so. One obvious problem faced by Anglican clergy was that LCM did not feel itself constrained by parochial boundaries.[62] *The Record* nevertheless declared that 'the dangers of infringing on Church discipline and order' was outweighed by 'the gigantic good' of evangelising the poor.[63] However, Donald Lewis pointed out that the LCM's ability to transcend the parochial plan of the established church was part of its appeal to a number of Evangelical Anglicans. At an early point in the LCM's development, Noel resigned his membership on the grounds that too few Anglicans were being employed as agents and that LCM was in danger of becoming a dissenting institution. He felt that LCM had only managed to prosper because of Anglican support. At this point, Nasmith withdrew and the LCM was reorganised with a committee, which was composed of an equal number of churchmen and Nonconformists.[64] The society engaged in a number of campaigns and projects. It visited 35,393 families, about one third of whom were without the Scriptures and were happy to receive a copy of the New Testament.[65] In 1839 they began to stand against Fairlop Fair, which managed to attract 70,000 people over a Sunday. The society's agents observed 'one hundred and seven drinking-booths, seventy-two gambling tables, and about twelve brothels'.[66]

---

[60] Ibid., pp. 56–7.
[61] Hodder, *Life and Work of Lord Shaftesbury*, p. 61.
[62] Lewis, *Lighten Their Darkness*, p. 54.
[63] *The Record*, 14 December 1855, cited by Lewis, *Lighten Their Darkness*, p. 53.
[64] Lewis, *Lighten Their Darkness*, p. 57.
[65] Ibid., p. 60.
[66] *LCM Magazine*, October 1839, cited by Lewis, *Lighten Their Darkness*, p. 65.

In order to meet the more specific needs of women, Mrs Ellen Ranyard founded the London Bible and Domestic Female Mission in 1857 or, as it came to be known, the Ranyard Bible Mission. Although the society was pan-Evangelical, Anglicans clearly predominated. Ranyard's original intention was that they should avoid engaging in social work, but most of her Bible women found it unavoidable. Thus, certain times were set aside for evangelistic work and others for giving material help. Mrs Ranyard received strong support through her friendships with Lord Shaftesbury, Bishop Anthony Thorold, the Kinnairds and the Pennefathers.[67] In 1859 the organisation of the Ranyard Bible Mission was considerably strengthened and the number of 'Bible women' rose from only thirty-five in 1859 to 137 by the end of the following year.[68] Its work was also greatly helped by the BFBS's provision of free grants of Bibles and Testaments.

Ranyard later extended the scope of her work by training some of her women as itinerant nurses in the wards of Guy's Hospital. Ellen Ranyard did much by writing and personal contact to encourage others to follow her methods. A number of similar organisations soon sprang up, such as the Church of England Parochial Mission Women's Association in 1860, but she made no attempt to link up their work with hers.

By the early 1830s Evangelical Anglicans were much divided over the best strategy for evangelising the poor. A number of Recordite laymen were of the view that a specifically Anglican Society that employed full-time lay-agents was vitally necessary. If necessary, they were prepared to ignore canon law and take independent action despite the opposition of the Evangelical clergy. Among their number was a small group of Islington laymen led by Frederick Sandoz who inserted a paragraph in *The Record* of 12 March 1835 calling attention to the need for a Church Home Missionary Society.[69] CPAS was formed 'for the purpose of benefiting the population of our own country by increasing the number of working clergymen in the Church of England, and encouraging the appointment of pious and discreet laymen as helpers to the clergy in duties not ministerial'[70] at a meeting held in the committee room of the CMS on 19 February 1836.

---

[67] See Heasman, *Evangelicals in Action*, p. 37, and Hodder, *Life and Work of Lord Shaftesbury*, p. 711.
[68] Lewis, *Lighten Their Darkness*, p. 221.
[69] Balleine, *History of the Evangelical Party*, p. 176.
[70] Hodder, *Life and Work of Lord Shaftesbury*, p. 113.

There was considerable contention over the ways in which the society proposed to employ its lay-agents. Some, including William Carus and Edward Bickersteth, were opposed to the introduction into the church of a new and distinct order of lay-teachers. Eventually, the decision was taken to modify their objectives and the following resolution was made: 'The Society will assist, as it may be able, in the supply of destitute places of lay agents, whether candidates for holy orders or others.' It was also resolved that lay agents should act 'under the direction of the incumbent, and be removed at his pleasure'.[71]

CPAS, which was strongly supported by bishops such as John Sumner[72] and Montagu Villiers,[73] grew steadily. By 1900 it was spending £66,000 and helping 656 ill-endowed parishes.[74] LCM also continued to expand till almost the end of the century. It reached a high point in 1890 when its income was £54,129 and it had 461 agents in the field.[75]

There were other important lay societies that operated in the parishes. As has been noted in chapter 3, many were primarily engaged in social work. Two other organisations that concerned themselves with evangelism were the Scripture Readers' Association and the Church Army.

The Scripture Readers' Association, which was founded in 1844, changed its name to the Church of England Scripture Readers' Association in 1849. It was organised by a committee that comprised of Evangelical laymen, which guaranteed the character and theology of the agents that it employed. The backing of Bishop Charles Blomfield of London and Bishop Sumner of Winchester strengthened the society, although their support resulted in some restrictions being placed on the Scripture Readers' Association's activities. The association prospered and in 1885 had an income of £12,312 with 126 agents in the parishes.[76]

Wilson Carlisle (1847–1942) founded the Church Army in 1882. He had been challenged by the effectiveness of William Booth's recently established Salvation Army and copied some of their methods. Carlisle was also doubtless aware of the Church

---

[71] Ibid., p. 113.
[72] Balleine, *History of the Evangelical Party*, p. 196.
[73] Villiers, *A Charge 1858*, p. 28.
[74] Inglis, *Churches and Working Classes*, p. 38.
[75] Lewis, *Lighten Their Darkness*, Appendix C.
[76] Ibid., Appendix C.

Gospel Army, which Evan Hopkins had begun in his parish of Holy Trinity, Richmond. Carlisle had served as deputy harmonium player[77] in D.L. Moody's London Campaign of 1875 and, like Booth, he was very aware of the power of music. When Moody and Sankey left London, Carlisle kept their choir together and with it arranged various missions in tents and halls in different parts of London.[78] Having worked for eleven years in a bank, he began training for the ministry at the London College of Divinity in 1878 and was ordained in 1880 as one of several curates at St Mary Abbot's, Kensington, under the Rev Carr Glyn. Here, fully supported by his vicar, he engaged in open-air preaching and trained lay-preachers to assist him in the work. This became the basis of the Church Army. Carlisle had early successes at Walworth and in Westminster where he also encountered a good deal of opposition. At the same time as the Westminster Mission, he began editing *Battle Axe*, which was published at a halfpenny a copy. It grew in popularity and in 1884 its name was changed to *The Church Army Gazette*.[79]

The Church Army was not sectarian. It operated as an integral part of the Church of England. Its officers were required to 'strive to keep their baptismal and Confirmation vows ... be regular and devout in the study of God's Holy Word, and in their attendance at Holy Communion'.[80] They were also to abstain from alcoholic drinks as beverages.[81] A training college was set up for men in 1883 at Oxford. The college was later moved to London. A college for women was opened in 1887.[82]

In spite of criticism from some quarters within the church,[83] and opposition from those outside,[84] the Church Army continued to expand. By 1891 there were 166 officer-evangelists and forty-four mission nurses, and about 40,000 meetings were held each year.[85] The first Church Army Labour Home in Marylebone, London, which provided food, accommodation and work for the very poor

---

[77] Dark, *Wilson Carlisle*, p. 43.

[78] Ibid., p. 44.

[79] Ibid., pp. 60–1.

[80] Ibid., p. 67.

[81] Ibid., p. 67.

[82] Ibid., pp. 64, 126.

[83] See Inglis, *Churches and Working Classes*, p. 45.

[84] Dark, *Wilson Carlisle*, p. 63.

[85] Hylson-Smith, *Evangelicals in the Church of England*, p. 181.

was opened in 1889. In 1895 the Army acquired a farm in Surrey and two years later Church Army sisters began working with destitute girls. By 1900 it had an income of £110,000, a troop of sixty-five vans manned by travelling evangelists, and more than 600 evangelists and nurses helping the parochial clergy.

In view of the impact made by laymen and laywomen in the parishes, it is not surprising that, in the later years of the nineteenth century, Evangelical bishops were strong advocates of their ministry. When Montagu Villiers became Bishop of Carlisle he supported an initiative to put a Scripture Readers' Association members in every market town in the diocese.[86] At his primary visitation of the diocese of Rochester, Joseph Wigram urged 'the aid and co-operation of the laity in tilling the vineyard of the Lord, and bringing souls into the folds of Christ'.[87]

Parochial Missions

Around the middle of the nineteenth century Evangelical Anglicans began to organise evangelistic missions in their parishes and sometimes in connection with others in their town or city. These missions usually consisted of a week of special services with a particular guest speaker. Some of these endeavours were linked with revivalist and holiness meetings (see chapter 11). One of the first such missions to be held was organised by John Cale Miller in Birmingham in 1856. Miller was also credited with reviving the practice of open air preaching. The idea of parochial missions developed more widely in the 1880s, particularly under the influence of the Baptist, Charles Spurgeon, and the campaigns of Moody and Sankey.

The later-Victorian years also saw the emergence of full-time Church of England Evangelists. Parochial missions often involved extensive visiting campaigns with people going from house to house with invitations to the meetings. When, for example, Anthony Thorold was at St Pancras, London, he organised a mission in his parish with the principal object being, 'the personal conversion to God of each worshipper'.[88] There was a large attendance on the part of the working classes, many of whom 'had not

---

[86] Munden, 'First Palmerston Bishop', p. 200.
[87] *The Chelmsford Chronicle*, 23 November 1860.
[88] Simpkinson, *Bishop Thorold*, p. 58.

been inside a place of worship for many years'.[89] This success
Thorold put down to eighty volunteers who made it their business
'to go out into their districts distributing invitations to the
services'.[90] Thorold conducted a mission at York in November
1871 and another at Oakley Square in December.[91] He was himself a committed Evangelist and published a small volume entitled
Parochial Missions in 1874.[92] In the introduction he wrote in
praise of the proposed London mission on account of its being
inaugurated by the bishops.[93] The essential features of a mission,
as Thorold saw it, were four: 'The weekday evening service, the
main point of which is the sermon. The after meeting ... Private
conference between the mission preacher and anxious inquirers ...
celebrations of the Holy Communion on the first and last Sundays
of the mission week.'[94] He also had some very practical advice for
organisers. For example, he urged that the missioner needs to be
'well-fed' with 'punctual meals' and that fasting during a mission
is a mistake because it results in the loss of much needed physical
energy.[95] Thorold had clearly learned the value of publicity from
the campaigns by American Evangelists. 'Money', he wrote, 'can
hardly be better spent than on printing.'[96]

A number of bishops were strong advocates of parochial missions.
Robert Bickersteth achieved a reputation for being a 'preaching
prelate' and on two occasions in 1875 and 1883 he assisted in
town-wide missions in Leeds.[97] Archbishop William Thomson took
part in three Sheffield missions which were held in 1872, 1876
and 1883.[98] His very close friend, Anthony Thorold, did all he could
to foster evangelistic missions in his Rochester diocese,[99] as did John
Ryle at Liverpool.[100] In fact, one of the last tracts Ryle wrote was
entitled *Thought about a Mission* and was published in 1890.

---

[89] Ibid., p. 59.
[90] Ibid., p. 59.
[91] Ibid., p. 60.
[92] Thorold, *Parochial Missions*.
[93] Ibid., p. 2.
[94] Ibid., p. 16.
[95] Ibid., p. 43.
[96] Ibid. p. 43.
[97] M.C. Bickersteth, *Robert Bickersteth*, p. 250.
[98] Kirk-Smith, *William Thomson*, p. 107.
[99] Simpkinson, *Bishop Thorold*, p. 168.
[100] Farley, *Ryle*, p. 119.

Ryle promoted organised missions within the Church of England wherever the opportunity arose and he was himself a frequent mission speaker. In January and February 1894 he organised a city-wide mission in Liverpool in which seventy-three churches participated and benefits of which were still felt thirty years later.[101]

A number of clergy shared John Miller's enthusiasm for open-air preaching. Among them were J.H. Titcomb, incumbent of St Andrew-the-less, Barnwell, Cambridge,[102] and Hugh McNeile, of St Judes, Liverpool, who was on one occasion prevented from preaching outside the city's Corn Exchange. W.E. Long of St Paul's, Bermondsey, held open-air services for some years in London.[103] Charles Sumner recommended open-air preaching in his charge to the clergy of the Diocese of Winchester in 1858.[104] This emerging interest in open-air preaching reflected a growing concern on the part of the Church of England as a whole to reach the working classes with the gospel.

Some Prominent Evangelical Parochial Successes

The anonymous writer of an article in *Macmillan's Magazine* felt compelled to acknowledge that one of the great strengths of the Evangelical party was the seriousness with which they undertook their parish work. He wrote:

> the Evangelical clergy as a body are indefatigable in ministerial duties, and devoted heart and soul to the manifold labours of Christian love. When the history of the Evangelical Party is written, it will be told of them that ... they yet worked manfully in the pestilent and heathen by-ways of our cities, and preached the gospel to the poor.[105]

There were many clergy whose dedicated pastoral work bore out this assertion. One among them, John Venn, came from true Evangelical stock, his grandfather, Henry Venn, having been Vicar of

[101] Ibid., pp. 119–20.

[102] *The Record*, 3 July 1857, cited by Bentley, *Transformation of the Evangelical Party*, p. 231.

[103] Hardman, *Evangelical Party*.

[104] C.R. Sumner, *Church Progress: A Charge*, pp. 46–7.

[105] Anon, 'The English Evangelical Clergy', *Macmillan's Magazine*, December 1860, cited by Balleine, *History of the Evangelical Party*, pp. 236–7.

Huddersfield and his father, John, having been Rector of Clapham. He became Vicar of St Peter's, Hereford, in 1833, an appointment that had 'given general satisfaction'.[106] During his long ministry in the city Venn demonstrated a genuine and energetic concern for the poor. He worked hard on behalf of the Sunday school, which had nearly three hundred pupils. The winter months at the beginning of 1839 were particularly severe and Venn organised a meeting to consider ways of relieving the poor in the parish. In January 1841 bread and coal were distributed throughout the city. Venn organised a Loan Society in 1841 in conjunction with the city mayor.[107] A coal department was set up and a yard rented at £8 per annum. 347 tons were sold at lower prices to the poor during the first winter of its operation. A mill, which ground cheap corn at cost price for the working classes, was established in 1846. Venn, it should be said, was no paternalist. This was clear from the stated aim of The Industrious Society of which he was founder: 'That the truest charity is that which enables the working man to maintain himself and his family in comfort and independence by his own industry.'[108] The total attendance at St Peter's on the Sunday of the 1851 Census was 2,400.[109]

Edward Foley was for twenty-three years Vicar of All Saints, Derby, from 1849 to 1872. During that time he gave himself unstintingly to educational concerns, most notably the ragged school, the Sunday school and the day schools. During his incumbency, three 'efficient schools' were built to replace two inefficient dame schools and a parochial library containing more than 1,000 volumes was also opened. Foley was deeply involved in many practical schemes including the improvement of water supply, the upgrading of the infirmary, the erection of The Midland Institution for the Blind at Nottingham and the Home for Penitent Females in Bass Street. Foley was an active member of the Derby School Board and Chaplain to the First Derby Militia. In addition, he was a faithful and conscientious pastor who preached 'with zeal and earnestness'.[110]

Thomas Sutton (1777–1851) was appointed to the living at Sheffield after having come under the influence of Charles Simeon of

---

[106] *Hereford Journal*, 15 June 1833.

[107] *Hereford Journal*, 10 March 1841.

[108] Information taken from J. Guise, *John Venn of Hereford 1802–1890: The Dilemmas of an Evangelical in a Cathedral City*, p. 90.

[109] Ibid., p. 62.

[110] See *The Derby Mercury*, 10 April 1872.

Cambridge. This resulted in him becoming a committed and devoted Evangelical. He was very active in the life and work of the huge parish, which encompassed the entire town. In order to exercise more effective pastoral care and evangelism, a number of district churches were built with pastoral responsibility for their surrounding localities. Sutton appointed their clergy and chose men who shared his views. He was constantly active in the work of charity. He supported the infirmary and was a founder member of the dispensary. When there was a severe outbreak of cholera in 1832, Sutton spared no effort as he visited the sick and raised money for the poor. He was a keen supporter of the BFBS and the CMS. He was also a staunch advocate of Christian education and believed that if the Government saw fit to bring in a system of national education, 'the reading of the Scriptures and instruction in the faith and duty of a Christian might be an essential and integral part of the system'.[111] In 1839 Sutton preached to the Chartists at their request from James 5:1–11 and he enjoyed good relations with the town's many Nonconformists. The *Sheffield and Rotherham Independent* were happy to affirm that, 'he was a good man, and full of the Holy Ghost and faith'.[112]

William Weldon Champneys was ordained in 1830 and served as a curate in Dorchester, Oxfordshire, and then at St Ebbe's in the city of Oxford where in his ministry to the poorest sections he made use of university students as visitors. In 1837 he became Vicar of St Mary's, Whitechapel, a parish of over 30,000 souls. It contained some of the worst slums in East London, and vice and crime were at a high level.[113]

Champneys was a fervent Evangelical and he soon gathered around him a group of lay-assistants and with their help the parish was systematically visited. Champneys was a man of grace and charm. He began to overcome the apathy which surrounded him through immense hard work and 'very simply preaching the gospel'. Champneys was, perhaps, 'the most effective slum clergyman of the mid-nineteenth century'. He held three plain but

---

[111] *Sheffield and Rotherham Independent*, 11 January 1851.

[112] *Sheffield and Rotherham Independent*, 11 January 1851; see also *Sheffield Free Press*, 14 January 1851.

[113] For fuller details of Champney's life and work see C. Bullock, 'Biographical Sketch', in *The Story of the Tent Maker*, W. Weldon Champneys; see also W.W. Champneys, *Parish Work: A Brief Manual for the Younger Clergy*.

cheerful services each Sunday in the parish church and, with assistance from the CPAS, three new district churches were built – St Paul's Dock Street, a church for sailors, St Mark's and St Jude's, which was financed by a West End congregation. Each was staffed with resident clergy. Day and Sunday schools were founded and a Young Men's Institute.[114] In addition, Mothers' Meetings and a Savings Bank, a Coal Club and Shoeblack Brigade were established. So successful were Champneys' labours that at the 1851 Census there were over 1,500 present at the morning service, 800 in the afternoon and more than 1,600 at night.[115] He was also a member of the Health of Towns Association and took an active role in seeking to improve the conditions of the area. There were three keys to his success: an emphasis on education; the extensive use of lay-visitors including LCM missionaries and Scripture Readers' Association members, of whom there were thirteen in 1853; and church planting.[116] In 1860 Champneys became Vicar of St Pancras parish church in London and was appointed Dean of Lichfield in 1867.

William Pennefather (1816–1873) was ordained priest in 1842 and was incumbent of churches in Aylesbury and Barnet where he began organising a conference for the promotion of deeper spiritual life. In 1864 he became Vicar of St Jude's, Mildmay Park, where he not only built a centre for his conferences, but also fought hard to minister to the social needs of his parish.[117] On his arrival he immediately resolved to erect an elementary school, which would provide education for the very poor, and to increase Sunday-school accommodation. The new conference centre also doubled up as a soup kitchen and dining centre for the poor. A second mission hall was constructed in 1863 and a curate or Scripture Reader always resided in the adjoining house.[118]

As was noted in the earlier chapter on social action, as a result of the cholera outbreak in 1866, Pennefather developed the Deaconess Training House, which he had established at Barnet in 1860, into a much larger institution based at Mildmay. It was patterned on the German model. The deaconesses were allotted to particular districts

[114] Balleine, *History of the Evangelical Party*, p. 238.
[115] Elliot-Binns, *Religion in the Victorian Era*, pp. 67–8.
[116] See J.B. Root, 'Champneys (William) Weldon' in Lewis (ed.), *Blackwell Dictionary of Evangelical Biography 1730–1860*.
[117] Braithwaite, *William Pennefather*, p. 391.
[118] Ibid., p. 401.

and visited and ministered to the sick.[119] Later, a small hospital and medical mission were established.[120] Pennefather preached a 'simple declaration of the truth as it is in Jesus' and with considerable power[121] to large congregations.[122] He had a great concern for working men, particularly cab drivers and navvies.[123]

William Cadman was curate to Montagu Villiers before becoming Vicar of St George's, Southwark, in 1852, a large slum parish of some 30,000 people. The very poor were for the most part housed in cramped courts that contained brothels and common lodging houses. On his arrival, church attendance was about twenty. Cadman divided the parish into six districts each with its own curate and helped by grants from the CPAS and assistance from the Scripture Readers' Association, as well as the LCM and the Ragged School Union, he recruited over 200 voluntary workers as district visitors. Every evening open-air services were held at the point where six roads met and attendances sometimes reached as many as a thousand. In 1856 the parish church, which had become overcrowded, was extended to take over 1,300 sittings and in 1857 the daughter church of St Paul's was opened.

Cadman moved to Holy Trinity, Marylebone, in 1859, where he remained until his death in 1891. This was an altogether different location and his new parish of 14,000 embraced the fashionable residences of Portland Place, Harley Street and Wimpole Street.[124]

Cheltenham was, perhaps, the most effective parish in a middle-class town parish outside London. Here, under the ministry of Francis Close, Charles Simeon found 'almost heaven on earth'.[125] After his ordination in 1821, Close was appointed as curate of

---

[119] Ibid., pp. 408–9.

[120] Ibid., p. 409.

[121] Ibid., p. 442.

[122] Ibid., p. 463.

[123] Ibid., pp. 467, 501.

[124] For Cadman see L.E. Shelford, *A Memoir of the Reverend William Cadman.*

[125] Hopkins, *Charles Simeon of Cambridge*, p. 210. Hopkins quotes Simeon: 'Here at Cheltenham I have almost heaven upon earth. The churches so capacious and so filled; the schools so large; so numerous, so beneficial; the people so full of love; the ministers such laborious and energetic men; and God so graciously with me in my exertions; in truth I can scarcely conceive any higher happiness on earth than I am now privileged to enjoy.'

Holy Trinity, Cheltenham. Then in 1826, following the untimely death of the incumbent of the parish church, Charles Jervis, Close was appointed to the living. He remained in the town for thirty years until his appointment to the Deanery of Carlisle in 1856.[126] Close was directly responsible for the building of four new churches, St Paul's in 1831, Christ Church in 1840, St Peter's in 1849 and St Luke's in 1854. Their clergy who were Close's appointees shared his strongly Protestant convictions.

Close was a strong advocate for education at all levels and in this field he has been acclaimed a minor national figure. He strengthened the existing Sunday school and built six day-schools in conjunction with the National Society. Close also reorganised the charity school in 1846 and overhauled the buildings of the town's Tudor grammar school. In 1843 Cheltenham College was opened for the sons of the middle classes, many of whom were settling in the town's new fashionable estates. With the growing Tractarian influence in the National Society, Close became concerned to train teachers with specifically Protestant convictions. This led to his founding in 1849 of the Cheltenham Training College on land donated by Miss Jane Cook. Its purpose was to train teachers with Evangelical and Protestant convictions.

Notwithstanding his strong conservatism, Close was concerned for the needs of the poor. He reorganised the Provident Society[127] and concerned himself with the building of the new hospital in Sandford Road which was opened in 1848.[128] After the cholera outbreak of 1832 Close helped to organise a better sewerage and drainage system for Cheltenham.[129] He divided the town into forty districts each with street visitors who were either businessmen or men of leisure. In this way, he kept in touch with the needs of the poor. In 1828 over 500 families were helped and a total of £360 was spent.[130] At one point in 1836, 200 women were being employed to make clothes for the poor.

---

[126] For Close's impact on the town see N.A.D. Scotland, 'Francis Close, "Cheltenham's Protestant Patriarch"', in J. Thrower (ed.), *Essays in Honour of Andrew Walls*, pp. 122–37.

[127] See A.F. Munden, 'Evangelical in the Shadows. Charles Jervis of Cheltenham', *Churchman* 96.2 (1982), pp. 142–51.

[128] Hart, *History of Cheltenham*, p. 235.

[129] *Cheltenham Parish Vestry Minutes*, 7 March 1833.

[130] G. Berwick, *Close of Cheltenham, Parish Pope: A Study in the Evangelical Background to the Oxford Movement*, chapter 6, p. 16.

Close attacked the theatre and preached against Cheltenham races in 1830.[131] So strong was his attack against 'the dissolute persons in attendance' that from 1831 to 1835 the meetings had to be transferred to Tewkesbury. Close was also a strict sabbatarian and he succeeded in persuading almost all the town's four hundred shopkeepers from trading on the Lord's Day. Close's dominance over the town and parish led to the poet Alfred Tennyson describing him as a 'pope'.[132] When he left the town in 1856 his opponents referred to his thirty-year rule as 'the Close season'.[133]

The list of nineteenth-century Evangelical clergy who ran their parishes to great effect is considerable. Charles Simeon, who was perpetual curate of Holy Trinity, Cambridge, from 1782 until his death in 1836 (1759–1836), was the great exemplar for all Evangelicals. Other influential figures included Hugh McNeile (1795–1879) at St Jude's, Liverpool;[134] Hugh Stowell (1799–1865) at Christ Church, Salford;[135] Daniel Wilson (1777–1858) at Islington; John Cale Miller (1814–1880), Vicar of St Martin's, Birmingham, from 1846 and Vicar of Greenwich from 1866; James Bardsley (1808–1886) at St Ann's, Manchester; Alfred Christopher (1820–1913), Rector of St Aldate's, Oxford, from 1859 to 1905;[136] James Flemming (1830–1908), Vicar of St Michael's, Chester Square, London, from 1874;[137] Edward Carr Glyn, Vicar of St Mary Abbots, Kensington; and William Marsh (1775–1864) at St Thomas, Birmingham, from 1829 to 1842.

Patronage

Charles Simeon (1759–1836) was perpetual curate of Holy Trinity, Cambridge, from 1782 until his death in 1836. In the long vacations at Cambridge, which were virtually four months, he toured England and Scotland preaching and spent time visiting and encouraging

---

[131] F. Close, *A Letter Addressed to the Inhabitants of Cheltenham on the Subject of the Races*, p. 6.
[132] Adams, *Memoirs of a Social Atom* Vol. 1, p. 23, n. 1. See also Close's obituary in *The Times*, 19 December 1882.
[133] Hart, *History of Cheltenham*, p. 200.
[134] Balleine, *History of the Evangelical Party*, p. 202–4.
[135] See Marsden, *Hugh Stowell*.
[136] See Reynolds, *Canon Christopher*.
[137] Finlayson, *Life of Canon Flemming*.

isolated Evangelicals. In order to secure the future for Evangelical parishes, Simeon began the practice of purchasing advowsons. His first acquisition was St Mary's, Cheltenham. By the time of his death in 1836 he had taken possession of twenty-one advowsons. By 1896 The Simeon Trust, which he had established in 1817, owned the advowsons of 150 livings. Among those purchased in his lifetime were Bath Abbey, Derby Parish Church and St Thomas and St Martin's, Liverpool. Simeon remarked of his trust that 'where others purchased income, I purchase spheres, wherein the prosperity of the Established Church ... may be advanced'.[138]

A critic writing in *Macmillan's Magazine* in 1860 stated that the 'Evangelical party is redeemed by the working of its parishes'.[139] Taken generally, Evangelical clergy were immensely hardworking and conscientious in their parishes, not only preaching the gospel message, but also engaging in a wide variety of educational and social endeavours, ranging from public health and fresh water supply to savings banks and local libraries. The problem for some was that, in the words of Owen Chadwick, they failed to recognise that 'a parochial system adapted to ministry in villages' was 'inflexible and unable to meet new circumstances'.[140] Those Evangelical clergy who were most effective were those who supplemented their existing parochial machinery with a variety of lay-agencies, mission halls, district churches and proprietary chapels, as well as promoting evangelistic and social reforming campaigns. Significantly, many of the most successful parochial incumbents also organised large visitation schemes with voluntary helpers managing particular districts.

---

[138] Carus, *Charles Simeon*, chapter 31.
[139] 'The English Clergy', *Macmillan's Magazine*, 3 December 1860.
[140] Chadwick, *Victorian Church* Part 2, p. 34.

16

The Shaping of an Age

It is not difficult to find dysfunctional aspects in any religious movement and the nineteenth-century Evangelicals are no exception. They were criticised both by their contemporaries, as well as by more recent writers. Sydney Smith, the literary commentator and author, made frequent jibes at the Clapham Sect.[1] Samuel Wilberforce denounced 'as wicked' some of Lord Palmerston's clerical appointments that had been prompted by Lord Shaftesbury.[2] Bishop Henry Phillpotts, the archetypal high church Bishop of Exeter, dealt some harsh blows to Evangelicals forcing them to wear the surplice at preaching services.[3] He further refused to institute George Gorham to the living of Brampford Speke because of the 'unsoundness' of his views on baptism.[4] Then, when the Privy Council decided against him, Phillpotts even went so far as to excommunicate John Sumner who, as Archbishop of Canterbury, arranged for the institution of Gorham against his wishes.[5] Among the harsher critics was Sabine Baring-Gould, rural incumbent and author of the hymn, 'Onward Christian Soldiers'. He criticised Evangelicals for swallowing whole Luther's doctrine of justification by faith,[6] for breeding sects such as the Plymouth Brethren and for their 'deficiency in learning' and their 'narrowness of view'.[7]

---

[1] A. Bell, *Sydney Smith*, p. 78.
[2] See Scotland, *Good and Proper Men*, p. 194.
[3] P.C. Hammond, *The Parson and the Victorian Parish*, p. 109.
[4] See N.A.D. Scotland, 'George Cornelius Gorham', in Lewis (ed.), *Blackwell Dictionary of Evangelical Biography 1730–1860*.
[5] Scotland, *John Bird Sumner*, p. 19.
[6] Baring-Gould, *Evangelical Revival*, p. 287.
[7] Ibid., p. 290.

The main weaknesses raised by the detractors of the Evangelicals were their intellectual narrowness, their other-worldly cultural horizons, particularly in the early years of the century, and their limited ecclesiology. Whether or not these criticisms were valid for Evangelical Anglicans as a whole, or were misconceptions based on a limited range of popular sources, is a question that may deserve further attention. As has been noted in earlier chapters, John Reynolds' study of Evangelicals at Oxford has demonstrated that Evangelicals produced a good number of 'firsts' in the university class lists. Additionally, they provided a number of Bampton lecturers.[8]

On the matter of Scripture, Evangelicals were late in making an intellectual defence of its authority and inspiration. In the early years of the century, their view was essentially that the *textus receptus* was a God-breathed volume that spoke infallibly on all matters of history, morals and science. There was, indeed, little attempt to recognise different genres of biblical writing and Evangelical interpretations of the biblical text regularly displayed a rigid literalism. This approach to Scripture was further reinforced by the Recordite campaigns on behalf of biblical inerrancy. By the same token, there was little or no attempt in the early decades to offer any kind of intellectual apologetic for the inspiration of the Bible.

All of this meant that most Evangelical Anglicans were less well equipped than some other sections of the established church to grapple with the challenges posed by Charles Darwin, *Essays and Reviews* and the writings of Bishop Colenso. It was not until William Thomson organised *Aids to Faith* as a riposte to *Essays and Reviews* that significant numbers of Evangelical clergy began to take on board the need for a more reasoned defence of biblical authority.

Not all of the nineteenth-century Evangelical clergy were rigid fundamentalists in their interpretation of Scripture. For example, Simeon, as has been noted, was not a literalist and Archbishop Sumner was clear that Genesis did not provide a scientific account of the origins of the universe.[9] By the turn of the century it had certainly become much more common place for Evangelicals to embrace at least some aspects of biblical criticism.

Evangelical ecclesiology was felt by many to be inadequate. Their strong emphasis on the invisible church meant that their attachment to the visible established Church of England was often

---

[8] Reynolds, *Evangelicals at Oxford*, pp. 28–30.
[9] Scotland, *John Bird Sumner*, p. 19.

limited or held to be of very secondary importance. Having said that, it is notable that the Evangelicals fought long and hard to preserve its Protestant foundations. Significantly, many of the Evangelical societies began with the word Church, for example, the Church Missionary Society and the Church Pastoral Aid Society. Victorian Evangelicals also did much through para-church organisations. However, it has been argued that they might have achieved a greater impact on politics and society if they had a stronger doctrine of the presence of Christ in the outward expression of the church.

It cannot seriously be claimed that the Evangelical party disregarded the sacraments; indeed, they were at the forefront of the movement for more frequent services of Holy Communion on Sundays. Nevertheless, high churchmen and Tractarians were of the opinion that the memorialist doctrine held by many Evangelicals was insufficient, and did not square with what they perceived to be the more Catholic view of the sacrament conveyed by the *Book of Common Prayer*.

The sacraments of baptism and, more particularly, Holy Communion became the focus of bitter controversy between the Anglo-Catholics and the Evangelicals. The latter clearly felt the rightness of their attack on those ritualistic practices which undermined the Reformed teaching of the Articles of Religion. However, the bitter court prosecutions promoted by the Church Association in the years following the passing of the Public Worship Regulation Act were perhaps a misjudgement of the situation. The resulting imprisonments of a number of Anglo-Catholics diverted many potential sympathisers away from Evangelical influence.[10]

In the matter of culture and the world beyond the confines of the church, there is no doubt that some Evangelicals, particularly in the earlier years of the century, adopted world-denying attitudes. They somehow lacked the confidence to see the material world and its pleasures in a positive and wholesome light. By the same token, many of their number found it hard to delight in the benefits of good books, fine arts and music. In some circles, even to have innocent fun was felt to be playing into the devil's hand.

These attitudes were well illustrated by Laura Ridding's impressions of her uncle, Samuel Waldegrave, the Bishop of Carlisle. She loved and respected him, but she could not tolerate his narrow view of the world. Hannah Baud noted that 'in the moral revolution

---

[10] N.A.D. Scotland, 'Evangelicals, Anglicans and Ritualism in Victorian England', *Churchman* 3.3 (1997), p. 264.

against untruth that he was fighting' Waldegrave would 'bowdlerize' Ridding's favourite Anderson tales. Indeed, Waldegrave went one step further and 'rewrote whole chunks of one of his niece's fairy stories, so that wherever the word "giant" appeared, it was amended to "the big man", "fairy" became "lady", "dwarf" became "little man" and "witch" was altered to "bad woman"'.[11] Laura found herself repelled by what she perceived as the Waldegraves' lack of interest in scholarly pursuits and their failure to enjoy times of celebration. She also noted with sadness that the Waldegrave influence banished playing cards from their home. Laura recognised that the Waldegraves represented Evangelicalism in its narrowest form but, nevertheless, their attitudes contributed to her turning away from her parents' convictions.

Numerous similar anecdotes of Evangelical narrowness could be cited but two further instances will have to suffice to carry the point. The *Saturday Review* of 29 December found it necessary to dub Joseph Wigram as 'a Bishop of Little Things' on account of his having denounced cricket, smoking and beards among the clergy during the course of his first charge to the diocese of Rochester.[12] He also warned of the dangers of dancing, cards and theatres.[13] The article concluded, 'Dr Wigram is at liberty to shave himself as closely as he pleases on the coldest mornings, but what right has he to pronounce from his episcopal throne the judgement that a beard is unseemly and marks the associate of fast young men?'[14] The feelings of Sir James Stephen whose father was a prominent member of the Clapham Sect resonated with the Waldegraves' attitude to life. He once smoked a cigar which he found so delicious that he never again smoked another.[15]

The narrowness of some sections of Evangelical Anglicanism was particularly visible in their sabbatarian attitudes. Not only were two and sometimes three Sunday services a requirement in many families, the rest of the day had to be endured without fun, games or relaxation. Shops were closed, as in the case of Cheltenham,[16] and Sunday bands were prohibited in London Parks,

---

[11] H. Baud, *Laura Ridding (1849–1939): The Life and Service of a Bishop's Wife*, p. 42.

[12] Ibid., p. 42.

[13] *The Saturday Review*, 29 December 1860, p. 829.

[14] Ibid., p. 830.

[15] Ibid., p. 830.

[16] Bradley, *Call to Seriousness*, p. 28.

as a result of pressure from Lord Shaftesbury and Archbishop Sumner. The campaigns for the Sunday closing of art galleries and museums and opposition to public transport were particularly harsh on the working classes who had little time in the rest of the week for leisure and cultural activities. However, as has been noted, Evangelical Anglicans in general began to move away from rigid sabbatarian ideals by the second half of the century.

Evangelicals were also open to the same criticisms that were levelled at the other sections of the established church. In their theology, for example, they were accepting of poverty and much of their social work was paternalistic in that it maintained dependency and reinforced what was believed to be a divinely-appointed social hierarchy. The Rev Robert Armitage typified their acceptance of poverty. He wrote in the *Church of England Magazine* in January 1839 that 'in every nation the vast multitude of men, women and children are poor; and, moreover, they must always be poor ... and it shall always be so; for God has said "the poor shall never cease out of the land".'[17] This assent to 'honourable poverty' and God-ordained roles in society was reflected in the school syllabuses adopted by Hannah More who ensured that children were only instructed to the level appropriate to their callings.

The foregoing paragraphs are indicative of the fact that Evangelical Anglicans, as indeed other sections of the established church, had their weak spots. It is, however, the thesis of this book that they nevertheless made an overwhelmingly positive impact on the society of which they were a part. Indeed, they played a formative role in shaping their age. It is, of course, a fact that Evangelical Nonconformity also exercised a major influence on the life and worship of nineteenth-century Britain. This was seen in their preaching, evangelism among the lower ranks and, in the case of the Primitive Methodists and the Salvation Army, among the liminal elements of society. Nonconformists also provided many leaders of working-class movements, such as Chartism, the Trade Unions and Co-operative societies. Aligned with the Liberal Party, Nonconformists were a powerful force in shaping morality, fighting for temperance and campaigning for unbiased religious education.[18] The Baptists, Methodists and the Society of Friends established a pattern for

---

[17] *The Church of England Magazine*, 18 January 1839, Vol. VIII, Number 204.

[18] See D.W. Bebbington, *The Nonconformist Conscience: Chapel Politics 1870–1914*.

benevolent factory owners who paid particular attention to the needs of their work forces. Among them were the matchmakers Bryant and May, Jesse Boot who founded the Chemist chain, the chocolate manufacturer George Cadbury, the biscuit maker John Carr, the starch and mustard manufacturer Jesse Colman, the confectioner Joseph Rowntree, the travel agent Thomas Cook, and the bookseller W.H. Smith.[19]

Perhaps their most obvious contribution, as indeed the word 'Evangelical' suggests, was in their active proclamation of the Christian gospel. Neither the high-church nor the broad-church parties matched their concern for both home and overseas mission. The Evangelicals were the founders of the CMS, the BFBS and the London Society for Promoting Christianity Among the Jews. Some of their clergy supported the work of SPG. Evangelical Anglicans also served as missionaries in inter-denominational organisations such as the LMS and the CIM. It is clear that Evangelical Anglican missionaries made a significant contribution to the establishment of a worldwide Anglican communion. Much of that family of episcopal churches in India, East Africa, Australia, and part of New Zealand and Canada was made up of congregations and parishes served by Evangelical clergy. Indeed, a significant number of nineteenth-century overseas bishops were Evangelicals. In all of this, the early influence of Charles Simeon was paramount.

In the matter of home missions, Evangelical Anglicans gave the lead to the established church. Their endeavours were made the more effective because they were willing to work with and, indeed, be a part of inter-denominational societies, the most obvious examples being the London City Mission and Mrs Ellen Ranyard's London Bible and Domestic Female Mission later known simply as the Ranyard Bible Mission. In addition, the exclusively Anglican Church Pastoral Aid Society, the Parochial Mission Women's Association and the Church Army made strong inroads among the poor in many needy urban parishes, particularly in London and the newly-expanding industrial towns and cities. They also worked in the countryside.

In their parishes Evangelical clergy worked long hours with great dedication engaging in a wide variety of social and philanthropic work alongside their overarching evangelistic concerns. Many proved themselves to be skilled managers as well as competent preachers. Their willingness to share their pastoral work with

---

[19] See I.C. Bradley, *Enlightened Entrepreneurs.*

laymen and laywomen was a great asset and enabled them to reach out to many more people, and, additionally, to establish lay-run mission halls and church rooms where shorter, brighter and non-liturgical services could be held. As Bishop Handley Moule reflected at the close of the century, 'It was a time of strong men in leading Evangelical posts'. He continued:

> Champneys (afterwards Dean of Lichfield), distinguished in the Oxford Schools, went to Whitechapel in 1837, and there did a work of remarkable thoroughness and power. M'Neile (afterwards Dean of Ripon) at Liverpool, and J.C. Miller at Birmingham, about the middle period, exerted a Christian influence of an uncommon kind each in his great city, which is felt in its results today; they certainly proved that the Evangelical believer and teacher can face and lead thought and life in great industrial centres with genuine mastery.[20]

Moule cited Close at Cheltenham, Cunningham at Lowestoft, Perry in Cambridge, Hoare in Holloway, Ramsgate and Tunbridge Wells, and Ryle and Groome in the Suffolk country as 'noble examples among many of wise pastoral management and the purest Christian earnestness'.[21] In these endeavours they developed their own spiritualities, which were as intense, serious and sustaining as those of their high church counterparts. In the middle Victorian years,[22] Evangelicals began holding parochial missions. The practice became more widespread from the 1870s onwards.[23] Among the first to see their possibility was Edward Bickersteth of Hampstead who later became Bishop of Exeter. His example was 'widely followed, with large spiritual results'[24] and The Church Parochial Mission Society was formed to organise such efforts.

In terms of nineteenth century social work, the Evangelicals were second to none. The abolition of the slave trade in 1807 and the ending of slavery in 1833 were outstanding achievements among many others. Lord Shaftesbury was without doubt the greatest single social reformer of the age. In a memorable speech shortly after his death, the Duke of Argyll declared that the social reforms of the last century 'were not mainly due to the Liberal party' but to

---

[20] Moule, *Evangelical School*, p. 53.
[21] Ibid., p. 54.
[22] Ibid., p. 60.
[23] Ibid., p. 60.
[24] Ibid., p. 60.

'the influence, character and perseverance of one man – Lord Shaftesbury'.[25] Lord Salisbury in response stated his belief that this was 'a very true representation of the facts'.[26] Other Evangelical Anglican names stand out among the great social reformers of the century: Hannah More, William Wilberforce, Thomas Clarkson, Thomas Fowell Buxton (who alone raised £46,000 for the destitute of London in 1817),[27] Florence Nightingale, Thomas Barnado, Josephine Butler, Wilson Carlisle and Quinton Hogg, Baptist Noel and Agnes Weston.

Evangelicals were past masters when it came to founding societies with a social or philanthropic objective. No individual had more influence in this regard than Lord Shaftesbury. He was instrumental in forming some of the most enduring organisations of the Victorian age and he acted as president and chairman of literally hundreds more. These institutions worked in practical ways and succeeded in solving many of the numerous and social problems of the age. In so doing, Heasman observed, 'they set the precedent for many of the techniques which followed' and played a significant role in laying the foundations of the twentieth-century social services.[28]

The Church of England was the major player in the field of education in the nineteenth century and in this the Evangelicals made leading contributions. Evangelicals also devoted much energy to the foundation and promotion of Sunday schools. Initially inspired by Robert Raikes, a Sunday School Society was set up with Henry Thornton as treasurer. The number increased steadily until the end of the nineteenth century, by which time it was calculated that three quarters of all those aged between five and fifteen in England attended Sunday schools.[29] Evening classes were also pioneered and for many working-class men and women this was the only education that they ever had.

The members of the Clapham Sect were among the very first to put forward the need for a national scheme of primary education. They were prominent supporters of the National Society from its beginnings, as well as promoters of primary schools and backers of Hannah More's schools in the Mendips. Francis Close of Cheltenham was prominent in the affairs of the National Society,

---

[25] Hodder, *Life and Work of Lord Shaftesbury*, p. 775.
[26] Ibid., p. 775.
[27] Moule, *Evangelical School*, p. 43.
[28] Heasman, *Evangelicals in Action*, p. 295.
[29] Bradley, *Call to Seriousness*, p. 44.

eventually leaving it to form the Church of England Education Society. Evangelical bishops, such as Sumner at Chester, made education one of the key aspects of their diocesan strategies.[30] In 1838 for example, he reported that fifty-nine schools had been built in the diocese during the previous three years.[31] Other Evangelicals who made a prominent contribution to education included Joseph Wigram, who was secretary of the National Society for many years, William Wilson, who promoted infant schools, and Francis Jeune, who was an influential headmaster of King Edward's School, Birmingham, where he remodelled the curriculum.[32] It was the case that Evangelicals provided education for both the poor and for the middle classes.

Evangelicals were also to the fore in the provision of teacher and clerical education. Bishops such as the Sumners, Robert Bickersteth and John Pelham were all active in establishing training colleges and Francis Close established a non-diocesan institution in Cheltenham. In the matter of clergy education, St Aidan's Birkenhead, St. John's Highbury, Wycliffe Hall, Oxford, and Ridley Hall in Cambridge were theological colleges with specifically Evangelical foundations. Additionally, the Church Missionary College at Islington, founded in 1825, also provided training for some clergy.

The Evangelicals contributed some notable names to the episcopate despite having no representatives on the bench at the beginning of the century. Their first appointment was Henry Ryder to the See of Gloucester in 1815 and Charles Sumner and his older brother, John, to Winchester and Chester respectively in 1827 and 1828. As conscientious reforming bishops they established a new pattern of episcopacy that addressed the needs of industrial society by building churches and schools and exercising pastoral care for their clergy. John Sumner in particular shed the aristocratic life style of many of his fellow bishops and moved freely among the people of his diocese and later within his province. The later 'Shaftesbury bishops' worked their dioceses from ground level and made themselves readily available to their clergy. John Bird Sumner was elevated to the primacy in 1848, Thomas Musgrave was Archbishop of York from 1847 to 1860 and William Thomson followed him from 1862 to 1890. Of the Evangelical bishops, Handley Moule reflected that 'perhaps no men ever gave themselves more

---

[30] Scotland, *Good and Proper Men*, p. 205.
[31] Scotland, *John Bird Sumner*, p. 58.
[32] Scotland, *Good and Proper Men*, pp. 48–9.

diligently to the diocese, and to it only, than did Pelham at Norwich, Waldegrave at Carlisle and Baring at Durham'.[33] The same could also be said of Ryle at Liverpool.

Throughout the century Evangelicals had shown themselves capable of not only getting their agenda into Parliament but also carrying the day on a number of key issues. These included opposition to the slave trade, Sunday observance, factory acts, lunacy laws, educational reforms and the Public Worship Regulation Act. Evangelicals also added powerful support to a number of other measures, including the Reform Bill of 1832 and the repeal of the Corn Laws in 1846. Significantly, Evangelicals had a major role in establishing public morality and making Christianity a religion of the home. Their influence was such that in Victorian society there was a generally accepted view of what was decent and in good taste. Their impact meant that even among the poor and those with very little education, there was a tacit acceptance of the Ten Commandments and a general agreement of what was right or wrong. The Evangelicals had also played a significant note in creating a Victorian middle-class morality. The earlier years of the century witnessed the emergence of lawyers, bankers, businessmen, civil servants, doctors and engineers. As they organised themselves into professional bodies and societies they found that the standards of behaviour advocated by the Evangelicals exactly resonated with their aspirations. Some of this undoubtedly helped to create a climate of private and public repression but, on the other hand, the 'seriousness of purpose', which also stemmed from high values, did much to motivate Evangelicals to persevere with their reformist and evangelistic activities.

In 1883 Edward Bickersteth, shortly to become Bishop of Exeter, took issue with those who followed the fashion 'to speak of the great Evangelical body in the Church of England as dwindling and decaying'.[34] 'Never', he asserted, 'was it so strong as at the present hour'.[35]

Significantly, there was a greater percentage of the population who worshipped in the Church of England at the beginning of the twentieth century than was the case at the beginning of the nineteenth. Evangelicals had clearly played a significant role in this increase. For this reason, if for no other, Handley Moule, as he looked

---

[33] Moule, *Evangelical School*, pp. 54–5.
[34] E.H. Bickersteth, *Evangelical Churchmanship*, p. 12.
[35] Ibid., p. 12.

back to the nineteenth century and then forward into the twentieth century that had just begun, was quietly optimistic about the future. 'I see', he wrote, ' "great doors and effectual" open in front, never greater nor more effectual than now.'[36] His words were testimony to a feeling shared by many of his contemporaries that Evangelicals had achieved a very great deal in nineteenth-century England. Indeed, they had played a major role in shaping the age.

---

[36] Moule, *Evangelical School*, pp. 54–5.

Bibliography

Unpublished Sources

Broadlands Papers (Southampton University Library)
Cheltenham Parish Vestry Minutes (Gloucestershire County Archives)
Church Missionary Society Letter Books (Birmingham University Library)
Church Pastoral Aid Society Committee Reports
Earl Grey Papers, 3rd Earl (University of Durham, Dept of Paleography)
Ellenborough Papers (Public Record Office, Kew)
Gladstone Correspondence (British Museum)
Golightly-Wigram Correspondence (Lambeth Palace Library)
Keswick Collection (Wheaton College, Illinois)
Longley Papers (Lambeth Palace Library)
Lord John Russell Letter Book
J.C. Miller Papers (Birmingham Central Library)
Mount Temple Collection (Hampshire Record Office)
Napier Papers (British Museum)
Panizzi Correspondence (British Museum)
Russell Papers (Public Record Office)
Sheffield Local Collection (Sheffield City Library)
Tait Papers (Lambeth Palace Library)
Wigram Family Papers (in the possession of Canon Sir Clifford Wigram)
Wilberforce Papers (Bodleian Library)

Newspapers and Journals

Bath Chronicle
Birmingham Journal
Cheltenham Journal
Durham County Advertiser
Essex Weekly News
Evangelical Christendom

Gentleman's Magazine
Guide to Holiness
Hansard
Hereford Journal
Pall Mall Gazette
Pulpit
Quarterly Review
Rochester and Chatham and Strood Gazette
Saturday Review
Sheffield and Rotherham Independent
Sheffield Free Press
The Chelmsford Chronicle
The Chester Chronicle
The Christian
The Christian Observer
The Christian's Pathway of Power
The Church of England Magazine
The Church of England Quarterly Review
The Derby Mercury
The Freeman
The Guardian
The Keswick Week
The Record
The Saturday Review
The Times
Yorkshire Post

Books, Articles and Theses

Abraham, W.J., *The Divine Inspiration of Holy Scripture* (Oxford: Oxford University Press, 1981)

Adams, W.E., *Memoirs of a Social Atom* (2 Vols.; London: Hutcheson & Co., 1903; reprinted New York: Augustus Kelley, 1968)

Algionby, F.K., *The Life of Edward Henry Bickersteth: Bishop and Poet* (London: Longmans, Green and Co., 1907)

Anon, *Account of the Union Meeting for the Promotion of Scriptural Holiness Held at Oxford August 29 to September 7, 1874* (Boston/New York: Willard Tract Repository, 1874)

Anon (Two of his Sons), *Memoir of T.D. Harford Battersby* (London: Seeley & Co., 1890)

Anon, 'The English Evangelical Clergy', *Macmillan's Magazine* (Dec 1860)

Anon, *Record of the Convention for the Promotion of Scriptural Holiness held at Brighton 29th May – 7th June 1875* (Brighton, 1875)

Ashton, O., 'Clerical Control and Radical Responses in Cheltenham', *Midland History*, Vol. VIII (1983), pp. 121–47

Ayer, J.C., *A Source Book for Ancient Church History* (New York: Charles Scribner & Sons, 1913)

Ayling, S., *John Wesley* (London: Collins, 1979)

Bailey, P., *Leisure and Class in Victorian Britain* (London: Routledge & Kegan Paul, 1978)

Bainton, R., *Here I Stand: A Life of Martin Luther* (New York: Abingdon Press, 1950)

Baker, F., *William Grimshaw 1708–63* (London: Epworth Press, 1963)

Balleine, G.R., *A History of the Evangelical Party in the Church of England* (London: Longmans, Green & Co., 1933)

Barabas, S., *So Great Salvation* (London: Marshall, Morgan & Scott, 1952)

Bardsley, J., 'Ritualism: Its Origin, Tendency and Antidotes', in *Truth for the Times* (London: William Hunt & Co., 2001)

Baring, C., *A Charge Delivered to the Clergy of the Diocese of Gloucester and Bristol at His Primary Visitation in October 1857* (London: Seeley, Jackson & Halliday, 1858)

Baring-Gould, S., *The Evangelical Revival* (London: Methuen & Co., 1920)

Barnard, H.C., *A History of English Education* (London: University of London Press, 1968)

Bateman, J., *The Life of the Rev Henry Venn Elliott* (Oxford: Oxford University Press, 1938)

Battiscombe, G., *Shaftesbury. A Biography of the Seventh Earl 1801–1885* (London: Constable, 1974)

Baud, H., *Laura Ridding (1849–1939): The Life and Service of a Bishop's Wife* (Unpublished PhD thesis; University of Gloucestershire, 2003)

Bayfield Roberts, G., *The History of the English Church Union 1859–1894* (London: Church Printing Company, 1989)

Baylee, J., *Verbal Inspiration* (London: Seeleys, 1854)

——, *Genesis and Geology: The Holy Word of God Defended from its Assailants* (London: Arthur Hall & Co, 1857)

——, *Verbal Inspiration: The True Characteristic of God's Holy Word* (London: S.W. Partridge & Co., 1870)

Bebbington, D.W., *The Nonconformist Conscience: Chapel and Politics 1870–1914* (London: Allen & Unwin, 1982)

——, *Evangelicalism in Modern Britain* (London: Unwin Hyman, 1989)

——, *Holiness in Nineteenth-Century England* (Carlisle: Paternoster Press, 2000)

Bell, A., *Sydney Smith* (Oxford: Clarendon Press, 1980)

Bell. H.C.F., *Lord Palmerston* (2 Vols.; London: Longmans, Green & Co, 1936)

Benson, A.C., *The Life of Edward White Benson* (2 Vols.; London: Macmillan & Co., 1899)

Bentley, A., *The Transformation of the Evangelical Party in the Church of England in the Later Nineteenth Century* (PhD thesis; Durham University, 1971)

Berwick, G., *Close of Cheltenham, Parish Pope: A Study in the Evangelical Background to the Oxford Movement* (Unpublished MS; Cheltenham Public Library, 1938)

——, *Life of Francis Close* (Unpublished MS; Cheltenham Public Library, 1945)

Best, G., *Shaftesbury* (London: Batsford, 1964)

——, *Temporal Pillars* (Cambridge: Cambridge University Press, 1964)

Best, G.F.A., 'The Evangelicals and the Established Church in the Early Nineteenth Century', *Journal of Theological Studies* 10.1 (1959), pp. 63–78

Bickersteth, E., *A Treatise on the Lord's Supper* (London: R.B. Seeley & W. Burnside, 1822)

——, *A Treatise on Prayer* (10th edn; London: R.B. Seeley & Son, 1826)

——, *A Discourse on Justification by Faith: Preached in the Course of Sermons on Points of Controversy between the Romish and Protestant Churches at Tavistock Chapel, Drury Lane on Tuesday 11 December 1827* (3rd edn; London: R.B. Seeley & Sons, 1828)

——, *A Scripture Help Designed to Assist in Reading the Bible Profitably* (London: R.B. Seeley & W. Burnside, 1829)

——, *Come Out of Rome: The Voice from Heaven to the People of God* (London, 1840)

——, *The Restoration of the Jews to Their Own Land and the Final Blessedness of our Earth* (London: R.B. Seeley & W. Burnside, 1841)

——, *Family Prayers* (London; R.B. Seeley & W. Burnside, 1842)

——, *Evangelical Churchmanship and Evangelical Eclecticism* (London: Sampson Low & Co., 1883)

Bickersteth, E.H., *Water From the Wellspring: Meditation* (London: Religious Tract Society, 1852)

——, *The Master's Home Call: A Memoir of Alice Frances Bickersteth* (London: Sampson Low & Co., 1872)

——, *Evangelical Churchmanship and Evangelical Eclecticism* (London: Sampson Law, Marston, Searle & Rivington, 1883)

Bickersteth, M.C., *A Sketch of the Life and Episcopate of the Right Reverend Robert Bickersteth DD Bishop of Ripon 1857–1884* (London: Rivingtons, 1887)

Bickersteth, R., *Romanism in its Relation to the Second Coming of Christ. A Lecture by the Rev R Bickersteth* (London: James Nisbet & Co, 1854)

——, *A Charge Delivered to the Clergy of the Diocese of Ripon at his Triennial Visitation, April 1861 by Robert, Lord Bishop of Ripon* (London: James Nisbet, & Co., 1861)

——, *Papal Aggression: A Sermon Preached in St John's Church, Clapham Rise* (London: D. Batten, 1885)

——, *The Universal and Perpetual Obligation of the Lord's Day* (London: The Religious Tract Society, 1887)

Birks, T.R., *Memoir of the Rev Edward Bickersteth, Late Rector of Watton, Herts* (2 Vols.; London: Seeleys, 1852)

——, *The Bible and Modern Thought* (London: The Religious Tract Society, 1861)

——, *The Victory of Divine Goodness* (London: Rivingtons, 1867)

Blomfield, A.F., *A Memoir of Charles James Blomfield* (2 Vols.; London: John Murray, 1863)

Boardman, Mrs W.E., *The Life and Labours of the Rev W.E. Boardman* (New York, 1887)

Book of Common Prayer (Oxford: Oxford University Press, nd)

Booth, C., *Life and Labour of the People in London* (3rd series; London: Williams & Norgate, 1902)

Booth, F.C., *Robert Raikes of Gloucester* (Redhill: National Christian Council, 1980)

Bowen, D., *The Idea of the Victorian Church* (Montreal: McGill University Press, 1968)

Bradbury, J.L., *Chester College and the Training of Teachers 1839–1875* (Chester: Governors of Chester, 1975)

Bradley, I.C., 'The English Sunday', *History Today* 2 (1972), pp. 355–64

——, *The Politics of Godliness: Evangelicals in Parliament 1784–1832* (DPhil thesis; Oxford University, 1974)

——, *The Call to Seriousness: The Evangelical Impact on Victorians* (London: Jonathan Cape, 1976)

——, *Enlightened Entrepreneurs* (London: Weidenfeld & Nicholson, 1987)

Braithwaite, R., *The Life and Letters of Rev William Pennefather BA* (London: John Shaw & Co., 1878)

Bready, J.W., *Lord Shaftesbury and Social Industrial Progress* (London: George Allen & Unwin, 1926)

——, *Dr Barnado, Physician, Pioneer, Prophet, Child Life Yesterday and Today* (London: George Allen & Unwin, 1930)

——, *England: Before and After Wesley. The Evangelical Revival and Social Reform* (London: Hodder & Stoughton Ltd., 1938)

Brooke, S.A., *Life and Letters of Frederick W. Robertson* (London: Smith, Elder & Co., 1868)

Brown, A.W., 'Notes on Calvinism and Arminianism', in *Recollections of Conversation Parties of the Rev Charles Simeon* (1863)

Brown, F.K., *Fathers of the Victorians: The Age of Wilberforce* (Cambridge: Cambridge University Press, 1961)

Brown, A.W., *Recollections of the Conversation-Parties of the Rev Charles Simeon* (London: Hamilton, Adams & Co., 1863)

Bull, J., *John Newton of Olney and St. Mary Woolnoth: An Autobiography and Narrative* (London: Religious Tract Society, 1868)

Bullock, C., 'Biographical Sketch', in *The Story of the Tent Maker, W. Weldon Champneys* (London, 1875)

Bullock, F.W.B., *The History of Ridley Hall, Cambridge* (2 Vols.; Cambridge, 1941)

Burg, C.A., *The Church Association* (London, 1873)

Burgess, H.J., *Enterprise in Education* (London: SPCK, 1958)

Burns, A., *The Diocesan Revival in the Church of England c. 1825–1865* (DPhil thesis; Oxford University, 1990)

——, *The Diocesan Revival in the Church of England c. 1800–1870* (Oxford: Clarendon Press, 1999)

Butler, J., *Personal Reminiscences of a Great Crusade* (London, 1910)

Butler, S., *The Way of All Flesh* (London: Penguin, 1995)

Buxton, C. (ed.), *Memoirs of Sir Thomas Fowell Buxton* (London: John Murray, 1848)

Cadman, W., 'The Sin of Neglecting the Poor', *The Pulpit* 69 (1856)

Calvin, J., *Institutes of the Christian Religion* (4 Vols.; Grand Rapids: Eerdmans, 1966)

Carpenter, S.C., *Church and People 1789–1889* (London: SPCK, 1933)

Carter, G.,' Prelates and Priests: The English Episcopate and the Evangelical Clergy', *Christianity and History Newsletter* 14 (Dec 1994), pp. 21–42

Carus, W., *Memoirs of the Life of Rev Charles Simeon* (London: J. Hatchard & Son, 1847)

Chadwick, O., *The Victorian Church* Parts 1 & 2 (London: A & C Black, 1970)

——, 'Indifference and Morality', in P. Brooks (ed.), *Christian Spirituality: Essays in Honour of Gordon Rupp* (London: SCM Press, 1975)

Champneys, W.W., *The Theatre: A Word to His Congregation in A Sermon Preached at St Ebbe's Church, Sunday Morning, July 3, 1836* (Oxford, 1836)

——, *Parish Work: A Brief Manual for the Younger Clergy* (London: Seeley, Jackson & Halliday, 1866)

Chavasse, F.J., *The Church of Christ* (London: James Nisbet & Co., 1898)

Church Association Tracts (6 Vols.; London: Church Association Protestant Publications, nd)

Clark, G.K., *Churchmen and the Condition of England* (London: Methuen & Co. Ltd., 1973)

Clarke, B.F.L., *Church Builders in the Nineteenth Century* (Newton Abbott: David & Charles Reprints, 1969)

Clarkson, T., *The Grievances of Our Mercantile Seamen A National and A Crying Evil by Thomas Clarkson, MA* (London/Ipswich: Longman, Rees, Orme, Brown & Co./S.Piper, 1845)

Cliff, P.B., *The Rise and Development of the Sunday School in England 1780–1980* (Redhill: National Christian Education Council, 1986)

Close, F., *The Book of Genesis* (London: J. Hatchard & Son, 1826)

——, *Miscellaneous Sermons Preached in the Parish Church of Cheltenham* (London: J. Hatchard & Son, 1829)

——, *A Letter Addressed to the Inhabitants of Cheltenham on the Subject of the Races* (1830)

——, *National Education and Lord Brougham's Bill Considered* (Cheltenham: William Wright, 1838)

——, *A Sermon Addressed to the Female Chartists of Cheltenham Sunday 25th August 1839* (London: Hamilton, Adams & Co., 1839)

——, *The Female Chartists' Visit to the Parish Church. A Sermon Addressed to the Female Chartists of Cheltenham, Sunday August 25th 1839* (London: Hamilton, Adams & Co., 1839)

——, *Sermon on the Occasion of the Visit of the Chartists to Cheltenham Parish Church* (London: Hamilton, Adams & Co., 1840)

——, *The Restoration of Churches is the Restoration of Popery: Proved and Illustrated from the Authenticated Publications of the Cambridge Camden Society: A Sermon Preached in the Parish Church of Cheltenham on Tuesday November 5th, 1844* (London: J. Hatchard & Son, 1844)

——, *Priestly Usurpation its Cause and Consequence: A Sermon Preached in the Parish Church of Cheltenham on Sunday March 30th, 1845* (London: J. Hatchard & Son, 1845)

——, *An Apology for the Evangelical Party* (London: J. Hatchard & Son, 1846)

——, *The Catholic Revival or Ritualism and Romanism in the Church of England* (London: J. Hatchard & Son, 1846)

——, *The Roman Antichrist, 'A Lying Spirit': Being the Substance of a Sermon Preached in the Parish Church of Cheltenham, 5th November 1846* (London: J. Hatchard & Son, 1846)

——, *Co-operation with the Committee of the Council on Education Vindicated and Recommended by the Revd Francis Close A.M. Incumbent of Cheltenham* (London: J. Hatchard & Son, 1848)

——, *The Secular System The Manchester Bill and the Government Scheme Contrasted by the Revd Francis Close AM* (London: J. Hatchard & Son, 1852)

——, *Footsteps of Error* (London: J. Hatchard & Son, 1863)

——, *The Stage Ancient and Modern its Tendencies on Morals and Religion. A Lecture by Francis Close, DD* (London: J. Hatchard & Son, 1877)

Collingwood, J. and M. Collingwood, *Hannah More* (Oxford: Lion, 1990)

Colloms., B., *Victorian Country Parsons* (London: Constable, 1977)

Conybeare, W.J., 'Church Parties', *The Edinburgh Review* (Oct 1853), pp. 273–342

Coombs, P., *A History of the Church Pastoral Aid Society 1836–1861* (MA thesis; University of Bristol, 1960)

Cornish, F.W., *A History of the English Church in the Nineteenth Century* Parts 1 & 2 (London: Macmillan & Co., 1910)

Coupland, R., *William Wilberforce* (Oxford: Clarendon, 1923)

Cubberley, E.P., *The History of Education* (Boston: Houghton Mifflin Co., 1948)

Cunningham,V., *Everywhere Spoken Against* (Oxford: Clarendon, 1977)

Daniel, W.H., *D.L. Moody and His Work* (Hartford: American Publishing Co., 1875)

Dark, S., *Wilson Carlisle The Laughing Cavalier* (London: James Clarke & Co., 1944)

Davidson, R.T. and W. Benham, *Life of Archibald Campbell Tait* (2 Vols.; London: Macmillan, 1891)

Davies, G.C.B., *The First Evangelical Bishop: Some Aspects of the Life of Henry Ryder* (London: Tyndale Press, 1958)

——, *Men for the Ministry* (London: Hodder, 1963)

Davies, H., *Worship and Theology in England* Vol. 3 (Grand Rapids: Eerdmans, 1996)

Davies, R.E., *Methodism* (Harmondsworth: Penguin Books, 1963)

Davis, G.T.B., *Dwight L. Moody: The Man and His Mission* (K.T. Boland, 1900)

Dawson, E.C., *James Hannington First Bishop of Eastern Equatorial Africa* (London: Seeley & Co., 1887)

Dealtry, W., *A Charge delivered at the Visitation in Hampshire, September, 1838 by W. Dealtry DD* (London: J. Hatchard & Son, 1838)

Dickens, C., *Little Dorrit* (London: Penguin, 1967 [1857])

Dickey, B., 'Evangelicals and Poverty', in J. Wolffe (ed.), *Evangelical Faith and Public Zeal* (London: SPCK, 1995)

Dimond, S.G., *The Psychology of the Methodist Revival* (London: Oxford University Press, 1926)

Ditchfield, G.M., *The Evangelical Revival* (London: UCL Press, 1998)

Dowland, D.W., *Nineteenth-Century Anglican Theological Training* (Oxford; Clarendon, 1997)

Dupuis, R.A.G. and G.N. Rosell, *The Memoirs of Charles G. Finney* (Grand Rapids: Zondervan, 1989)

Eardley, Sir C.E., *A Brief Notice of the Life of the Rev Edward Bickersteth* (London: Evangelical Christendom, 1850)

Edwards, D.L., *Christian England* (3 Vols; London: Fount, 1984)

Edwards, M.S., *Purge This Realm: A Life of Joseph Rayner Stephens* (London: Epworth Press, 1994)

Elliott-Binns, L.E., *The Early Evangelicals* (London: Lutterworth Press, 1953)

——, *Religion in the Victorian Era* (London: Lutterworth Press, 1964)

Eskenazi, T. et al. (eds.), *The Sabbath in Jewish and Christian Traditions* (New York: Crossroad, 1991)

Faber, G.S., *A General and Connected View of the Prophecies* (London: F.C. & J. Rivington, 1808)

——, *A Treatise on the Origin of Expiatory Sacrifice* (London: John Murray, 1827)

——, *The Primitive Doctrine of Justification Investigated* (London, 1837)

——, *Dissertations on the Prophecies* (London, 1845)

Farley, I.D., *J.C. Ryle: First Bishop of Liverpool* (Carlisle: Paternoster Press, 2000)

Figgis, J.B., *Keswick from Within* (London: Marshall Bros., 1914)

Findlay, J.F., *Dwight L. Moody American Evangelist 1837–1899* (Chicago: University of Chicago Press, 1969)

Finlayson, A.R.M., *Life of Canon Flemming* (London: James Nisbet & Co., 1909)

Finlayson, G.B.A.M., *The Seventh Earl of Shaftesbury 1801–1885* (London: Eyre Methuen, 1981)

Fitzgerald, M.H., *A Memoir of Herbert Edward Ryle* (London: Macmillan & Co, 1928)

Freeman, E.A., *Principles of Church Restoration* (London: J. Masters, 1846)

Gaussen, F.S.R.L., *Theopneustia: The Plenary Inspiration of the Holy Scriptures* (London: Passmore & Allabaster, 1891 [1841])

Gilbert, A.D., *Religion and Society in Industrial England: Church, Chapel and Social Change 1740–1914* (London: Longman, 1976)

Gill, J.C., *Parson Bull of Byerley* (London: SPCK, 1963)

Gill, R., *The Myth of the Empty Church* (London: SPCK, 1993)

Gill, S., *Women in the Church of England* (London: SPCK, 1994)

Gilley, S. and W.J. Shiels, *A History of Religion in Britain* (Oxford: Blackwell, 1994)

Girdlestone, R.B., *Wycliffe Hall, Oxford: Its Nature and Object* (Oxford, 1878)

Gisborne, T., *An Enquiry into the Duties of Men in the Higher and Middle Classes of Society in Great Britain* (2 Vols.; London, 1795)

——, *Friendly Observations Addressed to the Manufacturing Population of Great Britain Now Suffering under the Difficulties of the Times* (London: T. Caddell, 1827)

Goldstrom, J.M., *Education: Elementary Education 1700–1900* (Shannon: Irish University Press, 1972)

Goode, W., *The Modern Claims to the Possession of Extraordinary Gifts of the Spirit* (London: J. Hatchard & Son, 1833)

——, *The Doctrine of the Church of England as to the Effects of Baptism in the Case of Infants* (London: J. Hatchard & Son, 1850)

——, *The Divine Rule of Faith and Practice* (3 Vols.; London: John Farquar Shaw, 1855)

——, *The Nature of Christ's Presence* (London, 1856)

Gordon, J., *Evangelical Spirituality* (London: SPCK, 1991)

Goulburn, E.M., *John William Burgon, Late Dean of Chichester: A Biography, with Extracts from his Letters and Early Journals* (2 Vols.; London: John Murray, 1892)

Graham J., *A Sermon Preached ... March 16, 1841, Being the Day on Which the Foundation Stone was Laid of the Cambridge Victoria Benefit Asylum* (Cambridge, 1841)

Greaves, R.W., 'The Jerusalem Bishopric, 1841', *English Historical Review* 44 (July 1949), pp. 328–52

Green, V.H.H., *Luther and the Reformation* (London: B.T. Batsford, 1964)

Grubb, N.P., *C.T. Studd: Cricketer and Pioneer* (London: The Religious Tract Society, 1933)

Guise, J., *John Venn of Hereford 1802–1890: The Dilemmas of an Evangelical in a Cathedral City* (MA Dissertation; Cheltenham & Gloucester College of Higher Education, 1994)

Gulliver, D., *Dame Agnes Weston* (London & Chicester: Phillimore, 1971)

Haldane, A., *The Lives of Robert Haldane of Airthrey and his Brother, James Alexander Haldane* (London: Hamilton Adams, 1852)

Haldane, R., *The Evidence and Authority of Divine Revelation* (Edinburgh, 1816)

——, *The Bible its Own Witness* (Edinburgh: William P. Kennedy, 1866)

Hammond, J.L. and B. Hammond, *The Town Labourer 1760–1832* (London: Longmans & Co., 1917)

——, *Shaftesbury* (London: Constable, 1923)

Hammond, P.C., *The Parson and the Victorian Parish* (London: Hodder & Stoughton, 1977)

Hardman, B.E., *The Evangelical Party in the Church of England 1855–1865* (PhD thesis; Cambridge University, 1964)

Harford, J.B. and F.C. MacDonald, *Handley Carr Glyn Moule Bishop of Durham* (London: Hodder & Stoughton Ltd., 1922)

Harrison, B., *Drink and the Victorians* (Keele: Keele University Press, 1994)

Hart, G., *A History of Cheltenham* (Leicester: Leicester University Press, 1965)

Haslam, W., *From Death unto Life* (London: Morgan & Scott, nd)

Hastings, A., *A History of English Christianity 1920–1985* (London: Collins, 1986)

Havergal, M.V.G., *Memorials of Frances Ridley Havergal* (London: James Nisbet & Co., 1883)

Heasman, K., *Evangelicals in Action: An Appraisal of their Social Work in the Victorian Era* (London: Geoffrey Isles, 1962)

Hempton, D., ' Evangelicalism and Eschatology', *The Journal of Ecclesiastical History* 31.2 (1979), pp. 179–93

——, 'Bickersteth, Bishop of Ripon', *Northern History* 17 (1981), pp. 183–202

Hennell, M., *John Venn and the Clapham Sect* (London: Lutterworth Press, 1952)

——, *Sons of the Prophets* (London: SPCK, 1979)

Hennell M. and A. Pollard (eds.), *Charles Simeon 1759–1836* (London: SPCK, 1959)

Henry, M., *The Secret Life of Hannah Whitall Smith* (Grand Rapids: Zondervan, 1984)

Hessey, J.A., *Sunday: Its Origin, History and Present Obligation* (London, 1880)

Heurtley, C.A., *Justification – Eight Sermons* (London: F. & J. Rivington, 1846)

Hill, C., *Society and Puritanism* (London: Secker & Warburg, 1964)

Hill, T., *Letters and A Memoir of the Late Walter Augustus Shirley DD. Lord Bishop of Sodor and Man* (London: J. Hatchard & Son, 1849)

Hilton, B., *The Age of Atonement* (Oxford: Clarendon Press, 1991)

Hinchliff, P., *The Anglican Church in South Africa: An Account of the History and Development of the Church of the Province of South Africa* (London: Darton, Longman & Todd, 1963)

Hindmarsh, B., *John Newton and the Evangelical Tradition* (Oxford: Clarendon Press, 1996)

Hodder, E., *The Life and Work of Lord Shaftesbury* (popular edn; London: Cassell & Co., 1886)

——, *The Life and Work of the Seventh Earl of Shaftesbury, KG* (3 Vols.; London: Cassel & Co., 1886)

Hole, R., *Selected Writings of Hannah More* (London: William Pickering, 1996)

Hopkins, E.H., *The Holy Life* (London, 1875)

Hopkins, H.E., *Charles Simeon of Cambridge* (London: Hodder & Stoughton, 1977)

Hopkins, M.A., *Hannah More And Her Circle* (New York: Longmans Green & Co., 1947)

Horn, P.R.L., *Education in Rural England* (Dublin: Gill and MacMillan, 1978)

Howse, E.M., *Saints in Politics* (London: George Allen & Unwin, 1972)

Hudson, W.S., *Religion in America* (New York: Charles Scribner's & Sons, 1965)

Hutchinson, W.G., *The Oxford Movement. Being a Selection from Tracts for the Times* (London: The Walter Scott Publishing Co. Ltd., nd)

Hylson-Smith, K., *Evangelicals in the Church of England 1734–1984* (Edinburgh: T. & T. Clark, 1988)

Hymns Ancient and Modern (London: William Clowes & Sons, nd)

Ignotus, C., *A Golden Decade of a Favoured Town* (No Publisher, 1884)

Inglis, K.S., *Churches and the Working Classes in Victorian England* (London: Routledge & Kegan Paul, 1963)

Jacob, W.M., *The Making of the Anglican Church Worldwide* (London: SPCK, 1997)

Jarman, T.L., *Landmarks in the History of Education: English Education as part of the European Tradition* (London: John Murray, 1963)

Jay, E., *The Evangelical and Oxford Movements* (Cambridge: Cambridge University Press, 1983)

Jeune, F., *The Throne of Grace: Not a Confessional. A Sermon Preached Before the University of Oxford on Sunday, 18th October, 1846* (London: J. Hatchard & Son, 1846)

——, *A Charge Delivered to the Clergy and Churchwardens of the Diocese of Peterborough at his Primary Visitation in October 1867 by Francis, Lord Bishop of Peterborough* (London: James Parker & Co., 1867)

Johnson, G.W. and L.A. Johnson (eds.), *Josephine Butler: An Autobiographical Memoir* (Bristol: J.W. Arrowsmith, 1915)

Johnson, R.B., *The Letters of Hannah More* (London: Bodley Head, 1925), pp. 179–88

Jones, M.G., *Hannah More* (Cambridge: Cambridge University Press, 1952)

Kendall, H.B., *The Origin and History of the Primitive Methodist Church* (2 Vols.; London: Dalton, 1907)

Kent, J., *Holding the Fort* (London: Epworth, 1978)

Kingsley, F., *Charles Kingsley: His Letters and Memories of His Life* (2 Vols.; London, 1888)

Kingsley, F., *Charles Kingsley: His Letters and Memories of His Life* (popular edition; London: MacMillan & Co., 1899)

Kirk-Smith, H., *William Thomson, His Life and Times 1819–1890* (London: SPCK, 1958)

Kitchen, G.W., *Edward Harold Browne DD. Lord Bishop of Winchester, A Memoir* (London: John Murray, 1895)

Kitson Clark, G., *Churchmen and the Condition of England* (London: Methuen & Co., 1973)

Knight, F., *The Nineteenth-Century Church and English Society* (Cambridge: Cambridge University Press, 1995)

Laqueur, T.W., *Religion and Respectability: Sunday Schools and Working Class Culture 1780–1850* (New Haven: Yale University Press, 1976)

Law, W., *A Serious Call to a Devout and Holy Life* (London: Griffith, Farran Browne & Co., nd)

Lee, J., *A New Guide to Cheltenham and Its Environs* (1837)

Lewis, D. (ed.), *Blackwell Dictionary of Evangelical Biography 1730–1860* (2 Vols.; Oxford: Blackwell, 1995)

Lewis, D.M., *Lighten Their Darkness: The Evangelical Mission to Working-Class London 1828–1860* (Carlisle: Paternoster Press, 2001)

Liddon, H.P., *The Life of Edward Bouverie Pusey* (4 Vols.; London: Longmans, Green & Co., 1894)

Litton, E.A., *The Church of Christ in Its Idea, Attributes and Ministry* (London: Longman, Brown, Green & Longmans, 1851)

——, *Connection of the Church and the State: The Question of the Irish Church* (London: Stroud, 1868)

——, *Introduction to Dogmatic Theology on the Basis of the XXXIX Articles of the Church of England* (London: Elliot Stock, 1882)

——, *Manual of Worship and Ritual* (London: Church Association, 1884)

Loane, M., *John Charles Ryle 1816–1900* (London: Hodder & Stoughton, 1983)

Luther, M., *A Treatise on Christian Liberty* (Philadelphia: Fortress, 1982; first published in 1520)

Machin, G.I.T., *Politics and the Churches in Great Britain 1869–1921* (Oxford: Clarendon, 1987)

Madden, E.H., *Freedom and Grace: the Life of Asa Mahan* (Metuchen, NJ: Scarecrow Press, 1982)

Marsden, J.B., *Memoirs of the Rev Hugh Stowell* (London: Hamilton, Adams & Co., 1868)

Marsh, C., *The Life of the Reverend William Marsh* (London: James Nisbet & Co., 1867)

Marsh, P.T., *The Victorian Church in Decline* (Oxford: OUP, 1983)

Martin, M.C., 'Women and Philanthropy in Walthamstow and Leyton 1740–1870', *London Journal* 2.19 (1995), pp. 119–50

Matthews, T., *The A-Z of Wolves* (Derby: Breedon Books, 1999)

Maurice, F., *The Life of Frederick Denison Maurice* (2 Vols.; London: Macmillan & Co., 1885)

Mayor, S., *The Churches and the Labour Movement* (London: Independent Press, 1967)

McDonald, H.D., *Ideas of Revelation 1700–1860* (London: MacMillan, 1859)

McLachlan, H., *English Education under the Test Acts* (Manchester: Manchester University Press, 1981)

McNeile, H., *Popular Lectures on the Prophecies Relative to the Jewish Nation* (London: J. Hatchard & Son, 1830)

——, *Lectures on the Church of England* (London: J. Hatchard & Son, 1840)

Miller, J.C., *The Defective Ministerial Training of our Universities a Main Hindrance to the Efficiency of the Church of England: A Sermon Preached before the University of Oxford* (London: Thomas Hatchard, 1857)

——, *Bible Inspiration Vindicated: An Essay on Essays and Reviews* (Oxford/London: J.H. & J.A.S. Parker, 1861)

——, *The Confessional: A Lecture at St James Hall, Piccadilly, London, 12 March 1867* (London: William MacIntosh, 1867)

Monk, W. (ed.), *Dr Livingstone's Cambridge Lectures* (Cambridge, 1858)

Moody, W.R., *The Life of Dwight L. Moody* (Hartford: American Publishing Co., 1875)

Moore, E.R., *John Bird Sumner, Bishop of Chester 1828–1848* (Unpublished MA thesis; University of Manchester, 1976)

Moore, J., 'Cutting Both-ways- Darwin Among the Devout', *Christianity and History Newsletter* 14 (Dec 1994), pp. 43–9

Moorman, J.R.H., *History of the Church of England* (London: A. & C. Black, 1963)

More, C., *The Training of Teachers 1847–1947 A History of the Church Colleges at Cheltenham* (London: Hambledon Press, 1992)

More, H., *Village Politics 1793 with The Shepherd of Salisbury Plain c. 1820* (Oxford: Woodstock Books, 1995)

Morris, J., *Religion in Urban Croydon 1840–1914* (Woodbridge: Boydell Press, 1992)

Moss, A.R., *Valiant Crusade: The History of the RSPCA* (London: Cassell, 1961)

Moule, H.C.G., *Thoughts on Christian Sanctity* (London: Seeley & Co., 1866)

——, *Outlines of Christian Doctrine* (London: Hodder & Stoughton, 1889)

——, *The Evangelical School in the Church of England: Its Men and its Work in the Nineteenth Century* (London: James Nisbet & Co., 1901)

——, *Charles Simeon* (London: Inter-Varsity Fellowship, 1956)

Munden, A., *The Church of England in Cheltenham 1826–1856 with Particular Reference to Francis Close* (Unpublished MLitt thesis; Birmingham University, 1980)

——, *Cheltenham's Gamaliel* (Cheltenham: Dean Close School, 1997)

Munden, A.F., 'Evangelical in the Shadows. Charles Jervis of Cheltenham', *Churchman* 96.2 (1982), pp. 142–50

——, 'The First Palmerston Bishop: Henry Montagu Villiers, Bishop of Carlisle 1856–1860 and Bishop of Durham 1860–1861', *Northern History* 26 (1990), pp. 186–206

Murray, I., *Revival and Revivalism: The Making and Marring of American Revivalism* (London: The Banner of Truth Trust, 1994)

Murray, J., *Proclaim the Good News: A Short History of the Church Missionary Society* (London: Hodder & Stoughton, 1985)

Musgrave, T., *A Charge Delivered to the Clergy of the Diocese of Hereford 1839* (Hereford, 1839)

——, *A Charge Delivered to the Clergy of the Diocese of Hereford June 1845* (London: J.W. Power, 1845)

——, *A Charge Delivered to the Clergy of the Diocese of York, June 1849* (London: J.W. Parker, 1849)

——, *A Charge Delivered to the Clergy of the Diocese of York, June and July 1853* (London, 1853)

Neill, S., *A History of Christian Missions* (Harmondsworth: Penguin, 1964)

Newman, J.H., *Lectures on Justification* (London/Oxford: J.G. & F. Rivington/J.H. Parker, 1838)

——, *Apologia Pro Vita Sua* (Oxford: Oxford University Press, 1959)

——, *Letters and Diaries* (31 Vols.; Oxford: Clarendon, 1973–77)

Newsome, D., *The Parting of Friends: A Study of the Wilberforces and Henry Manning* (London: John Murray, 1966)

Nias, J.C.S., *Gorham and the Bishop of Exeter* (London: SPCK, 1951)

Noll, M. et al. (eds.), *Evangelicalism: Comparative Studies of Popular Protestantism in North America 1700–1900* (New York: Oxford University Press, 1994)

Norman, E.R., *Church and Society in England 1770–1970* (Oxford: Clarendon Press, 1976)

O'Brien, S., 'Eighteenth Century Publishing Networks in the First Years of Transatlantic "Evangelicalism", in M. Noll et al. (eds.), *Evangelicalism:. Comparative Studies of Popular Protestantism in North America 1700–1900*, (New York: Oxford University Press, 1994) pp. 38–57

Oastler, R., *Factory Legislation. A Letter Caused by the Publication of the Special Report of the Executive Committee of the National Association of Factory Occupiers, July, 1855* (London: Wertheim & Macintosh, 1855)

Obelkevich, J., *Religion and Society in Rural Lindsey* (Oxford: Clarendon, 1976)

Oliver, R., *Sir Harry Johnston and the Scramble for Africa* (London: Chatto & Windus, 1957)

Orchard, S.C., *English Evangelical Eschatology 1790–1850* (PhD thesis; University of Cambridge, 1961)

——, *English Evangelical Theology 1790–1850* (PhD thesis; Cambridge University, 1968)

Ormiston, J., *Hymns Ancient and Modern and Their Romanising Teaching* Tract 21 (London: Church Association, nd)

Orr, J.E., *The Second Evangelical Awakening. An Account of the Second Worldwide Evangelical Revival Beginning in the Mid-Nineteenth Century* (London/Edinburgh: Marshall, Morgan & Scott, 1953)

——, *The Light of the Nations* (Grand Rapids: Eerdmans, 1965)

——, *The Re-Study of Revival and Revivalism* (Los Angeles: School of World Mission, 1981)

Overton, J.H., *The English Church in the Nineteenth Century* (London: Longmans, Green & Co., 1894)

Packer, J.I., 'The Oxford Evangelicals in Theology' in J.S. Reynolds, *The Evangelicals at Oxford 1735–1871* (Oxford: Marcham Manor Press, 1975)

——, 'Robert Aitken', in D. Lewis (ed.), *Blackwell Dictionary of Evangelical Biography 1730–1860* Vol. 1 (2 Vols.; Oxford: Blackwell, 1995), <page range?>

Pakenham, S., *Cheltenham* (London: Macmillan, 1971)

Palmer, P., *Four Years in the Old World* (Walter C. Palmer Jnr, 1869)

Park, T., *St Bees College 1816–1895* (Barrow-in-Furness: St Bega Publications, 1982)

Parliamentary Papers, 1854, XIV, Report of the House of Commons Select Committee on Public Houses Sections 6, 7 *Register* 1802, xviii

Pedersen, S., 'Hannah More Meets Simple Simon: Tracts, Chapbooks, and Popular Culture in Late Eighteenth-Century England', *Journal of British Studies* (Jan, 1986)

Pelham, J.T., *A Charge Delivered to the Clergy and Churchwardens of the Diocese of Norwich by John Thomas, Lord Bishop of Norwich at His Visitation in 1865* (London: Rivingtons, 1865)

Pfander, K.G., *Balance of Truth* (London: Church Missionary Society, 1867)

Piersenné, J.A.R., *Belonging to No Party: The Christianity of Doctor Arnold* (privately published, 2002)

Piggin, S., *Making Evangelical Missionaries 1789–1858: The Social Background, Motives and Training of British Protestant Missionaries to India* (Abingdon: Sutton Courtenay Press, 1984)

——, *Firestorm of the Lord: The History and Prospects for Revival in the Church and the World* (Carlisle: Paternoster Press, 2000)

Platts, A. and G.A. Hainton, *Education in Gloucestershire* (Gloucester: Gloucester County Council, 1954)

Pocknee, C.E., 'Reservation in the Church of England and the Anglican Communion since 1549 until the Present Century', in A.A. King (ed.), *Eucharistic Reservation in the Western Church* (London: Mowbray, 1965), pp. 229–52

Pollard, A., 'Evangelical Parish Clergy 1820–1840', *Church Quarterly Review* 159 (1958), pp. 387–95

——, *Let Wisdom Judge: University Addresses and Sermon Outlines by Charles Simeon* (London: Inter-Varsity Fellowship, 1959)

——, 'Anglican Evangelical Views of the Bible 1800–1850', *Churchman* 74.3 (1960), pp. 166–74

Pollock, J.C., *Moody Without Sankey: A New Biographical Portrait* (London: Hodder & Stoughton, 1863)

——, *The Cambridge Seven* (London: Inter-Varsity Press, 1966)

——, *Wilberforce* (London: Constable, 1977)

Pratt, J.H. (ed.), *The Thought of the Evangelical Leaders: Notes of the Discussions of the Eclectic Society, London, During the Years 1798–1814* (Edinburgh: Banner of Truth, 1978 [1856])

Price, C. and I. Randall, *Transforming Keswick* (Carlisle: OM Publishing, 2000)

Proby, W.H.B., *Annals of the Low Church Party* (London: J.T. Hayes, 1888)

Pusey, E.B., *The Holy Eucharist a Comfort to the Penitent* (Oxford: John Henry Parker, 1843)

——, *The Holy Eucharist A Comfort to the Penitent. A Sermon Preached before the University in the Cathedral Church, in Oxford on the Fourth Sunday After Easter* (Oxford: John Henry Parker, 1843)

Rack, H.D., 'Domestic Visitation: a Chapter in Early Nineteenth Century Evangelism', *Journal of Ecclesiastical History* 24 (Oct 1973), pp. 357–76

Railton, N.M., *No North Sea* (Leiden: E.J. Brill, 2000)

Randall, I. and D. Hilborn, *One Body in Christ: The History and Significance of the Evangelical Alliance* (Carlisle: Paternoster Press, 2001)

Rattenbury, J.E., *Wesley's Legacy to the World* (London: Epworth, 1928)

Raven, C., *Christian Socialism 1848–1854* (London: Frank Cass & Co., 1968)

Reardon, B.M.G., *From Coleridge to Gore* (London: Longman, 1971)

Rennie, I., *Evangelicalism and English Public Life 1823–1850* (PhD thesis; University of Toronto, 1962)

Reynolds, J.S., *Canon Christopher of St Aldate's, Oxford* (Abingdon: The Abbey Press, 1967)

——, *The Evangelicals at Oxford 1735–1871* (Oxford: Marcham Manor Press, 1975)

——, *The Oxford Evangelicals 1871–1905* (Marcham Manor Press, 1975)

Roberts, M.J., 'Making Victorian Morals? The Society for the Suppression of Vice and its Critics', *Historical Studies* 21.83 (Oct 1981), pp. 157–73

Roberts, W., *Memoirs of the Life and Correspondence of Mrs Hannah More* (2nd edn; London, 1834)

Romaine, W., *The Life, Walk and Triumph of Faith by William Romaine with an Account of His Life and Work by Peter Toon* (Dublin: Attic Press, 1970)

Root, J.B., 'Champneys (William) Weldon' in D. Lewis (ed.), *Blackwell Dictionary of Evangelical Biography 1730–1860* (2 Vols.; Oxford: Blackwell, 1995), <Vol? page range?>

Rosman, D., *Evangelicals and Culture* (London. Croom Helm, 1984)

Rowan, E., *Wilson Carlisle and the Church Army* (London, 1905)

Rowell, G., *Hell and the Victorians* (Oxford: Clarendon, 1974)

——, *The Vision Glorious* (Oxford: Oxford University Press, 1983)

Royle, E., 'Evangelicals and Education', in J. Wolffe (ed.), *Evangelicals and Public Zeal: Evangelicals and Society in Britain 1780–1980* (London: SPCK, 1995), pp. 107–37

Russell, G.W.E., 'The Evangelical Influence', in *Collections and Recollections* (London: Thomas Nelson & Sons, 1903)

——, *A Short History of the Evangelical Movement* (London: Mowbray & Co., 1915)

Ryder, H., *A Charge to the Clergy of the Diocese of Lichfield and Coventry, at the Primary Visitation* (Stafford, 1824)

——, *Charge to the Clergy of the Diocese of Lichfield and Coventry* (London: A. Morgan, 1832)

Ryle, J.C., *Can They Be Brought In?: Thoughts on the Absence from the Church of the Working Classes* (London, 1883)

——, *Is All Scripture Inspired? An Attempt to Answer the Question* (London: William Hunt & Co., 1891)

——, *Knots Untied* (London: Charles J. Thyme, 1898)

——, *Holiness* (Exeter: A. Wheaton & Co. Ltd., 1956)

——, *Practical Religion* (New York: T. Crowell, 1959)

——, *Five Christian Leaders* (Edinburgh: The Banner of Truth Trust, 1963)

——, *Charges and Addresses* (Edinburgh: The Banner of Truth Trust, 1978)

Sargent, J., *Memoir of the Rev Henry Martyn BD* (Edinburgh: The Banner of Truth Trust, 1985)

Scotland, N.A.D., *Methodism and the Revolt of the Field in Lincolnshire, Norfolk and Suffolk 1872–1896* (Unpublished PhD thesis; Aberdeen University, 1975)

——, 'Rural War in Later Victorian Norfolk', *Norfolk Archaeology* 38.1 (1981), pp. 82–7

——, 'Francis Close, "Cheltenham's Protestant Patriarch" ', in J. Thrower (ed.), *Essays in Honour of Andrew Walls.* (Aberdeen: Aberdeen University, 1986) pp. 122–37

——, 'The Centenary of Dean Close School and the Contribution of Francis Close to Education', *History of Education Society Bulletin* (Autumn 1987), pp. 29–40

——, *John Bird Sumner: Evangelical Archbishop* (Leominster: Gracewing, 1995)

——, 'Evangelicals, Anglicans and Ritualism in Victorian England', *Churchman* 3.3 (1997), pp. 249–65

——, *Good and Proper Men: Lord Palmerston and the Bench of Bishops* (London: James Clarke & Co., 2000)

Scott, G.G., *A Plea for the Faithful Restoration of Ancient Churches* (London: John Henry Parker, 1850)

Scott, T., *Introduction to the Study of the Bible* (London: J. Hatchard & Son, 1881)

Seaman, L.C.B., *Victorian England* (London, Methuen and Co. Ltd., 1973)

Shelford, R.E.L., *A Memorial of the Reverend William Cadman* (London, 1899)

Shenk, W.R., *Henry Venn – Missionary Statesman* (Maryknoll, NY: Orbis Books, 1983)

Shirley, F.W.A., *The Supremacy of Holy Scripture* (Bampton Lectures, 1847; Oxford, 1847)

Simeon, J., *Let Wisdom Judge* (London: Inter-Varsity Press, 1959)

Simpkinson, C.H., *The Life and Work of Bishop Thorold of Rochester 1877–1891, Winchester 1891–1895* (London: Isbister & Co., 1896)

Sloan, W.B., *These Sixty Years* (London: Pickering & Inglis, 1935)

Smellie, A., *Evan Henry Hopkins* (London, 1920)

Smith, A., *The Established Church and Popular Religion* (London: Longmans, 1970)

Smith, D., *Transforming the World? The Social Impact of Evangelicalism* (Carlisle: Paternoster Press, 1998)

Smith, H.W., *The Unselfishness of God: A Spiritual Autobiography* (New York: Fleming H. Revell Co., 1903)

——, *The Christian's Secret of a Happy Life* (Grand Rapids: Zondervan, 1984)

Smith, K.S., *William Thomson Archbishop of York, His Life and Times* (London: SPCK, 1958)

Smyth, C.H., *Simeon and Church Order* (Cambridge: Cambridge University Press, 1940)

——, 'The Evangelical Movement in Perspective', *Cambridge Historical Journal* 7 (1943), pp. 160–74

Soar, P., *Tottenham Hotspur: The Official Illustrated History* (Hastings: Hilton Publishers, 1997)

Soloway, R.A., *Prelates and People* (London: Routledge & Kegan Paul, 1969)

Sprague, W., *Lectures on Revivals of Religion* (London: Banner of Truth Trust, 1959)

Stanley, B., *The Bible and the Flag* (Leicester: Apollos, 1990)

Stephen, Sir J., *Essays in Ecclesiastical Biography* (London: Longmans, Green, Reader & Dyer, 1885)

Stock, E., *The History of the Church Missionary Society* (3 Vols.; London: Church Missionary Society, 1899)

Stowell, H., *Tractarianism Tested by Scripture and the Church of England, in a Series of Sermons* (2 Vols.; London, 1845)

Stunt, T.C.F., 'Newman and The Evangelicals', *Journal of Ecclesiastical History*, 21.1 (January 1970), pp. 65–74

Sumner, C.R., *A Charge Delivered to the Clergy of the Diocese of Winchester in October 1833* (London, 1834)

——, *A Charge to the Clergy of Winchester1841* (London, 1841)

——, *The Home Work of the Parochial Ministry: A Charge* (London, 1854)

——, *Church Progress: A Charge* (London, 1858)

Sumner, G.H., *Life of Charles Richard Sumner DD Bishop of Winchester* (London: John Murray, 1876)

Sumner, J.B., *A Treatise on the Records of Creation* (2 Vols.; London: J. Hatchard & Son, 1816)

——, *A Charge Delivered to the Clergy of the Diocese of Chester at the Primary Visitation in August and September 1829* (London: J. Hatchard & Son, 1829)

——, *A Charge Delivered to the Clergy of the Diocese of Chester 1832* (London: J. Hatchard & Son, 1832)

——, *A Practical Exposition of the Gospel According to St John* (2 Vols.; London: J. Hatchard & Son, 1835)

——, *A Charge Delivered to the Clergy of the Diocese of Chester at the Triennial Visitation in 1838* (London: J. Hatchard & Son, 1838)

——, *A Charge Delivered to the Clergy of the Diocese of Chester in 1841* (London: J. Hatchard & Son, 1841)

——, *The Doctrine of Justification Briefly Stated* (London: J. Hatchard & Son, 1843)

——, *The Charge of John Bird Lord Archbishop of Canterbury to the Clergy of the Diocese at His Visitation 1853* (London: J. Hatchard & Son, 1853)

——, *Handwritten Notes on the Parishes of the Diocese of Chester* (MS EDR 5, box 5; Chester Records Office, nd)

Sweeny, J.T., *A Short History of The Diocese of Quebec 1793–1993* (Lennoxville: Church Society of the Diocese of Quebec, 1993)

Taylor, H., *Hudson Taylor and the China Inland Mission* (London: Marshall, Morgan & Scott, 1919)

——, *Hudson Taylor in Early Years* (London: China Inland Mission, 1932)

Thackeray, W.M., *The Newcomes* (ed. D. Pascoe; London: Penguin, 1996)

Thompson, E.P., *The Making of the English Working Class* (London: Victor Gollancz, 1963)

Thompson, H.P., *Into All Lands: The History of the Society for the Propagation of the Gospel in Foreign Parts 1701–1950* (London: SPCK, 1951)

Thompson, P., *An Unquenchable Flame: The Story of Captain Allen Gardiner* (London: Hodder & Stoughton, 1983)

Thomson, E.H., *The Life and Letters of William Thomson Archbishop of York* (London: John Lowe, 1919)

Thomson, W. *The Atoning Work of Christ* (Bampton Lectures, 1853)

——, *Aids To Faith* (London: John Murray, 1861)

——, *A Pastoral Letter to the Clergy and Laity of the Province of York by William Lord Archbishop of York, Primate of England and Metropolitan* (London: W. Close & Sons, 1864)

——, *A Charge to the Clergy of the Diocese of York Delivered at His Primary Visitation in October 1865 by the Most Reverent William Lord Archbishop of York, Primate of England and Metropolitan* (London: John Murray, 1865)

——, *The National Church. A Sermon Preached at the Opening of the Cathedral of St Albans on 2ⁿᵈ October 1885 by William Lord Archbishop of York* (Leeds: McCorquodale & Co., 1885)

Thorold, A.W., *Parochial Missions* (London: W. Isbister & Co., 1874)

——, *Bishop of Rochester's Ten Churches Fund 1887* (London, 1887)

Thrower, J. (ed.), *Essays in Honour of Andrew Walls* (Aberdeen: Aberdeen University, 1986)

Toon, P., *Evangelical Theology 1833–1856* (London: Marshall, Morgan & Scott, 1979)

Townsend, J.H., *Edward Hoare, MA* (London, 1896)

Trevelyan, G.O., *Life of Lord Macaulay* (2 Vols.; London: Longmans, 1876)

Trollope, A., *Barchester Towers* (London: J. Dent, 1912 [1857])

Venn, H., *The Native Pastorate and Organisation of Native Churches* (1857)

Venn, J., *Sermons by the Rev John Venn MA Rector of Clapham* (London: J. Hatchard & Rivingtons, 1814)

——, *The Life and A Selection from the Letters of the Late Rev Henry Venn MA* (London: Thomas Hatchard, 1853)

Vidler, A., *The Church in An Age of Revolution* (Harmandsworth: Penguin Books, 1968)

Villiers, H.M., *On the Necessity of Lay Agency in the Church* (London: Sampson, Low & Son, 1852)

——, *A Charge Delivered to the Clergy of the Diocese of Carlisle at the First Visitation of the Hon. Montagu Villiers, DD, Lord Bishop of Carlisle 1858* (London: James Nisbet & Co., 1858)

Wace, H., *The Bible and Modern Investigation: An Address on the Authority of Scripture* (London, 1903)

Wagner, G., *Barnado* (London: Weidenfeld & Nicholson, 1979)

Wakefield, G. (ed.), 'Spirituality', in *A Dictionary of Evangelical Spirituality* (London: SCM, 1983)

Waldegrave, S., *The Charge Delivered in July and August 1864 at His Second Episcopal Visitation by the Hon. And Right Rev Samuel Waldegrave DD Lord Bishop of Carlisle* (London: William Hunt and Co., 1864)

——, *New Testament Millenarianism: or the Kingdom and Coming of Christ as Taught by Himself and His Apostles by the Rt. Hon., and Right Rev Samuel Waldegrave DD, Lord Bishop of Carlisle* (London: William Hunt & Company, 1866)

——, *The Apostolic Commission on Auricular Confession and Priestly Absolution* (London: William Hunt, 1867)

——, *The Christian Ministry not Sacerdotal but Evangelistic. The Charge Delivered in September 1867 at his Third Episcopal Visitation by the Hon And Right Rev Samuel Waldegrave DD* (London: Hunt & Co., 1867)

——, *Ministering Kings to Our Established Church a Favour from God* (London: William Hunt & Co., 1868)

Walker, E., *A Sermon Preached in the Temporary Church, Cheltenham on Sunday May 25ᵗʰ in Aid of the Fund for the Relieving Distress in the Manufacturing Districts by the Rev E Walker MA, Rector of Cheltenham* (Cheltenham: Chronicle Office, 1862)

Waller, C.H., 'The Authoritative Inspiration of Holy Scripture as Distinct from the Inspiration of its Human Authors', *Imperial Bible Dictionary* (1885), pp. 1–58

——, *The Authoritative Inspiration of Holy Scripture as Distinct from the Inspiration of its Human Authors Acknowledged by Our Lord and Saviour Jesus Christ* (No date or publication details)

——, *The Word of God and the Testimony of Jesus* (London: Marshall Brothers, 1904)

Walton J.K. and J. Walvin (eds.), *Leisure in Britain 1780–1839* (Manchester: Manchester University Press, 1983)

Ward, H., *Robert Elsmere* (Oxford: Oxford University Press, 1989 [1888])

Ward, W.R., *Religion and Society in England 1790–1850* (London: Batsford, 1972)

Warren, M., *Social History of Christian Mission* (London: SCM, 1967)

Waterman, A.M.C., 'The Ideological Alliance of Political Economy and Christian Theology 1797–1833' *Journal of Ecclesiastical History* 34 (April 1983), pp. 231–44

——, *Revolution, Economics and Religion* (Cambridge: Cambridge University Press, 1991)

Weldon, J.E.C., *Recollections and Reflections* (London: Cassell & Co., 1915)

Wesley, J., 'Discourse on the Sermon on the Mount', in *Works* (3ʳᵈ edn; 1872), Volume 5

——, *A Collection of Hymns for the People called Methodists* (Wesleyan Conference Office, 1877)

Westbury Jones, J., *Figgis of Brighton* (London: Paternoster Press, 1917)

Weston, E.A., *My Life Among the Blue Jackets* (London: Nisbet & Co. Ltd., 1909)

Wickham, E.R., *Church and People in An Industrial City* (London: Lutterworth Press, 1969)

Wigley, J., *The Rise and Fall of the Victorian Sunday* (Manchester: Manchester University Press, 1980)

Wigram, J.C., *Ministerial Watchfulness: A Sermon Preached at the Visitation of the Rt Rev The Lord Bishop of Winchester in the Parish Church of Alton on Friday 17ᵗʰ October 1845* (London: Rivington, 1845)

——, 'The Advent of the Lord the Present Glory of the Church', in W.C. Wilson, (ed.), *The Blessing of the Lord's Second Advent: Six Lectures During Lent* (London, 1851)

——, *The Cottager's Family Prayers* (Chelmsford: T.B. Arthy, 1863)

——, *A Charge to the Clergy and Churchwardens of the Diocese of Rochester at his Second General Visitation in November 1864* (London: Rivingtons, 1864)

Wilberforce, R.G., *The Life of the Right Reverend Samuel Wilberforce* (3 Vols.; London: John Murray, 1883)

Wilberforce, R.I. and S. Wilberforce (eds.), *The Correspondence of William Wilberforce* (2 Vols.; London, 1840)

Wilberforce, W., *A Letter on the Abolition of the Slave Trade Addressed to the Freeholders and Other Inhabitants of Yorkshire* (London: T. Caddell, 1807)

——, *An Appeal to the Religion, Justice and Humanity of the Inhabitants of the British Empire on Behalf of the Negro Slaves in the West Indies* (London: J. Harchard and Son, 1823)

——, *A Practical View of the Prevailing Religious System of Professed Christians in the Higher and Middle Classes in this Country Contrasted with Real Christianity* (London: SCM Press, 1958 [1797])

Wilderspin, S., *Early Discipline Illustrated or the Infant System Progressing and Successful* (London: Wesley & David, 1832)

——, *The Infant System for Developing the Intellectual and Moral Powers of All Children* (London: Wesley & David, 1832)

Williams, C.P., 'Grand and Capacious Gothic Churches', *Tyndale Bulletin* 43.1 (1992), pp. 33–52

——, 'British Religion and the Wider World: Mission and Empire 1800–1940', in S. Gilley and W.J. Shiels, *A History of Religion in Britain* (Oxford: Blackwell, 1994), pp. 381–405

Williams, R., *Culture and Society* (London: Chatto & Windus, 1960)

Wilson, D., *Lectures on the Evidences of Christianity* (London, 1928)

——, *The Divine Authority and Perpetual Obligation of the Lord's Day* (London: Lord's Day Observance Society and Chas. J. Thynne, 1831)

——, *The Sufficiency of Holy Scripture as the Rule of Faith* (London, 1841)

Wilson, H.B. (ed.), *Essays and Reviews* (Oxford: J.W. Parker & Son, 1860)

Wilson, L., *Constrained by Zeal. Female Spirituality Amongst Nonconformists 1825–1875* (Carlisle: Paternoster Press, 2000)

Wilson, W., *The System of Infants' Schools by William Wilson AM Vicar of Walthamstow* (London: George Wilson, 1825)

——, *The Object, Authority and Use of the Holy Scriptures. A Sermon Preached in the Church of St Mary, Walthamstow, on Sunday, November 8th by W. Wilson BD Vicar* (London: George Wilson, 1829)

Wolffe, J. (ed.), *Evangelical Faith and Public Zeal: Evangelicals and Society in Britain 1780–1980* (London: SPCK, 1995)

Wolffe, J., *The Protestant Crusade in Great Britain 1829–1860* (Oxford: Clarendon, 1991)

——, *God and Greater Britain: Religion and National Life in Britain and Ireland 1843–1945* (London: Routledge, 1994)

Woods, C.E., *Memoirs and Letters of Canon Hay Aitken* (London: C.W. Daniel Co., 1928)

Yates, R., *Patronage in the Church of England* (London, 1823)

Yeo, E., 'Christianity in the Chartist Struggle', *Past and Present* (May 1981), pp. 109–39

Young, P.M., *Football on Merseyside* (London: Soccer Book Club, 1964)

Names Index

Subject Index